The Political Economy of Pι

C000085660

This volume examines the major trends in public finance in developed capitalist countries since the oil crisis of 1973. That year's oil shock quickly became an economic crisis, putting an end to a period of very high growth rates and an era of easy finance. Tax protests and growing welfare costs often led to rising debt levels. The change to floating exchange rates put more power in the hands of markets, which was associated with a growing influence of neo-liberal thinking. These developments placed state finances under considerable pressure, and leading scholars here examine how the wealthiest OECD countries responded to these challenges and the consequences for the distribution of wealth between the rich and the poor. As the case studies here make clear, there was no simple 'race to the bottom' in taxation and welfare spending: different countries opted for different solutions that reflected their political and economic structures.

Marc Buggeln is Lecturer in Contemporary History at Humboldt University, Berlin.

Martin Daunton was Professor of Economic History at the University of Cambridge from 1997 to 2015, and previously Astor Professor of British History at University College London.

Alexander Nützenadel is Professor of Economic and Social History at Humboldt University, Berlin.

The Political Economy of Public Finance

Taxation, State Spending and Debt since the 1970s

Marc Buggeln

Humboldt-Universität zu Berlin

Martin Daunton

University of Cambridge

Alexander Nützenadel

Humboldt-Universität zu Berlin

CAMBRIDGE
UNIVERSITY PRESS

CAMBRIDGE
UNIVERSITY PRESS

University Printing House, Cambridge CB2 8BS, United Kingdom

One Liberty Plaza, 20th Floor, New York, NY 10006, USA

477 Williamstown Road, Port Melbourne, VIC 3207, Australia

314-321, 3rd Floor, Plot 3, Splendor Forum, Jasola District Centre, New Delhi - 110025, India

79 Anson Road, #06-04/06, Singapore 079906

Cambridge University Press is part of the University of Cambridge.

It furthers the University's mission by disseminating knowledge in the pursuit of education, learning and research at the highest international levels of excellence.

www.cambridge.org
Information on this title: www.cambridge.org/9781316505595
DOI: 10.1017/9781316498958

First published 2017
First paperback edition 2018

A catalogue record for this publication is available from the British Library

ISBN 978-1-107-14012-7 Hardback
ISBN 978-1-316-50559-5 Paperback

Contents

Figures

Tables

List of Contributors

STEFANO BATTILOSSI is Associate Professor of Economic History and Jean Monnet Chair of the History of European Monetary and Financial Integration at Universidad Carlos III, Madrid. His research interests include international banking, financial regulation, fiscal policy and the development of securities markets in historical perspective, with a special focus on western Europe in the nineteenth and twentieth centuries. He has published papers in *The Economic History Review*, the *European Review of Economic History* and *Cliometrica*, and contributed chapters to the *Cambridge Economic History of Modern Europe* (Cambridge: Cambridge University Press, 2010), *The Oxford Handbook of the Italian Economy since Unification* (Oxford: Oxford University Press, 2013) and *The Oxford Handbook of Banking and Financial History* (Oxford: Oxford University Press, 2016). He is editor (with Y. Cassis) of *European Banks and the American Challenge: Competition and Co-operation in International Banking under Bretton Woods* (Oxford: Oxford University Press, 2002); and (with J. Reis) *State and Financial Systems in Europe and the USA: Historical Perspectives on Regulation and Supervision in the Nineteenth and Twentieth Centuries* (Farnham: Ashgate, 2010). He serves as managing editor of the *Financial History Review*.

W. ELLIOT BROWNLEE is Emeritus Professor of History at the University of California, Santa Barbara. His publications include *Federal Taxation in America: A History*, third edition (Cambridge: Cambridge University Press, forthcoming); 'Long-Run Fiscal Consolidation in the United States: The History at the Federal Level', in Gene Park and Eisaku Ide (eds.), *Deficits and Debt in the Industrializing Democracies* (London: Routledge, 2015), pp. 171–98; and (ed. with Eisaku Ide and Yasunori Fukagai) *The Political Economy of Transnational Tax Reform: The Shoup Mission to Japan* (Cambridge: Cambridge University Press, 2013). He is currently completing a book on the financing of the First World War in the United States.

MARC BUGGELN is a Lecturer at Humboldt University, Berlin. His publications include 'Steuern nach dem Boom. Die Öffentlichen Finanzen in den westlichen Industrienationen und ihre gesellschaftliche Verteilungswirkung', *Archiv für Sozialgeschichte* 52 (2012), 47–90; *Slave Labour in Nazi Concentration Camps* (Oxford: Oxford University Press, 2014); and (ed.) *Arbeit im Nationalsozialismus* (Munich: De Gruyter, 2014). He is currently working on a project titled 'Taxation in West Germany, 1949–1989'.

MARTIN CHICK is Professor of Economic History at the University of Edinburgh. His previous books include *Industrial Policy in Britain 1945– 1951: Economic Planning, Nationalisation and the Labour Governments* (Cambridge: Cambridge University Press, 1998); and *Electricity and Energy Policy in Britain, France and the United States since 1945* (Cheltenham: Edward Elgar, 2007). He is currently writing *Changing Times: A Political Economy of Britain since 1951* (Oxford: Oxford University Press, forthcoming).

MARTIN DAUNTON is Emeritus Professor of Economic History at the University of Cambridge, where he was Head of the School of the Humanities and Social Sciences until retiring in 2015. He is the author of *Trusting Leviathan: The Politics of Taxation in Britain, 1799–1914* (Cambridge: Cambridge University Press, 2001); *Just Taxes: The Politics of Taxation in Britain, 1914–1979* (Cambridge: Cambridge University Press, 2002); and of two surveys of British economic history since 1700. He is currently completing a book on the economic governance of the world since 1933.

CHRISTOPHE FARQUET has been a lecturer at the Paul Bairoch Institute of Economic History, University of Geneva, since 2014. His publications include 'Tax Avoidance, Collective Resistance, and International Negotiations: Foreign Tax Refusal by Swiss Banks and Industries between the Two World Wars', *Journal of Policy History* 25/3 (2013), 334–53; 'The Rise of the Swiss Tax Haven in the Interwar Period: An International Comparison', *EHES Working Papers in Economic History* 27 (2012), 1–40; and 'Lutte contre l'évasion fiscale: l'échec de la SDN durant l'entre-deux-guerres', *L'Economie politique* 44 (2009), 93–112. He is currently undertaking research for a history of the Swiss tax haven during the twentieth century in international comparison, and a history of capital flight from poor countries after the Second World War.

GISELA HUERLIMANN is a senior researcher at the Institute of History and chair of the History of Technology at ETH Zurich, and a senior lecturer at the University of Zurich. Her publications include 'Steuern', in

Monika Dommann, Christof Dejung and Daniel Speich Chassé (eds.), *Auf der Suche nach der Oekonomie* (Tübingen: Mohr Siebeck, 2014), pp. 287–314; *Steuern und Umverteilen. Effizienz versus Gerechtigkeit?* (Zurich: vdf-Verlag, 2012); and *'Die Eisenbahn der Zukunft'. Automatisierung, Schnellverkehr und Modernisierung bei den SBB 1955–2005* (Zurich: Chronos, 2007). She is currently undertaking research for a project examining social policy in the Swiss tax state during the 1950s.

EISAKU IDE is Professor of Economics at Keio University. His publications include (ed. with Gene Park), *Debt and Deficits in Industrialized Democracies* (London: Routledge, 2015); (with Gene Park) 'The Tax–Welfare Mix: Explaining Japan's Weak Extractive Capacity', *The Pacific Review* 27/5 (2014), 675–702; and (ed. with W. Elliot Brownlee and Yasunori Fukagai) *The Political Economy of Transnational Tax Reform: The Shoup Mission to Japan in Historical Context* (Cambridge: Cambridge University Press, 2013). He is currently investigating the origins of public debts accumulated in the 1990s and 2000s in Japan, focusing on the erosion of public trust, which undermines tax consent.

DAVID K. JESUIT is Professor of Political Science and Public Administration at Central Michigan University, Mount Pleasant. From 2000 to 2003 he served as project manager of the Luxembourg Income Study. His research has been published in *Political Research Quarterly*, *Social Science Quarterly* and *Socio-Economic Review*, among other journals. He was co-editor of and contributor to *Governance and Public Management: Strategic Foundations for Volatile Times* (London: Routledge, 2014).

BENJAMIN LEMOINE is a researcher in political science and socio-economics at CNRS and has been based at Paris Dauphine University (IRISSO) since 2013. His most recent publications include *L'ordre de la dette. Enquête sur les infortunes de l'état et la prospérité du marché* (Paris: La Découverte, February 2016); 'Dealing with the State. The Politics of French Sovereign Bond Transaction and Wholesaling', *Sociétés Contemporaines* (December 2013); and 'Measuring and Restructuring the State: Debt Metrics and the Control of Present and Future Political Order', in D. King and P. Le Galès (eds.), *Transforming European States* (Oxford: Oxford University Press, forthcoming). After developing a genealogical approach to the problem of public debt in France in order to show how sovereign debt techniques not only shape economic and social policies, but also political entities such as states and cities, he is now working on public debt diplomacy and the politics of sovereign debt restructuration, as well as the relationship between law, private finance and the reshaping of sovereign debt, where his current fieldwork is in Argentina, Greece and the United States.

PETER H. LINDERT is an economic historian, Distinguished Professor of Economics at the University of California – Davis, and a Research Associate of the National Bureau of Economic Research. His works on the welfare state and inequality include his prize-winning *Growing Public: Social Spending and Economic Growth since the Eighteenth Century* (Cambridge: Cambridge University Press, 2004); and (with Jeffrey G. Williamson) *Unequal Gains: American Growth and Inequality since 1700* (Princeton, NJ: Princeton University Press, 2016). With Leticia Arroyo Abad he is currently writing on the history of fiscal redistribution.

VINCENT A. MAHLER is Professor of Political Science at Loyola University, Chicago. He is the author of *Dependency Approaches to International Political Economy* (New York: Columbia University Press, 1984) and author or co-author of articles published in *Political Research Quarterly*, *The European Journal of Political Research*, *Social Science Quarterly*, *Comparative Political Studies*, *Polity*, *International Studies Quarterly*, *Comparative Politics*, *The American Political Science Review*, *International Organization* and other journals and edited collections.

ALEXANDER NÜTZENADEL is Professor of Economic and Social History at Humboldt University of Berlin. Publications include *Stunde der Ökonomen. Wissenschaft, Expertenkultur und Politik in der Bundesrepublik 1949–74* (Göttingen: Vandenhoeck & Ruprecht, 2005); (ed. with Christoph Strupp) *Taxation, State and Civil Society in Germany and the United States from the 18th to the 20th Century* (Baden-Baden: Nomos, 2007); (ed. with Cornelius Torp) *Economic Crisis and Global Politics in the 20th Century* (London: Routledge, 2013). He is currently working on a book on real estate markets and financial crisis 1870–1930.

REIMUT ZOHLNHÖFER is Professor of Political Science, University of Heidelberg. His most important publications include (with Herbert Obinger and Carina Schmitt) 'Partisan Politics and Privatization in OECD Countries', *Comparative Political Studies* 47/9 (2014), 1294–323; (with Georg Wenzelburger and Frieder Wolf) 'The Politics of Public and Private Pension Generosity in Advanced Democracies', *Social Policy & Administration* 48/1(2014), 86–106; and *Globalisierung der Wirtschaft und finanzpolitische Anpassungsreaktionen in Westeuropa* (Baden-Baden: Nomos, 2009). His current research projects include 'The Retreat of the Interventionist State in the Advanced Democracies since 1980' and 'Political Expectations and Responsibility Attribution'.

Acknowledgements

This volume has its origins in a conference on 'Leviathan After the Boom: Public Finance in the Industrialized Western Countries since the 1970s' held under the auspices of the Department of History of the Humboldt University, Berlin, at the Fritz-Thyssen-Stiftung in Cologne, 13–15 June 2013. We are very grateful to the Fritz Thyssen Stiftung für Wissenschaftsförderung for its generous support of the conference. We would like to thank Michael Wildt for his work as co-organiser. We also would like to thank all presenters, who could not be part of this volume, and the chairs and commentators at the conference for their engagement. The lively discussion at the conference was very helpful for the conception of this volume. Further thanks to the three blind peer reviewers who helped to sharpen our questions. The production of the volume was ably assisted by Ruth Willats, who standardised our English and style; and Auriol Griffith-Jones, who compiled the index. At Cambridge University Press, Michael Watson was a supportive editor. Thanks also to Ken Moxham for meticulous copy-editing and Robert Judkins for handling production so efficiently.

1   The Political Economy of Public Finance since the 1970s: Questioning the Leviathan

Marc Buggeln, Martin Daunton and
Alexander Nützenadel

When government takes on an independent life of its own, when Leviathan lives and breathes, a whole set of additional control issues comes into being ... Institutions evolve, but those that survive and prosper need not be those which are 'best', as evaluated by the men who live under them ... General escape may be possible only through genuine revolution in constitutional structure, through generalized rewriting of social contract. To expect such a revolution to take place may seem visionary.

> (James M. Buchanan, *The Limits of Liberty: Between Anarchy and Leviathan*, Chicago: University of Chicago Press, 1975, pp. ix–x)

Thomas Hobbes' image of the state as Leviathan was shaped by his pessimistic view of humanity. Unhindered by strict regulation, people would resort to murdering each other – or at least that was the philosopher's impression after witnessing the turmoil of the English Civil War. Man is wolf to man and his survival is only possible under strong leadership, which was why Hobbes argued that the state is entitled to wield limitless power. Over the following centuries, Hobbes' notion of the state was subject to massive criticism from the great thinkers of the Enlightenment and liberal theoreticians. They championed the rights of the individual and accordingly endeavoured to limit the power of the state and distribute its authority among various institutions. Since then, Hobbes' Leviathan has rarely been seen in a positive light and has almost universally symbolised a threatening, all too powerful state. This has led to widespread criticism of Leviathan, particularly since the eighteenth century.[1] States that combined democracy and capitalism generally withstood such liberal criticism and, until the early twentieth century, were hardly seen as Leviathan. By contrast, it was primarily dictatorships that were perceived as Leviathan.

---

[1] Thomas Hobbes, *Leviathan or the Matter, Forme and Power of a Commonwealth Ecclesiastical and Civil* (first English edition, 1651); Quentin Skinner, *Hobbes and Republican Liberty* (Cambridge: Cambridge University Press, 2008), and *Die drei Körper des Staates* (Göttingen: Wallstein, 2012).

It was not until the late 1960s that broad and influential movements emerged which saw the democratic state also as Leviathan. One of the most radical proponents of this view was James M. Buchanan (1919– 2013), Nobel laureate in economics (1986) and co-developer of the public choice approach of the Virginia School.[2] The introductory quotation to this chapter shows that the self-styled revolutionary proposed a radical change in the current state and its institutions. Buchanan dispelled the notion of selfless politicians and civil servants who were concerned only with the 'public interest'. In his view, politicians and bureaucrats wish to maximise tax revenues and spend more, whereas the electorate and taxpayers wish to minimise taxation. He warned that the democratic state had become increasingly powerful and was absorbing an increasing percentage of social resources, which he perceived as a deleterious influence on society. His assessment was based on a significant rise in tax and expenditure ratios in the wealthiest countries between 1900 and the late 1960s. Buchanan's main objective was to reduce tax revenues and government expenditure, particularly social spending. To achieve this, he urged greater tax competition, both between nation states and within federal states, limiting the power of the central state and reducing public spending by bolstering fiscal federalism so that competition between levels of jurisdiction would restrict Leviathan.[3]

Buchanan was by no means alone by the 1970s, and it was no longer only representatives of liberalism who were questioning how the democratic state was evolving. Indeed, criticism of the state was emerging on the radical left of the political spectrum. The democratic state now appeared less as a bulwark against the unruly forces of the market and more as an authoritarian state, the capitalists' sheriff, an information-devouring monster, a repressive socialisation machine. By now, a barrage of attacks had put the democratic Leviathan clearly on the defensive. Even among a number of European labour parties there was a growing sense that certain state interventions designed to allow people to make their own choices were engendering monolithic and bureaucratic systems that tended to limit personal freedom.[4]

---

[2] Although state intervention had been harshly rejected by earlier liberal economists, such as Friedrich Hayek, they rarely referred to the metaphor of the Leviathan.

[3] Geoffrey Brennan and James M. Buchanan, *The Power to Tax. Analytical Foundations of a Fiscal Constitution* (Cambridge: Cambridge University Press, 1980); and 'Towards a Tax Constitution for Leviathan', *Journal of Public Economics* 8/3 (1977), 255–73.

[4] For an overview of the range of criticism of the state, see Dominik Geppert and Jens Hacke (eds.), *Streit um den Staat. Intellektuelle Debatten in der Bundesrepublik 1960–1980* (Göttingen: Vandenhoek & Ruprecht, 2008); Daniel Rodgers, *Age of Fracture* (Cambridge, MA, and London: Harvard University Press, 2011), ch. 3. Important for the contemporary debate on a state crisis is Michel Crozier, Samuel P. Huntington and Joji Watanuki, *The Crisis of Democracy. Report on the Governability of Democracy to the Trilateral Commission* (New York: New York University Press, 1975).

In the United States in particular this criticism has continued to gain momentum in both conservative and liberal circles. Among Tea Party supporters it is no longer a matter of 'questioning Leviathan' but rather becoming a 'Leviathan slayer', a boast now found on websites associated with this political movement.[5] It is often no longer a question of pragmatically deciding which revenues should be used to finance particular expenditures. Instead, segments of the political spectrum now reject any increase in taxes or social spending, and the debate on public financing has been transformed into a highly charged dispute over fundamental principles.

After the Boom: The 1970s as a Starting Point

In most western European and North American countries, the 1960s was a period of grand dreams.[6] People looked to the future full of confidence that they would enjoy an era of boundless prosperity, where the capitalist economic system and the democratic state appeared to be a perfect match. Indeed, they seemed inseparable. Just as it seemed that the economic system would continuously improve thanks to planning and predictability, many felt that it was also possible to spur democracy on to ever greater heights. 'Let's dare more democracy', the acclaimed and popular slogan coined by Willy Brandt, post-war Germany's first Social Democratic chancellor, in 1969, was the most poignant expression of this sentiment, and was repeated in many Western countries at the time.[7]

However, these aspirations suffered a serious setback in 1973. That year's oil shock was triggered by a political crisis, but it quickly became an economic crisis when members of the Organization of Petroleum Exporting Countries (OPEC) voted to restrict the supply of oil, leading to drastic increases in the price of crude. Cheap oil had served as one of the main motors of the impressive growth rates in Western countries. Now, the petrol price increases severely exacerbated the incipient

---

[5] leviathanslayer.blogspot.de, last accessed 1 September, 2015.

[6] David R. Faber, *The Age of Great Dreams. America in the 1960s* (New York: Hill and Wang, 1994); Gabriele Metzler, 'Geborgenheit im gesicherten Fortschritt. Das Jahrzehnt von Planbarkeit und Machbarkeit', in Matthias Frese, Julia Paulus and Karl Teppe (eds.), *Demokratisierung und gesellschaftlicher Aufbruch. Die sechziger Jahre als Wendezeit der Bundesrepublik* (Paderborn: Schöningh, 2003), pp. 777–97. The main exception here was the United Kingdom, where matters were less optimistic amid a seemingly endless series of balance-of-payments crises and the progressive dismantling of the British Empire.

[7] Bernd Faulenbach, *Das sozialdemokratische Jahrzehnt. Von der Reformeuphorie zur Neuen Unübersichtlichkeit. Die SPD 1969–1982* (Bonn: Dietz, 2011), pp. 39–79.

economic crisis already felt in many Western countries.[8] Most leading Organisation for Economic Cooperation and Development (OECD) countries slipped into recession for the first time in years.[9] The rise in oil prices led to a dramatic increase in production costs for industry and also in the energy costs of private households, contributing to a fall in consumption outside the energy sector. In most Western countries the crisis consisted of high inflation rates, falling production, rising unemployment and balance-of-payments deficits. Most at the time hoped that this would be a brief reversal, but today we know that the first oil crisis marked the end of the boom and that over the following years the West would never again achieve the high growth rates of the 1950s and 1960s. In western Europe, growth in gross domestic product (GDP) per capita was 4.05 per cent from 1950 to 1973, but only 1.75 per cent from 1973 to 1997.[10] We also now know that this slow-down was more of a restoration of the norm, as the growth rates of the boom were unprecedented and many of the economic and institutional factors that had made the 'European miracle' possible – from technology transfers to working conditions and labour relations – began to peter out.[11] But for the actors in the early 1970s these had become the norm and they responded as if a return to growth could be expected and this new norm could be restored through state action.

---

[8] Karen R. Merrill, *The Oil Crisis of 1973–1974* (Boston, MA: Bedford Books, 2007); Mahmoud A. El-Gamal and Amy Myers Jaffe, *Oil, Dollars, Debt and Crises. The Global Curse of Black Gold* (Cambridge: Cambridge University Press, 2010); Jens Hohensee, *Der erste Ölpreisschock 1973–74: Die politischen und gesellschaftlichen Auswirkungen der arabischen Erdölpolitik auf die Bundesrepublik und Westeuropa* (Stuttgart: Steiner, 1996); Stefan Göbel, *Die Ölpreiskrisen der 1970er Jahre. Auswirkungen auf die Wirtschaft von Industriestaaten am Beispiel der Bundesrepublik Deutschland, der Vereinigten Staaten, Japan, Großbritanniens und Frankreichs* (Berlin: Logos, 2013).

[9] In some countries the economic slowdown began before the oil shock. And there is no doubt that the factors that fuelled the crisis were far more complex than merely a hike in the price of oil. In fact, the oil crisis also gave rise to an acute awareness of an economic crisis in the world's leading industrialised nations.

[10] Angus Maddison, *Economic Progress: The Last Half Century in Historical Perspective*, 1999, table 3a, at www.ggdc.net/MADDISON/ARTICLES/madpaper.pdf. See also Niall Ferguson, 'Introduction: Crisis, What Crisis? The 1970s and the Shock of the Global', in Niall Ferguson, Charles Maier, Erez Manela and Daniel J. Sargent (eds.), *The Shock of the Global. The 1970s in Perspective* (Cambridge, MA, and London: Harvard University Press, 2010), p. 9.

[11] Nicholas Crafts and Gianni Toniolo, 'Postwar Growth: An Overview', in Nicholas Crafts and Gianni Toniolo (eds.), *Economic Growth in Europe since 1945* (Cambridge: Cambridge University Press, 1996), pp. 1–37; Barry Eichengreen, *The European Economy since 1945: Coordinated Capitalism and Beyond* (Princeton, NJ: Princeton University Press, 2007), chs. 7 and 9. See also Werner Plumpe, *Wirtschaftskrisen. Geschichte und Gegenwart* (Munich: Beck, 2010), p. 99.

The end of the Bretton Woods system constituted another major challenge, albeit one that was paid far less attention at the time, although its long-term impact was just as significant. On 15 August 1971, President Richard Nixon suspended the convertibility of the US dollar into gold, and the subsequent attempts to return to a system of pegged exchange rates failed, leading to a new exchange rate system.[12] When they met on 11–14 March 1973, representatives of the countries of the European Community agreed to abandon the system of fixed foreign exchange rates and let their currencies float. This spelled the end of the worldwide currency exchange system of the boom era. The Bretton Woods regime was based on a desire to stabilise exchange rates and at the same time allow individual countries to pursue an active domestic monetary policy. These two aims could be reconciled only by limiting the movement of capital in response to different interest rates, which would otherwise put pressure on the fixed exchange rate – the so-called trilemma or 'impossible trinity'. This trade-off came under pressure from the growing freedom of capital movement after the currencies became convertible in 1958, the emergence of the Eurodollar market and the relaxing of capital controls in the 1970s. These changes gave rise to tensions within the Bretton Woods system and, alongside the failure to clear trade imbalances, contributed to its demise. As a result, the central banks now gained a considerable degree of autonomy and influence. At the same time, the greater scope for movement of capital between countries constrained independence in taxation policy, for if a country adopted policies that were too redistributive or costly for the markets to tolerate, it would be punished by capital flight.[13] The inflow of oil money from the OPEC countries and the rise of the Eurodollar market laid the foundations for the modern system of finance capitalism. The rise of the Eurodollar market also expanded the possibilities of evading taxation and contributed to the growth of tax havens.[14] Furthermore, the new phenomenon of stagflation – economic stagnation despite high inflation rates – gave renewed strength and

[12] Francis J. Gavin, *Gold, Dollars, and Power. The Politics of International Monetary Relations, 1958–1971* (Chapel Hill, NC: University Press of North Carolina, 2004).

[13] Harold James, *International Monetary Cooperation since Bretton Woods* (New York and Oxford: Oxford University Press, 1996); Barry Eichengreen, *Globalizing Capital. A History of the International Monetary System* (Princeton, NJ: Princeton University Press, 1996).

[14] See this volume, Chapter 6; Gabriel Zucman, *The Hidden Wealth of Nations. The Scourge of Tax Havens* (Chicago: University of Chicago Press, 2015); Ronen Palan, *The Offshore World. Sovereign Markets, Virtual Places, and Nomad Millionaires* (Ithaca, NY: Cornell University Press, 2003).

persuasiveness to (neo-)liberal criticism of Keynesian government policies.[15]

Due to lower growth rates, increases in tax revenue were negligible compared with the boom period. With expenditures continuing to grow at the same rate in nearly all areas, governments increasingly relied on borrowing to meet their financial obligations. This was helped by a refloating of oil money in the Western banking systems, especially the Eurodollar markets, which made credit very cheap in the mid-1970s. The formerly low level of government debt in the wealthy OECD countries steadily rose – and rose even more in many developing countries – and inflation rates reached levels not seen in decades.[16] All hopes of a return to rapid growth ended abruptly with the second oil crisis in 1979. This sparked loud demands in political circles for a reform of state finances.[17]

This is the story that can be told, with some national variation, for western Europe, North America and Japan. But for southern Europe, the story was different. In Spain, Portugal and Greece the 1960s was dominated by dictatorships that did not foster high expectations among the majority of the population. All three countries participated in the high growth rates of western Europe, but on average at a much lower level. Their tax rates were low and the welfare state was in its infancy. In contrast, the 1970s in these countries became an era of high expectations with the overthrow of the dictatorships and the introduction of democracy. All three countries were now governed by more or less social democratic parties, which led to greater expectations among the population. Their aim was to raise their countries to western European standards within a short period, but they faced doing so while western Europe was in the midst of an economic crisis.

How Politics Discovered Public Finances

James Buchanan's and others' criticism of the state as a rapacious and dangerous Leviathan was, of course, intensely political. To use their

---

[15] Charles Maier, '"Malaise". The Crisis of Capitalism in the 1970s', in Ferguson, Marer, Manda and Sargent (eds.), *The Shock of the Global*, pp. 27–32; Michael Bruno and Jeffrey D. Sachs, *Economics of Worldwide Stagflation* (Cambridge, MA: Harvard University Press 1995); Alan S. Blinder, *Economic Policy and the Great Stagflation* (New York: Academic Press, 1979).

[16] Wolfgang Streeck, *Buying Time. The Delayed Crisis of Democratic Capitalism* (London and New York: Verso, 2014).

[17] Göbel, *Ölpreiskrisen*; Frank Bösch, 'Umbrüche in die Gegenwart. Globale Ereignisse und Krisenreaktionen um 1979', *Zeithistorische Forschungen*, 9/1 (2012), 8–32.

own analytical categories, what they were proposing amounted to a shift in the fiscal constitution and thus differed from the more limited debates of the 1950s and 1960s. Any constitutional change is deeply contentious until the codes and rules of the new parameters are accepted as 'natural' and self-evident. The 1970s and 1980s were therefore characterised by deep political and ideological divisions as the new constitution took shape, on a par with the debates of the early twentieth century that led to the acceptance of a progressive and redistributive income tax, and to a related shift from market or charitable to collective, public provision. As a result, a more technical approach to taxation and public finance, with relatively low public engagement, gave way to a much more ideological and public debate as the critics of Leviathan moved from the periphery to the centre of politics. Fundamental assumptions about politics, society and economics were at stake.

Criticism of this nature had been voiced in some quarters in the 1950s and 1960s, but was marginal and had no clear sense of where it might lead. One example was the Union de Defense Commercants et Artisans (UDCA), founded in 1953 by the French right-wing politician Pierre Poujade. This was an anti-tax party, mobilising small shopkeepers, artisans and peasants against the government. However, the Poujade movement collapsed after the election of Charles de Gaulle and the establishment of the Fifth Republic in 1958.[18] In the United States, tax protest also mounted with the People's Initiative to Limit Property Taxation, which succeeded in enacting an amendment of the Constitution of California in 1978 to limit property tax to 1 per cent of the assessed value of real estate. Proposition 13 triggered a series of similar initiatives in other US states. The taxpayer revolt at the local and state levels had a strong impact on the presidential campaign and led to the election of the Republican candidate, Ronald Reagan, in 1980.[19] By 1985, Reagan could portray himself as a tax rebel in a long and honourable American tradition going back to the Boston Tea Party of 1773. As he expressed it in colonial Williamsburg, 'The tax system has earned a rebellion – and it is time we rebelled.' It was a clever piece of rhetoric, placing the President alongside the people against Leviathan. It was, of course, a partial account of American history, which was in reality in continuous tension between two approaches. On the one hand, taxation was theft, an attack on states' rights and family

---

[18] Stanley Hoffmann, *Le Mouvement Poujade* (Paris: Armand Colin, 1956). For a new tax resistance movement in the 1970s in France, see Alexis Spire, 'The Spread of Tax Resistance: The Antitax Movement in France in the 1970s', *Journal of Policy History* 25/3 (2013), 444–60.

[19] See this volume, Chapters 3 and 5.

responsibilities. Low taxes would lead to incentives and prosperity. On the other hand, taxation would rein in the power of big business, protect opportunities by constraining rent-seeking behaviour and create social solidarity. The progressive agenda sometimes was to the fore, as it was under President Franklin Roosevelt; at other times, hostility to taxation was in the ascendant.[20] Why did the second approach dominate in the 1970s and 1980s, moving from the periphery to the centre of debate? The shift occurred not only in the United States, for taxation lost its legitimacy to a greater or lesser extent in many OECD countries. There was a decline in acceptance that income and wealth were generated by society as whole, and a growing belief that income and wealth belonged to the individual, with anything taken by the state seen as expropriation. Political support for taxation weakened and was linked to a shift from direct to indirect taxes, from taxation to borrowing, from a tax state to a debt state.

Public choice theory offers one way to explain the change, in terms of the self-interest of voters seeking to maximise their utility and deciding whether paying taxes for the collective provision of public services was beneficial. There are two ways of explaining the change in their perception of the costs and benefits of taxation. The first is to look at the relationship between the franchise and taxation. Between 1945 and around 1970 most voters fell below the income tax threshold, and certainly below the higher-rate threshold. Thus they were likely to benefit from public spending without contributing to it, and so would vote for it. As wages rose and tax thresholds did not increase in line with inflation, more voters began to pay tax or were liable at a higher-rate – indeed, they could experience a very high marginal rate by losing benefits and coming into the purview of direct taxes. The politics of direct taxation had changed: after the war, the median voter earned a modest income, falling below the threshold for income tax. This gave rise to strong electoral support for direct taxation. However, by the 1970s the median voter was paying income tax at a high rate and this eroded support for direct taxation.

A second way of looking at the changing assumptions of taxpayers and the electorate is to consider the relationship between the incidence of taxation and the receipt of benefits. In some countries, such as Britain, social benefits were funded by direct taxes largely paid by

---

[20] Romain D. Huret, *American Tax Resisters* (Cambridge, MA: Harvard University Press, 2014); Isaac William Martin, *Rich People's Movements. Grassroots Campaigns to Untax the One Percent* (Oxford: Oxford University Press, 2013). For a comparative approach, see 'Tax Resistance: A Global History?', special issue of the *Journal of Policy History* 25/3 (2013), eds. Romain D. Huret and Nicolas Delalande.

middle-class voters. Initially, the middle class might have felt that they were getting a reasonable deal, for they might disproportionately benefit from greater access to healthcare and secondary and higher education; and at a time of high employment, there was less concern that benefits were being used to support the 'undeserving' poor. A public choice analysis might suggest that the attitude of middle-class taxpayers would change by the 1970s. The somewhat generalised pattern of welfare provision after the war seemed more attractive at the time, but rising incomes and advances in healthcare created a demand for more individualised and targeted provision. Pressure for increased social spending would lead to higher income taxes and a resentment of 'scroungers'. According to Avner Offer, affluence led to myopic choice rather than rational choice: a search for instant gratification and a loss of self-control.[21] There is a more general point that greater disposable income and paying higher taxes for a basic level of provision seemed less attractive to a generation with different assumptions about consumer choice created in the decades of affluence in the 1950s and 1960s. Why not opt out of the state system and purchase what they wanted? By contrast, in some countries direct taxes were much less important and the costs tended to fall on consumption: thus whereas in the United Kingdom consumption taxes comprised 27.6 per cent of total taxation in 1970, they accounted for 50.5 per cent in Ireland, 38.3 per cent in Italy and 36.5 per cent in France.[22] This different tax structure modified the assumptions of the electorate, for the middle class was less inclined to pay high-income tax rates to fund benefits for less well-off members of society. Could it be that a less progressive tax regime mitigated the hostility of voters with incomes above the median to providing redistributive welfare benefits? Marc Buggeln highlights some of the dynamics created by these different tax regimes. In Britain, high levels of taxation of average incomes created demands for tax reform, leading to a shift to consumption taxes after 1979. However, he also shows that in France, the Socialist government of President François Mitterrand moved in the opposite direction, reversing the trend towards higher sales taxes and introducing a 'solidarity tax' in 1981, which required the wealthy to

---

[21] Avner Offer, *The Challenge of Affluence: Self-Control and Well-Being in the United States and Britain since 1950* (Oxford: Oxford University Press, 2006). For a comparison between the United States and Japan, see Sheldon Garon, *Beyond Our Means: Why America Spends While the World Saves* (Princeton, NJ: Princeton University Press, 2012).

[22] Eurostat (ed.), *Structures of the Taxation Systems in the European Union 1970–1997* (Luxembourg: Office for Official Publications of the European Communities, 2000), p. 148.

fund employment and welfare benefits. The electoral response of voters and the calculations of politicians were shaped by the incidence of taxation and the receipt of benefits at different income levels.[23]

Of course, these arguments are open to the criticism that they incorporate the assumptions of the critics of Leviathan: individual utility-maximising voters or taxpayers decide what is in their own interests. Although there is some merit in the public choice approach, it does not tell the whole story. Society is not made up of individuals, but of groups, and their identity is shaped not only by the prevailing material conditions, but also by language and rhetoric. We need to ask what was considered to be fair, just and equitable, and one of the major changes from the 1970s was precisely the sense that any assessment rested with the individual. In his analysis of American society, Dan Rodgers has termed this the 'age of fracture' – a movement away from concepts of national consensus, managed markets and citizen responsibility to a more fluid sense of gender and racial identities, narrower definitions of collective responsibility and the replacement of solidarity in terms of class or race by fluid, multiple identities. Keynesian macroeconomics was overtaken by flexible, instantly acting markets and by the individual interest of public choice theory. As Rodgers puts it, solidarity and collective institutions gave way to a more individualised sense of human nature based on choice, agency, performance and desire. 'Strong metaphors of society were supplanted by weaker ones. Imagined collectivities shrank; notions of structure and power thinned out.' He argues that social assumptions shifted through a 'contagion of metaphors', as central features of game theory such as the prisoners' dilemma and free riders moved from economics departments into law and the social sciences, and out into the wider public discourse. The notion of 'choice' was employed more frequently and became an inherent claim on both the progressive left – for example, a woman's right to abortion – and the conservative right – the freedom to choose how to spend one's own money. Both used the rhetoric of choice, though for different ends.[24]

Historians have grappled with the reasons for this change. In broad terms, it is often said that it amounts to a rise of neo-liberal ideas which

---

[23] See this volume, Chapter 5.

[24] Rodgers, *Age of Fracture*, pp. 3–12. See also Pierre Rosanvallon, *The Society of Equals* (Cambridge, MA, and London: Harvard University Press, 2013), ch. 4; Edward D. Berkowitz, *Something Happened. A Political and Cultural Overview of the Seventies* (New York: Columbia University Press, 2005); Bruce J. Schulman, *The Seventies. The Great Shift in American Culture, Society, and Politics* (New York: The Free Press, 2001); Konrad H. Jarausch (ed.), *Das Ende der Zuversicht? Die siebziger Jahre als Geschichte* (Göttingen: Vandenhoeck & Ruprecht, 2008).

have been carefully described by a number of historians,[25] but that is merely to restate what needs to be explained. It also misses the point, for the changes were experienced on the left as it moved away from more rigid notions of state planning and control to allow more freedom and choice.[26] We can think of a number of possible lines of enquiry to explain these wider cultural shifts and how they varied among countries.

The nature of political mobilisation began to change in the 1960s. The mass political parties that emerged in the nineteenth century were coalitions of different interests, making concessions to construct a general platform for which members would campaign, even if they were not entirely happy about all the elements. This pattern weakened from the 1960s, with greater mobilisation on single issues rather than a common platform. Issues such as feminism and sexual politics, or the politics of consumption, suffer from what Geoff Eley has called the 'tyranny of structurelessness', with their decentralised and non-bureaucratic forms of mobilisation. In his view, the 'empowerment of participation' of 1968 was difficult to convert into a response to the emergence of global capitalism.[27] Of course, these changes in political mobilisation varied between countries and were shaped by differences in their party structures and electoral systems.

Another possible explanation for the shift is the change in the structure of capitalist society. By the 1970s, profits were being squeezed in many industrial economies and particularly in Britain. A report by the OECD in 1977 found that gross profits in the corporate sector since 1970 were lowest in the United Kingdom out of nine industrial countries, at less than half the level in the United States, France and Germany.[28] Consequently, investment was low as a proportion of GNP, with less capital per worker than in many countries; investment in manufacturing was only 5.4 per cent of gross capital stock in 1960-8. In the case of Japan and Germany, capital investment in manufacturing

[25] Angus Burgin, *The Great Persuasion: Reinventing Free Markets since the Depression* (Cambridge, MA, and London: Harvard University Press, 2012), emphasises Milton Friedman as a great persuader. See also Philip Mirowski and Dieter Plehwe (eds.), *The Road from Mont Pèlerin: The Making of the Neoliberal Thought Collective* (Cambridge, MA, and London: Harvard University Press, 2009).

[26] Luc Boltanski and Ève Chiapello, *Le nouvel esprit du capitalisme* (Paris: Gallimard, 1999); Sven Reichardt, *Authentizität und Gemeinschaft. Linksalternatives Leben in den siebziger und frühen achtziger Jahren* (Berlin: Suhrkamp, 2014).

[27] Geoff Eley, *Forging Democracy: The History of the Left in Europe, 1850–2000* (Oxford: Oxford University Press, 2002), pp. 378, 468.

[28] Andrew Glyn and Bob Sutcliffe, *British Capitalism, Workers and the Profits Squeeze* (Harmondsworth: Penguin Books, 1972), pp. 66–8; OECD, *Towards Full Employment and Price Stability* (Paris: OECD, 1977).

during the golden age was much higher, at 9.4 and 19.1 per cent of gross capital stock, respectively. The oil price shock after 1973 and the rising costs of borrowing in the 1980s led to a drop in investment in manufacturing in most countries: in Britain it fell to 3.1 per cent of gross capital stock in 1980–8, and even more strikingly in Germany and Japan to 10.2 and 5.8 per cent. In Germany and Japan, about two-thirds of the fall in investment can be explained by declining profitability; in Britain, the effect of profitability on investment was modest.[29]

The squeeze on profits meant that the social contract between labour, capital and the state on which the boom rested was breaking down. After the war, the social contract was based on workers trading lower current consumption for higher living standards in the future, based on the belief that industrialists would reinvest their profits; commitment to the deal was underwritten by the government through tax-breaks on condition that firms invested, by schemes for industrial support and by welfare benefits for the workers. Barry Eichengreen sees this neo-corporatist 'web of interlocking agreements' forming an exit barrier that increased the cost of bringing the post-war settlement to an end.[30] However, by 1970 the contract was breaking down as profits fell, squeezed by the demands for higher wages which could no longer be covered by gains in productivity. The crisis was felt in most of Europe and led to a search for new solutions. In Britain, the answer was to increase competition both internally and by joining the European Economic Community (EEC) – a shock that weakened rather than revived British industry. In Germany, industry was better able to respond as a result of different forms of corporate governance and industrial relations, with co-determination as the price for union support during the crisis.[31]

Structural change in the capitalist economy cannot provide the whole answer, for the chronology is not entirely plausible: ideas and assumptions started to shift too soon. A better way of looking at the pressure for change is Rodgers' argument that 'the crisis that had launched the

---

[29] V. Bhaskar and Andrew Glyn, 'Investment and Profitability: The Evidence from the Advanced Capitalist Countries', in Gerald Epstein and Herbert Gintis (eds.), *Macroeconomic Policy after the Conservative Era* (Cambridge: Cambridge University Press, 1995), pp. 190–1.

[30] See Eichengreen, *The European Economy*, pp. 31–47; and 'Institutions and Economic Growth: Europe after World War II', in Crafts and Toniolo, *Economic Growth in Europe*, pp. 38–72.

[31] Werner Plumpe, '"Ölkrise" und wirtschaftlicher Strukturwandel. Die bundesdeutsche Wirtschaft im Zeichen von Normalisierung und Globalisierung während der 1970er Jahre', in Alexander Gallus, Axel Schildt and Detlef Siegfried (eds.), *Deutsche Zeitgeschichte – Transnational* (Göttingen: Wallstein, 2015), pp. 101–23.

age was a breakdown in economic predictability and performance'.[32]
A similar point is made by Daniel Stedman Jones in his account of the
transatlantic emergence of neo-liberalism. It was the result of the economic crisis of the 1970s and the acceptance on the left as much as the
right of the need for new policies to fill a policy vacuum in response to
the collapse of the Bretton Woods system and the onset of stagflation.
John Hicks – an economist closely associated with the triumph of
Keynesianism – pointed out in lectures in April 1973 that the *General
Theory* which was devised to deal with deflation offered no solution to
the problem of rising inflation, and especially the combination of high
inflation and high unemployment which seemed impossible in classical
Keynesianism. Consequently, there was a crisis of Keynesian economics, although Hicks still hoped that 'reformulated Keynes is much more
like Keynes than it is like the cruder forms of neo-classical doctrine'.[33]
Others were less sanguine. Ideas for an alternative approach had been
evolving in a network of think tanks and pressure groups and could
now be tested. In Stedman Jones' words, 'just as in 1932 or 1945,
the 1970s were a rare moment when the pieces of the political and
economic jigsaw were strewn all over the place, in need of painstaking
rearrangement' – and the pieces were moved around as much by the
Labour government in Britain in the 1976 financial crisis and by Jimmy
Carter's administration in the Volcker shock of 1979, as by the right.[34]

The stagflation crisis also put considerable pressure on the formerly
successful collaboration between social democratic governments and
labour unions. If social democratic governments wanted to avoid very
high inflation they had to persuade the unions to accept a very moderate wages policy.[35] The most successful country in this respect was
Austria where the unions decided to follow the wishes of the government and exercised self-restraint, so that the government itself did not
need to take firm action against inflation and could implement public
spending programmes in favour of employment. With this form of
Keynesian stability policy, Austria was able to keep inflation and unemployment comparatively low. Elsewhere, this approach did not work. In
Germany, the unions restricted their wage demands somewhat in 1974

---

[32] Rodger, *Age of Fracture*, p. 256.

[33] John R. Hicks, *The Crisis in Keynesian Economics* (Oxford: Oxford University Press,
1974). See also Maier, '"Malaise"', pp. 32–8.

[34] Daniel Stedman Jones, *Masters of the Universe: Hayek, Friedman and the Birth of
Neoliberal Politics* (Princeton, NJ, and London: Princeton University Press, 2012),
pp. 215–16.

[35] Fritz W. Scharpf, *Sozialdemokratische Krisenpolitik in Europe* (Frankfurt: Campus,
1987); English translation *Crisis and Choice in European Social Democracy* (Ithaca,
NY: Cornell University Press, 1991).

but returned to a more aggressive stance in 1975. The independent Bundesbank responded with a sharp increase in the interest rate and as the Social Democratic Party/Free Democratic Party government was not willing to lock horns with the Bundesbank it accepted its anti-inflation policy. The result was high unemployment. This forced the unions to return to more moderate demands to avoid an inevitable and even more dramatic increase in unemployment. In Sweden too, the government and unions were not able to agree on a coordinated stabilisation policy, which was one of the reasons why in 1976 the governing Social Democratic Party lost power for the first time since the war.[36]

The problems were quite different in the new democratic states of southern Europe – Greece, Spain and Portugal. All three countries opted not for the French and Italian tax regimes, which were based on high consumption taxes to overcome widespread tax evasion, but for the much more progressive central European tax regime, which was based firmly on a progressive income tax. All three states soon adopted tax laws in favour of such an approach, but were not able to administer them through a well-trained tax bureaucracy. The result was extensive tax fraud and evasion, something all three countries have had problems in combating to this day.[37] This left them with the problem of how they could finance their emerging welfare systems. All three countries, as in Italy, overcame the problem of tax fraud through the use of the central bank, which was strongly dependent on the government, to monetise large and recurrent budget deficits. This was and remains a highly controversial issue, as it is in our volume. While Benjamin Lemoine argues that this is an equitable way to avoid dependency on creditors, Stefano Battilossi analyses inflationary finance and its interaction with the extensive regulation of domestic banking (financial repression) from a public finance perspective and argues that this policy mix tends to create severe distortions in the economy.[38] In reality, the southern European states were able to solve some of the problems of government finance through this policy until the run-up to European

---

[36] Scharpf, *Sozialdemokratische Krisenpolitik*, chs. 4, 6 and 7.

[37] Sara Torregrosa Hetland, 'Did Democracy Bring Redistribution? Insights from the Spanish Tax System, 1960–90', *European Review of Economic History* (2015), 1–22; and 'Bypassing Progressive Taxation: Fraud and Base Erosion in the Spanish Income Tax (1970–2001)', IEB Working Paper 2015/31; Juan Prieto Rodriguez, Maria Jose Sanzo Perez and Javier Suarez Pandiello, 'Análisis economic de la actitud hacia el fraude fiscal en Espana', *Hacienda Publica Espanola: Revista de Economia Publica*, 177 (2006), 107–28; Demetrios J. Delivanis, 'Griechenland', in *Handbuch der Finanzwissenschaft*, vol. IV (Tübingen: Mohr, 1983), pp. 905–26; Chiara Bronchi and José C. Gomes-Santos, 'Reforming the Tax System in Portugal', *OECD Economics Department Working Papers* 302 (2001).

[38] See this volume, Chapters 11 and 12.

monetary unification in the late 1980s, when they switched, with some reluctance, to a path of disinflation, financial liberalisation and fiscal consolidation.[39]

The crisis of Keynesianism was more than a change in economic policy. It was also linked to a general scepticism towards macroeconomics and quantitative approaches, and the predictability of economic outcomes. The state should limit its role to creating an efficient institutional framework for markets, but distance itself from demand management and economic fine-tuning. The problems of Keynesian economic policy and rising scepticism about it were the context for the policy changes of the Thatcher government after 1979 and the Reagan administration after 1981: the difficult economic conditions of the 1970s of low growth, the two oil crises and the collapse of the Bretton Woods system meant that the shift to greater reliance on the market was born from a sense of the failure of the post-war order.[40]

It was not just that economists came up with different policies in response to perceived failure; it was also possible for politicians to sell a more optimistic future to a weary electorate in place of what Lester Thurow in 1980 termed a zero-sum society where a gain for one was a loss for another.[41] The new ideas offered a more confident approach in which growth and prosperity were possible through what has been called 'populist market optimism', expressed in the significant tax cuts of 1979 and 1981 in Britain and the United States. These ideas were popularised in two best-sellers published in the United States. The first was Jude Wanniski's *The Way the World Works* which advocated a supply-side approach, arguing that a 'wedge' of taxation interrupted trade between producer and consumer; if it could be reduced, the economy would flourish. The Democrats offered spending to help the poor; rather than oppose spending, the Republicans should promise tax cuts which, they claimed, would restore full employment and so contain pressure for public spending and reduce the size of the public sector.[42] The second was George Gilder's *Wealth and Poverty*, which presented an optimistic account of economic growth once entrepreneurs had been unshackled from the fetters of taxation; Reagan made sure that the members of his cabinet were given copies.[43] The radical tax reductions

---

[39] See this volume, Chapter 12.

[40] Rodger, *Age of Fracture*, p. 44.

[41] Lester Thurow, *The Zero-sum Society and the Possibilities for Change* (New York: Basic Books, 1980).

[42] Jude Wanninski, *The Way the World Works: How Economies Fail – and Succeed* (New York: Basic Books, 1978).

[43] George Gilder, *Wealth and Poverty* (New York: Basic Books, 1981); Rodger, *Age of Fracture*, pp. 69, 72.

introduced by Reagan and Thatcher represented the most extensive overhaul of the tax system in the United States and United Kingdom since the end of the Second World War. These developments were political thunderclaps that reverberated around the world and left an indelible mark on fiscal policy, creating a new fiscal constitution.[44]

The New Fiscal Constitution since the 1980s

The end of the boom and then the radical shifts in policy after 1979 provide the starting point for this collection of essays and demonstrate a fundamental shift in the fiscal constitution in the 1980s. While the first oil crisis and the demise of the Bretton Woods system made it hard for countries to pursue Keynesian economics and combine low unemployment with redistribution that could narrow the gap between high- and low-income earners, the second oil crisis made this policy highly improbable because the rise in oil prices was combined with the Volcker shock. When the OPEC countries tripled the price of oil in 1979, the consequences were nearly the same as in 1973: high inflation, more unemployment, falling production and deficits in the balance of payments. But Paul Volcker, the new chairman of the Federal Reserve appointed by President Carter, decided to fight at least one part of the consequences with vigour: inflation. The Federal Reserve had already started to follow the Bundesbank's monetarist policy in autumn 1978 by raising the interest rate. But when the second oil crisis struck the United States the Fed increased the interest rate again in the second half of 1979. This created shock waves in the highly indebted developing countries and triggered an international debt crisis.[45] But during the 1980 election Volcker returned to an expansionary path and inflation again started to rise. Only after Reagan took office did Volcker change his policy once more, this time more dramatically, driving real interest rates in the United States up to 6 per cent in 1982 and 8 per cent in 1983–4.[46] Once again OPEC money flowed into the Western

---

[44] See this volume, Chapters 2–5. See also W. Elliot Brownlee and Eugene C. Steuerle, 'Taxation', in W. Elliot Brownlee and Hugh Davis Graham (eds.), *The Reagan Presidency. Pragmatic Conservatism and Its Legacies* (Lawrence, KS: University Press of Kansas, 2003), pp. 155–81.

[45] Jeffry A. Frieden, *Debt, Development, and Democracy. Modern Political Economy and Latin America, 1965–1985* (Princeton, NJ: Princeton University Press, 1991); Osvald Sunkel and Stephany Griffith-Jones, *Debt and Development Crises in Latin America. The End of an Illusion* (Oxford: Oxford University Press 1986).

[46] Robert L. Hetzel, *The Monetary Policy of the Federal Reserve. A History* (Cambridge: Cambridge University Press, 2008), ch. 13; Andrew Glyn, *Capitalism Unleashed. Finance, Globalisation, and Welfare* (Oxford: Oxford University Press, 2006), pp. 25–8.

banking system, but this time it did not make credit cheap for the governments.

As a result of the greater freedom of the capital markets, all the other Western countries had to follow the United States by raising their interest rates if they did not want to be stripped of capital that otherwise would flow into the United States. The high interest rates now made it very expensive for states to stimulate their economy through state spending on the basis of borrowing. The other problem was that the high interest rates reduced the incentive to invest. If investors could obtain a high rate of return from financial investment, why should they invest in infrastructure and property in Western countries offering moderate growth rates, considerable insecurity about the future path of the economy and lower profitability? This made it nearly impossible for states not to offer investors lower taxes, tax-breaks or subsidies for investments; if not, the chances of keeping unemployment low seemed to be diminishing.[47]

The politics of the Social Democratic or Socialist governments in Europe from 1979 to 1984 demonstrate these problems quite clearly. The most obvious case was France where the newly elected Socialist president, François Mitterrand, adopted a policy that Timothy B. Smith called '(Pseudo) Keynesianism in one country'.[48] Mitterrand raised state spending dramatically to stimulate the economy while introducing redistributive justice. The outcome was massive capital flight, which in turn led to three devaluations of the franc and a rise in unemployment. In 1982, after slipping into an ever deeper crisis, Mitterrand and the Socialists changed course. Now they turned to a policy of austerity and tax-breaks for investors and the wealthy.[49] In Sweden the Social Democrats adopted a more capital-friendly policy as soon as they returned to office in 1982 by opting for a radical devaluation of the Swedish krona to boost the country's export industry. At the same time, they did not cut state spending and offered some tax-breaks for investment. As a result, they were able to keep unemployment comparatively low, but state debt became a problem and the payment of interest as part of central state spending rose from less than 5 per cent in 1977 to 23 per cent in 1985. Furthermore, because the costs of imported goods were rising, real wages deteriorated. They had already fallen each year between 1978 and 1981 by about 1 per cent; now they

[47] Scharpf, *Sozialdemokratische Krisenpolitik*, ch. 11.
[48] Timothy B. Smith, *France in Crisis: Welfare, Inequality and Globalization since 1980* (Cambridge: Cambridge University Press, 2004), p. 97.
[49] See this volume, Chapter 5.

fell each year from 1982 to 1984 by around 4 per cent.[50] So, if we look at the politics of European Socialist or Social Democratic governments from 1979 to 1984 we can see that there was a trade-off between low employment and any attempt to move to equalise income distribution.

Because of this trade-off, policy-makers in most countries at that time resorted to one of two forms to improve conditions for investment. In Germany, tax policy was increasingly influenced by debates on national competitiveness. This began in the 1980s when low growth rates and a large, and partly internationally uncompetitive, industrial sector was increasingly linked to high labour costs and an unfavourable tax regime for foreign investors. After the fall of the Berlin Wall and the reunification of East and West Germany in 1990, the debate was even more pronounced.[51] While initially some politicians had promised 'flourishing landscapes' and rapid economic recovery in East Germany, the structural weakness of East Germany's industry soon became apparent. The high costs of reunification and the problem of declining international competitiveness had two consequences: the welfare system was used to compensate for a large part of the financial burden of reunification;[52] and the need for high taxation rates had to be adapted to a system that did not harm Germany's economic position in the world.

The long-term shift to direct and redistributive taxes that had been in place since the war (or even earlier) had already been reversed, with a greater reliance on indirect taxes in many countries, in particular value added tax (VAT) in the European Community. Tax harmonisation, which started in the late 1960s to enhance competition within the common trade area, focused mainly on indirect taxes. One effect was that countries with low indirect tax rates, such as Germany, had the option to increase their VAT rate, while only a few countries lowered their rates. Although there was talk in some countries and in some ideological quarters of 'rolling back the state', the overall level of tax remained relatively constant or even slightly increased. Most groups call for lower taxes, yet do not want the resulting cuts in spending to adversely affect the benefits they receive. What did change was the *structure* of taxation. In some cases, politicians turned to what have been called 'stealth taxes' – charges that are hidden and almost surreptitious – such as duties on

---

[50] Scharpf, *Sozialdemokratische Krisenpolitik*, pp. 304–14.

[51] Wencke Meteling, 'Internationale Konkurrenz als nationale Bedrohung. Zur politischen Maxime der "Standortsicherung" in den neunziger Jahren', in Ralph Jessen (ed.), *Konkurrenz in der Geschichte. Praktiken –Werte – Institutionalisierungen* (Frankfurt and New York: Campus, 2014), pp. 289–315.

[52] Gerhard A. Ritter, *Der Preis der deutschen Einheit. Die Wiedervereinigung und die Krise des Sozialstaats* (Munich: Beck 2007).

petrol linked to the rate of inflation, or increases in social insurance contributions that are not defined as taxes. The striking change was the move away from redistribution, with reductions in the top rates of direct taxes and an increase in employees' social contributions, which had important social and economic consequences, not least for patterns of inequality of wealth and income. The argument was that incentives would be restored and prosperity created, though the shift in policy might also have led to recession and unemployment.[53] The trend towards higher indirect taxes had negative monetary effects too, leading to higher prices which forced central banks to impose more restrictive monetary policies.

The new approach was therefore linked to a stricter approach to monetary policy, moving away from the loose monetary policies that had been possible after the shift to floating exchange rates. Of course, some countries had retained a relatively tight monetary policy – above all Germany; now others followed, such as the United States with the Volcker shock and the various efforts in Britain to impose discipline through the Medium Term Financial Strategy or by linking the pound to the Deutschmark.[54] The tightening of monetary policy was combined with the deregulation of financial markets. In the United States, the first step was the lifting of controls that set limits to the rate of interest which could be paid on consumer savings deposits in 1980. It allowed credit to flow freely through the country and increased financial sector profits.[55] In a closed economy raising the interest rate would have led to a crowding-out of private borrowers, which would have forced the Reagan administration to impose fiscal austerity. But fiscal deregulation and globalisation helped high interest rates to encourage a huge inflow of foreign money, which made credit available for public

---

[53] See this volume, Chapters 2–5; Junko Kato, *Regressive Taxation and the Welfare State. Path Dependence and Policy Diffusion* (Cambridge: Cambridge University Press, 2003); Duane Swank and Sven Steinmo, 'The New Political Economy of Taxation in Advanced Political Economies', *American Journal of Political Science* 46 (2002), 642–55; Philipp Genschel, 'Globalization, Tax Competition and the Welfare State', *Politics & Society* 30/2 (2002), 245–75. Discussion of a possible race to the bottom in taxation grew stronger at the end of the 1990s. See OECD, *Harmful Tax Competition* (Paris: OECD, 1998).

[54] Ernst Baltensprenger, 'Geldpolitik bei wachsender Integration (1979–1996)', in Deutsche Bundesbank (ed.), *Fünfzig Jahre Deutsche Mark. Notenbank und Währung in Deutschland seit 1948* (Munich: Beck, 1998), pp. 475–560; Hetzel, *Monetary Policy*, ch. 14; Duncan Needham, *UK Monetary Policy from Devaluation to Thatcher, 1967–1982* (Basingstoke: Palgrave Macmillan, 2014). A highly critical account of the Bundesbank's policy can be found in David Marsh, *The Most Powerful Bank: Inside the German Bundesbank* (London: Heinemann, 1992).

[55] Greta Krippner, *Capitalizing on the Crisis. The Political Origins of the Rise of Finance* (Cambridge, MA: Harvard University Press, 2011), pp. 58–9.

and private borrowers.[56] A second wave of financial deregulation was introduced during Bill Clinton's presidency. Most important was the Gramm–Leach–Bliley Act of 1999, which removed sections of the Glass–Steagall Act of 1933. The 1933 Act had restricted commercial banks' engagement in securities activities and imposed strict separation between commercial and investment banks.[57] Financial deregulation furthered financialisation so that a growing percentage of profits in the United States consisted of financial activities, while in the early 1980s many US manufacturers were driven into bankruptcy as a result of the high dollar rate.[58] It also resulted in the growth of credit markets for poor and middle-income citizens and the highly speculative derivatives market for the wealthy, which Colin Crouch sees as the basis for the short success story of a privatised Keynesianism in the 1990s and early 2000s.[59] Although most European countries had a much less regulated banking sector than the US,[60] they also adopted some further deregulation, not least Britain with the so-called 'Big Bang' of 1986 which deregulated the financial markets and led to a massive growth in the financial services sector. While in 1976 only five out of nineteen OECD countries were considered by the International Monetary Fund to have an open capital market, in 1995 all were rated as having such a market.[61]

The emergence of a more powerful international financial sector in the 1980s was linked with another policy shift: privatisation and the use of capital markets rather than taxes to fund infrastructure. This unfolded more rapidly in some countries than in others.[62] One way of responding to the growth of Leviathan was to argue that the public sector was inefficient because it lacked the incentives of competition and so led to rising costs. This did not entail only selling state utilities, such as gas and electricity, to private concerns, but also funding projects

---

[56] Krippner, *Capitalizing*, p. 142.

[57] Carl Felsenfeld and David L. Glass, *Banking Regulation in the United States*, 3rd edn (New York: Juris, 2011), pp. 94–8.

[58] Krippner, *Capitalizing*, ch. 2; Robert Brenner, *The Economics of Global Turbulence. The Advanced Capitalist Economies from Long Boom to Long Downturn, 1945–2005* (London and New York: Verso, 2006), pp. 187–90.

[59] Colin Crouch, 'Privatised Keynesianism: An Unacknowledged Policy Regime', *The British Journal of Politics and International Relations* 11 (2009), 382–99.

[60] Monica Prasad, *The Land of Too Much. American Abundance and the Paradox of Poverty* (Cambridge, MA: Harvard University Press, 2012).

[61] Glyn, *Capitalism Unleashed*, p. 65.

[62] See this volume, Chapter 9; James Meek, *Private Island. Why Britain Now Belongs to Someone Else* (London: Verso, 2014); Massimo Florio, *The Great Divestiture: Evaluating the Welfare Impact of the British Privatizations, 1979–1997* (Cambridge, MA: MIT Press, 2004); Norbert Frei and Dietmar Süß (eds.), *Privatisierung. Idee und Praxis seit den 1970er Jahren* (Göttingen: Wallstein, 2012).

with private money. This process had started earlier, with the first Eurobond issued in 1963 for the Italian company Autostrade, but now became more significant.[63] Public sector net investment fell, and the shift from Keynesian management was linked to a reduction in the state ownership of and investment in fixed capital assets as a result of privatisation and the greater use of private concerns.

Tension started to emerge between the demands on governments to continue funding social welfare, not least for better healthcare and support for an ageing population, and the weakening support for taxation. In many OECD countries there were heated debates about whether and how far the welfare state should be cut back, but in the end politicians often refrained from drastic cuts, so the spending ratio for social policy in most countries remained at least stable or even continued to rise.[64] So the question remained: how could more generous social provision be combined with lower taxes if the supposed benefits of higher growth were not being realised? It did prove possible to square the circle and reduce the national debt during periods of economic prosperity, as during the Clinton administration,[65] but increasingly, the circle was squared only by borrowing, resulting in a structural budget deficit even in the boom years.[66] Here the adoption of the euro has a role to play, for countries with a persistent record of default and a weak fiscal regime – Greece, Portugal and Italy – were able to borrow on more favourable terms thanks to their membership of the Eurozone, and the debt-to-GDP ratio started to rise to unsustainable levels.[67]

The shift to the use of debt ran into difficulties with the onset of the recession in 2008. The argument of opponents of deficit finance was now more widely accepted, that the result was to impose charges on the future and to threaten state bankruptcy – an argument that defeated those who believed that the recession offered an opportunity to use cheap loans to invest for future growth. The result in some countries was to tighten fiscal rules to constrain what was seen as a 'deficit bias'

[63] Arnold Picot, Massimo Florio, Nico Grove and Johann Kranz (eds.), *The Economics of Infrastructure Provisioning. The Changing Role of the State* (Cambridge, MA: MIT Press, 2015); Akintola Akintoye, Matthias Beck and Cliff Hardcastle (eds.), *Public–Private Partnerships. Managing Risks and Opportunities* (Oxford: Blackwell, 2003).

[64] Peter H. Lindert, *Growing Public. Social Spending and Economic Growth since the Eighteenth Century*, vol. 1: *The Story* (Cambridge: Cambridge University Press, 2004), pp. 12–14, 27.

[65] See this volume, Chapter 3; Christopher J. Bailey, 'Clintonomics', in Dilys Hill and Paul Herrnson (eds.), *The Clinton Presidency. The First Term, 1992–1996* (Basingstoke: Palgrave Macmillan, 1999), pp. 85–103; Joseph Stiglitz, *The Roaring Nineties: A New History of the World's Most Prosperous Decade* (New York: W. W. Norton, 2004).

[66] Streeck, *Buying Time*.

[67] See this volume, Chapter 12.

created by the rising relative costs of public services due to more advanced healthcare provision or its labour-intensive nature, and by the demands of some social groups for welfare. Reducing debt after the Second World War was possible because of high economic growth, low interest rates and often high inflation rates, all of which were policy options. Although interest rates are now low as a result of quantitative easing, so are growth and inflation, which means that debt reduction was widely considered to entail austerity rather than an increase in fiscal extraction.[68] Furthermore, the euro eradicates the capacity of large debtors such as Greece to devalue their currency; and German economic policies contribute to a strong euro. Consequently, there is a serious political problem of who should bear the burden of any cuts.

In the wake of the two oil crises, the richest OECD countries experienced a turnaround in the trend towards greater social equality. While people from all walks of life had enjoyed a fairer distribution of wealth during the boom years, the well-known Kuznets curve now proved to be wrong in its generalisation and the gap was widening again between the lowest and highest income groups. In his highly acclaimed book *Capital in the Twenty-First Century*, Thomas Piketty has shown that this is especially true for the concentration of wealth.[69] In this volume David Jesuit and Vincent Mahler show that this concentration process is far slower when it comes to disposable incomes, because taxes and transfers continued to rise in most developed countries at least until the 1990s, so that the growing gap in market incomes was reduced.[70] Nevertheless the trend has also been reversed in disposable incomes, and in some countries, especially the United States, the gap has widened significantly since the 1970s. Piketty now strongly urges the use of taxation and especially of progressive income taxation and a global capital tax to combat this trend.

The Focus of This Book

Many of the issues raised by Piketty figure prominently in our volume. In contrast to Piketty, however, this collection does not seek to identify capitalistic principles over the centuries, such as the constant tendency of the rate of return on capital to outstrip growth. Rather, this volume primarily takes the economic and political changes of the 1970s as its

---

[68] Nick Crafts, 'Reducing High Public Debt Ratios: Lessons from UK Experience', *Fiscal Studies*, epub., 23 December 2015.

[69] Thomas Piketty, *Capital in the Twenty-First Century* (Cambridge, MA: Harvard University Press, 2014).

[70] See this volume, Chapter 8.

starting point and examines how the wealthiest OECD countries responded to the ensuing challenges. The contributors consider the political economy of different places and times, and the nature of political regimes and ideologies. In Marc Buggeln's chapter, for example, we see that countries differed in their tax policies which were influenced by path dependencies and political structures as well as by common challenges. As Buggeln points out, even Reagan and Thatcher, who are often placed together, differed considerably in their tax policies. The United States did not adopt value added tax, unlike most European countries, and its debt increased considerably, whereas in Britain it fell. Other chapters ask why countries in southern Europe adopted an approach to public finance through 'financial repression'. There is, therefore, a recurring interest in the balance between the forces leading to convergence and the counter-pressures for divergence.

One pressure for convergence has been mentioned in the literature: a neo-liberal convergence among Western countries and in Western financial policy in the 1970s which replaced Keynesian economics as the predominant doctrine.[71] But does this stand up to scrutiny? True, Keynesianism lost its role as the leading economic doctrine of the post-war decades, but it never completely disappeared from economic science and policy. For example, the German 'stability law' of 1967 is still in force and there have been various attempts to re-establish elements of Keynesian economics in both academic and political circles. On the other hand, it is unclear what influence neo-liberal economists really had on governments of the day. Have neo-liberal tax and fiscal policies won? And what is actually 'neo-' about neo-liberalism? From one perspective, Thatcher was implementing a well-developed neo-liberal agenda, but from another, as Martin Daunton explains, she was expressing a desire for moral regeneration with its origins in her religious upbringing, and the ideas on tax reform came from economists who cannot be defined as neo-liberal and whose influence was mediated through Treasury officials. And for all the lip-service paid to neo-liberalism and rolling back the state, actual reductions in government spending have been modest at best, as Buggeln shows for four EU countries where taxation was a higher proportion of GDP in 1990 than in 1970.

[71] Peter Hall, 'The Movement from Keynesianism to Monetarism: Institutional Analysis and British Economic Policy in the 1970s', in Sven Steinmo, Kathleen Thelen and Frank Longstreth (eds.), *Structuring Politics. Historical Institutionalism in Comparative Perspective* (Cambridge: Cambridge University Press, 1992), pp. 90–113; Marion Fourcade-Gourinchas and Sarah L. Babb, 'The Rebirth of the Liberal Creed: Path to Neoliberalism in Four Countries', *American Journal of Sociology*, 108/3 (2002), 533–79.

Another possible source of convergence was the increasing pressure of global tax competition which forced countries to reduce taxation on both high-income earners and corporations to prevent capital flight and the use of tax havens. Piketty raises the highly contentious fairness-related issue of an increasing flight of wealthy citizens to tax havens since the 1970s, a problem that provokes outrage in the face of empty coffers. Switzerland is an interesting case of a country that for decades profited from its reputation as a secure tax haven offering guaranteed banking secrecy. This unique position was challenged by financial deregulation and the emergence of offshore banking in various countries during the 1970s. Christophe Farquet explains how the Swiss government successfully defended its advantages against the challenges of international competition. Gisela Hürlimann also indicates that tax competition was a driving force in tax reforms in the Swiss cantons, which at the same time led to greater social inequality. She shows how Switzerland's still-evolving welfare state has delivered a spending surge, especially since the onset of the international financial crisis, financing these expenditures with growing tax revenues that have been further swollen by the inflow of foreign capital attracted to its low tax regime. This once again demonstrates how small states have been able to achieve significant victories in tax competition, while larger states were unable or unwilling to counter them. Certainly, tax competition was used by politicians such as the UK Chancellor of the Exchequer, Nigel Lawson, to justify changes in the country's taxation structure. Buggeln shows that most countries in western Europe followed in reducing the top rate of income and corporation tax. Again, all OECD countries refrained from financial repression and relied almost exclusively on the market to borrow.

Indeed, there is another strand in the literature that stresses the differences between forms of the state rather than convergence towards a single pattern. Concepts such as 'Varieties of Capitalism' (Hall and Soskice) and 'Three Worlds of Welfare Capitalism' (Esping-Andersen) point to significant differences between Western countries which have remained relatively constant over a long period. Consequently, the present volume strives to shed more light on the relationship between convergence and divergence. Societies facing similar problems of rising social expenditure could still come to different solutions according to their political and economic structures.

In addressing these issues, this book brings together perspectives from a variety of disciplines that have been engaged in research on taxation and public finance, including history, economics, sociology and political science. By drawing on case studies from different disciplines and geographical areas, this book sheds light on how the process of historical change in taxation and public spending is to be understood from economic, social and political perspectives. This book does not claim to cover all parts of the world. Rather, the focus is on the advanced industrialised countries which are members of the OECD. Rather than providing an overall compendium of public spending since the 1970s in all industrialised countries, we focus on specific problems and debates. The approach is sometimes explicitly comparative between a pair or group of countries to see how differing political systems responded to common pressures. In Peter Lindert's chapter the approach is more synoptic, looking at the role of pressure groups in shaping redistribution in thirty-four countries. Again, the approach is sometimes concerned with transnational connections, for politicians in one country often referred to actions elsewhere to justify their actions, or to argue that they were driven by tax competition. Other studies provide an in-depth analysis of one country, showing the interplay between domestic actors and interests.

While there is an extensive literature on structural changes in tax systems, there is less research on the relationship between public finances, fiscal administration and politics.[72] While most of the literature looks at state income *or* expenditures, this volume brings together both sides of fiscal policy through an inclusive approach in which public finances are viewed through the lens of political economy. This is done in a number of ways.

Above all, public finances serve as a 'hinge' between the state, the economy and society. In no other sector are the political and economic spheres so closely intertwined. It is not simply the case that the state and other political institutions are largely financed through taxation, but also that much of the state's intervention in the economy and society is transmitted by the fiscal system, including the efficient allocation of economic resources, the provision of public goods and redistribution between regions, social groups and generations. Taxation is a field where different social groups, political parties and institutions act in their own interests and try to maximise their benefit or add to their institutional power.

Lindert uses quantitative data to investigate the power of interest groups. His findings suggest that democracies tend to favour small interest groups, especially those on the losing side of the free-market

---

[72] Alberto Alesina and Roberto Perotti, 'The Political Economy of Budget Deficits', *NBER Working Paper Series*, 4637 (1994), 1–31; Duane Swank and Sven Steinmo, 'The New Political Economy of Taxation in Advanced Capitalist Democracies', *American Journal of Political Science* 46/3 (2002), 642–55.

economy, such as farmers. However, the cost of any concessions made to them is likely to fall over time, for they constitute a declining share of the population. By contrast, he argues that the voice of groups that form a larger part of the population, such as pensioners, becomes weaker as a result of any gains being spread more thinly and by enraging younger taxpayers. Jesuit and Mahler take the opposite view that pensioners have been able to protect the generous benefits obtained during the years of affluence which are now very difficult to reduce. As a result, there is an intergenerational transfer in favour of the so-called 'pinch generation' – members of society who experienced full employment and rising affluence in the boom years – who have now reached old age and retain their generous benefits at the expense of the young, who face unemployment and declining standards of living, and have fewer expectations of a sufficient pension in old age or property ownership.[73] Nor can Lindert's approach make sense of the massive economic power of the financial services sector, which is both a source of tax revenue and has considerable political influence in shaping fiscal policy. Redistribution does not always go to the declining sectors. Nor do interest groups simply emerge from a material base; they are defined in terms of political language and rhetoric, and need to be mobilised.[74]

The question of how different groups and interests mobilise and shape public finances is a recurrent theme in this volume. Path dependency is important, for the tax system itself created vested interests, such as insurance companies and pensions funds which enjoyed generous tax-breaks in Britain. Interest groups not only shape taxation, but are themselves defined by the tax system. As Daunton shows, Thatcher's Conservative government wished to weaken vested interest groups' hold on investment, but removing their preferential treatment would alienate both these institutions and the individuals whose decisions rested on existing tax-breaks. Reforming the tax system entails a break with path dependency and this is not easy and can be achieved

---

[73] The title of a book by the Conservative MP David Willetts, *The Pinch: How the Baby Boomers Took their Children's Future – and Why They Should Give It Back* (London: Atlantic Books, 2010). The most thorough historical study on pension policy in Germany and Britain from 1945 until today tends more to Lindert's position and shows that the pensioners were not able to build a strong interest organisation. Because of that the reduction in pensions has been possible in recent years in both countries without much protest, even if the extent should not be overestimated: Cornelius Torp, *Gerechtigkeit im Wohlfahrtsstaat. Alter und Alterssicherung in Deutschland und Großbritannien von 1945 bis heute* (Göttingen: Vandenhoeck & Ruprecht, 2015).

[74] Frank Trentmann, *Free Trade Nation. Commerce, Consumption, and Civil Society in Modern Britain* (Oxford: Oxford University Press, 2009).

only in certain circumstances.[75] These need to be fully appreciated, for the political economy of countries differed, with greater or lesser flexibility or resistance to change, and with weaker or stronger veto players.[76]

Hence the contributors to this volume are interested in the institutions created to handle public finance on the side of revenue and spending, including tax law, public administration, central banks and budget committees. Differences are found between countries with a federal or a unitary system; between the checks and balances of presidential structures and the greater freedom of the executive in parliamentary systems; between proportional representation which is more likely to lead to coalitions with veto players or first-past-the-post systems which are more likely to lead to one-party governments that can impose their political will. Taking the examples of Denmark and the Netherlands – countries with many similarities – Reimut Zohlnhöfer demonstrates how the Dutch party system allowed successive governments to move more quickly in implementing the reforms they considered necessary than the Danish party system. Similarly, Elliot Brownlee and Eisaku Ide show that tax compliance is closely connected to trust in one's own state and is found more often where people believe that what they pay in tax delivers important goals.

Indeed, one of the most striking differences is between those countries that have a well-developed tax administration that rests on consent, legitimacy and compliance, and those countries where the fiscal regime is fragile, notably the countries of southern Europe. In these cases, there was a reliance on non-tax revenues or securing loans outside the capital market. Stefano Battilossi sees structural similarities in the growing fiscal imbalances in southern Europe where low growth, more social spending and an inefficient tax system were responsible for rising deficits. But regardless of this difference, after the Second World War nearly all governments increasingly relied on implicit revenues through financial repression and seigniorage. Benjamin Lemoine shows that in France after the war the state relied on non-market debt financing through the 'Treasury Circuit', until it was deliberately blocked by new voices within the ministerial bureaucracy in order to control inflation and to make the state increasingly reliant on the financial markets as the only source of credit, more on the lines of Britain and the United States.

---

[75] These issues are addressed in Paul Pierson, *Politics in Time: History, Institutions and Social Analysis* (Princeton, NJ: Princeton University Press, 2004).

[76] George Tsebelis, *Veto Players. How Political Institutions Work* (Princeton, NJ: Princeton University Press, 2002).

The evolution of public finance did not only entail changes in the structure of taxation, for resistance to tax increases and demands for higher social welfare gave rise to a persistent 'deficit bias' that could only be filled by resorting to loans. Since the 1970s, almost all Western industrialised countries have seen a significant rise in public debt, which had fallen in many countries during the boom years. Since then, economic policy debates have focused on the question of how much debt a state should assume and what consequences this might have for its citizens and the economy. Debates have addressed not only the burdens that debt places on society and, under certain conditions on future generations, but also the options available to the state itself, the resources of which have been increasingly focused on paying interest and reducing debt. In nearly every industrialised country, concern about public debt has become so powerful that it now overshadows every other budgetary question. As a result, there has been a trend since the 1980s towards what Wolfgang Streeck calls the 'debt-consolidation state' or an enforced 'politics of austerity' (Paul Pierson), which has resulted in renewed efforts to reduce both expenditures and debt.[77] This attempt to cut debt has been justified in part by an appeal to Carmen Reinhart and Ken Rogoff's '90 per cent rule' that growth falls by 1 per cent when debt exceeds 90 per cent of GDP.[78] Their analysis has been hotly contested on the grounds that debt is not always inimical to growth and there has always existed an opposing view that public debt can be harmless and sometimes even beneficial.

Above all, it was in Greece, Spain and Portugal that governments turned to public borrowing as a way to fund the modernisation of welfare state structures that had been neglected by preceding dictatorships, but in a period of delayed growth. Stefano Battilossi shows that these states not only increased their public borrowing, but also employed various other tools in order to limit the size of the debt. However, joining the European Union meant that these tools became increasingly unviable, leading to a rapid expansion of public debt, although the catastrophic consequences would only come later, after the crisis erupted. The political implications of debt varied between countries, depending on whether it was serviced by an effective taxation

---

[77] Streeck, *Buying Time*, ch. 2; Paul Pierson, *Dismantling the Welfare State? Reagan, Thatcher and the Politics of Retrenchment* (Cambridge: Cambridge University Press, 1995); and (ed.), *The New Politics of the Welfare State* (Oxford: Oxford University Press, 2001).

[78] Carmen Reinhart and Kenneth Rogoff, 'Growth in a Time of Debt', NBER Working Paper 15639 (January 2010); and 'Debt, Growth and the Austerity Debate', *New York Times*, 25 April 2013.

system and whether the debt was held by foreigners or within the national economy, as in Japan.

The ministerial bureaucracy highlighted by Lemoine is one example of important players that have so far received little attention in the literature. He indicates that a leading spokesman in the change in French public finance was Jean-Yves Haberer, a young finance inspector with experience of the capital markets in the United States, and who opposed the views of established officials in the Treasury. Similarly, in Britain officials in the Treasury and their economic advisers were proposing tax reforms that owed much to a shift from viewing taxation through marginal utility – an approach that shaped progressive tax regimes – to optimal tax theory and a changed understanding of incentives and equity. This theoretical shift complemented the more ideological approaches of leading politicians towards creating a society based on enterprise and individualism. The nature of the relationship between economists, officials and politicians is a major topic, one that certainly cannot be reduced to a simple triumph of neo-liberalism. Some of the leading proponents of reform in Britain – including the Nobel Prize-winning economists James Meade and James Mirrlees – were social democrats, and their approach influenced officials' thinking. Official protagonists play an important role for Martin Chick too, because the adoption of new accounting systems changes the course of public investments in the future, resulting in far-reaching consequences for the long-term structure of the British state.

Countries differed in the permeability of the public bureaucracy to new economic ideas with the shift from Keynesian or social market responses, and in the ability of officials to shape policy. Historians and political scientists have provided excellent explanations of the reception of Keynes in different countries, depending on the existing state structures and capacities which facilitated or blocked the use of public works.[79] We now need a much deeper appreciation of how and why a new economic thinking displaced Keynesianism. How important were ideas in reshaping the state compared with electoral calculation or interest group politics? What was the role of economic experts and the dominance of political discourse in their approach of economic individualism? Fiscal policy is especially prone to political and ideological

[79] See, for example, Peter A. Hall (ed.), *The Political Power of Economic Ideas: Keynesianism Across States* (Princeton, NJ: Princeton University Press, 1989); Margaret Weir and Theda Skocpol, 'State Structures and the Possibilities for "Keynesian" Responses to the Great Depression in Sweden, Britain and the United States', in P. B. Evans, D. Rueschemeyer and T. Skocpol (eds.), *Bringing the State Back In* (Cambridge: Cambridge University Press, 1985).

conflicts. The fiscal structure is much more than a legal or administrative problem, but rather mirrors the political and social constitution of a country. Incoming governments often begin their term of office by reforming the tax system – or at least they promise to do so. Often, these reforms are linked to controversies within the economic and social sciences, as the endless discussion between Keynesians and monetarists shows. Linking fiscal policy and its contentions to the role of economic experts and scientists is a constant issue found in this volume.

This collection of essays starts with the shift in the nature of the state and public finance in the early 1970s. There is general agreement that the 1970s represented a critical turning point, but the issue of how to classify the subsequent decades is still hotly debated. Are we now facing another shift in the form of the state in the face of the challenge of the financial crisis and economic uncertainty, with major changes in the world economic order? For instance, it remains to be seen to what extent the classification proposed by Streeck – with the transition from a tax state to a debt state to a fiscal consolidation state – will prove to be viable.[80] There is now an extensive body of research addressing the demise of one model of the state and pointing to a transformation of the 'democratic constitutional/interventionist state' since the beginning of the crisis in the 1960s–70s. Although many still dream of reviving that model, the way back has largely been blocked by privatisation, economic globalisation and international tax competition. The concept of the 'guarantor state', which characterised the golden age of economic growth and social welfare expansion after 1945, has been lost for ever. New analytical models are proposed, such as the post-Fordist state or those interpreting the state as a complex configuration of social relations and networks.[81] However, they can only partly explain the deep transformations of the recent fiscal constitution. The enormous fiscal imbalances resulting from the financial crisis since 2008 have questioned the existing explanations and models of fiscal policy.

Several factors have to be considered. First, in many countries, public debt has risen to unprecedented levels and appears to be unsustainable. While older forms of fiscal repression are doomed in the present international monetary system, in many countries a rising fiscal burden leads to economic recession and new social inequalities. There is a downward

---

[80] Streeck, *Buying Time*.
[81] Bob Jessop, *The State. Past, Present* (Cambridge: Polity, 2016); Gunnar Folke Schuppert (ed.), *Der Gewährleistungsstaat – Ein Leitbild auf dem Prüfstand* (Baden-Baden: Nomos, 2005); Stephan Leibfried, Evelyne Huber, Matthew Lange, Jonah D. Levy, Frank Nullmeier and John D. Stephens (eds.), *The Oxford Handbook of Transformations of the State* (Oxford: Oxford University Press, 2015).

spiral of economic and fiscal problems which threatens not only the affected countries, but has unforeseen contagion effects in other countries and regions. Second, the problems of public and private debt are closely intertwined. As Moritz Schularick has pointed out, private debt in recent decades has risen far faster than public sector debt.[82] Moreover, the growth in state deficits largely stems from costs associated with preventing private bankruptcies. Hence, only an overall examination of the private and public sectors and their respective interactions can provide insights into the origins and consequences of fiscal imbalances. Third, the present financial crisis marks the indisputable end of the fiscal state which emerged as one of the characteristics of the Westphalian system. Even though fiscal policy is formally still a matter of national sovereignty, the power of state institutions has rapidly eroded during the crisis – especially within the Eurozone, but also beyond it. While monetary policy is controlled by international rules and institutions, international fiscal regulation is lacking. A successful and sustainable reform of the fiscal system therefore needs to be embedded in international norms, rules and regulations. Fourth, it is more than probable that rising national and international fiscal imbalances are at the core of a new social question. As in the 1970s, fiscal policy might move back to the centre of political contention, but with different ideological front lines and social groups involved. Who will pay for the massive costs of rescuing the banks is only one of the questions that remain to be answered. Fifth, from this it becomes clear that fiscal policy will probably gain in importance as a means to deal with new problems, among them the growth of intergenerational inequality. The political economy of public finance is therefore more than history. It remains central to any scientific analysis that brings together historians, political scientists and economists in a fruitful dialogue.

---

[82] Moritz Schularick, 'Public and Private Debt: The Historical Record (1870–2010)', *German Economic Review*, 15 (2013), 191–207.

2 Creating a Dynamic Society: The Tax Reforms of the Thatcher Government

Martin Daunton

The election of Mrs Thatcher's Conservative government in 1979 has acquired an almost mythical significance in the history of economic policy in Britain and the wider world. In the words of a memorandum of 1984,

the Government's prime tax objective is to reduce the overall level of taxation … Tax reductions will improve incentives to work, risk-taking and enterprise. They will contribute to the release of market forces, which will improve the 'supply-side' of the economy, thus increasing output and generating more job opportunities … [T]ax reductions should contribute to a more dynamic and adaptable economy, in which choices are more market determined and less influenced by the State.[1]

But if the measure of success was 'rolling back the state', the government failed. In 1978, the final full year of the Labour government, total tax revenue as a percentage of GDP was 32.7 per cent, before rising to a peak of 38.5 per cent in 1982. By the time Mrs Thatcher left office in 1990, total taxation had fallen to 35.5 per cent of GDP, still above the level when she came to power.[2] Reducing the level of taxation would, it seemed to the Chancellor of the Exchequer in 1984, depend on two things: encouraging economic growth; and ensuring that the additional resources were not 'siphoned off into higher public spending'.[3] Much of the debate over taxation came down to the second objective – 'to reform the tax structure to reduce economic distortion' in order to stimulate growth by the more efficient use of resources and personal initiative:

A broader tax base with fewer special exemptions will reduce tax created distortions and allow marginal rates to be reduced and resources to be allocated more efficiently. Tax reform is no substitute for tax reductions but, with a given level

---

[1] The National Archives [TNA], T470/201, 'Tax policy and the jobs exercise: summary'. Memorandum by the Chancellor of the Exchequer, 21 November 1984.

[2] Organisation for Economic Cooperation and Development, *Revenue Statistics 2012* (Paris: OECD Publications, 2012), pp. 97–8.

[3] TNA, T470/201, 'Tax policy and the jobs exercise: summary'. Memorandum by the Chancellor of the Exchequer, 21 November 1984.

of revenue, it can increase the influence of the market and reduce that of the State on resource allocation and thereby minimise the damage that taxation does to economic performance.[4]

A major concern was how to reshape taxation to liberate market forces from state intervention that led to the misallocation of resources and the stifling of initiative. Nigel Lawson, the Chancellor of the Exchequer from 1983 to 1989, remarked in 1986 that the aim was 'creating a simpler and fairer tax structure and one that is more favourable to enterprise, growth and employment'.[5] It was an attempt to reshape British society along new lines.

The ambition posed difficult choices about what cuts and reforms would best stimulate enterprise: incentives for high incomes to create a more dynamic society; removing low-income earners from the poverty and unemployment traps to stimulate their work ethic; improvements in profitability to encourage investment; or changes in tax-breaks to move away from institutional investment to direct ownership of equities. The relative merits of these different approaches were contested within the Conservative Party and Treasury, with the balance changing over time, and reflecting debates that pre-dated Mrs Thatcher.[6]

The need for reform was apparent before 1979 to all political parties, with a sense that the British tax system had reached an impasse. In 1976, the Labour Chancellor of the Exchequer, Denis Healey, contemplated a Royal Commission on the overall design of the tax system, including the appropriate distribution of taxes on income, expenditure and wealth; the balance between income tax and taxes on goods and services; the treatment of personal savings, including for retirement; disincentives created by high rates of income tax; and the role of corporation tax.[7] These were precisely the issues addressed by Thatcher's government. The consensus in 1976 was that a comprehensive study by a Royal Commission was not realistic and that a more piecemeal approach was more practical. In any case, the Institute for Fiscal Studies had recently embarked on a major review under the chairmanship of the economist James Meade; this appeared in 1978.[8] The need for reform was therefore generally accepted,

---

[4] Ibid.

[5] TNA, CAB/129/220/7, C(86)7, Cabinet: 'Green paper on personal taxation'. Memorandum by the Chancellor of the Exchequer, 21 February 1986.

[6] Thinking in opposition is discussed by A. Williamson, *Conservative Economic Policymaking and the Birth of Thatcherism, 1964–1979* (Basingstoke: Palgrave Macmillan, 2015), ch. 3.

[7] TNA, T366/167, A. H. Lovell, Royal Commission on Taxation, 18 March 1976; Topics recommended, without major qualification, as suitable for a standing Royal Commission; Draft budget brief: Royal Commission on taxation, n.d.

[8] TNA, T366/205, The Meade Report, A. H. Lovell, December 1977.

but the solutions embodied distinctive normative assumptions about the nature of British society and the motivations of individuals.

The Meade Report: A Social Democratic Vision

The Meade Report offered a comprehensive reform of the fiscal system to ensure that it no longer distorted the economy through different rates on capital gains, inheritances, gifts, earned income and investment income. The solution was a tax on lifetime expenditure and a progressive annual wealth accessions tax on inherited wealth. The expenditure tax was a tax on the total spending of an individual or household aggregated from earned and unearned income, gifts, capital gains and so on. This tax would assist business, for resources devoted to development of the enterprise would be free of tax; and it would impose a heavy burden on consumption by the rich, including from capital resources. More tax would be imposed on earnings spent on immediate consumption and less tax on current earnings used to finance consumption in the future, thus encouraging prudential and long-sighted decision-making. In addition, a progressive annual wealth accessions tax would be levied on the cumulative total of gifts and inheritances received at a progressive rate. This was justified because inherited wealth was the result of luck rather than skill and effort. Meade favoured a tax to prevent great inequalities of wealth and the concentration of large fortunes. Further, the tax would encourage active holding of wealth rather than passive recipients, and would create equity between more permanent unearned income from property and less reliable income from work.

Meade argued that the new system would be even-handed between different sources of income and wealth; would prevent punitive rates at the top; avoid the poverty trap at the bottom; and allow a more enterprising society, based on social integration. This tax system would provide revenue for a costly 'new Beveridge scheme' which would set a floor to the standard of living of all people by raising tax thresholds and benefits above the minimum standard of living; and it would encourage enterprise by taxation of high levels of personal consumption and inherited wealth.[9] Enterprise was to be complemented by compassion in a social democratic vision of British society.

The report's vision of society had similarities with but also divergences from policies adopted after 1979. Meade argued that his report was in agreement with Conservative thinking on enterprise and

---

[9] Institute for Fiscal Studies, *The Structure and Reform of Direct Taxation: Report of a Committee Chaired by Professor J. E. Meade* (London: Allen and Unwin, 1978).

initiative, and on minimising distortions and disincentives. It proposed a tax on consumption rather than income; it would encourage private (and especially small) businesses; it would simplify the capital market by removing the complex interplay between income, corporation and capital gains taxes; and it would remove excessive marginal rates at both ends of the income scale. Meade assured the new Conservative chancellor, Geoffrey Howe, that these policies would lead to 'an upsurge of private initiative and enterprise'.[10] There were, nevertheless, differences over attitudes to equality and individualism.

In Meade's view, society was threatened by growing inequality of wealth, largely through inheritance, which would lead to dominance by a wealthy elite and a loss of dynamism. The Conservative policy group on economic policy that was set up in 1965 was similarly wary of the dominance of inherited wealth, pointing out that existing large fortunes could avoid taxation, but that the tax system hindered the creation of modest fortunes. What was needed was a tax system that would allow the accumulation of up to £25,000 without penalty so that there was 'a real and positive encouragement to the acquisition of a modest capital' that offered a stronger incentive than income.[11] The election manifesto of 1970, *A Better Tomorrow*, promised a move from a property-owning democracy to a 'capital-owning democracy of the future', in which 'individuals and families who save and accumulate wealth serve the nation as truly as they serve themselves', and the theme was repeated in *The Right Approach to the Economy* in 1977 with its ambition of creating a 'habit of personal capital cumulation, making vast numbers of people owners as well as earners'. Meade would agree so far, but he differed in his greater emphasis on the positive virtues of equality. *The Right Approach* did not wish to see concentrations of wealth, but saw the solution not in redistribution so much as in encouraging more people to acquire and transmit property.[12] Meade went further in arguing that 'unacceptable inequalities of opportunity, wealth and privilege' threatened a dynamic society. He was, as a Treasury official pointed out,

[10] London School of Economics, Meade 6/2, Meade to Howe, 23 November 1977, quoted in Martin Chick, 'Reforming the Structure of Direct Taxation: The Political and Administrative Response to the Meade Report (1978)', *Edinburgh Research Explorer* (2013); www.research.ed.ac.uk/portal/en/publications/reforming-the-structure-of-direct-taxation-the-political-and-administrative-response-to-the-meade-report1978%281cOe20d8-c19a-4368-945b-4800ab61d67d%29.html.

[11] M. Daunton, *Just Taxes: The Politics of Taxation in Britain, 1914–1979* (Cambridge: Cambridge University Press, 2002), pp. 306–8.

[12] G. Howe, K. Joseph and D. Howell, *The Right Approach to the Economy: Outline of an Economic Strategy for the Next Conservative Government* (London: Conservative Central Office, 1977), ch. 3 on taxation.

following a 'liberal and radical philosophy' with 'a consistent thread of what might be called old fashioned liberal thinking'. He argued that an individual did not 'own' the proceeds of his or her talents. Meade's proposals were designed to reduce the intergenerational transfer of advantage and to ensure that society was flexible and open to opportunity. He wished to create a just economy by removing the 'self-reinforcing influences which help to sustain the good fortune of the fortunate and the bad fortune of the unfortunate'. Howe was sceptical, sensing socialism.[13]

In their response to Meade, Inland Revenue officials admitted anomalies in the existing tax system which produced varying net returns on different investments, but they argued that reform was possible within the existing system. The Inland Revenue damned the report as 'disappointing – its original proposals are not practicable and its practicable proposals are not original'. The Treasury feared that this 'hatchet job' created the impression of a closed mind and complacency when the need for reform was widely recognised. Douglas Todd of the Treasury was 'pro-Meade' and complained that the Revenue was 'less than generous'. In general, the Treasury was not unsympathetic to Meade: the report's ideas might be abstract and lacking in feasibility, but its approach to such issues as distortions could be adopted in 'a piecemeal and evolved fashion' without an expenditure tax. The Treasury did not reject Meade's ideas out of hand, referring to the report at various points in the ensuing discussions.[14] Indeed, the Treasury produced a paper in 1982 on 'taxation in the longer term', inspired by Ian Byatt, the deputy chief economic adviser, who considered the way that different parts of the tax system interacted and affected the economy in terms of profitability, incentives and the allocation of savings. The Inland Revenue was horrified at what they saw as advocacy and the adoption of Meade's unworldly criticism of the tax system as incoherent rather than realising that each 'distortion' was the result of a conscious political decision.[15] There was a fundamental difference of intellectual approach within the Civil Service, with Treasury officials such as Todd and Byatt

[13] James Meade, *The Just Economy* (London: Allen and Unwin, 1976), p. 155; LSE, Meade 6/2, G. Howe to J. Meade, 25 November 1977, quoted in Chick, 'Reforming the structure of direct taxation'; TNA, T366/205, Report of the Meade committee.

[14] TNA, T364/149, Meade Committee Report: paper, Inland Revenue, December 1977, quoted by Chick, 'Reforming the structure of direct taxation'; T366/205, Douglas Todd, Meade Report, 16 January 1978 covering his 'Report of the Meade Committee, J. H. Gracey, Meade Report, 11 November 1977; The Meade Report, A. H. Lovell, December 1977.

[15] TNA, T430/36, 'Taxation in the longer term': note by the Deputy Chief Economic Adviser, September 1982; no title, Treasury, 1 October 1982; J. Green to P. Middleton, 'Taxation in the longer term', 18 October 1982; T470/37, I. C. R. Byatt to Chancellor, 21 December 1982.

accepting the need to consider substitution effects and optimal tax theory as developed by economists such as James Mirrlees.[16]

In the five or six years following the election victory of the Conservatives in 1979, Treasury officials embarked on extensive discussions of the tax system, proposing a number of ways in which piecemeal reform could be introduced. There was considerable continuity to the debates from the formulation of ideas by the Conservative Party in opposition in 1965 and in government between 1970 and 1974 to the government of Mrs Thatcher. The basic problems were clear, and the professional civil servants produced detailed papers on distortions in the tax system. What the Conservative politicians provided was an overarching philosophy to justify reform and decide among priorities. In the words of Howe in his budget speech of 1979, it was necessary to reform a tax system 'that might have been designed to discourage innovation and punish success'. Howe stressed that

We need to strengthen incentives, by allowing people to keep more of what they earn, so that hard work, talent and ability are properly rewarded. We need to enlarge freedom of choice for the individual by reducing the role of the State. We need to reduce the burden of financing the public sector, so as to leave room for commerce and industry to prosper.[17]

Taxation was part of a much wider ambition of reshaping British society to create a new sense of enterprise, dynamism and personal responsibility.

Distortion of Investment Decisions

A major concern was that the tax system distorted investment decisions to the detriment of the efficient utilisation of resources, and that taxes should be changed to allow more direct personal engagement with capitalist enterprise.

In the 1970s, both the Labour and Conservative Parties agreed that institutional investors were harming the British economy; but they differed on the cure. Labour favoured some form of state direction and coordination of the institutional funds; the Conservatives were naturally more inclined to encourage institutional investors to take an active interest in the management of firms.[18] They were also concerned about

---

[16] See J. A. Mirrlees, 'An Exploration in the Theory of Optimum Income Taxation', *Review of Economic Studies* 38 (1971), 175–208; and 'Optimal Tax Theory: A Synthesis', *Journal of Public Economics* 6 (1976), 327–58.

[17] Parliamentary Debates, 5th series, vol. 968, Commons, 12 June 1979, col. 240.

[18] The debates are considered in the forthcoming book of Aled Davies on social democracy and the City to be published by Oxford University Press.

the 'dearth of private risk capital' which harmed small businesses, the source of dynamism and economic growth. The solution was the 'accumulation of property in private hands'. In the words of *The Right Approach*, 'occupational pension rights and savings through life assurance schemes already offer the majority of households in Britain the chance during working life to acquire a proper stake (albeit at one remove) in the ownership of the wealth of the community. But we would like to promote more direct forms of personal ownership as well.'[19]

The issue was considered by the committee on the functioning of financial institutions chaired by Harold Wilson, the former Labour prime minister, which found that the proportion of listed UK ordinary shares held by financial institutions had risen from 21 per cent in 1957 to 50 per cent by the end of 1978. Direct ownership by individuals had fallen from 66 per cent in 1957 to about 32 per cent in 1978. The Wilson committee was concerned that the institutions did not monitor performance or ensure that investment assisted economic growth. Wilson's solution was to extend tax relief to *all* forms of contractual medium- and long-term savings, with safeguards against early withdrawal. The result would be neutrality among institutions; the committee did not recommend preferential treatment of direct investment in equities or businesses.[20]

The tax system offered widely varying 'fiscal privilege' to different investments. A report by the Institute for Fiscal Studies estimated the 'fiscal privilege' for 1978–9 to 1982–3 at actual inflation rates was 132 per cent for a life insurance contract lasting five years, 104 per cent for a house with a mortgage of half its value, and 56 per cent for a pension contribution ten years from retirement. By contrast, direct shareholding by an individual had a tax liability of 60 per cent and a unit trust (a portfolio of stock exchange securities in which small investors bought units) one of 81 per cent. The report argued that 'there seems no obvious reason why we should wish deployment of personal savings to be controlled by a small number of possibly unadventurous financial institutions, and yet that is what the system has encouraged'.[21] What should be done?

In 1981, an official working group recommended a general reduction in taxation to make equities more appealing rather than introducing new biases or an explicit tax-break for direct ownership. They were

---

[19] Howe, Joseph and Howell, *The Right Approach*, ch. 3.
[20] PP 1979/80 Cmnd 7937, *Committee to Review the Functioning of Financial Institutions*, pp. 72–3, 203, 250–3, 255–6, 258–60.
[21] John Hills, *Savings and Fiscal Privilege* IFS Report Series 9, 1984, discussed in TNA, T470/252, 'Savings and fiscal privilege: summary', n.d.

cautious about reducing tax-breaks on life insurance, which would annoy powerful companies; and a change in the tax treatment of pensions would require employers to invest more to cover liabilities, leading to a further undesirable growth in the funds. The Institute for Fiscal Studies thought that a possible solution was to divide savings into privileged and unprivileged groups, with tax-breaks for the types of savings the government wished to encourage. Each individual should have an annual allowance for savings; institutions could then compete for business, and savers would have greater freedom to switch funds with personal control over the allocation of assets.[22]

The Conservative government went further, stressing the virtues of direct investment in equities rather than parity between forms of investment. This amounted to a major shift in the underlying philosophy of the tax system, away from long-term prudential savings with high exit charges if it were decided to take money sooner (pensions, life insurance) to more entrepreneurial investment in shares with personal control and easy access to funds. Not only would such savings attract a tax-break, but income from investment would no long attract a higher tax rate as 'unearned' and passive. It overturned the fiscal principles laid down by two Liberal chancellors in 1853 and 1907, and rejected Meade's advocacy of higher taxation of unearned income.

Tax-breaks on life insurance policies were introduced by William Gladstone in 1853 as a way of blocking demands for differentiation of the income tax between 'earned' and 'unearned' income. The case for differentiation was that income from landed estates and stocks did not depend on personal enterprise, with the asset surviving for dependants. By contrast, income from trade, industry or employment depended on the individual, without leaving an asset to produce a continued flow of income. Here was the rationale for taxing earned income from wages, salaries and profits at a lower rate to reflect the need to save for retirement and dependants. Gladstone feared that differentiation would define one class against another, and instead offered a tax-break for life insurance. These policies could pay out on death to support dependants or build up an 'endowment' to provide an income in old age. They were available to everyone who behaved prudently through long-term, contractual and prudential savings with very high exit charges. The tax-break continued despite the fact that differentiation between earned and unearned income was introduced by the Liberal government in

[22] TNA, T470/137, 'Working Group on Tax and Savings', P. E. Middleton to Chancellor, 3 February 1981; and Report of the Working Group on Tax and Savings; Hills, *Savings and Fiscal Privileges*.

1907 at a time when radical attacks on the unearned increment of land were politically appealing, thus removing the initial rationale of the concession. Although the tax-break was reduced during the First World War, rising levels of income tax still made investment in life insurance attractive, especially in endowment policies for old age. In 1921, the tax concession was extended to occupational pension funds run by employers and it was made more generous in 1956 and again in 1970. By the 1970s, occupational pension schemes accounted for a third of personal savings, an unusually high proportion in international terms.[23]

Tax-breaks on life insurance and differentiation of the income tax made political sense to Liberal chancellors when they were introduced: in 1853 to block differentiation, which threatened to set social classes against each other, and in 1907 to adjust the party to the challenge from Labour. The tax-break continued after 1907, despite the removal of the initial justification, and was extended to employers' pension funds as a way of encouraging support in old age. But the growth of institutional investment and the decline in personal capitalism worried Conservative chancellors who wished to create more entrepreneurial forms of saving that would appeal to a more affluent middle class and create a more dynamic economy.

Another major tax-break was for the purchase of owner-occupied housing. The Conservatives were committed to a property-owning democracy, but the generous tax benefit was not entirely intentional. Initially, imputed rental income was set against mortgage interest, which was increasingly unreal in the absence of up-to-date valuations; if a new valuation were made, it would entail a politically unpopular three- or four-fold increase. As a result, taxation of imputed income was abandoned in 1963 with a considerable loss of revenue in addition to the tax relief on mortgages. Higher tax payers were disproportionately beneficiaries.[24]

The situation was causing concern for a number of reasons. The treatment of different forms of investment was criticised for creating

---

[23] M. Zimmeck, 'Gladstone Holds His Own: The Origins of Income Tax Relief for Life Insurance Purposes', *Bulletin of the Institute of Historical Research* 58 (1985), 167–88; L. Hannah, *Inventing Retirement: The Development of Occupational Pension Funds in Britain* (Cambridge: Cambridge University Press, 1986), pp. 33–4, 47–51; data on savings from Government Actuary, *Occupational Pensions Schemes 1979, Sixth Survey* (London: HMSO, 1981), p. 2.

[24] J. Black and D. Stafford, *Housing Policy and Finance* (London: Routledge, 1988), pp. 93–4; TNA, T470/152, 'Owner-occupied housing: fiscal incentives and financial and economic consequences'; 'Owner-occupied housing: economic and financial aspects of tax relief'.

rigidities and distortions, favouring risk-averse, passive, long-term prudential investment which hindered the creation of an entrepreneurial society. The favourable tax treatment of housing led to over-investment compared with other assets, so that 'the personal sector (the property owning democracy) holds more of its wealth in the form of housing and less in the form of claims (shares, etc.) on other forms of physical capital'. The result might simply be higher house prices to the detriment of first-time buyers, with mortgage lending leaking into consumer spending and monetary growth. Labour mobility was also reduced. Owner-occupiers were less mobile than were private tenants because of price differentials between areas and transaction costs.[25] Furthermore, work-based pensions were not readily transferrable, thus creating an incentive to stay with the current employer.[26]

Adam Ridley, a leading adviser to Howe, argued for a radical rethink of the 'very arbitrary and widely varying pattern of rates of return on the different kinds of investment outlets', leading to investment in housing and life insurance rather than

investment in ordinary shares or in one's own (or someone else's) business ... The more one entrenches such undesirable biases against spontaneous personal financing of the revival of enterprise, the more one is forced to construct complex, artificial and relatively ineffective devices to redress the balance ... How much better it would be if there was a plentiful supply of private money which flowed naturally into private business expansion.[27]

On this view, the creation of wider share-ownership was not linked to privatisation of telecommunications or electricity so much as to the encouragement of small enterprises. In 1979, Keith Joseph, one of the authors of *The Right Approach*, stressed the need for tax relief for individuals investing in the equity of small businesses.[28]

How far were Thatcher and her colleagues willing to go in making changes that would upset large interest groups and significant parts of the electorate?

---

[25] TNA, T470/152, 'Owner-occupied housing: fiscal incentives and financial and economic consequences'; 'Owner-occupied housing: economic and financial aspects of tax relief'; T470/109, draft minute from the Chancellor to the Prime Minister, 'Tax policy'; T470/214, 'Housing and labour mobility'.

[26] TNA, T470/ 214, 'Reducing impediments to labour mobility: pension right', S. K. Holman, 29 July 1983.

[27] TNA, T470/152, Adam Ridley to Howe, 'Mortgage relief', 16 February 1983.

[28] TNA, Prem/25, Keith Joseph to Margaret Thatcher, 25 June 1979 and 'Acceleration of enterprise: note by the Secretary of State for Industry', 29 June 1979.

In 1983, the Treasury drafted a note for Howe to explain the rationale for change to Thatcher:

> Our tax policy is based on our economic and political philosophy. Our economic belief is that we should create the environment in which enterprise and wealth creation can flourish. Our political belief is that we should enlarge the role of the individual and diminish the role of the state. We want to encourage personal decision taking, personal responsibility and self-reliance. We want to reduce the role of Whitehall.

The existing reliefs had emerged over time, and 'they represent layer upon layer of past political prejudices, many of them socialist' and 'inconsistent with our aim of enlarging individual choice and responsibility'. Indeed,

> What is objectionable is the fact that the State is intervening at all. It is nannying. It distorts economic decision taking. It erodes personal choice. It inhibits personal responsibility. State intervention in the form of tax reliefs is in many ways as unsatisfactory as state intervention in the form of public expenditure, nationalisation or state controls ...
>
> We need to work towards a simple, understandable 'low rate, low relief' tax system, leaving individuals free to take their own decisions rather than be guided by the dead hand of past political prejudice and State intervention. Such a system will enable us to reduce rates of tax and rid ourselves of costly bureaucracy.

Since some people would lose from a change in reliefs, the best way of proceeding was in conjunction with a general cut in taxation so that 'those whose *relative* tax burden is increased do not at the same time face an *absolute* increase in their tax liability'.[29] Tax reform was therefore closely linked to reductions in income tax.

One approach was to create neutrality between investments, either by removing tax-breaks or by extending them to a wider range. Although Thatcher was initially attracted by broader tax reliefs, a narrower tax base would require higher rates elsewhere. A second line was to remove particularly favourable tax-breaks, possibly on pensions, and so widen the tax base – the easiest but also an unpopular solution.[30] An alternative approach was to introduce a new bias rather than to create equality, changing the entire regime by removing tax-breaks on long-term institutional investments with explicit encouragement to direct investment. Whatever choice was taken would have serious political and economic consequences.

---

[29] TNA, T470/109, Draft minute from the Chancellor to the Prime Minister, n.d. [1983].
[30] TNA, T470/154, A. J. G. Isaac to Financial Secretary, 2 December 1983.

Pensions were treated very favourably. Pension contributions were made out of untaxed income, which particularly benefited those on higher marginal rates; the investment income of the funds had a tax advantage; and any lump sum paid to pensioners at retirement in addition to the annual pension was not taxed. Although some reform seemed sensible, there were political difficulties. Taxing the investment income of the funds would reduce their ability to cover their pension liabilities, and would lead to higher contributions to cover their loss of revenue, thus leading to even more cautious, unenterprising institutional investment. Taxing the lump sum seemed logical: why should contributions into the scheme come from untaxed income, and then incur no tax on the benefit? By imposing a tax on the benefit, there would be no threat to the viability of the funds, and contributions and institutional investment would not increase. However, taxing the only capital sum that most people received would be highly unpopular.[31] The eventual outcome was to retain existing tax relief on pensions and to extend it to new, 'portable' personal pensions from 1988, which could move with the individual between jobs, so addressing labour mobility and giving more direct control over investment. Employees could also opt out of their employer's scheme and make their own arrangements, or pay additional contributions in a separate plan of their own choice – an extension of individual choice that led to a scandal of mis-selling of pensions by financial advisers.[32]

More progress was made on life insurance. In 1984, the Chancellor removed life insurance premium relief on all new contracts.[33] Tax-breaks on housing loans were also reduced – a particularly sensitive topic given the large number affected. Howe was wary about raising the existing ceiling on loans from £25,000 which would merely increase house prices and remove the possibility of raising income tax thresholds to assist low

---

[31] TNA, T470/140, D. J. Barton to Chancellor, 'Taxation and savings and investment', 17 October 1983; T470/140, Ian Stewart, Economic Secretary to Chancellor, 'Taxation of savings and investment', 25 October 1983; T470/154, 'Note of a meeting on the taxation of savings', 21 November 1983; A. J. G. Isaac to Financial Secretary, 'Taxation of pensions', 2 December 1983; and Financial Secretary to Chancellor, 'Taxation of pensions funds', 14 December 1983; T470/141, 'Note of a meeting to discuss further work on taxation of savings and investment', 11 Downing Street, 2 November 1983; 'Note of a meeting on the tax treatment of pensions', 15 November 1983.

[32] Parliamentary Debates, 6th series, vol. 94, Commons, 18 March 1986, col. 176; vol. 112, Commons, 17 March 1987, cols. 824–5.

[33] TNA, T470/253, Tax reform meeting, 22 June: 'Life assurance', J. C. Simpson to A. J. G. Isaac, 22 June 1984; 'Life assurance', G. W. Monger, 9 July 1984; Parliamentary Debates, 6th series, vol. 56, Commons, 13 March 1984, col. 293.

earners. He did increase the ceiling to £30,000, but this was a considerable reduction in real terms and in 1991 relief was restricted to the basic rate.[34]

The major change was the introduction of a new tax-break for direct personal investment in equities, which was linked to a shift in the higher rates of taxation of unearned income from savings. In 1972, the Heath government unified the income tax rates for earned and unearned income but introduced an investment income surcharge of up to 15 per cent on top of the income tax – thus retaining differentiation between earned and unearned income at a more modest level. At the same time, inflation eroded savings in real terms: the Meade Report estimated that the value of savings after tax fell in real terms by as much as 22.3 per cent in 1976. Savers looked more like victims than a fiscal target.[35] The Thatcher government embarked on a major change in the taxation of savings.

In 1979, Howe increased the threshold for the investment income surcharge, and his successor as chancellor, Nigel Lawson, entirely removed differentiation between earned and unearned income in 1984. Lawson castigated it as 'an unfair and anomalous tax on savings and on the rewards of successful enterprise. It hits the small business man who reaches retirement without the cushion of a company pension scheme ... In the vast majority of cases it is a tax on savings made out of hard-earned and fully-taxed income'. He argued that the major beneficiaries were elderly retired people who lived off their investments: over half of those who paid the surcharge were aged over sixty-five, and of these, half would otherwise pay only the basic rate of tax.[36]

The government also changed the tax treatment of savings to encourage a capital-owning democracy. Most savings designed to smooth income between stages of an individual's life cycle now received a tax-break, as Meade had envisaged, but the main emphasis was on a form of savings that he had not advocated: direct personal ownership of equities. Rather than neutrality, a new bias was introduced. In 1958, the Wider Share-Ownership Council advocated employee share-ownership in order to involve workers in the success of their employers' enterprises and

---

[34] TNA, T470/152, 'Owner-occupied housing: fiscal incentives and economic consequences', n.d.; 'Owner-occupied housing: economic and financial effects of tax reliefs'; Michael Heseltine to Howe, 'Mobility – housing aspects', 28 January 1981; G. Howe to M. Heseltine, 4 March 1981; Working Group on Taxation and Savings, 'Mortgage interest relief and stamp duty', October 1981; T470/152, Howe to Prime Minister, 'Mortgage interest relief', 24 February 1983.

[35] Institute for Fiscal Studies, *Structure and Reform of Direct Taxation*, p. 107; C. Munro, 'The Fiscal Politics of Savings and Share Ownership in Britain, 1970–80', *Historical Journal*, 55 (2012), 763.

[36] Parliamentary Debates, 5th series, vol. 968, Commons, 12 June 1979, col. 260; 6th series, vol. 56, 13 March 1984, cols. 293–4.

diffuse wealth. The idea was taken up by some senior figures in the Conservative Party in 1975, but it remained a minority view: did workers want to save in their employers' companies, and was it relevant in Britain where there was not the same sense of unity between workers and employers as in Germany? Further, it seemed too close to the extension of industrial democracy and workers' directors being explored by the Labour government at the same time. As Howe pointed out to Thatcher in 1978, the party's policy on encouraging wealth was 'still too nebulous' and 'must rest, therefore, overwhelmingly on council house sales'.[37]

The right of tenants to buy their public housing was hardly a solution for the wider middle class, and was not fulfilling the ambitions of *The Right Approach*. In 1981, Howe went some way to meet Joseph's call for incentives for individual investors in small firms with the Business Start-Up Scheme.[38] The major change came in 1986, when Lawson launched a policy that would have a wider appeal: tax-breaks on personal equity plans (PEPs) for direct individual investment in UK shares, designed to attract small savers who had never previously owned shares. At this stage, unit trusts were not included for they were open to the criticism that they did not lead to direct contact with the management of firms and hence an appreciation of the operation of business.[39] Nevertheless, the coverage of PEPs was subsequently extended to allow investment in unit trusts and in non-UK shares. Lawson boasted of the shift from institutional investment to direct share-ownership:

Just as we have made Britain a nation of home owners so it is the long-term ambition of this Government to make the British people a nation of share owners, too; to create a popular capitalism in which more and more men and women have a direct personal stake in British business and industry.

By 1987, Lawson reported there were 8.5 million individual shareholders, or 20 per cent of the population – a tripling of the number since 1979.[40] Of course, the change was fostered by the privatisation of telecommunications in 1984 and gas in 1986, which were soon followed by other public utilities. Privatisation had other motivations, but soon offered the prospect of increasing the number of shareholders more

---

[37] Williamson, *Conservative Economic Policymaking*, pp. 84–5, 273–4; on changing approaches to a property-owning democracy, see M. Francis, '"A Crusade to Enfranchise the Many": Thatcherism and the "Property-Owning Democracy"', *Twentieth-Century British History*, 23 (2012), 275–97.

[38] Parliamentary Debates 6th series vol 1000, Commons, 10 March 1981, cols. 781–2.

[39] For example, Enoch Powell, *Saving in a Free Society* (London: Institute of Economic Affairs, 1960), p. 106.

[40] Parliamentary Debates, 6th series, vol. 94, Commons, 18 March 1986, cols. 177–8; vol. 112, Commons, 17 March 1987, col. 824.

easily than by encouraging investment in small businesses. The sale of shares in the privatised industries did not lead to a significant deepening of the market. Many shares were held for only a short time to make a quick profit, so that the change was less deep-seated than Lawson implied, and the proportion of shares in UK listed companies directly held by private investors continued to fall, from 47.4 per cent in 1969 to 17.1 per cent in 1993 and 16.0 per cent in 2000.[41] The proportion held by institutions continued to rise for some time: pension funds held 9.0 per cent of UK quoted shares in 1969 and insurance companies 12.2 per cent, growing to 17.7 and 21.0 per cent respectively by 2000. The scale of unit trusts was modest, accounting for 2.9 per cent of UK quoted shares in 1969, 6.6 per cent in 1993 and only 1.1 per cent in 2000.[42] The outcome was less the emergence of shareholder capitalism than what Hyman Minsky termed 'money manager capitalism', with shares held by funds with an emphasis on short-term performance and the current valuation of firms rather than their long-term growth.

The prudential commitment mechanisms of life insurance and pensions were weakened with a shift to more short-term investments, which could be accessed without penalty.[43] Attitudes had shifted away from Gladstonian rectitude to encourage what John Kay and Mervyn King termed 'entrepreneurs' assets' rather than 'civil servants' assets'.[44]

Profits and Corporate Taxation

The debate over the role of institutional investors was linked to a concern in the mid-1970s that falling profitability was harming investment and frustrating the creation of a dynamic economy. In 1981, the Treasury reported that the net pre-tax real rate of return for industrial and commercial companies (excluding North Sea oil) was 3.2 per cent, falling from 13.2 per cent in 1960 and 8.7 per cent in 1970. Byatt warned that 'the secular decline in company profits has probably reached the point where many firms have an inadequate incentive to produce', and he pointed out that the real rate of profit had fallen below the real cost of capital since the mid-1970s. A liquidity crisis was

---

[41] M. Vincent, 'Dream of wide shareownership failed', *Financial Times*, 7 December 2011.

[42] Data from Office for National Statistics, www.ons.gov.uk/economy/investmentspensionsandtrusts/bulletins/ownership%20of%20ukquotedshares/2015-09-02.

[43] See Avner Offer, *The Challenge of Affluence: Self-Control and Well-Being in the United States and Britain since 1950* (Oxford: Oxford University Press, 2006).

[44] Munro, 'Fiscal Politics', 773–4; Howe, Joseph and Howell, *The Right Approach*, p. 34; J. A. Kay and M. A. King, *The British Tax System* (Oxford: Oxford University Press, 1978), p. 13.

avoided only by destocking and shedding labour. What should be done to rectify a state of affairs that threatened economic recovery?[45]

There were several possibilities. A reduction in the public sector borrowing requirement (PSBR) and lower interest rates might be more effective in stimulating growth than cuts in taxation, but if taxation were reduced, should it be personal taxation, National Insurance or corporate taxes? There were cases for and against each option. A reduction in personal income tax would help by making dividends from equities more attractive compared with other forms of savings, which received generous tax-breaks. Another possibility was a cut in employers' National Insurance contributions or the National Insurance surcharge. The surcharge was an additional employers' contribution announced by the Labour chancellor in July 1976 in response to the International Monetary Fund (IMF) crisis in order to reduce the PSBR. At the time, Howe criticised the surcharge for reducing profits, but in office he realised that reducing National Insurance contributions or abolishing the surcharge was not necessarily the most effective response to low profitability. Some of the reduced payment might simply be diverted to higher wages; in any case, only about a third of the reduction in payment would go to manufacturing firms who were seen as most in need of assistance, with the rest going to financial services and public sector employers. A reduction in corporation tax was favoured by Ian Byatt, who argued that it produced 'a bewildering range of marginal rates of tax on investment', and encouraged firms to use loans rather than equity finance. In the absence of a major reform to remove these distortions, a lower rate would at least reduce the harm, help restore profitability and encourage a supply-led recovery.[46]

In 1982, the cabinet decided to give priority to companies rather than individuals in order to assist economic recovery by 'steps to strengthen the country's industrial and commercial base. This, rather than reductions in the real rate of personal taxation, was the best way to respond

---

[45] TNA, T470/81, 'Taxation and the supply side', I. C. R. Byatt, 11 September 1981; T470/93, 'Corporate taxation: background to the budget', D. J. L. Moore to Chancellor, 22 December 1982 and attached paper; T432/68, Fiscal Policy Committee FPC(82)1st meeting, 18 January 1982.

[46] Parliamentary Debates, 5th series, Commons, vol. 915, 22 July 1976, cols. 2017, 2021; vol. 916, 2 August 1976 col. 1231; vol. 922, 8 December 1976, cols. 539–88; TNA, T470/81, 'Taxation and the supply side', I. C. R. Byatt, 11 September 1981; T366/748, Note of a meeting held in the Chancellor of the Exchequer's room, House of Commons, 6 August 1980; R. I. Tolkein, 8 August 1980; T432/68, Fiscal Policy Committee FPC (82), 1st meeting, 18 January 1982, FPC(82)1, 15 January 1982, 'Corporate taxation: background to the budget'; CAB128/75, CC(82), 3rd conclusions; T430/36, I. C. R. Byatt to P. Middleton, 'Reducing corporation tax', 23 September 1982; untitled paper, 1 October 1982.

to the problem of unemployment and to open up the prospect of creating jobs'.[47] Consequently, Howe reduced the National Insurance surcharge from 3.5 to 2.5 per cent for private employers so that the benefits went to business rather than the public sector, and he modified capital taxation which was 'holding back business success and penalising personal endeavour'. Over two-thirds of the reduction in taxes went to business.[48]

The strategy was taken further in 1984 when Lawson proposed a 'far-reaching reform of company taxation'. He abolished the National Insurance surcharge for private employers and announced his intention of reducing corporation tax, which was 'far too high, penalising profit and success, and blunting the cutting edge of enterprise'. He removed reliefs that distorted decisions in order to encourage 'investment decisions based on future market assessments, not future tax assessments'.[49] Above all, he reduced corporation tax in stages from 52 per cent to 35 per cent by 1986/7. This was one of the lowest levels in the OECD: the rate in West Germany was as high as 64.5 per cent, in Japan 54 per cent, France 50 per cent and the United States 46 per cent. Business taxes (excluding North Sea revenues) fell from 28.4 per cent of total taxation in 1978/9 to 24.9 per cent in 1984/5.[50] He concentrated on cuts in business taxation as part of the general strategy of removing distortion between forms of investment and encouraging the return of personal investors. 'These changes hold out an exciting opportunity for British industry as a whole: an opportunity further to improve its profitability, and to expand ... Higher profits after tax will encourage and reward enterprise, stimulate start innovation in all its forms, and create more jobs.'[51]

The 1984 budget marked a major shift in company taxation, but Lawson acknowledged that 'we have not yet tackled the personal

[47] TNA, CAB128/75, CC(82), 3rd conclusions, 28 January 1982; Prem 19/700, 25 January 1982; and Robert Armstrong to Prime Minister, Economic Strategy C(82)10, 27 January 1982.

[48] Parliamentary Debates, 6th series, vol. 19, Commons, 9 March 1982, cols. 741, 754; vol. 39, col. 154.

[49] Parliamentary Debates, 6th series, vol. 56, Commons, 13 March 1984, cols. 295–6.

[50] Figures from TNA, T470/201, 'Tax policy and the jobs exercise: memorandum by the Chancellor of the Exchequer', 21 November 1984.

[51] Parliamentary Debates, 6th series, vol. 56, Commons, 13 March 1984, cols. 297–8; TNA, CAB128/78/5, CC(84), 5th conclusions, Cabinet: 'Conclusions of a meeting of the Cabinet', 9 February 1984; CAB128/80, most confidential record to CC(84), 5th conclusions, 9 February 1984; T470/109, I. C. R. Byatt to J. M. Green, 'Tax policy in the medium term', 24 May 1983; T470/173, Chevening tax issues paper, 1 January 1984; T470/174, draft minute for the Chancellor to send to the Prime Minister; T470/201, 'Tax policy and the jobs exercise: memorandum by the Chancellor of the Exchequer', n.d. [1984]; T470/251, A. H. Lovell, 'Company tax package', 21 February 1984.

income tax system, which remains essentially as it emerged after the war', and was 'almost universally seen as unfair and indefensible'.[52] What could be done to reform individual taxation and improve incentives for work and enterprise? There was a choice between tax-breaks for the higher-income levels, or solving the problems of the poverty and unemployment traps for low incomes.

Individual Incentives

When the Conservatives came to power it was not clear at what point high marginal rates harmed incentives. Meade argued that the top rate should be cut to 70 per cent; the Treasury suggested that 75 per cent or even as low as 65 per cent might be justified, but that there was no strong case for going further than that.[53] In 1978, the Medium Term Tax Strategy of the Treasury aimed to increase incentives by reducing the top income tax rate from 83 to 75 per cent through an increase in VAT.[54] The government, and especially Lawson, went much further.

The Conservative government started to reduce reliance on income tax as soon as it came to office, with a drop from 32.6 per cent of total taxation in 1978/9 to 29.3 per cent in 1979/80.[55] Howe was in no doubt that 'excessive rates of income tax bear a heavy responsibility for the lacklustre performance of the British economy'. He proclaimed his first budget of 1979 a turning point, shifting from the taxation of earnings to spending as 'the only way that we can restore incentives and make it more worthwhile to work and, at the same time, increase the freedom of choice of the individual'. He turned to VAT. When the Conservatives introduced VAT in 1973, the rate was 10 per cent. In 1974, the Labour government reduced the rate to 8 per cent, with a higher-rate of 12.5 per cent on some luxury goods. The Treasury felt that indirect taxes could be increased without serious distributional consequences: although VAT was less progressive than the income tax, it was not regressive for poorer households, which spent more of their income on zero-rated goods.[56]

[52] TNA, CAB 129/220/7 C(86)7, 21 February 1986, Cabinet: 'Green Paper on personal taxation', memorandum by the Chancellor of the Exchequer, Nigel Lawson, 21 February 1986.

[53] TNA, T171/1450, 'Income tax: higher rates and bands', Inland Revenue, February 1979, quoted by Chick, 'Reforming the Structure of Direct Taxation'.

[54] TNA, T378/88, A. H. Lovell, 22 January 1978, paras. 6, 12, 14, 16 and 19, quoted in Chick 'Reforming the Structure of Direct Taxation'.

[55] TNA, T470/35, 'Where are we going? Taxation in the medium term'. Note by FP and DEU, n.d.

[56] TNA, T470/77, 'Indirect taxes – impact on households', Douglas Todd, 12 February 1981; T470/167, A. M. Fraser to Chancellor, 'Indirect taxation: further planning', 10 May 1984; 'Extension of the VAT base', B. H. Knox to Chancellor, 27 July 1984.

In 1979, Howe replaced the two bands with a single higher-rate of 15 per cent in order to reduce reliance on income tax; it was further increased to 17.5 per cent in 1991, in part to hold down the level of the unpopular Community Charge (commonly known as the poll tax).[57]

Where should the cuts in income tax be concentrated? In 1979, Howe focused on the higher rates, which, he argued, applied not only to senior executives, middle managers, professionals and small business, but even to skilled workers – 'the people upon whom so many of our hopes for initiative, greater enterprise and national prosperity must depend'. He cut the top rate of 83 per cent on earned incomes to 60 per cent, and raised the threshold. In reality, few paid the top rate of 83 per cent on earned incomes, and even fewer the unearned rate of 98 per cent, but the change was symbolically important. His aim was to bring the top rate into line with the European average: the top rate in France was 60 per cent, but in Germany 56 per cent and the US only 50 per cent – and in Britain it came into effect at lower incomes. The number of people paying higher rates above the standard rate fell from 1.2 million to 650,000. He also raised the tax threshold for lower incomes, taking 1.3 million people out of the income tax, and reduced the basic rate from 33 to 30 per cent, with the ambition of eventually cutting it to 25 per cent. Howe presented these changes as a major shift, leaving people with more money and allowing them, rather than the government, to decide how to spend it. Even after these changes, Howe worried that higher incomes were still more heavily taxed than in other industrialised countries: 'We have over the years spent far too much time and effort trying to "level down". This is no good to anybody. It is much more important to have a successful and prosperous society, and we cannot have a successful and prosperous society without successful and prosperous individuals.'[58] Indeed, the changes were more modest than the 'headline' rate of tax, for the crucial point was the effective rate after taking into account thresholds and allowances. The effective rate for a married man with two children on average earnings continued to rise from 18 per cent in 1979 to 20 per cent in 1983.[59]

The Chancellor had to decide whether future reductions in income tax should concentrate on changes in rates or in thresholds and allowances, and how to balance incentives at both the bottom and the top.

---

[57] Parliamentary Debates, 5th series, vol. 968, Commons, 12 June 1979, col. 250; 6th series, vol. 188, 19 March 1991, cols. 180–1.

[58] Parliamentary Debates, 5th series, vol. 968, Commons, 12 June 1979, cols. 258–62.

[59] Paul Johnson, Frances Lynch and John Geoffrey Walker, 'Income tax and elections in Britain, 1950–2001', *Electoral Studies*, 24 (2005), 400.

There were two problems. First, the income tax threshold in Britain was lower than in other countries. In 1984, a single person started paying income tax with an income of £2,005 and a married man without children of £3,155; the figures in France were £3,840 and £4,250, in the United States £2,580 and £4,220, and in Germany £1,980 and £3,455.[60] Second, social security benefits might be lost by taking a job or increasing earnings, so that people on low incomes might pay a very high marginal rate and be caught in the poverty and unemployment traps.

One of the leading critics of the unemployment trap was Ralph Howell, a right-wing Conservative MP. He pressed Howe for action:

It is high time we realised just how bad the present tax system is and to what extent it is destroying the will to work. Most working people in this country are extremely conscientious but an ever larger number are realising that they are caught on a treadmill and would be better-off if they either worked less hours or did not bother to work at all.

In his view, 'why work?' had become 'Britain's number one problem'. He urged Howe to remove 'this depressing disincentive to the will to work ... In making tax changes your aim must be to reward – not to punish – a man for working harder'.[61] Howe took a wider view, stressing the need for economic growth to increase the incomes of those in work and thus increase the gap with out-of-work benefits.[62] Nevertheless, he saw the need for 'deep, sustained radical thinking' and even a second Beveridge study by independent experts. In the event, officials were asked to consider the long-term evolution of welfare, and whether it was affordable given economic growth and demographic trends.[63]

One possibility was tax credits, which were seriously considered by the Conservative government of 1970–4. Tax credits would replace family allowances – cash payments to everyone with children – and personal income tax allowances: an individual would either receive a net payment after deduction of any tax due or make a net payment if the credit were smaller than the tax liability. The attraction of the scheme was that it graduated income tax by family circumstances and would

---

[60] TNA, T470/154, 'Note of a meeting on the taxation of savings', 21 November 1983; T470/201, 'Tax policy and the jobs exercise', memorandum by the Chancellor of the Exchequer.
[61] TNA, T366/754, R. Howell to G. Howe, 16 January 1981; Ralph Howell, *Why Work? A Challenge to the Chancellor* (London: Conservative Political Centre, 1976).
[62] TNA, T366/754, G. Howe to R. Howell, 3 February 1981; G. Howe to R. Howell, Personal, 3 February 1981.
[63] TNA, T366/773, G. Howe to Patrick Jenkin, 11 December 1980.

help remove the poverty and unemployment traps.[64] Although Howe supported tax credits in 1974, Thatcher had turned against the scheme by 1977 on the grounds that it meant 'reinforcement of the "transfer machine" … further socialization of income … further entrenchment of expectations and removal of the motive to personal thrift'. Attention turned in other directions, on the grounds that child benefit achieved most of the advantages offered by tax credits. Similarly, a fully integrated or unified tax and benefits system was not only too complicated, but would have the disadvantage of blurring the 'distinction between what individuals earn by their own effort and what they receive from the state', running against the aim of creating individualism and self-reliance. Attention therefore turned to smaller, ad hoc interventions.[65]

The choice was between cutting the basic rate of income tax and raising the threshold, which had different distributional outcomes. A reduction in the basic rate was more valuable relative to income, benefiting higher earners towards the top of the basic band. An increase in the threshold was of the same absolute value for everyone, reducing the average rate more for the lower paid and taking some out of the tax, thus creating an incentive for unemployed people to take on a low-paid job. The Inland Revenue favoured an increase in thresholds, which were low by historical and international standards. The Treasury disagreed and strongly favoured a cut in the basic rate, arguing that thresholds did nothing to improve the supply side of the economy by increasing incentives to take on more work or responsibility: they argued that the marginal reward for working harder was not affected once a person passed the threshold to pay tax.[66] An official report on incentives for the low-paid concurred. Most low-paid people wanted to work out of a sense of pride – the real problem was a lack of suitable jobs or their own social disadvantage. Consequently, cutting thresholds and increasing the gap between in- and out-of-work incomes for the low-paid would have little effect, and the emphasis should be on

[64] PP1971–2, Cmnd 5116, Proposals for a tax credit system; PP1972–3, XXXIV.1 Select Committee on Tax Credit, Report and Proceedings.
[65] TNA, T470/111, 'Note of a meeting held at 3 pm on Monday 2 August in the Chancellor's room at HM Treasury, to discuss taxation policy', 12 August 1983; T470/156, 'Tax credits', A. J. G. Isaac, May 1979; A. G. J. Isaac to Financial Secretary, 'A minimum scheme of tax credits', 28 July 1983; Tax credits, n.d.; F. Sutcliffe-Braithwaite, 'Neoliberalism and Morality: The Making of Thatcherite Social Policy', *Historical Journal* 55 (2012), 505–7, 510; N. Lawson, *The View from No. 11: Memoirs of a Tory Radical* (London: Bantam, 1992), pp. 596–8.
[66] TNA, T366/755, A. M. W. Battishill, 'Inland Revenue manpower and tax reduction', 2 July 1980; 'Inland Revenue manpower and tax reductions', D. Wass to Chancellor, 25 June 1980; I. Airey to Chancellor, 26 June 1980; J. H. Gracey, 'Inland Revenue manpower and tax reductions', 26 June 1980.

'industrial workers on average earnings and for those towards the upper end of the basic rate scale'. Priority should therefore be given to cutting the basic rate, for 'it is still the highly skilled worker, the middle manager and junior professional man ... on whom the burden of tax continues to fall with considerable severity'.[67]

Howe was certainly concerned about the lack of progress on the poverty and unemployment traps, and he informed Thatcher in 1981 that 'the damage it does goes far wider than just those people who have been positively affected – it can affect the attitude to work over a very wide range of incomes. We must seek to tackle this problem, against the upturn of the economy'. He thought – contrary to the Treasury – that in order to improve incentives to work, 'the gap between in- and out-of-work incomes must be increased, either by raising in-work incomes or decreasing out-of-work incomes'. But he felt trapped. He did not have the means to increase in-work incomes by raising tax thresholds which were indexed against inflation and, for a married man, had dropped from two-thirds of average earnings in 1950 to just over a third. Nor could he afford to increase child benefits. By contrast, out-of-work benefits were indexed against earnings and therefore rose faster. But it would be politically difficult to take action against the 'unsustainable false expectations' of higher benefits. When the opportunity arose in 1982 and 1983, he gave priority to increasing thresholds in real terms rather than to cutting the basic rate, and pointed to the need for more fundamental reform to take the low-paid out of income tax in order to solve the unemployment and poverty traps.[68]

When Lawson became chancellor in 1983 he took a somewhat different line. He announced his intention of reforming personal taxation and finding a more radical solution to the poverty and unemployment traps by linking them to another issue: the tax position of women and families. The structure of personal allowances was much the same as it had been in 1942: married men received 150 per cent of the single allowance; a wife received a single person's allowance. A working

---

[67] TNA, T366/776, A. H. Lovell to J. B. Unwin, 'Incentives for the low paid', 3 January 1980; E. F. Kemp to A. H. Lovell, 'Incentives for the lower paid', 8 January 1980; E. F. Kemp to Bailey and Chancellor, 'Incentives for the lower paid', 23 January 1980; 'Work incentives for the lower paid: report by officials'; 'Incentives for the lower paid': draft E committee paper for the Chancellor of the Exchequer.

[68] TNA, T470/39, G. Howe to Prime Minister, 'Working group on tax incentives', 26 [illegible] 1981; T470/39, WIIC(81)2, 10 February 1981, 'Work incentives and income compression'; CAB/129/213/12, C(81)37, 17 July 1981, Cabinet: 'Tax and public expenditure'. Memorandum by the Chancellor of the Exchequer; Parliamentary Debates, 6th series, vol. 19, Commons, 9 March 1982, col. 756; vol. 39, 15 March 1983, col. 156.

couple therefore received 250 per cent of the single allowance, and a couple with a non-working spouse 150 per cent. Hence a couple with both partners in work would pay less tax than a family with one earner on the same income. Lawson argued that the tax system hit married couples at the time of greatest need, when they had a young family and the wife stayed home. One possible solution was a 'transferrable allowance': everyone would have a standard tax-free allowance and could transfer the unused element so that a husband could use the allowance of his non-working wife, thus reducing his tax bill and lifting families out of the poverty and unemployment trap. This suggestion was abandoned on the grounds that it would largely benefit single-earner married couples rather than two-earner married couples, and the cost of the scheme might be better used in cutting the basic rate of tax or increasing allowances. In 1988, Lawson announced that, from 1990, husbands and wives could make separate tax returns: they would each have the same personal allowance plus an additional married man's allowance. The wife was no longer taxed at her husband's marginal rate, but any unused personal allowance in respect of income from employment could not be transferred. However, the couple could transfer assets between themselves to use both personal allowances and so reduce liability to taxation of capital gains and investment income.[69] Lawson was removing the anomalous and outmoded tax treatment of women in a way that offered some modest assistance to the poverty and unemployment traps, but especially to better-off married couples who were able to share their investment income.

Although Lawson increased the threshold for the basic rate in real terms in 1984 and 1985, he concentrated on reducing the standard rate of income tax. In 1986, he reduced the basic rate to 29 per cent; in 1987, the basic rate was cut to 27 per cent. In 1988, he again increased the basic rate threshold so that it was now 25 per cent higher in real terms than in 1979, and he cut the basic rate to 25 per cent. At the

---

[69] Parliamentary Debates, 6th series, vol. 129, Commons, 15 March 1988, cols. 997–8; TNA, CAB/129/220/7, C(86)7, 21 February 1986: Cabinet: 'Green Paper on personal taxation. Memorandum by the Chancellor of the Exchequer, Nigel Lawson, 21 February 1986; CAB/128/83/8 Cabinet conclusions, 'Reform of personal taxation', 27 February 1986; PP 1985/6, Cmnd 9756, *The Reform of Personal Taxation: Presented to Parliament by the Chancellor of the Exchequer by Command of Her Majesty March 1986*; TNA, PREM19/1708, 'Proposed Green Paper on personal taxation', David Norgrove (Private Secretary to the Prime Minister) to Rachel Lomax (Treasury), 4 December 1985; John Redwood to Prime Minister, 'How can £5.25 bn of tax relief be best spent?', 6 January 1986; 'Reform of personal taxation', note of a meeting at 10 Downing Street, 16 January 1986; 'Reform of personal taxation', note of a further meeting at 10 Downing Street, 29 January 1986.

same time, he consolidated all the higher rates of tax between 40 and 60 per cent at a single rate of 40 per cent which, he argued, was necessary given the general reduction in the top rates in other countries.[70] Overall, the changes were more beneficial to higher incomes, a trend that was taken further in the recession of the early 1990s when the tax system became considerably less progressive, benefiting the rich at the expense of the poor.[71]

Incentives at the top were given priority over incentives at the bottom. In opposition in the 1960s, the Conservatives developed the notion of an opportunity state that would integrate members of society by cutting taxes at the top and offering benefits to the poor in compensation for indirect taxes, leading to a more dynamic society that would also be fair. In office in 1970–4, this vision was already fading. Increasingly, the focus was on an enterprise society in which income and wealth inequality became more extreme, and policies more divisive and self-interested. It was a far cry from the aims of Meade as the good fortune of the fortunate was reinforced rather than mitigated.

Conclusion

In 1988, Lawson remarked that 'the emergence of the capital-owning democracy has been one of the most remarkable features of the 1980s'. The Thatcher government used the tax system to reconstitute British society, moving it away from reliance on long-term, prudential institutional investment to individual control of assets in personal equity plans or portable pensions, linked with the end of higher taxation of unearned income and an increase in profitability. These changes were more striking than any reduction in the share of taxation in GDP or even in the movement from direct to indirect taxation. The ideas had antecedents in both the Labour and Conservative Parties, both of which recognised the problems of institutional investment, worried about the poverty and unemployment traps and saw the virtues of VAT in producing revenue. In part, the approach of the Meade Report was pursued, in particular the attempt to remove distortions in investment. But there were also major differences, namely Conservative encouragement of personal investments and a greater emphasis on incentives for the rich rather than equality.

---

[70] Parliamentary Debates, 6th series, vol. 94, Commons, 18 March 1986, cols. 181–3; vol. 129, 15 March 1988, cols. 1012–13.
[71] Christopher Giles and Paul Johnson, 'Tax reform in the UK and changes in the progressivity of the tax system, 198595', Fiscal Studies 15/3 (1994), 64–86.

The policies of the Thatcher government went back to the thinking of the working party on economic policy in opposition in the second half of the 1960s and the Heath government with the desire to create a more enterprising and capitalist society. They were also widely supported within the Treasury by economists such as Byatt and officials such as Todd, who were well aware of thinking on optimal tax theory. The Thatcher government was not taking the same line as President Ronald Reagan in the United States, of reducing taxes in order to 'starve the beast' and so force the government to do less; in Britain, taxation did not fall as a proportion of national income, and revenues benefited from the windfall of North Sea oil and the growth of financial services. Thatcher's policies were not a simple expression of neo-liberalism, but should be understood in a more nuanced manner in relation to the particular issues facing British society and the need to shift the structure of incentives and reform the current institutional structures. In many ways, Thatcher owed as much to her early Methodist upbringing and the goal of a moral rejuvenation of Britain, based on a shift from paternalistic, state-centred policies to self-reliance in families and communities. It was a different approach from the economistic individualism of neo-liberalism.[72]

Of course, officials and politicians were well aware of the impact of tax changes on insurance companies or pensions schemes, and had to take account of potential opposition. However, most of the policy debates were somewhat technical and internal, without much popular engagement, except rarely in cases such as the imposition of VAT on domestic fuel, or the poll tax. The majoritarian system of parliament meant that the government could implement its changes without the veto points found in countries with proportional representation. What the changes in the tax system did capture was the emergence of a growing sense of self-reliance and choice over the allocation of income. The tax policies of Howe and Lawson expressed and encouraged this massive cultural shift more than the egalitarian and integrative social democratic vision of Meade.

---

[72] Sutcliffe-Braithwaite, 'Neoliberalism and morality', 510, 520.

3 Fiscal Policy in Japan and the United States since 1973: Economic Crises, Taxation and Weak Tax Consent

W. Elliot Brownlee and Eisaku Ide

Contemporary Fiscal Challenges

The fiscal problems that face almost all the high-income nations today seem to be multifaceted and formidable in scale. These problems emerged, broadly speaking, in the wake of oil shocks and inflation during the 1970s and became even more intractable during and following the Great Recession of 2007–9. Among the problems have been increasing budget deficits and public debt. The pace, extent and nature of these problems have varied among the high-income nations, but a common trend of increasing reliance on debt finance has led some students of the history of public finance and fiscal policy to declare the decline or end of the 'tax state', propose dating the beginning of that transition in the 1970s, suggest that 'debt state' is a better way to describe the financial core of the contemporary state in the advanced nations and to propose that this means a chronic loss of fiscal capacity.[1]

In this chapter we seek to understand the sources of the growing reliance on deficits and debt among high-income nations by examining the history of the fiscal policies of Japan and the United States since the Second World War. Studies of international fiscal affairs often tend to view the histories of the United States and Japan as exceptional and therefore difficult to incorporate into comparative analysis. However, we have coupled these two nations for several reasons. First, they are two of the three largest economies in the world and any interpretation of contemporary global fiscal policy needs to encompass their situation and histories. Second, each has a high level of national debt by any standard. In Japan, debt as a percentage of GDP has reached an all-time high in that nation's history. Moreover, the level of 230 per cent in 2014 was the highest of any OECD nation at the time. In the United

---

[1] For suggestions of this, see Wolfgang Streek, 'The Crises of Democratic Capitalism', *New Left Review* 71 (September–October 2011), 5–29; and Greta R. Krippner, *Capitalizing on Crisis: The Political Origins of the Rise of Finance* (Cambridge, MA: Harvard University Press, 2011).

States, the debt-to-GDP ratio has risen to approximately 103 per cent of the level of GDP, or to a level approaching those attained during the aftermath of the American Revolution and Second World War. The current level exceeds the comparable ratios in Canada, France, Germany and all the Scandinavian nations. Third, both nations have relatively small public sectors and relatively low levels of public investment and expenditures for social services compared to nations in western Europe. Fourth, the two make the least tax effort among the largest high-income nations as measured by the ratio of tax revenues to GDP. Clearly, on one level, the high levels of debt in the United States and Japan must be understood in part in terms of a relatively low tax effort, and this is the aspect of the 'debt problem' that we focus on in this chapter. We seek to understand this by placing it in the larger context of the fiscal history of both the United States and Japan since the Second World War, with special attention to the period since the 1970s. We hope that in the process of understanding the commonalities and differences in the fiscal history of the two nations, this chapter will contribute to a broader understanding of contemporary fiscal capacity in the other high-income nations.

Prelude: The 'Era of Easy Finance', 1945–73

Until the global economic reversals that began in the 1970s, the United States and Japan enjoyed economic successes that featured high rates of economic growth and a great degree of price stability. These economic successes were central to the system of social cohesion which, in both nations, experienced considerable success in moderating internal economic discord. Supplementing the cohesive force of economic growth and price stability in each nation were interlocking features of public policy. First, in the realm of fiscal affairs, national spending programmes – military spending and highway construction in the United States and post-war reconstruction in Japan – supported employment and stimulated consumer demand. Second, their welfare states were moderate in size but expanding in scope. Third, their public revenue systems were relatively progressive in incidence but kept the overall level of taxation low. In addition, issuing debt in the form of long-term loans almost always supplemented tax revenue, contributing to the financing of central government in the two nations, especially during the war. With this financial model in place, national debt was not a structural problem but rather an instrument that could advance the interests of society. In other words, the modern fiscal state in both nations was always much more than the 'tax state', as described by the economist Joseph Schumpeter in the early twentieth century.[2]

Broad-based, centrist political coalitions maintained these systems. However, there were important differences in the way these coalitions governed and in the outcomes the policies produced, particularly in the realm of economic redistribution. One of the most important was that the US coalition embraced a higher degree of tax progressivity. That reflected a history of greater concentrations of wealth and income which had, through the financing of the Second World War, stimulated redistributive taxation, followed by responses from the economic elites to reverse this. In other ways, though, the two fiscal systems were remarkably similar, reflecting the fundamental correspondences in the structure of their system of social cohesion.

In the United States and Japan a sharply progressive income tax provided the core of wartime taxation.[3] After the war, inflation in both countries engendered hostility among taxpayers who resented the unlegislated increases to taxation, resulting from so-called bracket-creep. Moreover, during the war the Japanese government had introduced deep horizontal inequity into the personal income tax system by adopting a rigorous withholding system while failing to adopt an effective way to determine the incomes of self-employed workers who were not subject to withholding. In the late 1960s this became known as the '9-6-4 problem' (*Ku-Ro-Yon Mondai*), for while the Tax Bureau of the Ministry of Finance had the administrative capacity to reach 90 per cent of payroll income through the withholding system, it could reach only 60 per cent of the income of independent businesses and just 40 per cent of the income earned by farming households. Loosely administered self-assessment in income tax enabled the government to curry favour with small business owners and farmers, who constituted the backbone of traditional society in Japan. But the system bred cynicism, distrust, a sense of inequality and tax resistance among wage workers and salaried employees. As a consequence, from the end of

---

[2] Richard Bonney, Patrick K. O'Brien, W. Mark Ormrod and others have been pioneers in developing the concept of the modern fiscal state and moving beyond Schumpeter's 'tax state' model to incorporate debt finance and thus understand the crucial links between successful nation states and financial markets. See Richard Bonney (ed.), *Economic Systems and State Finance* (Oxford: Clarendon Press, 1995); and Richard Bonney (ed.), *The Rise of the Fiscal State in Europe, c.1200–1815* (Oxford: Clarendon Press, 1999). For an extension of the concept of the modern fiscal state to the experience of China and Japan, see Wekai He, *Paths toward the Modern Fiscal State: England, Japan, and China* (Cambridge, MA: Harvard University Press, 2013).

[3] W. Elliot Brownlee, 'The Shoup Mission to Japan: Two Political Economies Intersect', in Isaac William Martin, Ajay K. Mehrotra and Monica Prasad (eds.), *The New Fiscal Sociology: Taxation in Comparative and Historical Perspective* (Cambridge: Cambridge University Press, 2009), pp. 238–40.

the war through the era of high economic growth in Japan, employees whose taxes were withheld regarded tax relief as an even higher priority than did their counterparts in the United States.

Tax-cutting at the national level began during the early post-war years in both the United States and Japan and continued into the 1970s. These cuts involved both reductions in income tax rates and widening of any loopholes designed to reduce the cost of capital. Tax-cutting, however, exercised little constraint on what the governments wished to do. During this era of easy finance the combination of economic expansion and some inflation yielded substantial increases in income tax revenues.[4] As a consequence, both nations' governments could expand significantly a wide range of programmes largely without legislated tax increases, even while making significant tax cuts.

In the United States, military spending dominated the federal budget throughout this period; nevertheless, the tax bonanza enabled federal spending on domestic programmes to grow from about 6 per cent of GDP in 1954 to almost 15 per cent in 1975. In addition, the federal government made implicit financial commitments and engaged in significant off-budget spending. For example, Fannie Mae and Freddie Mac (government-sponsored enterprises active in the secondary mortgage market by securitising mortgages in the form of mortgage-backed securities), along with a variety of tax expenditures within the income tax, played a critical role in subsidising the families and businesses that transformed suburban and Sunbelt America during the post-war decades.

In this same period, Japan established and expanded both its health insurance and its universal state pension schemes, and increased public works, financed in part through the Fiscal Investment and Loan Programme (FILP).[5] This programme, commonly known as the second budget, enabled the government to use public funds from postal savings and public insurance to make low-interest loans to governmental financial institutions, semi-governmental corporations and local governments.

---

[4] The term was coined by Eugene Steuerle, 'Financing the American State at the Turn of the Century', in W. Elliot Brownlee (ed.), *Funding the American State, 1941–1995: The Rise and Fall of the Era of Easy Finance* (Cambridge and Washington, DC: Cambridge University Press and Woodrow Wilson Center Press, 1996).

[5] Pressure from the United States reinforced this programme of vigorous spending. The pressure became intense after the so-called 'Nixon shock' of 1971 (the adoption of a policy of free-floating exchange rates). The strengthening of the yen after the Nixon shock led the US government to urge Japan to increase its domestic consumption, a request the Japanese government attempted to comply with.

By 1976, investments made through FILP equalled in size the spending for on-budget public works and social insurance of all types.[6]

In both nations impressive economic growth, economic stimulation from spending on national defence, national-level subsidies for suburban development in the United States and of the 'construction state' in Japan, and the growth of social programmes favoured by the middle classes combined to mute popular demand for building a comprehensive welfare state.[7] That would have required eschewing tax cuts and, arguably, increasing the rate of taxation. Politicians in the United States and Japan rarely had to discuss how expanding expenditure for defence, public works and conventional welfare state functions could be financed. Partly as a result of the absence of debate about tax increases, in the two nations, taxpayers – both individual and corporate – lost sight of the connection between the taxes they paid and public expenditure. This lack of 'tax consciousness' set the stage for a subsequent loss of faith in government.

Economic Shocks and Fiscal Responses, 1973–80

During the last decades of the twentieth century natural fiscal slack – the slack produced by economic growth increasing the tax base – shrank dramatically in both nations. With the oil shock of 1973, long-term (secular) growth slowed, and an especially severe international recession took hold in 1974–5. The 'Great Inflation' ensued later in the decade, and a second oil shock came in 1979. A weakening of productivity, which had begun in the late 1960s, continued in both Japan and the United States.

In the face of slowing or declining productivity the two nations adjusted fiscal policy in significant ways. However, they placed their primary emphasis on maintaining defence spending in the United States and to some extent its functional counterpart – the construction state – in Japan. Both defence spending and the construction state received support from a broad range of communities, key industries, powerful politicians and an implicit Keynesian commitment to supporting demand. Both nations responded to economic difficulties by reaffirming this commitment. The principal fiscal adjustment in each nation was to

---

[6] The leading analysis of FILP is Gene Park, *Spending without Taxation: FILP and the Politics of Public Finance in Japan* (Stanford, CA: Stanford University Press, 2011).

[7] The central elements of the construction state were established in the mid-1970s in order to maintain the political order established during the era of high economic growth. See Ide Eisaku, 'Touchi no Zentaizo to shite no Doken Kokka' [The Construction State as the Whole Picture of the Governance], in Ide Eisaku (ed.), *Nihon Zaisei no Gendai-shi, I* [A Modern History of Japan's Public Finance, vol. 1] (Tokyo: Yuhikaku, 2014).

ramp up tax cuts. This approach represented a Keynesian stimulus on the one hand, and a response to middle-class resentment of inflation and business concern about the cost of capital on the other.

When Japan and the United States faced the first oil crisis and the severe recession that followed it, both their governments undertook fiscal stimulation that relied heavily on tax cuts. In his budget for fiscal year (FY) 1974, Prime Minister Tanaka Kakuei took the lead in making large-scale cuts to taxation of personal income, both to mitigate the depressing effects of the oil crisis and to respond to the continuing demands of employees to fix the '9-6-4' problem. But OPEC's quadrupling of oil prices had a greater impact on the Japanese economy than Tanaka had expected, driving the budget deficit much higher than the government anticipated and hoped to maintain. In response, in 1974 the government began to increase corporation tax in order to make up for the revenue shortfall that followed the cuts to personal income tax. Unfortunately, this tax hike worsened, in Keynesian terms, the economic stagnation that the oil crisis had generated, and falling corporate earnings resulted in a sharp decline in corporate tax revenue, despite the tax increase. After the compilation of the FY 1975 budget, the government took steps to offset the depressing effects of the tax increase with a huge offering of deficit-financing bonds.[8]

In the United States the administration of President Gerald R. Ford took similar steps after first attempting to offset inflation through budget cuts and monetary restriction. In January 1975 Ford endorsed what was then the biggest peacetime deficit in US history, including a massive tax cut designed to stimulate consumption. Congress did not cut marginal tax rates but provided all taxpayers and their dependants with a tax credit and increased the standard deduction.[9] The influence on policy of neo-liberal economists like Milton Friedman and think tanks like the Heritage Foundation was becoming stronger in the United States, but at this stage had little effect on fiscal policy, in part because of policy conflicts among leading Republicans.[10] The Ford administration's tax-cutting strategy was traditional Keynesian-style, demand-side stimulation, and did not reflect the anti-government ideology of the

---

[8] Hirata Keiichiro, Chu Saichi and Izumi Minomatsu (eds.), *Showa Zeisei Kaiko to Tenbo, Jyo-kan* [Retrospect and Prospect of Taxation in the Showa Era, vol. 1] (Tokyo: Okura Zaimu Kyokai, 1979), pp. 708–9.

[9] W. Elliot Brownlee, *Dynamics of Ascent: A History of the American Economy*, 2nd edn (New York: Alfred A. Knopf, 1979), pp. 464–6.

[10] We prefer the term 'retro-liberal' to 'neo-liberal', but to avoid confusion we use the conventional rubric in this chapter. For the case for using the term retro-liberal, see W. Elliot Brownlee, *Federal Taxation in America: A History* (Cambridge: Cambridge University Press, 2016), pp. 175–7.

neo-liberals or represent a wholesale assault on the legacy of the New Deal.[11]

In both nations fiscal stimulation contributed to strong economic recovery starting in the summer of 1975 and continuing, although at a slower pace, through 1977. At the same time, however, supply-side shocks continued to drive up prices.[12] The administration of President Jimmy Carter concentrated its inflation-fighting efforts on administrative mechanisms while continuing Ford's stimulus programme, including minor tax cuts, largely in the form of inflation adjustments. In 1977, Carter eased the stimulus somewhat but, through a mission headed by Vice President Walter Mondale, he put pressure on both the Japanese and German governments to undertake expansionary fiscal policies (described in Japan as the Japan–Germany locomotive) to promote an international Keynesian programme of augmenting global demand. Carter's pressure became known as the 'Carter shock' within the Japanese government. The German government was reluctant to cooperate, but Japanese leaders, despite their concerns about the serious implications of such a policy for budget deficits, responded with a major fiscal stimulus.[13] The government embraced expansion in its supplementary budget of 1977 and, at the Bonn Summit of 1978, Prime Minister Fukuda Takeo promised to achieve 7 per cent real term economic growth. In the FY 1978 budget he increased public works expenditures by 34.5 per cent over the previous year. This dramatic move resulted in further increases in the national debt. The ratio between outstanding obligations in the general account budget and GDP had been just 9.8 per cent in 1975, but increased steadily to 25 per cent by 1979. During the same period, in the United States the ratio of federal debt held by the public to GDP was relatively stable at around 25 per cent.[14]

---

[11] On neo-liberal influences on the Ford administration, see David Stedman Jones, *Masters of the Universe: Hayek, Friedman, and the Birth of Neoliberal Politics* (Princeton, NJ: Princeton University Press, 2012), p. 243; and Herbert Stein, 'The Fiscal Revolution in America, Part II', in Brownlee (ed.), *Funding the Modern American State*, pp. 256–63.

[12] On the importance of the oil shocks, see Alan S. Blinder, 'The Anatomy of Double-Digit Inflation in the 1970s', in Robert E. Hall (ed.), *Inflation: Causes and Effects* (Chicago: University of Chicago Press, 1982), pp. 261–82.

[13] The Japanese business community was worried about a rapid rise in the exchange rate of the yen and urged the government to adopt an expansionary fiscal policy. See Keizai Dantai Rengo-kai (ed.), *Keizai Dantai Rengo-kai Gojyu-nen-shi* [A Fifty-Year History of the Japan Business Federation] (Tokyo: Keizai Dantai Rengo-kai, 1999), pp. 101–4.

[14] The US side of this episode in international economic relations is well reported in W. Carl Biven, *Jimmy Carter's Economy: Policy in an Age of Limits* (Chapel Hill, NC: University of North Carolina Press, 2002), pp. 85–121.

Beginning in 1978, both the US and Japanese governments became acutely concerned about soaring inflation and the scale of deficits and debt, and sought to shift the course of their fiscal policies. But first, in early 1978, Carter once again proposed tax cuts. However, he had always been more of an inflation hawk than his advisers and, in October 1978, he finally announced a plan to cut the deficit by tightening expenditures.[15] In 1978, Ohira Masayoshi, who had held the position of finance minister in the Tanaka cabinet, took office as prime minister, but with a sense of personal responsibility for having increasing levels of national debt. Ohira embraced a Ministry of Finance (MOF) plan to introduce a general consumption tax (i.e. a value added tax) as a way of both reducing the deficit and resolving the '9-6-4 problem'.[16] MOF argued that adopting a general consumption tax would enhance horizontal equity and relieve the government of the need to take the much more unpopular course of stepping up efforts to collect the income tax owed by independent businesses and farming households.

Neither Carter nor Ohira enjoyed any immediate success. Carter's cabinet was not enthusiastic about his austerity proposals and, when details of the budget were leaked, Congressional Democrats, led by Senator Edward Kennedy, forced Carter to abandon the idea. At the same time, widespread frustration over inflation-driven increases in tax rates produced the dramatic success of the 1978 taxpayers' revolt in California. The passage of Proposition 13, which capped property taxes and limited the ability to increase other state taxes, encouraged Congress to contemplate making significant cuts in income taxes. Only Carter's threat of a veto prevented Congress from passing a version of the Kemp–Roth tax bill, which called for three years of deep cuts (10 per cent each year) in income taxes. Carter remained firmly opposed to tax cuts for the rest of his administration, even during his failed 1980 re-election campaign when he stood against Ronald Reagan.[17]

---

[15] On Carter's approach to fiscal policy, see ibid., pp. 130–4, 186–207; and Stein, 'The Fiscal Revolution in America, Part II', p. 263.

[16] At this time the terminology of '9-6-4' became entrenched in public discourse and, despite the two trillion yen tax cut of 1974, by which MOF sharply increased the employment income deduction from 25 per cent to 40 per cent, employees remained deeply resentful about their relatively heavy tax burden. 'Showa 53–56nen no Shuzei-kyoku Gyosei' [Administration of the Tax Bureau from 1978 to 1981], Ministry of Finance, Research Institute, 20.

[17] On Kemp–Roth, see W. Elliot Brownlee, *Federal Taxation in America: A History* (Cambridge: Cambridge University Press, 2016), pp. 178–80. On Carter's opposition to tax cuts in 1980, see Biven, *Jimmy Carter's Economy*, pp. 204–6.

In 1979 Ohira's plans were disrupted by the second oil crisis. An election was imminent and, for the first time since the post-war Occupation, a Japanese government would test at the polls a proposal for a major tax increase. In the face of the oil crisis, leaders of Ohira's Liberal Democratic Party (LDP) lost confidence in the willingness of middle-class voters to accept the introduction of VAT and so, in 1979, Ohira abandoned the proposal. Even so, his government lost office, largely because it had been advocating the tax. However, continuing concern within MOF and the cabinet about the deficit blocked any attempt to make significant cuts in personal income taxes.[18]

Divergent Fiscal Paths, 1980–1

During 1980–1, the United States and Japan took significantly different paths in using fiscal policy to address the economic problems associated with the Great Inflation. In the 1980 US presidential election the Republican candidate, Ronald Reagan, won in part because he promised to make dramatic tax cuts, both across-the-board and cuts designed to reduce the cost of capital. With the former he promised relief for the millions of Americans who had suffered the implicit tax levied by the Great Inflation and, at the same time, endured unlegislated tax increases through the process of bracket-creep. Reagan called for tax relief as part of a larger attack on government, focusing on waste, on what he described as the bloated costs of welfare and on the seeming inability of Keynesian economics to deal with stagflation. In so doing, Reagan encouraged a middle-class backlash against much of the legacy of the New Deal and President Johnson's Great Society. The capital-favouring proposals responded to both traditional business hostility to taxation, especially when applied to capital income and high-income earners, and growing support for neo-liberal ideology among conservative economists and business-backed think tanks. After Reagan's victory, Congress followed through with the Economic Recovery Tax Act of 1981 (ERTA). The Act slashed tax rates across the board, indexed income tax rates, cut the top income tax rate to 50 per cent and significantly increased depreciation allowances for corporations. The unusually severe Great Inflation of the late 1970s, along with the slowing of secular growth, had provided the Reagan administration with a case for abandoning the caution with which both the

---

[18] Okura Masataka, 'Ippan Shouhi-zei Koso no Zasetsu' [Failure of the General Consumption Tax Plan], in Hiroshi Ando (ed.), *Sekinin to Genkai, Ge-kan* [Responsibility and Limitation, vol. 2] (Tokyo: Japan Kinyu Zaisei Jijyo Kenkyukai, 1987), pp. 100–26.

Truman and Eisenhower administrations had approached tax-cutting after an earlier episode of soaring inflation.[19]

While Congress was dressing the ERTA 'Christmas tree', the Japanese government, led by Prime Minister Suzuki Zenko, was also providing some tax relief. But in Japan relief went only to the beleaguered personal income taxpayers and applied only to any future tax increases. At the same time, the Suzuki government imposed a sharp increase in corporate income taxes,[20] the largest tax increase of any kind in post-war Japan (with the exception of several that the government had imposed during the American Occupation). The government had reckoned on two things. First, labour's low share of national income meant that large corporations had been able to economise on operating expenses and thus could afford high corporate income tax payments. Second, labour's low share of national income meant that the success of the government's programmes of social integration, particularly the funding of the construction state, required the government to reduce the fiscal burden borne by the middle classes employed in the corporate sector.[21]

A number of factors help to explain why the Japanese government's fiscal measures were less geared to favour business and also why the US government cut taxes dramatically while the Japanese government raised them.[22] The first question is the easier to answer: a major source of public disaffection with the fiscal arrangements undergirding the Japanese state continued to be the '9-6-4' problem. Given the determination of the Japanese government to raise significant new tax revenues, and that there was potent resistance to increasing taxes on small businesses and farms, the Japanese government faced a choice: it could either raise income taxes and risk further increasing tax resistance

[19] On the Economic Recovery Act of 1981, see Brownlee, *Federal Taxation in America*, pp. 186–8; and Monica Prasad, 'The Popular Origins of Neoliberalism in the Reagan Tax Cut of 1982', *Journal of Policy History*, 24 (2012), 351–83.

[20] Partly as a result of the increases in corporate tax rates in Japan and the United States, during the mid-1980s the contribution of corporate income tax to central government tax revenues in Japan remained relatively steady at about 30 per cent, while the comparable share in the United States declined from around 22 per cent to about 13 per cent. See the comparative OECD corporate income tax data available at http://stats.oecd.org/Index.aspx?DataSetCode=REV.

[21] Satoshi Sekiguchi, 'The Corporate Income Tax in Postwar Japan and the Shoup Recommendations: Why Did the Corporate Income Tax Become So High?', in W. Elliot Brownlee, Eisaku Ide, Yasunori Fukagai et al., *The Political Economy of Transnational Tax Reform: The Shoup Mission to Japan* (Cambridge: Cambridge University Press, 2013), pp. 388–9.

[22] The 1981 increase in corporate taxation contributed to a significant increase in the average effective tax rate on corporations in Japan above that in the United States. See Hiromitsu Ishi, *The Japanese Tax System* (Oxford: Clarendon Press, 1989), pp. 195–201.

among the corporate employees who paid disproportionately high-income taxes; or it could broaden the base of taxation by imposing a general consumption tax and alienate much of the business community as well as many consumers. However, the government's attempt to introduce a general consumption tax had failed in 1979, so the only feasible option seemed to be to increase corporate taxes. The corporate tax rate was at about the same level as in other industrialised nations, but the government attempted to persuade the corporations that increasing their taxes was not only in their best interests but also those of the LDP and the nation at large.[23]

There are several answers to the second puzzle. First, the Reagan administration had a very different social agenda from that of its Japanese counterpart. One of Reagan's central objectives was to slow down or even reverse the growth of the welfare state his administration had inherited. Making dramatic tax cuts while protecting the military budget, which was the Reagan administration's greatest priority, would accelerate a general attack on the welfare state by squeezing discretionary domestic spending. In contrast, the Japanese government sought to protect both the construction state and conventional welfare services, which were broadly popular with the LDP's political base. Second, neo-liberal enthusiasm for both shrinking government and dramatically reducing taxation on capital income and high-income earners had, at this point, gained much greater ground among influential opinion-makers in the United States. Third, the technocrats working in the Department of the Treasury, who tended to oppose deep tax cuts and to favour broadening or diversifying the tax base, had far less influence over tax policy than did technocrats in MOF, who had the same general concerns. Unlike the Treasury, MOF and its Tax Bureau had always exerted greater power within the government, and the government in turn had more muscle in structuring the tax debate than did the presidential administrations in the United States. A fundamental explanation for this difference was constitutional. Under a parliamentary system, Japanese governments had the initiative in proposing revenue reform. In contrast, the US Constitution required that the most democratic legislative body, the House of Representatives, introduce revenue legislation. Also, the Japanese Constitution restricts the Diet's budgetary review to either acceptance or rejection of the cabinet's proposals, and in Japan a budget never has the status of a law. Together, these two

[23] Mizuno Masaru, *Zaisei Kaisei Gojyu-nen: Kaiko to Tenbo* [Fifty Years of Tax Reform: Retrospect and Prospect] (Tokyo: Okura Zaimu Kyokai, 2006), pp. 177–9.

provisions enabled Japanese governments to exercise greater autonomy in setting budgetary policy. Fourth, Suzuki's government, in fact, had serious reservations about the corporate tax increase, and immediately afterwards the government, under pressure from the Keidanren (the Japan Business Federation), switched its fiscal policy to an emphasis on cutting expenditures as a means to reduce the nation's tax burden, including that on businesses. The final reason, closely related to all the others, is that the 1980 election had given the Reagan administration a broad mandate for change, and the administration regarded itself as being in the vanguard of a neo-liberal revolution.

Convergent Taxation, Divergent Spending, 1981–93

Reagan's massive 1981 tax cuts had profound budgetary consequences. When he assumed office as president in 1981, the national debt was roughly one-third of GDP, lower than at any time since the 1930s Depression. ERTA, however, along with a severe recession in 1981–2, caused the national debt to soar. The Act produced what the economist Herbert Stein called the 'Big Budget Bang'.[24] In 1983 the budget deficit approached $200 billion, roughly four times the size of the deficits in the second half of the 1970s.

What followed immediately after the passage of ERTA in 1981, and continued until 1993, was the most significant series of peacetime tax increases in US history, other than those of the New Deal era. Bipartisan worries about increasing interest rates fuelled the major policy shift. Pressure from the business community was crucial. Most importantly, investment bankers were worried that large deficits would crowd out private capital and high interest rates would threaten recession. In addition, American exporters demanded a reduction in interest rates to reduce the attractiveness of federal debt to Japanese investors whose dollar holdings enabled Japanese exporters to maintain the advantage of a low-priced yen. At the same time, leaders in both political parties wanted to avoid cuts in Social Security, Medicare and national defence.

Three presidents – Ronald Reagan, George H. W. Bush and Bill Clinton – were instrumental in adopting the series of tax increases: Reagan with the loophole-closing Tax Equity and Fiscal Responsibility Act of 1982 (TEFRA), the 1983 acceleration of Social Security taxes and the Deficit Reduction Act of 1984 (DEFRA), which closed more

---

[24] Stein, 'The Fiscal Revolution in America, Part II', p. 266.

loopholes; Bush with the Omnibus Budget Reconciliation Act (OBRA) of 1990, which raised the top marginal personal income tax rate from 28 per cent to 31 per cent; and Clinton with OBRA 1993, which raised the top marginal personal income tax rate again, to 39.6 per cent. Also, Reagan provided crucial leadership for the Tax Reform Act of 1986. That Act provided rate cuts for the wealthiest, reflecting the growing appeal of neo-liberal supply-side enthusiasm, but also included the first major attempt since the New Deal to slash federal tax expenditures, particularly those benefiting businesses and investors. In addition, the Act provided major tax benefits for the working poor, including a major expansion of Earned Income Tax Credit (EITC).[25] As a result of all these measures, reinforced by rapid economic expansion, the United States seemed firmly on track for a significant deficit reduction. In January 1998, Clinton submitted the first balanced federal budget in three decades.[26]

While the three tax-raising presidents reduced the federal deficits, they had a mixed record in improving tax consciousness or public confidence in the tax system. Throughout his period of tax-raising, Reagan continued to rail against big government in general and welfare spending in particular, reinforcing the public's perception that their income taxes went primarily to fund wasteful social spending. Moreover, in discussing its tax increases, the Reagan administration never admitted it was, in fact, raising taxes. Reagan described the Social Security tax increases as an acceleration of increases that had already been scheduled, while he largely ignored the benefit cuts. Furthermore, he described TEFRA and DEFRA as tax reforms rather than tax increases. Reagan's defence of the Tax Reform Act of 1986, however, did enhance public trust in the tax system. The Act quelled the preceding uproar over outrageous tax shelters and satisfied some that progress was being made towards horizontal tax equity, or treating equals equally, and tax simplicity, just as many proponents of the

---

[25] The major losers in 1986 were the many individuals, corporations and industries for which the loss of tax preferences was greater than their gains from the reduction of the top rates.

   The net effect of the Reagan administration's tax policies was to leave tax progressivity essentially unchanged. See W. Elliot Brownlee and Eugene Steuerle, 'Taxation', in W. Elliot Brownlee and Hugh Davis Graham (eds.), *The Reagan Presidency: Pragmatic Conservatism and its Legacies* (Lawrence, KS: University Press of Kansas, 2003), pp. 173–4.

[26] For surveys of the tax increases in the Reagan, Bush and Clinton administrations, see ibid., pp. 163–9; and Brownlee, *Federal Taxation in America*, pp. 178–216.

measure had hoped.[27] However, Reagan's two successors abandoned the base-broadening reform strategy and supported instead significant expansion in tax expenditures.

By stressing the goal of deficit reduction rather than support for government programmes, the three presidents also undermined public support for taxation to finance social spending. The three administrations did not link tax increases to social spending, and Bush, as well as Reagan, continued to foster the impression that social spending was wasteful and dominated the federal budget. Clinton may have believed that controlling deficits through a tax increase would pave the way for subsequent expansion of domestic programmes and even the enactment of some form of national health insurance, but he did not make that part of his case to the public for OBRA 1993. Regardless of Clinton's long-term strategy, he like his two predecessors exercised fiscal restraint, not only by raising taxes but also by reversing what had been a trend of increasing spending on civilian programmes as a share of GDP. Reagan, Bush and Clinton stabilised such spending at approximately the 15 per cent level and, at the same time, cut spending as a share of GDP on infrastructure, education, job training and alternative energy development. Thus, the three presidents met the challenges of the end of the era of easy finance by increasing taxes and reducing spending on significant social programmes, while failing to increase public understanding of the nation's fiscal system.

The victory in 1981 for a 'Reagan revolution' in tax policy had no Japanese counterpart. But a comparison of the fiscal experience of the United States and Japan throughout the 1980s reveals that while the sequence of fiscal measures differed between the two nations during the 1980s, both governments made cuts in personal income taxes and adopted other major tax increases. In the case of Japan, the increases came in the form of higher corporate taxes and would soon come as well through the introduction in 1988 of a significant VAT-style consumption tax. Japan's combination of tax cuts and tax hikes resembled in a general way the combination of rate cuts and base-broadening tax increases in the United States during the same decade. Furthermore, as in the United States, the tax increases introduced during the 1980s in Japan were a pragmatic response on the part of conservatives in both the government and Japan's financial institutions to large deficits.

---

[27] For an analysis of the effects of the Tax Reform Act of 1986 on public opinion, see Brownlee and Steuerle, 'Taxation', pp. 173–4; and Brownlee, *Federal Taxation in America*, pp. 240–1. For supporting polling data, see Andrea Louise Campbell, 'What Americans Think of Taxes', in Martin, Mehrotra and Prasad, *The New Fiscal Sociology*, pp. 65–6.

In addition, and only slightly later than in the United States, the tide of enthusiasm throughout the Western world for neo-liberal economics had a significant impact on taxation.[28]

During the 1980s government leaders in Japan, as in the United States, struggled to respond to calls for budget balancing through tax increases (a process known as reconstruction of public finances) amid conflicting calls to reduce expenditures and provide tax relief (in Japan, especially for waged and salaried employees). In Japan the first success-ful relief for individuals came in 1984, three years later than the cut in personal income tax in the United States. In 1984, the government of Prime Minister Nakasone Yasuhiro introduced a reduction in personal income taxes of 760 billion yen via increases in the standard deduction, the spousal exemption, the dependants exemption and the deduction for employment income. At the same time, however, partly to provide the funds for individual income tax reductions, the Tax Bureau of MOF moved to adopt another major increase in corporate income tax. The business community organised to fight back. But the Tax Bureau stood firm and, with some important business support from within the Japan Business Federation, continued to insist that the corporations accept some increase in their taxes.[29] In the end, the two sides agreed to a temporary (two-year) increase in the rate. In return, the government allowed corporations to establish a commission, the Provisional Council for the Promotion of Administrative Reform, to promote ways of reducing expenditures.[30] The Council had a strong influence on the Nakasone government's administrative reforms, including the privatisation of

[28] In explaining the influence of neo-liberal ideology in both Japan and the United States, we tend to favour an interpretation that stresses the importance of class (business group power). For an excellent discussion of competing interpretations, see Monica Prasad, *The Politics of Free Markets: The Rise of Neoliberal Economic Policies in Britain, France, Germany, and the United States* (Chicago: University of Chicago Press, 2006), pp. 15–42. Prasad emphasises the role of the social institutions that produced progres-sive initiatives and intensified adversarial politics. This factor undoubtedly played a part in the United States but we see less evidence of it in Japan, where the tax system was the least progressive of the twenty-two OECD nations in its distributional effects.

[29] Iwata Kazuo, an influential member of Japan's Business Federation and a member of a MOF tax commission, sharply criticised MOF for being too eager to raise business taxes and too reluctant to raise other taxes or cut expenditures. However, he agreed with MOF that the corporate tax increase would not have any serious, immediate effects on Japan's international competitiveness and capital investment. Umezawa Setsuo, director-general of the Tax Bureau, persuaded Iwata to accept the increase, emphasising that MOF was asking for fiscal assistance not only from the business com-munity but also from the general public through indirect taxes. *Showa 57–60nen no Shuzei-kyoku Gyosei* [Administration of the Tax Bureau from 1982 to 1985] (Ministry of Finance, Research Institute, pp. 20–1).

[30] This commission replaced the Second Provisional Commission for Administrative Reform (*Dai-ni Rincho*), which had completed its work in 1983.

Japan's national railways, and the successors to the Council contributed powerfully to 'small government', neo-liberal reform in the 1990s and the following decade.

Following the two-year compromise the Tax Bureau continued to press for another tax increase. In 1984 it shifted its focus from increasing corporate taxation to enacting a VAT-style consumption tax. Such a tax had been under discussion off and on since 1949 when the Shoup Mission had first proposed the tax for Japan. But, in the face of vigorous opposition from a powerful coalition of small business interests, the government had not attempted to introduce the tax. Nonetheless, the Bureau had retained an active interest in it, particularly as it had met with success in western Europe during the 1960s. The Bureau had come to regard VAT as administratively attractive and believed that it might be accepted by the business community as a reasonable alternative to higher corporate taxes. This was the course the Bureau adopted in 1984. It sought to persuade the business community that VAT would inevitably be enacted and would be preferable to higher corporate income taxes. At the same time, the Bureau and MOF persuaded the Nakasone government once again to use the Constitution-based power of the cabinet to shape tax policy.[31] In part because of that concession, the organised community of large corporations agreed to support a general consumption tax. But powerful groups of retail businesses delayed the introduction of VAT for three years and contributed to the fall of the Nakasone government in 1987. The unwavering commitment of the Tax Bureau to a consumption tax and the power it exercised over governments had led to the collapse of two earlier administrations, Ohira's and Nakasone's. In 1989, after the change in cabinets, the government introduced a VAT and this helped bring down another government, that of Takeshita Noburu. While enacting the tax, his government made the reform more acceptable to business by reducing both personal income tax and corporation income tax. In 1989 the highest marginal rates of personal income tax were cut from 60 per cent to 50 per cent and the corporate income tax rate was cut from 42 per cent to 40 per cent. The concession was a response to growing support in the business community for importing neo-liberal tax ideas from the United States and Great Britain. Nevertheless VAT had survived the business challenge.

Various factors explain why Japan adopted VAT and the United States did not. In Japan, various conditions prevailed that were not

---

[31] Yoshikuni Jiro, *Sengo Houjin Zeisei-shi* [History of Post-War Corporate Taxation] (Tokyo: Zeimu Kenkyukai, 1996), p. 862.

present in the United States: technocratic enthusiasm for the tax within the government; the power of a tax technocracy led by the Tax Bureau (which indirectly helped bring down three governments); a government and public that put greater emphasis on horizontal rather than vertical equity; a business community persuaded that VAT revenues would go in part towards reducing other taxes paid by business, including their contributions to the pensions of a rapidly ageing population; and the constitutional power of the cabinet, operating within the context of a parliamentary system, to structure national budget options.[32]

The general pattern of tax reform in Japan during the 1980s resembled and converged with that of the United States, despite the latter's failure to adopt VAT. But in that decade, on the expenditure side of the fiscal ledger, the Japanese government, rather than applying the brakes to its social spending, expanded the construction state, its alternative to a European-style welfare state. Indeed, the construction state came into full bloom during the late 1980s, with increasing attention to projects that would serve the urban middle classes and thereby help to broaden the LDP's political base. The government funded this approach by dramatic increases in FILP loans. The divergence was possible because, in the late 1980s, deficits troubled the government and the financial leadership of Japan less than their counterparts in the United States. The high savings rate of the Japanese public and the effectiveness of the postal banking system in channelling those savings into low-interest loans to the government enabled moderate deficit finance. And a great asset boom took hold in Japan in the late 1980s, which appeared to reduce the relative burden of the resulting debt. Consequently, the size of national debt relative to GDP was highly stable, and even declined from 41.1 per cent in 1985 to 37.0 per cent in 1990.

Japan's divergence from the United States in spending and debt finance became more pronounced during the early 1990s, when Japan further accelerated the expansion of the construction state. The central reason for this was another major shock: the bursting in 1990 of what turned out to be a huge asset bubble which had masked slow productivity growth. By 1992 Japan was experiencing the kind of deflationary

---

[32] In the United States technocrats worried a great deal about technical issues, especially the challenge of harmonising VAT with state sales taxes. The Democrats usually opposed introducing a large, regressive tax, even though it might fund services whose benefits were distributed progressively. And business lobbyists generally believed that the Democrats would use VAT revenues to expand social programmes rather than reduce other taxes. These concerns surfaced during debates over VAT during the Carter and Clinton administrations. See Brownlee, *Federal Taxation in America*, pp. 180–1, 224–5.

stress the United States would begin to suffer after 2007. During what became known as the 'lost decade' of the 1990s, the demand of the middle classes for social services increased sharply, and in response the Japanese government moved the construction state machine into high gear.[33] Reinforcing Japan's rapid expansion of public investment in the 1990s was the resumption of the arm-twisting that the US government had employed during the 'Carter shock' to stimulate an expansionary fiscal policy. In what was called the 'Structural Impediments Initiative', agreed to by the United States and Japan in 1990, the Bush administration pressed the Japanese government to increase public investment. The Bush administration had two related objectives in mind: directly stimulating global economic demand and increasing the demand for American exports by strengthening the value of the yen. The Japanese government promised to formulate a 'Basic Plan for Public Investment' and then spent 430 trillion yen on public investment over a ten-year period. In 1993, at the same time that it raised taxes, the Clinton administration pressed Japan to expand its stimulus programme. The administration hoped that the programme, along with tax increases in the United States, would help adjust exchange rates in a way that promoted American exports. In response, the Japanese government increased the stimulus target from 430 trillion yen to 630 trillion yen. By 1996 public investment in Japan had expanded, reaching more than 6 per cent of GDP, compared with about 3 per cent in the United States and France.[34]

Neo-Liberal Gains, 1993–2014

During the mid-1990s, fiscal policy diverged even further in the world's two largest economies in response to a similar force in both nations: a political backlash against the tax increases that both governments had imposed as part of their earlier attempts at fiscal consolidation. In both nations, the foundation for this backlash had been laid by the tax hikes of the 1980s, which represented the first major tax increases since the Second World War in the United States and the Occupation era in the case of Japan. The tax increases, in turn, stimulated threatened

---

[33] Eisaku Ide and Sven Steinmo, 'The End of the Strong State? On the Evolution of Japanese Tax Policy', in Martin et al., *The New Fiscal Sociology*, pp. 119–37. Also, the government clearly recognised that a significant decline in the birth rate was approaching and keenly felt that the 1990s would be the last chance to fund the social infrastructure. See 'Kokyo Toshi Kihon Keikaku' ['Basic Plan for Public Investment'] formulated by the Economic Planning Agency.

[34] Ide Eisaku, *Nihon Zaisei Tenkan no Shishin* [Japan's Public Finance Direction of the Transformation] (Iwanami Shoten, 2013), p. 37.

taxpayers to seek broad support for their challenges to the tax system and the programmes of social integration that it funded.

Neo-liberal mobilisation intensified during the 1980s. During the Reagan and Bush administrations business lobbyists, Republican politicians and think tanks expanded and strengthened an intellectual and political infrastructure that could challenge yet more expensive deficit-fighting initiatives. In Japan, as early as 1981, business lobbyists were preparing for a difficult future. They formed a committee, the Second Provisional Commission for Administrative Reform (*Dai-ni Rincho*), which came to exert a powerful political influence on the Nakasone cabinet.[35]

In the United States, the Clinton tax increases of 1993 intensified organised attacks on income taxation from outside government. A phalanx of neo-liberal think tanks with extreme supply-side agendas and grass-roots organisations, such as Grover Norquist's Americans for Tax Reform, became increasingly vocal and powerful. This forceful expression of what the sociologist Isaac Martin has called 'Rich People's Movements' found enthusiastic support within government from Newt Gingrich and the other Republican leaders who had taken control of both Houses of Congress in 1994. In their 'Contract for America' proposal they included a balanced-budget amendment and proposals to resume the tax-cutting that had ended in 1981.[36] However, this neo-liberal offensive accomplished relatively little during the second half of the 1990s. Most of the nation's financial leaders resisted any tax cuts that would reverse successes, and the Clinton administration's brilliant 'triangulation', which emphasised differences between his position and those of both the Republicans and Democrats in Congress, frustrated neo-liberal reform initiatives. In addition, the neo-liberals disagreed among themselves on tax priorities and failed to develop a coherent reform programme that could energise broad-based support.[37]

In Japan the anti-tax business movement enjoyed greater success in the late 1990s, reinforced by both economic stagnation and the groundswell of neo-liberal thinking within Japan's policy communities. Six significant tax cuts resulted during the late 1990s. In the process, the government made additional cuts in the top marginal rates of

---

[35] Mizuno Masaru, Director of the Co-ordination Division of the Tax Bureau, recalls that tax increases in 1981 caused deep concern within the business community about the threat of the possibility of future radical increases in corporate taxes. Mizuno Masaru, *Zeisei Kaisei Gojyunen; Kaiko to Tenbo* [Fifty Years of Tax Reform: Retrospect and Prospect] (Tokyo: Okura Zaimu Kyokai, 2006), p. 279.

[36] Isaac William Martin, *Rich People's Movements: Grassroots Campaigns to Untax the One Percent* (New York: Oxford University Press, 2013), pp. 182–94.

[37] Brownlee, *Federal Taxation in America*, pp. 225–44.

personal income and corporate income taxation, reducing them from 50 per cent in 1989 to 37 per cent in 1999 and from 42 per cent in 1987 to 30 per cent in 1999 respectively. The government wholly accepted the political assertions of the business world and claimed that the cuts would increase Japan's international competitiveness. The government did enact one significant tax increase: an increase in VAT from 3 per cent to 5 per cent in 1997. But this did not represent any net increase in tax yield given the size of the cuts in personal income taxation. Unlike the United States, the bursting of the asset bubble provided a powerful economic incentive for the government not only to satisfy the demands of the business community for lower taxes, but also to stimulate domestic consumption. As a consequence of the tax cuts, Japan's debt soared as a percentage of GDP during the late 1990s.[38]

At the turn of the century the stage was set, in both nations, for a reinvigorated neo-liberal assault on their respective systems of social cohesion. In the United States, neo-liberals, frustrated by Clinton's political acumen and their inability to bring about fiscal reform, were ready to resume the 'Reagan revolution'. In Japan, because of the 'lost decade' of the 1990s, the public at large was experiencing deep disillusionment with government – something that would surface in the United States later, particularly in 2010. An increasingly cynical Japanese public had come to doubt the ability of the government to stimulate economic recovery and break out of its deflationary malaise. However, public opinion leaders and the public at large did not interpret economic stagnation as being the result of a liquidity trap. Increasingly, they viewed the 'lost decade' as primarily the consequence of fundamental flaws in Japan's construction state.

The US elections of 2000 put the Republican Party in control of both the presidency and Congress for most of George W. Bush's years in office. Even though he had won the election while losing the popular vote, he and his administration were ready to exploit the fact that this was the first time the Republicans had enjoyed such control since the 1920s, permitting an extended period of tax-cutting similar in important ways to the tax-cutting led by Secretary of the Treasury Andrew Mellon during the 1920s. The Bush tax cuts yielded some across-the-board benefits, but focused heavily on extending favours to the wealthiest Americans and enhancing returns on capital investment. Neo-liberal ideology drove tax reform and featured the claim that the supply cuts favouring wealth and capital were necessary to enhance productivity. This claim conveniently

---

[38] Gene Park and Eisaku Ide, 'The Tax–Welfare Mix: Explaining Japan's Weak Extractive Capacity', *The Pacific Review* 27/5 (21 August 2014), 675–702.

ignored that fact that total factor productivity in the United States had revived in the late 1990s.[39] Neo-liberalism had little immediate impact on the spending side of the federal budget. The Bush administration waged expensive wars in the wake of the 9/11 terror attacks, expanded entitlement benefits, especially in the form of a high-cost prescription drug programme within Medicare, and launched an ambitious and expensive bailout of the financial sector after the onset of the Great Recession in late 2007. The Leviathan did not starve. Instead, it was able to feed on low-cost borrowed money, which the Bush administration preferred to take rather than raise anyone's taxes, especially during a recession or the threat of recession. Of particular assistance in keeping interest costs to the federal government low was the growing demand of China for US debt, a demand driven by China's effort to keep its currency from appreciating and jeopardising its markets in the United States. In contrast to the previous two administrations, the Bush administration did not make any serious effort to reduce the flow of investments from Japan or China into federal debt. In a sense, the administration was willing to penalise American exporters and those who relied on interest income in order to reward Americans, including the federal government, who benefited from borrowing at exceptionally low interest rates. Thus, neo-liberal designs on the size of government had little immediate impact. However, at the end of the Bush presidency, a variety of factors – the severity of the Great Recession, the slow pace of recovery from it, high rates of unemployment, stagnating or declining real incomes, the scale of financial bailouts and exaggerated threats of debt-driven financial disasters – intensified public anxiety and populist resentment of government. This anxiety and resentment, coupled with the Bush tax cuts, set the stage for the Tea Party movement and its effective takeover of the Republican Party in 2010 after the presidential victory of the Democrat candidate, Barack Obama, in 2008. The Republicans proceeded to declare war not only on deficits but also on almost all the elements of the discretionary domestic spending that had survived three decades of cutting and on the movement towards universal healthcare launched by the Obama administration. Congress enacted tax increases on the wealthy to help fund the Affordable Care Act. But the hard line of Tea Party Republicans in Congress against repealing the Bush tax cuts and against expansion of additional deficit spending for economic stimulation ratcheted up the pressure on domestic discretionary programmes. This imposed even greater economic hardship

---

[39] Robert J. Gordon, 'Revisiting U.S. Productivity Growth over the Past Century with a View of the Future', Working Paper 15834 (2010), NBER Working Paper Series. Available at www.nber.org/papers.

on both middle-class and poor families, particularly those suffering from the persistence of high rates of unemployment.

In Japan, in contrast, neo-liberalism focused on reducing the spending side of the budget and, in particular, on rolling back the construction state. Contributing in a major way to this sentiment was growing scepticism on the part of the urban middle class, who now enjoyed well-developed infrastructure in the cities, regarding the economic value of continued public investment in rural areas. The growing belief in the wastefulness of spending on the part of the national government strengthened the desire of MOF technocrats as well as some business leaders to reduce deficits and the rate of growth in Japan's debt. In 2001, the government of Prime Minister Koizumi Junichiro came to power with a plan to shift away from heavy reliance on the construction state and tax-cutting, and to reduce even further Japan's limited welfare state. Most dramatically, the government reduced spending on public works. Expenditures on these via both FILP and the general account budget had begun to decline before the Koizumi government took power, but between 2001 and 2007 public investment declined from about 5 per cent of GDP to 3 per cent of GDP, about the same level as in the United States and France.[40] Other steps taken included reducing the central financing of local government, lowering the rate of growth in social security expenditures, reducing public assistance and ending the extended period of relentless tax-cutting. As a consequence, the system for social integration which the LDP had crafted was in disarray.

The Koizumi government held office until 2006, and the consequences of its neo-liberalism were profoundly negative. Its efforts to stimulate the economy produced only sporadic relief from long-term stagnation. Meanwhile, labour's share of income declined and the rate of atypical (part-time and outsourced) employment increased.[41] The government's brake on the growth in social security expenditures and in-kind services, coupled with reductions in public assistance, occurred just when the need and demand for such programmes were increasing

---

[40] Ide, *Nihon Zaisei Tenkan no Shishin*, p. 37.

[41] The average income of all households declined from 6.6 million yen in 1996 to 5.6 million yen in 2010. *Kokumin Seikatsu Kiso Chosa* [Comprehensive Survey of Living Conditions] (Kosei rodo Sho, 2012). The ratio of atypical employment increased by only 3.5 per cent from 1990 to 1998. But from 1998 to 2006 (the last year of the Koizumi cabinet), it increased by 9.7 per cent. *Rodoryoku Chosa* [Labour Force Survey] (Soumu-sho Tokei-kyoku).

owing to continuing stagnation. Poor families suffered most acutely, especially from the retrenchment in public assistance.[42] The cuts in budgets for public works bit into a traditional source of employment and income benefits for low-paid workers whether in the rural or urban areas. Added pressure on social services followed the increasing labour force participation rate of women, creating greater demands for public spending in the areas of childcare, kindergarten education, care for the elderly and nursing services.[43] The suspension of tax cuts further weakened the ability of the middle classes to save and prepare for retirement.[44] Under the pressure of increased demand for social services the institutions delivering them became increasingly dysfunctional. At the same time, much of the weakened middle class began to feel resentful as income became increasingly concentrated in the highest income groups, and the sense of middle-class generosity on behalf of lower-income citizens waned. The depth of public cynicism, reinforced by the weakness of the service state and the end of tax cuts, made it impossible for the Koizumi administration, even if it had been willing, to impose the kind of tax increases that might have helped solve the dual problems of unprecedented deficits and a service state in the throes of a crisis. Public confidence in government sank to new depths, despite Koizumi's personal popularity.[45] All these conditions set the stage for the emergence of a second major political party – the Democratic Party of Japan (DPJ) – and then, after that party failed, a reconstituted LDP under the leadership of Prime Minister Abe Shinzo. His government has taken the advice of the Tax Bureau and the Ministry of Finance and engineered a significant increase in VAT, but it remains to be seen whether the Abe reforms will be sufficiently comprehensive to prepare the

---

[42] During 2005–7 cases of starvation came to light in Kitakyushu city, and in 2007, one middle-aged man starved to death after his application for public assistance was refused. He left the message 'I want to eat a rice ball.' By the end of the Koizumi era the term *Kakusa Shakai* [differential society] had come into vogue.

[43] The participation rate of women aged 25–34 years rose from 56.6 per cent in 1990 to 72.3 per cent in 2010. Historical Data 3 (7), 'Labor Force and Labor Force Participation Rate by Age Group – All Japan', *Labor Force Survey*, 2011. On the increased demands this created, see Ide, *Nihon Zaisei Tenkan no Shishin*, ch. 4.

[44] The percentage of people in 1978 who viewed retirement pessimistically was 43.8 per cent, but increased after 1998 and reached 85.3 per cent in 2005. 'Heisei 20nen-do Kokumin seikatsu Senko-do Chosa' ['National Survey of Lifestyle Preferences in FY 2008'] (Naikaku-hu, 2009).

[45] The joint investigation between Japan and the United States, undertaken by *Yomiuri* newspaper, indicated that trust in the government has continued to decline since the late 1990s and has fallen to much lower levels than in the United States.

Japanese welfare state to meet the growing crisis of the middle classes.[46] Meanwhile, in both nations, the rolling back of the welfare state has eroded the living standards of the middle classes, placed a heavier burden on the poor, worsened the distribution of income and, in the process, slowed the rate of recovery from the Great Recession.

Fiscal Needs and Tax Reform: The Future

In both the USA and Japan, the erosion of the middle classes, the worsening of conditions for the poor and other factors may eventually help drive strong popular demand for an expansion of government responsibility for social cohesion. Meeting such demands may require significant tax increases. The fiscal history of Japan and the United States outlined in this chapter suggests that enacting such increases will face great challenges.

Since the Second World War, in both nations, political leaders have found a wide variety of reasons to cut taxes and have done so far more frequently than they have raised taxes, leaving the USA and Japan with the weakest tax-raising ability among the major industrial nations. An extremely wide range of goals on the part of government and other political actors has produced tax cuts. Neo-liberal goals have been a major source for tax-cutting enthusiasm in both nations since the 1970s, but divergent social goals have also contributed. Certainly, the reasons for cutting taxes have included stimulating investment according to supply-side dogma and containing the growth of the welfare state (in the United States 'Starving the Beast', particularly when applied to discretionary domestic spending), following the rationale provided in both nations by neo-liberal economics. But many of the tax cuts should be understood, as well, as a result of the traditional anti-tax and anti-government politics pursued by wealthy elites. Also, the goals of tax cuts have at times included providing tax relief across the economic spectrum, offering tax deductions and exemptions to various groups deemed disadvantaged, and promoting consumption in a Keynesian demand-side fashion.

The other side of the coin is that, since the Second World War, the justification for raising taxes has been hesitant and circumscribed, reflecting a high degree of political defensiveness in the face of anti-tax

---

[46] The Democratic Party of Japan decided to increase VAT from 5 per cent to 8 per cent in 2014 and then to 10 per cent in 2015. Abe accepted this policy and introduced the increase scheduled for 2014. However, the economic stagnation that followed forced the cabinet to postpone the tax increase scheduled for 2015. It is worth noting that only 1 per cent of the 5 per cent increase would be used for social security spending.

sentiments. The prime rationale for tax increases has been the containment or reduction of deficits and debt. Some proponents of successful increases sought to protect public programmes such as defence spending, the construction state and social security entitlements, but they cloaked their intentions under the cause of deficit reduction and almost never had in mind strengthening the funding for domestic discretionary programmes.

Another rationale for tax increases, one less common than deficit reduction, has been broadening the tax base and thereby making it fairer from a horizontal standpoint in the sense of taxing equals more equally. In Japan these efforts have included the adoption and increasing of VAT, and, in the United States, the passage of DEFRA, TEFRA and the Tax Reform Act of 1986. Some of these base-broadening measures strengthened the revenue capacity of the income tax, but their architects argued the case for them as being revenue-neutral.

Proponents of increases in progressive taxes, of course, also advocated fairness, focused on the enhancement of vertical equity. Also at times they highlighted the ability to raise large revenues at the highest income levels with relatively small increases in progressive rates. This was the case in the increases supported by Presidents George H. W. Bush, Bill Clinton and Barack Obama. But, in only one case – Obama's high-income tax to help fund the Affordable Care Act – was the increase linked to enhancing a specific programme. It is worth noting here an important difference between the United States and Japan: in the relatively short history of post-war tax increases in Japan, there have been virtually no instances of tax increases advanced for the sake of increasing tax progressivity. In Japan, tax equity is discussed almost exclusively in terms of its horizontal dimension.[47]

If demands emerge for important new public investments and services, the necessary tax increases will require the kind of explicit justifications that have been absent in Japan and the United States since the Second World War. In other words, reformers in the United States and Japan will have to make the case for an expanded public sector and tax increases simultaneously and in an integrated fashion – something that no federal government in the United States has done since the

---

[47] An OECD analysis of inequality suggests that, over two decades beginning in the mid-1980s, progressive redistribution through the tax system was lower in Japan than in any of the other twenty-two OECD nations studied. In contrast, the United States ranked nearly at the top of this group in terms of progressive tax redistribution. See Organisation for Economic Cooperation and Development, *Growing Unequal? Income Distribution and Poverty in OECD Countries* (Paris: OECD, 2008), especially pp. 111–15. www.oecd-ilibrary.org/social-issues-migration-health/growing-unequal_9789264044197-en (accessed 29 September 2014).

1930s and no central government in Japan has ever done. In the process, Japan and the United States will almost certainly need to embrace more of what might be described as fundamental tax reform. To succeed in this project, government leaders would have to argue both that new social programmes will require significant new tax revenues ('the price of civilisation') and that the increased taxes will be accompanied by substantial reforms that make the tax system much fairer (defined in both horizontal and vertical terms), efficient and transparent. This would provide a way to link fundamental tax reform to the building of tax consciousness, tax consent and, in turn, the enhancement of the modern state in both nations.

4   Swiss Worlds of Taxation: The Political Economy of Fiscal Federalism and Tax Competition

Gisela Huerlimann

'The Swiss have used federation effectively in keeping their society more or less free for centuries', James M. Buchanan wrote admiringly in 1975,[1] and as recently as 2001 this prominent proponent of public choice theory praised the unique system of Swiss direct democracy and effective federalism which granted the country

> the continuing support from classical liberals who seek institutions of governance strong enough to prevent the ever-present threat of lapse into anarchy, but also institutions of governance that are themselves limited by enforceable constitutional checks and balances from succumbing to the ever-present temptations to behave as Leviathan.[2]

Is Switzerland, therefore, a classic case for 'questioning Leviathan'? Buchanan's repeated praise of Swiss state containment seems to find its empirical evidence in the welfare regime literature. Based on data on public expenditure from the early 1980s, Gøsta Esping-Andersen famously grouped Switzerland within a group of *liberal* welfare states in his *Three Worlds of Welfare Capitalism*.[3] Referring to the revenue structure and based on data for the mid-1960s, B. Guy Peters also categorised Switzerland as a member of a liberal, mainly Anglo-American group of countries, which showed a preference for taxing incomes, earnings, property and wealth over consumption taxes.[4] Highly federalist states do not constitute the norm by which international revenue, debt, public expenditure and welfare spending data are collected and aggregated. This is also one of the reasons why various authors have struggled to categorise the Swiss welfare regime according

---

[1] James M. Buchanan, *The Limits of Liberty: Between Anarchy and Leviathan* (Chicago: Chicago University Press 1975), p. 18.

[2] James M. Buchanan, 'Direct Democracy, Classical Liberalism, and Constitutional Strategy', *Kyklos* 54/2–3 (2001), 241.

[3] Gøsta Esping-Andersen, *The Three Worlds of Welfare Capitalism* (Princeton NJ: Princeton University Press 1990).

[4] B. Guy Peters, *The Politics of Taxation: A Comparative Perspective* (Cambridge, MA: Blackwell, 1991), pp. 58–64.

to Esping-Andersen's typology.[5] Some have concluded that the notion of twenty-six different worlds of welfare[6] – and let us add, of taxation – is a more apt way to describe the reality of a political and fiscal landscape shaped by the twenty-six Swiss cantons with their significant autonomy in setting tax rates, even deciding tax regimes and deciding regional expenditure. This chapter focuses on the revenue side of the tax-and-welfare state – on the redistributive dimensions afforded to taxation as an element of fiscal welfare,[7] and on the relationship between tax justice and market fairness. This relates to a conceptual assumption expressed in the political economy of the two spheres of Swiss taxation. The first sphere contains aspects of regular taxation that conform to the general principles of taxation, such as efficiency, rationality, universality, equity and the ability to pay. The second sphere brings together preferential tax regimes for particular groups of individuals as well as companies. It tends to ignore classic taxation principles and stresses the laws of the market. The lump-sum taxation of wealthy foreigners who have no salaried occupation in Switzerland is in this latter sphere. Whereas the first cantonal rule allowing for this preferential treatment dates back to 1862,[8] privileged taxation for holding companies was implemented in 1903 first, in line with similar regimes introduced in other countries.[9] The two spheres have coexisted in a relationship of tension and rivalry, of complementarity and also of spill-over as the tax policy period since the mid-1990s shows. This is the fourth period within a periodisation model that analyses developments and debates since the late 1950s and informs the structure of this chapter. While the chapter concentrates on the period since the 1970s, the narrative starts with a summary of developments since the end of the First World War, when the new federalist fiscal compromise began to take shape.

---

[5] See Francis G. Castles and Deborah Mitchell, 'Worlds of Welfare and Families of Nations', in F. G. Castles (ed.), *Families of Nations: Patterns of Public Policy in Western Democracies* (Aldershot: Dartmouth, 1993), pp. 93–128; Michael Nollert, 'Sonderfall im rheinischen Kapitalismus oder Sonderweg im liberalen Wohlfahrtskapitalismus? Zur Spezifität des Sozialstaats Schweiz', in Kurt Imhof and Thomas S. Eberle (eds.), *Der Sonderfall Schweiz* (Zürich: Seismo 2007), pp. 153–71.

[6] Klaus Armingeon, Fabio Bertozzi and Giuliano Bonoli, 'Swiss Worlds of Welfare', *West European Politics* (2004), 27(1), pp. 20–44.

[7] Richard Titmuss, 'The Social Division of Welfare: Some Reflections on the Search for Equity', in Richard M. Titmuss (ed.), *Essays on the Welfare State* (London: Allen & Unwin 1958), pp. 34–55.

[8] Mario Morger, *Die Besteuerung nach dem Aufwand aus ökonomischer Sicht* (Bern: Eidg. Finanzdepartement EFD, 2010).

[9] Richard Oesch, *Die Holdingbesteuerung in der Schweiz: Eine Studie über ihre Grundlage und Ausformung* (Zürich: Schulthess Polygraph, Verlag, 1976); Ronen Palan, Richard Murphy and Christian Chavagneux, *Tax Havens: How Globalization Really Works* (Ithaca, NY: Cornell University Press, 2010).

Wars and Crisis Alter the Initial Fiscal Compromise

Indirect taxes are the prerogative of federal government, while direct[10] taxes should be the privilege of the cantonal and local governments: this conviction, based on the federalist division of labour during mid-nineteenth-century state-building, was voiced by members of the federal parliament as well as business representatives well into the 1960s, even though the federal government had started to levy a provisional income tax during the First World War, and would continue to levy it. Conceived as an extraordinary measure, this 'war tax' was the model for the federal anti-crisis tax during the Great Depression. The exceptional period of the Second World War even saw the anchoring of the three main pillars of the future federal tax structure: a 'national defence tax' on income, profits and wealth, which would become the 'direct federal tax'; a turnover tax; and a withholding tax on income on net wealth interests, also dubbed a 'tax dodger's tax' because it was reimbursed if the assets were declared. In the 1950s, when this makeshift emergency law was scheduled to be turned into a regular constitutional arrangement, the federal tax on income and profits and the turnover tax were compared to conjoined twins[11] due to their key political interconnectedness and the mutual lock-in of the political camps, each opposed to one of the so-called twins. While many federalist liberals,[12] most conservatives and the majority of business interests continued to object to income and wealth taxes at the federal level, they conceded to them out of necessity and on condition that indirect taxes would stay in force and make up the lion's share of federal taxation in the long run, as had once been the case with customs duties. The Social Democrats, trade unions and consumer organisations, on the other hand, denounced the turnover tax as a regressive, socially unjust measure, which they accepted only because the federal government had also raised progressive direct taxes. By 1958, this renewed and modified federalist compromise, leading to a more cooperative fiscal federalism, was inserted into the federal constitution. This,

---

[10] The terms are still widely used in Switzerland. 'Indirect' refers to consumption taxes (in the past, customs duties were also implied) and 'direct' refers to taxes on income, wealth, profits, and so on.

[11] The term was coined by the then Swiss Finance Minister Max Weber, in *Proceedings of the Swiss National Assembly*, 18 March 1953, p. 119. Online: www.amtsdruckschriften.bar.admin.ch/detailView.do?id=20035420#1 (accessed 4 November 2014).

[12] Liberals in the western European sense of free-market liberals; federalist in the sense of advocates for cantonal hegemony and for limiting the size of the federal government.

though, was on a temporary basis and so required regular renewal.[13] The same bill institutionalised the cantons' share of federal tax revenue and the system of fiscal equalisation.

The 1958 legislation was coupled with fairly significant tax cuts and included the revoking of the federal wealth tax, much to the chagrin of the left. In 1963, for the first extension of this federal finance legislation, the administration's attempt to rescind some of the deductions and allowances and to set the tax rates more flexibly not only failed, but was reversed by a powerful alliance of liberal and conservative policy-makers and business lobbies who managed to have tax brackets 'stretched' and tax deductions increased.[14] This pattern became archetypical. The political alliance on the right managed to keep direct federal taxes in check and also supported attempts from the left to reduce the tax liabilities of workers, on condition that the general tax burden would decrease, or at least would not rise. As a result of these political bargains, almost half a million former taxpayers were entirely exempted from the federal income tax by 1965.

Redistributive Wisdom and Enthusiasm for More Harmony and Equality, 1966–78

The second half of the 1960s and the early 1970s saw a convergence of concerns over the growing gap between the limited federal revenue potential and increasing demands for expenditure, paltry social insurance benefits and the problems of equity raised by unequal taxation and tax competition. In order to counter the appeal of proposals from the left to integrate the private company pension schemes into the public social security system, parliament and the government doubled old age benefits, enacted higher social security contributions and, in 1972, introduced the three-pillar system which made basic occupational schemes – most of them on a company basis – mandatory and created tax incentives for individual savings plans.[15] The 1970s debate on the redistributive effects of taxation was also motivated by economic scholarship, which focused on income and wealth distribution and redistribution and the incidence of

---

[13] 'Arrêté fédéral du 31.01.1958 instituant de nouvelles dispositions constitutionnelles sur le régime financier de la Confédération'. This new bill was accepted in the federal vote of 11 May 1958; Olivier Longchamp, *La politique financière fédérale (1945–1958)* (Lausanne: Antipodes, 2014).

[14] Federal Act for a continuation of the federal finance regime, voted on 8 December 1963; in force 1 January 1965.

[15] Bernard Degen, 'Entstehung und Entwicklung des schweizerischen Sozialstaats', in Schweizerisches Bundesarchiv (ed.), *Geschichte der Sozialversicherungen* (Zürich: Chronos 2006), pp. 17–48; Matthieu Leimgruber, *Solidarity without the State? Business and the Shaping of the Swiss Welfare State, 1890 –2000* (Cambridge: Cambridge University Press, 2008).

fiscal policy, mirroring similar international research.[16] The report of the UN Economic Commission for Europe (UNECE) on post-war income development and distribution was closely scrutinised in Switzerland.[17] The fact that the UNECE study did not include data on Switzerland's income and wealth distribution moved one Social Democratic member of the Swiss parliament in 1971 to request that the federal government correct the omission with its own data and analysis, and suggest measures to even out the inequalities.[18] The answer of the federal government in 1972 was well placed in what was to become mainstream economic thinking in the 1980s and 1990s, and was famously expressed in Arthur Okun's *Big Tradeoff*.[19] The federal minister of finance tied the thorny subject of income (re)distribution to the fundamental question of whether or not to agree with a free-market economy and therefore also accept its potential disadvantages. The task of economic policy was to maintain a balance between economic growth and an 'income distribution [that was] as equitable as possible'.[20] While the government agreed to meet the demand for more statistical data, it rejected the transformative request of the Social Democrat proposition. But the logic of market freedom due to market fairness was threatened by unfair privileges. Criticism of the lure of Switzerland's tax policy, such as preferential treatment for base companies and Swiss non-compliance with regard to supplying information on tax evaders, had earlier been voiced by the US and German governments in the first half of the 1960s.[21] But the weight of international reservations

---

[16] See, for example, René L. Frey, *Von der Sozial- zur Verteilungspolitik* (Basel: WWZ, 1971); Albert Noth, 'Die personelle Einkommensverteilung in der Schweiz' (PhD thesis, University of Fribourg, 1975).

[17] Secretariat of the Economic Commission for Europe, *Incomes in Postwar Europe: A Study of Policies, Growth and Distribution* (Economic Survey of Europe in 1965, Part 2) (Geneva: United Nations, 1967).

[18] The parliamentary proposal by René Felber MP referred to the French version of 1969. Swiss Federal Archives, E6300B#2004/37#27*: MP Felber, parliamentary proposal of 16 December 1971 concerning the income distribution.

[19] Arthur Okun, *Equality and Efficiency: The Big Tradeoff* (Washington, DC: The Brookings Institution, 1975).

[20] In Nello Celio's words: 'entre la croissance de l'économie et une distribution des revenus aussi équitable que possible'. The German draft for the speech made by his staff used the term: 'möglichst gerechte Einkommensverteilung'. Swiss Federal Archives, #E6300B#2004/377#27*.

[21] John F. Kennedy, *Special Message to the Congress on Taxation*, 20 April 1961, online: www.presidency.ucsb.edu/ws/?pid=8074 (accessed 12 August 2015), by Gerhard Peters and John T. Woolley, The American Presidency Project; John F. Kennedy, *Special Message to the Congress on Gold and the Balance of Payments Deficit*, 6 February 1961, point 10, online: www.jfklink.com/speeches/jfk/publicpapers/1961/jfk23_61.html (accessed 12 August 2015); Bericht der Bundesregierung über Wettbewerbsverfälschungen, die sich aus Sitzverlagerungen und aus dem zwischenstaatlichen Steuergefälle ergeben können, 23 June 1964, pp. 4–5, 8, online: http://dipbt.bundestag.de/doc/btp/04/04026.pdf (accessed 12 August 2015).

about the Swiss 'tax haven' was mostly felt when renegotiating double tax agreements (DTA) with various European countries during the mid- and late 1960s. France and Germany's demands to reduce tax exemptions under the DTA rule for business activities that mainly profited from shifting their profits from their home countries to Switzerland found indirect empirical evidence in the impressive increase of stock corporations and holding companies in Switzerland. The number of stock corporations increased by 78 per cent between 1955 and 1964 and almost doubled between 1964 and 1975, from 46,267 to 92,149 companies.[22] Some of these newly founded or newly located companies were owned by foreign investors and also by holding or domiciled companies. But the growth and entry of such companies and their effects were not evenly distributed within Switzerland.

After Geneva, Zurich, Ticino and the canton of Grisons, the tiny canton of Zug, an aggressive tax competitor, had received a large number of foreign-owned companies by the mid-1960s.[23] It would not only become renowned for its 'letterbox' companies, but also as the site of European and American multinationals, such as Philipp Brothers (Phibro LLC), which moved its European headquarters there in 1956 and thus laid the foundation for the later commodity hub, which would eventually involve the trading and mining company Glencore.[24] While Zug had ranked among the wealthier third of the cantons until the 1940s, its wealth and growth began to lag behind in the early post-war era. In 1946, the canton revised its tax laws once again and extended tax privileges for holding, domicile and hybrid companies.[25] In 1960, Zug came ninth in the cantonal ranking of regional aggregate income per capita. By 1965, it had risen to third place, and by 1970 came second.[26] Zug also had prospering industries, but its tax policy undoubtedly added capital and led to more employment. However,

---

[22] 'Bewegung der Aktiengesellschaften seit 1902', in Eidg. Statistisches Amt (ed.), *Statistisches Jahrbuch der Schweiz 1965* (Basel: Birkhäuser, 1965), p. 394; table T6.2.3.1, in Bundesamt für Statistik (ed.), *Statistisches Lexikon der Schweiz* (Bern, 1964): Im Handelsregister am Jahresende eingetragene Firmen nach Rechtsform 1883–2003: 46,267; 1975: 92,149.

[23] 'Bestand der Holdinggesellschaften', in *Statistisches Jahrbuch der Schweiz 1965*, p. 398; sowie: Bewegung seit 1953, ibid.

[24] H. Waszkis, *Philipp Brothers. The Rise and Fall of a Trading Giant, 1901–1985* (Surrey: Metal Bulletin Books, 1987), pp. 154–6; Daniel Ammann, *The King of Oil: The Secret Lives of Marc Rich* (New York: St Martin's Press, 2009).

[25] Michael van Orsouw, *Das vermeintliche Paradies. Eine historische Analyse der Anziehungskraft der Zuger Steuergesetze* (Zürich: Chronos, 1995).

[26] Calculations based on data in the Historical Statistics of Switzerland Online (HSSO). Online: www.fsw.uzh.ch/hstat/nls_rev/ls_files.php?chapter_var=./q, table Q.19. Population Income of Cantons in Current Swiss Francs 1890–2001 (selected years), Economic history of Switzerland during the twentieth century (accessed 20 November 2014).

one canton's gains could also mean another canton's loss. And this was resented even by the liberals.

In March 1970, federal councillor Nello Celio, the federal finance minister and a representative of the liberal Free Democratic Party, called for an end to 'this competition among the cantons'.[27] Celio was referring here to the intensified bid for preferential taxation for companies and high-income earners. But the cantonal worlds of taxation were traditionally highly disparate when it came to regular taxation. In 1970, the nominal tax charge by cantonal and communal taxation for very high-income earners varied between 16.5 per cent and 23.7 per cent, while the tax rate for low to medium-income earners ranged between 3.6 per cent and 7.6 per cent.[28] While cantonal tax competition had been tolerated as a legitimate measure for attracting investors and fostering prosperity, or simply as a concession to cantonal tax sovereignty, the late 1960s and early 1970s saw growing unease about the drawbacks of rapid growth, as symbolised in uncontrolled housing sprawl or the spread of the motorway network, and uneven economic development. Furthermore, the federal government acquired ever more tasks in the field of infrastructure and economic policies and spent increasing sums on subsidising structurally weak regions. Suspicion grew that tax competitors might weaken other cantons by encouraging tax-related migration, as well as by engendering international resentment. The Swiss debate also mirrored the intense tax harmonisation zeal within the European Economic Community, which had started in the early 1960s.[29]

Minister Celio's comment made in 1970 was echoed in a spate of propositions for tax harmonisation by parliamentarians on both the left and the right, and from the cantonal ministers of finance, who tried to circumvent federal legislation by negotiating a voluntary agreement. While the latter aimed at a modest harmonisation, one restricted to standardising the tax base, deductions and a tax levy, others proposed a single federal income and wealth tax which would unify the highly divergent cantonal taxes. This far-reaching proposal was first put

---

[27] Nello Celio, *Proceedings of the National Assembly*, 11 March 1970, p. 140.

[28] Original source: 'Administration fédérale des contributions', in Bureau fédérale de la statistique (ed.), *Charge fiscale en Suisse 1970* (Berne: BFS, 1971). The first comparison applies to an income of CHF 200,000 (in 2013 terms CHF 595,209); the lowest tax rate was in Liestal (Basel country) and the highest in Lausanne (Vaud). The second comparison relates to an annual income of CHF 15,000 (in 2013 terms CHF 44,641) with the lowest tax rate in the city of Basel and the highest in Lausanne.

[29] EEC Fiscal and Financial Committee, *The EEC Reports on Tax Harmonization*. Unofficial translation by Dr H. Thurston (Amsterdam: International Bureau of Fiscal Documentation, 1963); 'Programme on Tax Harmonisation, Commission Communication of 8 February 1967', *Bulletin Supplement* 8 (1967).

forward by representatives of the Independent Party and, in 1973, had become a popular initiative[30] with the telling subtitle: 'For more tax fairness and the abolition of tax privileges'. It suggested that cantonal taxes on income and wealth be replaced by a single federal tax to be raised by the cantons, combined with a sophisticated system of fiscal equalisation and allowing the cantons and communes to add surcharges if needed. In addition, the initiative proposed the harmonisation of cantonal estate and gift taxes, and the introduction of steering taxes (Pigouvian taxes),[31] such as a duty on all alcoholic beverages and a tax on energy consumption as a response to climate change. While the initiative contained an unmistakable redistributive thrust, its primary concern was rooted in the long-standing liberal tradition of tax justice professed in the principles of horizontal equity and the equality of sacrifice.[32] The Independent Party's initiative had a clear focus on the ethical dimension of tax fairness by ruling out 'tax privileges'. But in the vein of contemporary liberal-egalitarian philosophy, the initiative also stipulated redistribution to counter unequal opportunities, such as inherited wealth.[33]

Until the late 1970s, tax convergence and equalisation for reasons of justice and 'rationality' enjoyed considerable support among open-minded liberals and conservatives. This is reflected in a parliamentary proposal made by a Christian Democrat MP in late 1973, which was very similar to the far-reaching initiative of the Independents.[34] The fact that renowned economists and financial experts had influenced the latter's initiative[35] made its reform programme appealing even to the free-market-oriented newspaper *Neue Zürcher Zeitung*.[36] The concurrent popular initiative launched by the Social Democratic Party 'for tax harmonisation, stronger taxation of the rich and for tax relief

[30] A popular initiative at the federal level is a proposition or bill signed by at least 100,000 voters. Parliament has to decide on its claim. It usually rejects the proposition or comes up with a counter-proposal. The initiative is then, with or without a counter-proposal, put to the popular vote.

[31] Following Pigou's model for taxes which aims to discourage adverse consumption or production and thus internalise so-called market externalities. Arthur C. Pigou, *The Economics of Welfare*, 4th edn (London: Macmillan, 1932).

[32] Fritz Karl Mann, *Steuerpolitische Ideale: Vergleichende Studien zur Geschichte der ökonomischen und politischen Ideen und ihres Wirkens in der öffentlichen Meinung, 1600–1935* (Jena: Gustav Fischer, 1937).

[33] John Rawls, *A Theory of Justice* (Cambridge MA: The Belknap Press of Harvard University Press, 1971).

[34] Laurent Butty, National Councillor, parliamentary proposal for tax harmonisation, 14 December 1973.

[35] Heinz Haller and Walter Biel, *Zukunftsgerechte Finanzreform für die Schweiz* (Zürich: Ex Libris Verlag, 1971).

[36] 'Versuch zu einer steuerlichen Gesamtlösung', *Neue Zürcher Zeitung* (13 April 1973).

for lower incomes' was less radical in its position vis-à-vis the federalist system, more traditional in its class politics approach and more overtly redistributive. The project was merely the culmination of a series of similar initiatives launched in ten cantons in 1972–3 after the electorate of Basel Country had approved such a tax in late 1972 as a temporary measure for resolving the budget deficit. The proposals suggested higher income taxes for the rich, and a few included higher net wealth taxation.[37] The federal initiative proposed a two-fold tax system: an income tax with proportional tariffs on low- and middle-income earners and a surcharge with progressive tariffs on higher-income groups. The tariffs for the latter would be uniform across the country, which meant that this surtax would be a federal tax on the rich. International tax data played an important role in the political campaign as the proponents of this 'tax-the-rich initiative' compared the maximum tax charge for high-income earners in Switzerland to other European countries in order to show that Switzerland's top earners faced less onerous tax liabilities than their counterparts in France, Germany, Austria, Denmark or Great Britain even under a more stringent tax regime.[38] The comparative OECD data seemed to suggest that Switzerland was in uncomfortable company, that of relatively poorer and economically less developed countries such as Portugal, Spain and Turkey, as well as of a different case, Japan.[39] Both initiatives were rejected in the popular votes of 1976 and 1977 respectively, but nevertheless were fairly well supported.[40] Before they were put to the vote, both parliament and the electorate had accepted an emergency government bill to increase the rates of all three major federal taxes.[41] These temporary measures, some of which

[37] Various authors, 'Kommt die Reichtumssteuer?', *Wirtschafts Revue, Das schweizerische Wirtschaftsmagazin* (1974), 3.

[38] Swiss Social Archives, Zurich, Holding: 28.61 QS 1973: *Reichtumssteuer-Initiative*, pamphlet by the Swiss Social-Democratic Party, November 1973, p. 19.

[39] Ibid., p. 18. The data are derived from the OECD 1972 (data for 1968–70). The tax rate as a percentage of gross social product (GSP) was Switzerland: 18.3 per cent; Portugal: 16.5 per cent; the United Kingdom: 31.6 per cent; Germany: 23.2 per cent; and the United States: 22.7 per cent. If social contributions are included, Switzerland still ranked nineteenth out of twenty-three.

[40] The Independent Party's proposal won 42.2 per cent of the yes vote in March 1976; the Social Democrat proposal received 44.6 per cent of the yes vote in December 1977.

[41] The turnover tax rate was increased from 5.6 per cent to 8.4 per cent (a temporary measure); the marginal income tax rate was increased from 10.45 per cent to 11.5 per cent (this increase would become permanent); the marginal rate on net profits was increased from 8.8 per cent to 9.8 per cent (another temporary measure); and the withholding tax rate on net wealth interests was raised from 30 per cent to 35 per cent (this also would become permanent). The popular vote on this federal bill for an increase of federal tax revenue took place on 8 June 1975.

became permanent, were intended to reverse the unprecedentedly high federal budget deficit. After a first plunge into the red in 1971, the deficit more than quadrupled until 1975, and would touch a record low in 1976 and again in 1979.[42]

These deficits reflected a dramatic deterioration in the economy, starting in the early 1970s. Switzerland registered one of the lowest growth rates among the industrialised countries. In the *annus horribilis* of 1974/5, Swiss GDP was −7.3 per cent compared to −1.7 per cent for Germany and −0.7 per cent for the United States.[43] In the average of the years 1970–8, Swiss GDP grew 0.7 per cent a year, while GDP growth in the other western European countries was 3.5 per cent a year and the US annual growth rate was 2.9 per cent.[44] The Swiss economy suffered a record loss of jobs – 10 per cent of all industrial jobs were axed between 1974 and 1977[45] – and a significant downturn in consumer spending. Yet the official unemployment rate never exceeded the 0.7 per cent recorded in 1976.[46] While the strategy of dismissing the immigrant labour force (which left through sheer force of circumstance and was then denied re-entry) benefited native Swiss workers and massaged the statistics, the official data were also distorted by the fact that a mere 20 per cent of the Swiss workforce were covered by an unemployment scheme by the mid-1970s.[47] Following a federal emergency bill in 1976, the Swiss Social Security Funds, which provided insurance benefits for the elderly, the bereaved and the disabled, and compensation for loss of income during military service, opened a branch for the

---

[42] Federal deficits (all in millions of CHF) are as follows: 1971: −294; 1975: −1,309; 1976: −1,573; 1979: −1,715. Federal Tax Administration, Statistical Services: Clôture des comptes de la Confédération (time-series table A1.1), compiled for the author in November 2014.

[43] Ibid., p. 2.

[44] Francesco Kneschaurek, *Der 'Trendbruch' der siebziger Jahre und seine wirtschaftlichen Konsequenzen* (Diessenhofen: Rüegger, 1980), p. 31. Comparative data for 1950–73 show that growth in Switzerland had also been smaller than growth in the other western European economies (with the exception of the United Kingdom and Sweden) even before the crisis; see Nicholas Crafts and Gianni Toniolo, 'Aggregate Growth 1950–2005', in Stephen Broadberry and Kevin H. O'Rourke (eds.), *The Cambridge Economic History of Modern Europe*, vol. 2 (New York: Cambridge University Press, 2010), p. 301.

[45] Manfred G. Schmidt, *Der schweizerische Weg zur Vollbeschäftigung: Eine Bilanz der Beschäftigung, der Arbeitslosigkeit und der Arbeitsmarktpolitik* (Frankfurt am Main and New York: Campus Verlag, 1985).

[46] Data compiled by Bernard Degen and published as 'Arbeitslosigkeit', an entry in *Historisches Lexikon der Schweiz*. Online: www.hls-dhs-dss.ch/textes/d/D13924.php (accessed 9 December 2013).

[47] George Sheldon, 'Der Schweizer Arbeitsmarkt seit 1920: Langfristige Tendenzen', *Die Volkswirtschaft* 1–2 (2010), 15–19.

federal unemployment insurance.[48] At the same time, old age and disability benefits were raised significantly. This expansion of welfare entitlements and social benefits was mainly financed by the classic model of payroll contributions by employers and employees, while direct taxes played only a subsidiary role.

For most of the liberal partisans and big business interests, the traditional approach to dealing with income distribution consisted of an amalgam of market liberalism, bargaining with the trade unions without state interference and government support for ailing industries in times of need. This tied in well with a general preference for the principle of subsidiarity,[49] which resulted in an attempt to rein in the growth of the federal government in general and of market regulation in particular. From such a perspective, the growing public deficits and the increasing importance of federal redistribution schemes seemed to indicate a need once again to consider a liberal turn.

Formal Tax Harmonisation, Liberal Policy-Making and the Bridging role of VAT, 1979–94

In September 1979, a few months after the Conservative Party came to power in the United Kingdom, the Swiss Free Democratic Party stuck to the liberal zeitgeist by campaigning under the slogan 'More Liberty, Less Government' in the national elections.[50] The liberals increased their vote in 1979 and again in 1983 when they ousted the Social Democrats, who had formed the single biggest group in the National Assembly since 1975, and managed to maintain their lead until 1991.[51] Consequently, the 1980s saw a surge of liberal opinion-making in the field of tax policy. This tied in with the structural economic change accentuated by the recession and which was shown in the decline of the classic industrial branches and the burgeoning of financial services, as well as by growing

---

[48] This bill, which had prompted the immediate introduction of the federal unemployment insurance approved by the Swiss electorate in 1976, was made into a regular law in 1982.

[49] The principle of subsidiarity is anchored in the Swiss Federal Constitution of 1999, Art. 5a. Online: https://www.admin.ch/opc/en/classified-compilation/19995395/index.html (accessed 10 September 2015). See also Andreas Ladner, 'Switzerland: Subsidiarity, Power-Sharing, and Direct Democracy', in Frank Hendriks, Anders Lidström and John Loughlin (eds.), *The Oxford Handbook of Local and Regional Democracy in Europe* (Oxford: Oxford University Press, 2011) pp. 196–217.

[50] In German, the slogan reads: 'Mehr Freiheit, weniger Staat'.

[51] Data from the Swiss Federal Statistical Office, *Nationalratswahlen: Mandatsverteilung nach Parteien*, table T 17.2.3.4.1.

international competition in the context of the second wave of globalisation. Tax competition appealed to the logic of both international competition and supply-side economics. This is exemplified by the staunch defence of cantonal freedom to engage in tax competition made by liberal MPs in the tax harmonisation debates. While the liberal MP for the canton of Zug defended the motives of foreign companies in seeking a tax shelter in Switzerland, his colleague from Glarus argued for privileging outcomes over procedures: 'After all, our people want prosperity. Although these companies do not have humanitarian aims, they still help to build this prosperity. And with the revenue obtained by these companies, humanitarian aims can still be achieved.'[52]

Other than in the unruly and openly redistributive 1970s, such positions proved to be influential and helped to revise the tax harmonisation agenda. The neo-subsidiarity drive reduced the amount and scope of those cantonal tax matters that should be regulated through federal legislation. Consequently, the preferential taxation regimes for base companies and the lump-sum tax privilege for wealthy foreigners were both removed from the list of what should be ruled and harmonised. Other proposals for reform motivated by tax fairness concerns and/or with redistributive aims were similarly dismissed. A split or separate taxation for married couples, a federal tax on private capital gains and a federal tax on inheritance and estate taxes had been put forward in the 1970s. But by the mid-1980s none of these measures had been introduced into the legislative process for tax harmonisation. Furthermore, any 'material' harmonisation of cantonal tax disparities, such as an adjustment of tax brackets and rates, was not included in the tax harmonisation legislation voted on in 1990.[53]

In the 1980s and early 1990s, the family and middle-class households became the main target of tax reform. The left had requested or supported compensation for fiscal drag or bracket-creep – the rise of tax liabilities under a progressive tax due to a rise in nominal income and augmented by inflation – in the early 1960s on the grounds of justice for their more prosperous constituency. While the mildly 'Keynesian'-minded government experts contested claims that would reduce overall revenue, the parliamentary majority insisted on a constitutional amendment in 1971 and had tax discounts introduced in 1973 and 1975.

---

[52] Peter Hefti, 'Proceedings of the Council of States Committee on Tax Harmonisation, meeting from 6–7 September 1984', in Swiss Federal Archives, E6100B-02, 1989/1975, Steuerharmonisierung: Kommission Ständerat, Protokolle, vol. 15, p. 55.

[53] Loi fédérale sur l'harmonisation des impôts directs des cantons et des communes, 14 December 1990. Online: https://www.admin.ch/opc/fr/classified-compilation/19900333/index.html (accessed 12 March 2015).

By the 1980s, liberals and organised business interests capitalised on the fiscal drag issue in order to appeal to the middle class. They used it also as a vehicle for tax cuts, thus restricting federal revenue and advocating a brake on federal expenditures. The other core object of reference for doing justice was the family, embraced equally by the conservatives, liberals and the left. After the federal accounts in 1986 returned their first budget surplus since 1971, a liberal initiative in favour of 'more equitable taxes for married couples and families' inspired an instant tax relief programme by the federal government. The political stakeholders quickly agreed on a more favourable tariff for married taxpayers, by increasing deductions for children and for the 'second earner'. This family focus not only masked the socio-economic differences along occupational lines, income groups and educational skills, it also helped to keep women 'captured' within the logic of a fiscal 'household unit',[54] in which husbands earned the family income and working wives would at best feature as 'additional earners' in joint taxation, which was made partly deductible to ease the burden of progression.

While split or individual taxation of married couples remained an unresolved issue in the federal revenue, another piece of controversial legislation was finally wrapped up: the value added tax (VAT).

The federal government had closely followed the European debate and policy surrounding the harmonisation of turnover taxes and VAT ever since the publication of the Neumark Report in 1962.[55] This interest coincided with the rapprochement between Switzerland and the EEC.[56] The Swiss VAT debate gained momentum after the EEC published its VAT directive in April 1967 and Germany introduced the VAT system.[57] The market-oriented reasons for a common VAT in

---

[54] Kathleen A. Lahey, 'The "Capture" of Women in Law and Fiscal Policy: The Tax/Benefit Unit, Gender Equality and Feminist Ontologies', in K. Brooks, A. Gunnarsson, L. Philipps and M. Wersig (eds.), *Challenging Gender Inequality in Tax Policy Making. Comparative Perspectives* (Oxford: Hart Publishing, 2011), pp. 11–35.

[55] EEC Report 1963. Fritz Neumark had chaired the EEC Fiscal and Financial Committee and was the main contributor to the EEC Reports on Tax Harmonisation. The German report first appeared in 1962. The Swiss Federal Tax Administration summarised its content for the federal finance minister in July 1963.

[56] Switzerland had requested an association with the EEC in 1961–2. After de Gaulle vetoed the United Kingdom's application to become a member of the EEC, new applications were suspended. The process was taken up again in the late 1980s, but it ended in rejection in the Swiss ballots of 1992.

[57] 'First Council Directive of 11 April 1967 on the Harmonisation of Legislation of Member States Concerning Turnover Taxes' (67/227/EEC), in *Official Journal* 071 (14 April 1967), pp. 1301–3. Online: http://eur-lex.europa.eu/legal-content/EN/TXT/?uri=CELEX:31967L0227 (accessed 1 September 2015).

the EEC chimed with the long-standing criticism in Switzerland of the market-distorting effects which the turnover tax had because it did not allow for an input tax deduction, had a long list of exemptions, did not cover services and could not be fully passed on to consumers. Keen to diminish the importance of the unloved federal income tax, in 1972 the liberals called for the immediate introduction of VAT and suggested limiting the federal income tax to mere fiscal equalisation purposes among the cantons.[58] The challenge consisted in overcoming the poor reputation consumption taxes suffered within the left, trade unions and consumer organisations, as well as small businesses, the service sector and the tourism industry. From 1967 onwards, fiscal experts within the trade unions adopted a more favourable approach to VAT.[59] Centrist Social Democrats began to follow suit in 1971.[60] Disillusionment with the effect of fiscal drag on their middle-class constituency was one reason for this change of heart, along with the example of the Swedish Social Democrats, who welcomed the introduction of VAT in 1969 to finance the welfare state, and out of simple political realism. A substantial increase of the marginal federal income tax rate was inconceivable in the fine-tuned Swiss system of checks and balances. But in the light of decreasing customs duties, VAT appeared to be the only means of maintaining or enlarging federal investments in welfare, education and infrastructure. However, traditional veto points in the Swiss referendum system deferred the system change. Voters rejected VAT in 1977 and 1979, and again in 1991. Yet, another recession with yet another federal deficit crisis,[61] along with the new realities of the European Community, made the swift introduction of VAT vital. Two Social Democrat ministers in the federal government played a key role in winning over the majority of voters in the 1993 referendum vote on VAT.[62] One of them was Otto Stich, later the federal finance minister, who had been one of the protagonists of the

---

[58] Swiss Federal Archives, E6300B#2004/377#27*: various parliamentarian proposals. Proposal by Alfred Weber concerning the Federal Tax System (9 March 1972).

[59] Schweizerischer Gewerkschaftsbund, 6 November 1967, Bericht z. H. des Bundeskomitees.

[60] Kommission für Wirtschafts- und Finanzpolitik der SPS, *Gefordert: Die Umgestaltung des schweizerischen Steuersystems. Ein Vorschlag der wirtschafts- und finanzpolitischen Kommission der Sozialdemokratischen Partei der Schweiz* (Bern: SPS, 1971).

[61] The federal account turned negative in 1990 (−779 million CHF) and recorded an unprecedented −9,740 million CHF in 1993. See Federal Tax Administration, Statistical Services: Clôture des comptes de la Confédération (time-series table A1.1), compiled for the author in November 2014.

[62] The federal finance bill including VAT was put to the vote on 28 November 1993, together with a bill on special consumption taxes and another on measures to support the social security system.

tax harmonisation debate in the 1970s. The projected healthcare reform of 1994, by which private healthcare insurance became mandatory and entitlement therefore universal, was promoted by Stich's fellow Social Democrat, federal councillor Ruth Dreifuss. The clue consisted in earmarking a portion of the new VAT for welfare purposes and thus for expenditure-side redistribution. The bitter pill of regressive per capita healthcare premiums was sweetened by the fact that a portion of VAT would subsidise these premiums for families and the disadvantaged.[63] Further VAT receipts were earmarked for the ailing Social Security Funds and for major railway infrastructure investment.

The revenue effect proved to be quite significant. The share of the turnover tax/VAT in the federal fiscal revenue rose from 29.8 per cent in 1994 to 35.8 per cent in 1995. Nevertheless, the importance of direct federal taxes increased again in the context of the growth period 2004–7, rising to 29 per cent (see Figure 4.1). The increase in revenue from the federal income tax, with its more pronounced progressivity, directly relates to the growth of higher market incomes in the first decade of the twenty-first century. This reflects an internationally recognised trend of a rising income and wage gap at the top 10 and top 1 per cent end of the income ladder. This trend has been identified as one of the main driving forces behind growing income inequality.[64] Even more significant, though, was the increase of fiscal revenue from the federal tax on company earnings. In 1996, this amounted to 7.5 per cent of the federal fiscal revenue. By 2001, the return from company earnings peaked at 13.1 per cent, and after suffering losses during the dot.com crisis recovered to 12.9 per cent in 2007. Between 2000 and 2008, federal tax revenue from company earnings increased by 8 per cent a year.[65] Tax revenue from company earnings from the late 1990s had much to do with tax reforms during the latest period of Swiss tax policy, which saw a generalisation of the preferential tax treatment for holding, domicile and mixed companies in the context of cooperative fiscal federalism.

---

[63] Federal Act on Health Care Insurance, voted on 4 December 1994.

[64] See, for example, Mike Brewer, Luke Sibieta and Liam Wren-Lewis, *Racing Away? Income Inequality and the Evolution of High Incomes*, Briefing Note 76 (London: The Institute for Fiscal Studies 2008); Thomas Piketty, *Capital in the Twenty-First Century* (Cambridge, MA: Harvard University Press, 2014); for Switzerland, see Reto Foellmi and Isabel Martinez, *Volatile Top Income Shares in Switzerland? Reassessing the Evolution between 1981 and 2008*, Discussion Paper 2012-27 (St Gallen: School of Economics and Political Science, 2012).

[65] 'Einnahmenentwicklung direkte Bundessteuer', in Eidgenössisches Finanzdepartement EFD (ed.), *Bericht des EFD* (Bern, 23 March 2015), pp. 2–4.

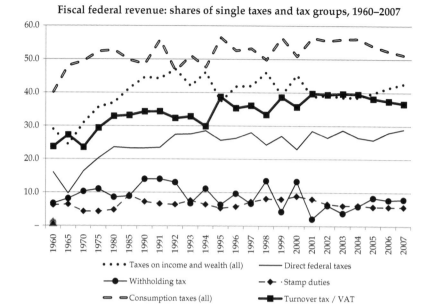

Figure 4.1. The relative importance of turnover tax/VAT and direct federal taxes.

Note: Taxes on income and wealth comprise all direct federal taxes, the withholding tax and stamp duties, alongside other minor taxes not included in this dataset. Direct federal taxes include the federal tax 'on income' and the federal tax 'on company earnings' (profits), as well as capital taxes (not included in Figure 4.1). The turnover tax was replaced by VAT in 1995.

Source: Swiss Federal Tax Administration, statistics section, data compilation by the author (November 2014).

Globalisation and Neo-Liberalism: The Mid-1990s to 2008

The 'welfarisation' of VAT, which thus accompanied the expansion of the welfare system, was one way of dealing with the diverse challenges of the 1990s, which also saw the greatest unemployment crisis in Switzerland since the 1930s. The official unemployment rate rose from a mere 1 per cent in 1991 to 4.5 per cent in 1993 and peaked at 5.2 per cent in 1997.[66] State deficits also reached record levels. The federal government closed

---

[66] See G. Rais and P. Stauffer, *Die Schweizer Wirtschaft von den Neunzigerjahren bis Heute: Wichtige Fakten und Konjunkturanalysen* (Neuchâtel: Bundesamt für Statistik, 2005).

its account for 1993 with a deficit of over 9.7 billion CHF.[67] The cantonal and local accounts also plummeted into the red, although to a much lesser extent as a result of passing various responsibilities to the federal level. Apart from austerity adjustments which reduced the size of and the eligibility period for unemployment benefits, local and cantonal government increasingly turned from administering social aid towards a welfare-to-work policy.[68] This 'activation' scheme corresponded to a more general reliance on the market, which was a central feature of the liberalisation agenda of the General Agreement on Tariffs and Trade (GATT) 1994 and the European Common Market following the Maastricht Treaty of 1992. It also influenced a number of reforms in Switzerland in the telecom sector and, to a lesser extent, the railways.[69]

More far-reaching privatisation demands, as formulated by neo-liberals in 1995,[70] met with little success in the Swiss system. Federalist and direct democratic convictions privileged a broad and egalitarian allocation of public investments and services over efficient concentration. Nevertheless, the pressures arising from globalisation and a change of political power relations promoted a more explicit defence of business interests also at the federal level. In the 1990s and early 2000s the national conservative Swiss People's Party (SVP) enjoyed the most astonishing electoral increase the parliament had ever recorded. Fiscally conservative and fiercely advocating tax competition, it has influenced tax policy ever since, siding with the free-market orientation of the liberals, albeit with the exception of a protectionist, pro-farmer attitude.[71] This process culminated in the explicit appraisal of cantonal tax competition and tax reductions as a means of attracting new revenue by federal ministers in the 2000s, and in controversial corporate tax reforms at the federal level.[72]

---

[67] Federal Tax Administration, Statistical Services: Clôture des comptes de la Confédération (time-series table A1.1), compiled for the author in November 2014.

[68] Giuliano Bonoli and Cyrielle Champion, 'Federalism and Welfare to Work in Switzerland: The Development of Active Social Policies in a Fragmented Welfare State', *Publius: The Journal of Federalism*, 45/1 (2015), 77–98.

[69] For an evaluation of the EU liberalisation agenda and the Swiss transport system, see also Gisela Hürlimann, *Die Eisenbahn der Zukunft. Automatisierung, Schnellverkehr und Modernisierung bei den SBB 1955–2005* (Zürich: Chronos, 2007).

[70] David de Pury et al., *Mut zum Aufbruch. Eine wirtschaftspolitische Agenda* (Zürich: Orell Füssli, 1995).

[71] Swiss Federal Statistical Office, *Nationalratswahlen: Mandatsverteilung nach Parteien*, table T17.2.3.4.1.

[72] For the federal company and corporate tax reform see www.efd.admin.ch/dokumentation/gesetzgebung/00573/02299/index.html?lang=fr (accessed 9 October 2015); and Daniel Jositsch, 'Unternehmenssteuerreform II "Ein Hohn gegenüber dem Rechtsstaat"', *Der Beobachter*, 21 December 2011.

In 1997, the Swiss parliament launched the first of a series of legislative Acts to fundamentally reform Swiss corporate taxation.[73] In this first reform package, federal policy-makers solidified and generalised the cantonal preferential tax regimes for holding and domicile companies. They did so by implementing these tax privileges into the very harmonisation legislation that in the 1970s had been discussed to rule out this type of preferential taxation.[74] The federalist division of labour meant that a given canton would attract new base companies with its preferential tax scheme. These companies paid zero cantonal profit taxes and a nominal capital tax, while they owed the regular federal corporate tax which had been changed into a proportional tax. By 2013, the federal revenue from base companies under 'special taxation' constituted almost half of the entire federal revenue from company earnings.[75] This is a clear-cut example of how 'innovation among the constituent units' of a federal state can spill over to the federal level, as it has been described for the realm of public welfare policy.[76] Beyond this innovation spill-over within the multi-tiered fiscal system, the second bill of this corporate tax reform series also saw a spill-over of procedures and standards from the sphere of preferential taxation to that of regular taxation. The 2008 bill reduced the tax liabilities of shareholders (as well as companies) by cutting taxes on dividends and thereby privileging capital income over wage income. Criticism concerning the redistributive consequences of this tax reform culminated in a lawsuit when it became apparent that it also resulted in far bigger revenue losses than the federal government had announced. This was a consequence of the capital contribution principle. This legal innovation had been lobbied for successfully by business interests. It allowed companies to repay their shareholders the premiums and additional payments they had provided since 1997 free of tax.

---

[73] For the government's perspective, see www.efd.admin.ch/dokumentation/gesetzgebung/00573/02299 for parts I and II of the corporate tax reform series; and www.efd.admin.ch/themen/steuern/02720 for part III. For a critical perspective, see, inter alia, the arguments of the left-wing think tank Denknetz at www.denknetz-online.ch/unternehmenssteuerreform-iii-usr-iii; and for the liberal perspective as represented by the major umbrella organisation for business and employer interests 'economiesuisse', see www.economiesuisse.ch/de/themen/ste/unternehmensbesteuerung/Seiten/default.aspx (all accessed 3 March 2015).

[74] Federal Tax Harmonisation Act (StHG), Art. 28 Abs. 2 StHG.

[75] The joint intake from the taxation of holding, domicile and mixed companies amounted to an average of 47.86 per cent for the years 2008–10; see 'Massnahmen zur Stärkung der steuerlichen Wettbewerbsfähigkeit (Unternehmenssteuerreform III)', in Eidg. Finanzdepartement (ed.), *Bericht des Steuerungsorgans zuhanden der EFD* (Bern, 11 December 2013), p. 16.

[76] Bonoli and Champion, 'Federalism and Welfare to Work in Switzerland', 77.

The need to adjust cantonal legislation to the Federal Tax Harmonisation Act launched a series of cantonal tax reforms which went far beyond formal standardisation and accelerated the trend of cutting income, corporate and net wealth tax rates. Many of these moves were argued for in the light of intensified international competition in the wake of globalisation and the tax policies of other cantons. But innovation was needed to stay in the game. The authorities of the rural canton of Obwalden, a net receiver of subsidies and of payments from the fiscal equalisation funds, tested the margin of the agreed constitutionality when they reformed their income tax law and introduced an openly regressive tariff for higher incomes. This tax structure was declared unconstitutional by the Swiss Federal Court in 2007 because it went against the ability-to-pay principle. But the court's verdict did not prescribe the application of a progressive income tariff.[77] This gave way to the option of a proportional or flat tariff, similar to those introduced in some east European countries from the 1990s.[78] Such deviations from the general pattern of progressive income taxes were only possible in a minority of small and rural cantons, while the revenue expenditure structure in most of the cantons forced them to adhere to the established paradigm and satisfy voters and businesses with tariff reductions, or rely on subsidies from fiscal equalisation. The intensified tax competition, which only abated in 2011, can therefore be read as an indirect and seemingly paradoxical result of harmonisation. By restricting harmonisation to a formal standardisation, federal regulation unfolded a 'liberalising' effect because the absence of common rules in certain realms became a licence for self-rule – at least until the 'outer world's' reaction to some of the use (and abuse) of cantonal fiscal liberties provoked the federal government's intervention.

Back to International (Market) Justice – and a Conclusion

In the aftermath of the global financial and debt crisis of 2008 and beyond, heightened international pressure against harmful tax practices and any legislation and procedure which eased tax evasion has led to a historic reorientation of the Swiss political and business elites. When the major Swiss bank UBS began to hand over client data to the US authorities in 2009 in order to avoid criminal charges and the withdrawal of its banking licence in the US market, the Swiss authorities gave

[77] Schweizerisches Bundesgericht (2007). Urteil vom 1. Juni 2007. I. ö.-r. Abteilung. 2P.43/2006 /fco.
[78] Anthony John Evans and Paul Dragos Aligica, 'The Spread of the Flat Tax in Eastern Europe: A Comparative Study', *Eastern European Economics* 46/3 (2008), 49–67.

their backing;[79] had they failed to do so it would have constituted a violation of article 47 of the Swiss Federal Banking Act, which imposes a custodial sentence on any bank employee who supplies information to a third party about professional confidential data ('bank secrecy').[80] Since then, the Swiss government has agreed to apply OECD standards concerning the automatic exchange of tax-related information. This move came after decades of resistance towards and reservation about similar claims by foreign governments or the OECD.[81] Furthermore, the federal council in 2014 launched a third corporate tax reform bill which will abolish the taxation privileges for holding, domicile and mixed companies, after the EU authorities successfully claimed that this preferential scheme unfairly distorted market competition and violated the Free Trade Agreement of 1972. This (re)turn to an internationally tax-compliant, and thus fair, mode of competition is costly for many cantonal, as well as the federal, treasuries. Measures for compensating the expected fiscal loss from the abolition of the old regime include corporate tax allowances for research and development expenses (i.e. patents, licences and intellectual property boxes).[82] As this will not suffice, policy-makers plan for further reductions of the effective company tax rates with a selected set of measures. The plan for introducing a federal tax on private capital gains, though, was rejected in a public hearing.[83]

Taking up and slightly subverting James M. Buchanan's appraisal of Swiss fiscal federalism discussed in the introduction to this chapter, it

[79] The UBS agreement with the United States was first declared legal by the Swiss Financial Market Supervisory Authority (FINMA). See 'FINMA Makes Possible Settlement between UBS and the US Authorities and Announces the Results of its Own Investigation' (18 February 2009). Online: www.finma.ch/en/news/2009/02/mm-ubs-xborder-20090218/ (accessed 30 August 2015).

[80] Federal Banking Act of 8 November 1934, article 47.

[81] See the documents on the website of the Swiss State Secretariat for International Financial Matters: www.sif.admin.ch/sif/en/home/themen/internationale-steuerpolitik/automatischer-informationsaustausch.html (accessed 10 September 2015). For the earlier resistance of the Swiss OECD delegates and Swiss authorities to acknowledging the tax evasion potential of Swiss bank secrecy, see OECD Archives, Paris: Recommendation of the Council of 21 September 1977 on Tax Avoidance and Evasion [C(77)149/FINAL]; European Council, Recommendation 833 (1978) concerning cooperation between the member states in order to combat international tax avoidance and evasion (Pettersson); Organisation for Economic Cooperation and Development, *Taxation and the Abuse of Bank Secrecy* (Paris: OECD, 1985).

[82] Rainer Hausmann, Oliver Krummenacher and Philipp Roth, 'The License Box as an Alternative Tax Model to the Mixed Company', *Der Schweizer Treuhänder/L'Expert Comptable Suisse*, January/February 2012, 87ff.

[83] See State Secretariat for International Financial Matters, Bern, 5 June 2015: Dispatch on the Corporate Tax Reform Act III ('Botschaft zum Unternehmenssteuerreformgesetz III'). The Corporate Tax Reform Act III was adopted by the Swiss Parliament in June 2016 and has to undergo a referendum rote in February 2017.

seems that the Swiss currently use their federal government to effectively keep their society (and, above all, their economy) free from retaliation and international compliance pressure. The reasons for the increased governing will and ruling powers of bodies like the European Union or the OECD – the Leviathan of the early twenty-first century?[84] – are many. Among them are the challenges of 'globalisation', as expressed in transfer pricing, profit shifting and other stratagems of multinational business and the global capital elite.[85] Current Swiss tax reforms mirror international fiscal reregulation, which is the most recent proof that the Swiss world of taxation is distinctively transnationally entangled. It is arguable whether the classic notion of a multi-tiered Swiss tax system should be expanded to a transnational level, not only in view of the latest developments, but also with an eye on the interconnections going back to the 1960s analysed here. Such a perspective takes into account that the tax competitive measures at the cantonal level have been conceived and adapted in an international business and wealth environment since the early twentieth century, and that the explicit reference to international competition and globalisation since the 1990s has only marked the last stage.

The political economy of the Swiss fiscal system can furthermore be understood as an effective division of labour between the cantons, communes and the federal government when dealing with domestic and transnational tax fairness and redistributive justice. The fiscal equalisation system, managed by the federal government, has ensured that inter-cantonal tensions arising from fiscal disparities would not endanger national identity. Fiscal redistribution (also on an inter-personal level) should therefore always be contextualised within its inter-regional dimension. Compared to general welfare regime research standards, Switzerland might still seem to be more of a 'liberal'-type – indeed a Buchananian – paradise. In the early twenty-first century, the Swiss tax-to-GDP ratio is still significantly lower than in most west European countries. Amounting to 28.2 per cent in 2012, it scored even less than the United Kingdom (35.2 per cent) or Spain (32.9 per cent), was similar to Japan (28.6 per cent in 2011) and slightly above the United States (24.3 per cent).[86] The growing income gap and intensified tax

---

[84] The author here also refers to an impression shared in confidence with her by leading officials of the Swiss Federal Tax authorities in August 2015 concerning the role of the OECD in tax matters.

[85] Among other reports, see Organisation for Economic Cooperation and Development, *Addressing Base Erosion and Profit Shifting* (Paris: OECD, 2013).

[86] See OECD Revenue Statistics – Comparative tables, data extracted from OECD.Stat (4 November 2014).

competition may have caused a relatively equal income distribution to become more unequal. This is suggested by newly computed data at the cantonal level for the period 1973–2010, although the trend is mixed.[87] But even tax competition has not yielded to a non-means-tested social insurance and social security system. The coincidence in time and substance of welfare expansion along the lines of the social contribution model – or with the help of indirect taxation – preceding periods of more restricted or more competitive direct taxation sheds light on a specific Swiss welfare regime model which deserves further analysis.

---

[87] Swiss Federal Tax Administration 2013: Statistical Key Figures from the Direct Federal Tax on Individuals; data aggregation and Gini computation by the FNS project Sinergia, No. 130648, 'The Swiss Confederation: A Natural Laboratory for Research on Fiscal and Political Decentralization'.

5   Taxation in the 1980s: A Five-Country Comparison of Neo-Liberalism and Path Dependency

Marc Buggeln

There is widespread agreement among researchers that the early 1970s were a turning point in the history of the Western industrialised countries. In these sweeping analyses, national financial policy generally plays only a limited role. Researchers tend to focus on efforts to reduce the welfare state and the transition to a neo-liberal approach, which demanded a reduction in the economic participation of the state. Although researchers generally highlight the importance of US President Ronald Reagan and UK Prime Minister Margaret Thatcher, they rarely mention, or only briefly outline, the essential role of tax programmes in the policies introduced by both politicians.[1] The following analysis, however, places special emphasis on the issue of the changing conditions for national tax policy in the Western industrialised countries, based on the assumption that these policies, as Thomas Piketty argued, were of critical importance. This chapter consists of a comparative study of five countries. First, the changes introduced by Thatcher in the United Kingdom will be analysed and briefly compared with those implemented by Reagan in the United States. This will be followed by an examination of the extent to which similar reforms were launched in West Germany, France and Sweden, and to what extent the frequently predicted 'race to the bottom' already existed in the 1980s.

Two additional issues will play a significant role. First, Junko Kato has advanced the thesis that the welfare state has experienced robust growth only in those countries in which value added tax (VAT) was introduced before the first oil shock in 1973. Kato argues that ever since the crisis it has been possible to extend the tax base only with regressive taxes, which tend to burden the general population, rather than with progressive taxes, which impose greater payments by wealthier citizens.[2]

---

[1] See, for example, Anselm Doering and Raphael Manteuffel, *Nach dem Boom. Perspektiven auf die Zeitgeschichte seit 1970* (Göttingen: Vandenhoeck & Ruprecht, 2008), pp. 45–52.

[2] Junko Kato, *Regressive Taxation and the Welfare State: Path Dependence and Policy Diffusion* (Cambridge: Cambridge University Press, 2003).

The second issue to be examined is the importance of path dependencies. In view of their decisive influence, analysts often group countries into clusters. Such a tax policy model has been proposed by B. Guy Peters. Based on the tax practices of twenty-two OECD countries, in 1965 he identified the following four categories: (1) the Anglo-American group, which is characterised by comparatively high property and corporate taxes, fairly high-income taxes and rather low sales taxes; (2) the Scandinavian group, which favours high-income and sales taxes, but low corporate taxes; (3) a continental group, which Peters describes as having 'broad-based taxation'; this group consists of Austria, the Netherlands, Spain and Germany, and is characterised by the comprehensive use of all important types of taxes; and (4) a southern European group, made up of France, Italy, Portugal and Greece, which assumes there will be widespread tax evasion and thus relies principally on sales taxes.[3] Peters goes on to say that, based on OECD tax data, he was able to verify this classification up to 1987 and notes that the four clusters remained relatively constant until that point. The only exception he found was France, which he found, switched in the 1980s from a southern European to a continental European type of taxation. Overall, he maintains that the clusters have tended to merge, as the Anglo-American and southern European countries gradually moved towards broad-based taxation.[4] Nevertheless, a measure of caution should be exercised when examining Peters' data because he does not supply the statistics that he used to reach his conclusions.

There Is No Alternative: The Iron Lady and Her Taxes

Margaret Thatcher first had to convince members of her own party when she started campaigning for the turnaround that she hoped to achieve. The British Conservative Party had helped fuel the expansion of the welfare state and had long pursued Keynesian economic policies. Thatcher, on the other hand, saw four main problems which had to be resolved to make Britain more competitive: the trade unions were too powerful, government was weak, the private sector was overburdened, and wasteful government spending was prevalent. Thatcher viewed this last problem as the key issue because, in her opinion, the other three were caused or exacerbated by a spendthrift state.[5]

---

[3] B. Guy Peters, *The Politics of Taxation: A Comparative Perspective* (Cambridge, MA: Blackwell, 1991), pp. 58–64 and ch. 6.

[4] Ibid., pp. 66–7.

[5] Adrian Williamson, *Conservative Economic Policymaking and the Birth of Thatcherism, 1964–1979* (Basingstoke: Palgrave Macmillan, 2015); Dominik Geppert, *Thatchers konservative Revolution. Der Richtungswandel der britischen Tories 1975–1979* (Munich: Oldenbourg, 2002).

After her election victory in 1979 her first initiatives were decidedly radical. Inspired by neo-liberal economists, she made the money supply her key indicator, the rationale being that the amount of money in circulation could be used to control the entire economy and thereby reduce inflation. From Thatcher's perspective, this indicator had the added advantage that the trade unions had almost no influence over it.[6] Thatcher also immediately introduced cuts in social spending, but here she proceeded gradually and with greater caution. This was nevertheless an abrupt change of course for public expenditure policy, but the changes on the revenue side were even more radical. Thatcher and her first Chancellor of the Exchequer, Geoffrey Howe, reduced the top rate of income tax on earned income from 83 per cent to 60 per cent. To help finance this, VAT was raised from a standard 8 per cent and 12.5 per cent on certain items to a single rate of 15 per cent. At the same time, fuel duty was increased. In fact, with these increases they overcompensated for the decrease in revenues from lowering income taxes.[7] Both the tax and the expenditure rates increased.

Although the country was in the grip of a recession, Thatcher and Howe continued to pursue a restrictive budget in 1981/2. Their primary objective was to improve the supply situation, which explains why they reduced income tax rates for the wealthy and corporate taxes for companies. At the same time, they suspended inflation-adjusted income tax rates, increased excise duty and imposed a one-off tax on bank deposits. This triggered an additional deflationary impulse that exacerbated the crisis.[8] Thatcher's popularity and that of the Conservative Party now reached an all-time low.

These developments ultimately led the Conservative government to moderate its tone somewhat from mid-1981. In light of the undeniable problems, the government was obliged to abandon its policy of viewing the money supply as the key indicator. Barry Eichengreen calls this the end of the only attempt in an advanced industrialised country to practise a pure form of neo-liberal theory.[9] The course of tax policy also

---

[6] Duncan Needham, *UK Monetary Policy from Devaluation to Thatcher 1967–1982* (Basingstoke: Palgrave Macmillan, 2014), pp. 134–68.

[7] Jonathan Leape, 'Tax Policies in the 1980s and 1990s: The Case of the United Kingdom', in Anthonie Knoester (ed.), *Taxation in the United States and Europe: Theory and Practice* (Basingstoke: Macmillan, 1993), pp. 276–311; Bob Rowthorne, 'Government Spending and Taxation in the Thatcher Era', in Jonathan Michie (ed.), *The Economic Legacy 1979–1992* (London: Academic Press, 1992), pp. 261–93.

[8] Duncan Needham and Anthony Hotson (eds.), *Expansionary Fiscal Contraction: The Thatcher Government's 1981 Budget in Perspective* (Cambridge: Cambridge University Press, 2014).

[9] Barry Eichengreen, *The European Economy since 1945: Coordinated Capitalism and Beyond* (Princeton, NJ: Princeton University Press, 2008), p. 280.

changed in one respect: the decreases in tax revenues in the 1982/3 budget were significantly larger than the newly introduced taxes, which led to an overall shortfall of £3.2 billion. In other words, Thatcher had switched from a restrictive to an expansive course. But the general direction remained the same: direct taxes decreased further while indirect taxes increased. The expansive budget coincided with a general recovery in the global economy and produced a slight increase in GDP of 1 per cent in 1982, increasing to 3.8 per cent in 1983. Without this economic recovery, Thatcher would have had hardly any chance of being re-elected in June 1983. She was also carried to victory by two events that had little to do with economic policy: first, the Labour Party came close to self-destruction amid diverse internal policy disputes; and second, Thatcher's aggressive stance, and ultimate victory, in the 1982 Falklands War was greeted with widespread approval in Britain.

After the 1983 election, Thatcher's ally Nigel Lawson succeeded Geoffrey Howe as Chancellor of the Exchequer. Together, Lawson and Thatcher pressed ahead with radical tax changes. On the supply side, the government now focused on gradually reducing the top rate of corporate tax from 52 per cent to 35 per cent. However, Lawson also expanded the tax base by including smaller companies and reducing tax allowances, with the result that tax revenues remained constant or rose slightly. Tax reductions for large companies were accompanied by the elimination of a surtax on capital income, along with the waiving of the employer's contribution to the social security system, the National Insurance scheme.[10] That the financial policies pursued during this period proved comparatively uncontroversial was thanks to two large sources of income for the government. First, oil exploitation in the North Sea reached its peak and over £8 billion flowed into state coffers in 1985 alone.[11] Second, the government received a considerable cash injection from the privatisation of state-owned companies.[12]

In 1987, Thatcher celebrated yet another election victory. Lawson announced his intention to pursue drastic changes, which focused on further amendments to income tax legislation. His main initiative was to reduce the number of tax bands, so that there were now only two – one at 25 per cent and one at 40 per cent. Consequently, in the nine

---

[10] Leape, *Tax Policies*, pp. 287–96; and Reimut Zohlnhöfer, *Globalisierung der Wirtschaft und finanzpolitische Anpassungsreaktionen in Westeuropa* (Baden-Baden: Nomos, 2009), pp. 92–3.

[11] Jim Tomlinson, *Public Policy and the Economy since 1900* (Oxford: Oxford University Press, 1990), p. 346.

[12] Harvey Feigenbaum, Jeffrey Henig and Chris Hamnett, *Shrinking the State: The Political Underpinnings of Privatization* (Cambridge: Cambridge University Press, 1998); see also this volume, Chapter 9.

years under Thatcher the top tax rate for earned incomes more than halved from 83 per cent to 40 per cent.[13] But the reform was poorly timed. Tax reductions for the wealthy coincided with an uproar over wide-ranging cuts to social services and a rise in the inflation rate. Criticism rained down on Thatcher not only from the Labour Party, but also from among the ranks of her own party and sectors of the media that normally favoured her policies.[14]

Another tax initiative ended in Thatcher's downfall. Her goal was to eliminate the existing local property tax (known as the rates), which was primarily paid by homeowners, and replace it with a per-capita tax, officially called the Community Charge, but more commonly known as the poll tax. The government introduced this new tax during the 1989/90 fiscal year in Scotland and in 1990/1 in England and Wales. As a result, every adult now had to pay the same amount of Community Charge, regardless of his or her income, the amount being set by each local authority. Thatcher's main aim in introducing the tax was to limit the increase in local government expenditures. The tax was popular among the more affluent members of society, while it was particularly despised by local authorities and blue-collar workers. A protest movement sprang up in Scotland and quickly spread throughout the United Kingdom. In March 1990, an anti-poll tax demonstration in London was attended by an estimated 100,000–200,000 people and sparked violent clashes with the police. In the wake of this civil unrest, Thatcher lost the support of many members of her own party, who eventually nominated another MP, Michael Heseltine, to lead the party. When Thatcher failed to achieve the necessary majority in the first round of voting, she resigned in November 1990.[15]

Two Neo-Liberals? Thatcher, Reagan and the Social Impact of Their Policies

Although Thatcher's and Reagan's policies are often mentioned in one breath, there were considerable differences in the policies they actually pursued. When it comes to budget policy, aside from an initial loss of revenue as a result of making tax reductions, Reagan was responsible for expanding government expenditures, primarily by increasing the

---

[13] Before that period, there was an additional tax on unearned income which took the top marginal tax rate to 98 per cent. Zohlnhöfer, *Globalisierung*, p. 73.
[14] John Campbell, *Margaret Thatcher*, vol. II: *The Iron Lady* (London: Jonathan Cape, 2003), p. 579.
[15] Campbell, *Thatcher*, pp. 709–47.

military budget.[16] During his first year in office (1981), the deficit was 21.6 per cent of GDP, but by 1986 it had soared to over 37 per cent.[17] By contrast Thatcher managed to keep government expenditures relatively stable during her first term in office, and thus reduce the UK deficit. The increase in revenues in the United Kingdom is explained by another significant difference. Thatcher balanced the reduction in direct taxes by increasing VAT and employers' contributions to National Insurance, whereas in 1981 Reagan lowered taxes without introducing measures to finance this. He did not introduce a federal VAT and the United States remains one of the last of the wealthiest eighteen OECD countries without such a tax.[18] But in terms of tax policy, there were obvious shared features, whose impact can be observed in the distribution of social burdens. Both Thatcher and Reagan began to lower the top income tax rate shortly after they entered office. In the United States the income tax rate for affluent Americans dropped from 70 per cent to 28 per cent within just six years. And, as we have seen, in the United Kingdom the top income tax rate more than halved from 83 per cent in 1975 to 40 per cent in 1990. What is more, both countries reduced the corporate tax rate.

The key issue for evaluating the policies of Reagan and Thatcher revolves around the consequences for income distribution. In the United Kingdom, and especially the United States, a relatively progressive tax system had, at least until then, compensated for a relatively weak system of social services. Among the rich OECD countries, the United States placed in the midfield while Britain ranked among the nations with the most egalitarian income distribution. This changed dramatically in the 1980s. A detailed analysis of tax changes in Britain under Thatcher and her successor, John Major, between 1985 and 1995 shows that the reforms resulted in a 28 per cent reduction in the equalising impact of the tax system.[19] It also shows that roughly 50 per cent of the money distributed from the government's tax reductions benefited the richest 10 per cent of the population.[20] Lower- and middle-income families in the United States did not benefit from Reagan's tax reductions because these were offset by increases in social

[16] Michel French, *US Economic History since 1945* (Manchester: Manchester University Press, 1997), p. 144.

[17] James M. Poterba, 'Budget Policy', in Martin Feldstein (ed.), *American Economic Policy in the 1980s* (Chicago: University of Chicago Press, 1994), p. 241.

[18] See this volume, Chapter 7.

[19] Christopher Giles and Paul Johnson, 'Tax Reform in the UK and Changes in the Progressivity of the Tax System 1985–95', *Fiscal Studies* 15/3 (1994), 85.

[20] Paul Johnson and Graham Stark, 'Ten Years of Mrs Thatcher: The Distributional Consequences', *Fiscal Studies* 10 (1989), 33.

security contributions.[21] The situation tended to improve among the top 10 per cent of the population. A new study shows that it was, above all, the 1 per cent of the US population with the absolute highest level of income that benefited far more than the average American from the tax reforms under Reagan.[22] This increase in social inequality ensured that Thatcher and Reagan maintained a remarkable level of respect from their neo-liberal advisers. In a posthumously published interview, Milton Friedman gave the following advice to European leaders: 'In a nutshell, they should all emulate Margaret Thatcher and Ronald Reagan.'[23]

The Tax Policies of the CDU–CSU/FDP Coalition in West Germany

It took a couple of years before the conservative party in West Germany was able to follow the lead set by its political counterparts in the United States and United Kingdom. The previous governing coalition of the centre-left Social Democratic Party (SPD) and the pro-business Free Democratic Party (FDP) had collapsed on 17 September 1982 amid intense wrangling over the budget.[24] Helmut Kohl, the chancellor of the new conservative coalition (Christian Democratic Union–Christian Social Union (CDU–CSU) and the FDP), called the change in government an 'intellectual and moral turning point' and pledged, right from the outset, a dramatic departure from the policies of his predecessors in office. It was a political watershed that in many ways resembled the course charted by Reagan and Thatcher. Kohl announced a reduction of the government deficit and a broad tax reform featuring significant tax reductions.[25]

After Kohl's successful re-election in 1983, the main goals remained fiscal consolidation and reducing the rate of inflation. The coalition agreement contained the following far-reaching resolutions:

The growth of expenditures in the 1984 federal budget is to be limited to approximately 2 per cent and for the 1985–1987 medium-term financial planning period

---

[21] Willi Leibfritz, John Thornton and Alexandra Bibbee, *Taxation and Economic Performance* (Paris: OECD, 1997), pp. 106–11.

[22] Thomas Piketty and Emmanuel Sanz, 'Income Inequality in the United States, 1913–1998', *Quarterly Journal of Economics* 68/1 (2003), 1–39. This fact seems to be underestimated in this volume in the otherwise admirable Chapter 3.

[23] *Die Welt*, 17 November 2006.

[24] Martin H. Geyer, 'Rahmenbedingungen: Unsicherheit als Normalität', in Martin H. Geyer (ed.), *Geschichte der Sozialpolitik in Deutschland seit 1945*, vol. 6: *1974–1982 Bundesrepublik Deutschland* (Baden-Baden: Nomos, 2008), pp. 105–9.

[25] Roland Sturm, 'Die Wende im Stolperschritt – eine finanzpolitische Bilanz', in Göttrick Wewer (ed.), *Bilanz der Ära Kohl* (Opladen: Leske & Budrich, 1998), pp. 183–4.

it is to be limited to an annual increase of approximately 3 per cent. For government budgets, the aim on the whole is to maintain their growth significantly below the nominal increase of the gross domestic product.[26]

The clearly dominant characteristic of the 1983 and 1984 budgets was consolidation on the expenditure side. On the revenue side, the government's policy initially was marked by restraint. The government did little here and collected more tax revenue thanks to bracket-creep ('cold progression').[27]

Unlike Thatcher and Reagan, Kohl was fortunate in that he did not assume the responsibilities of government until the recession had ended in most industrialised countries. The same holds true for German industry, which enjoyed slow growth in 1983, followed by accelerated growth in sales in 1984. Furthermore, the government benefited from the high dollar exchange rate. In addition to fuelling German exports, this boosted the profits of the Bundesbank and considerably reduced the amount of new debt incurred by the German government. Buoyed by these successes, the government decided to forgo introducing any major cutbacks in social services during the second half of the legislative period. Thus, after the initial signs of a recovery, the government now switched to a policy of tax relief.

In December 1983, the FDP urged that, by the beginning of 1986, the German government should introduce tax rate reductions to encourage investment and boost the economy.[28] One of the main reasons for the timing was that the date of the next German parliamentary election was January 1987, so a tax reduction on 1 January 1987 would have little time to make an impact. The CSU readily agreed to support the measure.[29] On 21 February 1984, the coalition partners met to discuss the tax plans, but were only able to agree on a targeted reduction of roughly 25 billion Deutschmarks.[30] On 23 March, the weekly newspaper *Die Zeit* published an article quoting the finance minister Gerhard Stoltenberg, who stated that the reform would have to be introduced in two stages: in 1986, with increased benefits for families, and in 1988 with income tax reductions. Stoltenberg demanded financing measures

---

[26] Coalition agreement of 22 March 1983 as appendix 4 to the parliamentary group meeting of 23 March 1983, in *Archiv für Christlich-Demokratische Politik* (ACDP), 08-001-1070/2.

[27] Hans-Peter Ullmann, *Der deutsche Steuerstaat. Geschichte der öffentlichen Finanzen* (München: Beck, 2005), pp. 205–7; Andreas Wirsching, *Abschied vom Provisorium. Geschichte der Bundesrepublik Deutschland 1982–1990* (Stuttgart: DVA, 2006), p. 266; and Zohlnhöfer, *Globalisierung*, pp. 310–13.

[28] *Wirtschaftswoche*, 25 November 1983, p. 26; *Frankfurter Rundschau*, 22 December 1983.

[29] *Der Spiegel*, 5 December 1983, p. 32.

[30] Wirsching, *Abschied*, p. 273.

to cover half of these reductions. Both the CSU and the FDP firmly opposed financing the measures with tax increases and dividing the reform into two stages. By contrast, the governors of the CDU-led German states were urging reform in two stages and more comprehensive financing measures.[31] Due to their veto position in the Bundesrat (the legislative chamber that represents the states), no reform could be forced through against the will of the state governors. During a coalition meeting in May, it was agreed that the long list of proposed subsidy cuts was even less appealing than raising VAT and the decision was subsequently deferred to a later date.[32] It was not until 20 June that the coalition partners were finally able to reach a compromise. This involved introducing the reform in two stages, in 1986 and 1988, in line with what the state governors wanted. In return, it was agreed that there would be no extraordinary financing measures. In terms of the amount of tax and benefit relief, they agreed on 18.7 billion DM, which was somewhere between the 10–12 billion DM proposed by the state governors and the 25 billion DM demanded by the parliamentary groups.[33]

The January 1987 election returned the coalition to another four years in office, with each of the coalition partners promising further tax reductions. However, just two weeks after the election, when the coalition committee met to discuss the tax reform for the first time, the differences between the parties immediately surfaced. Stoltenberg favoured a progressive, linear tax scheme[34] with moderate reductions, which would be partly compensated for by increasing VAT, while the FDP and the CSU opposed this and called for greater tax cuts, primarily a reduction in the top tax income bracket. This met with fierce resistance from the CDU Executive Committee.[35] *Die Zeit* dubbed it a 'fiscal religious war'.[36] The CSU and the FDP openly threatened not to re-elect Kohl as chancellor when this was put to the vote in parliament on 11 March. Kohl's response was to tell his own party, the CDU, that he would call for a vote of confidence if the party failed to declare its willingness to support a reduction in the top income tax bracket.

---

[31] CDU/CSU parliamentary group meetings of 3 April 1984 and 2 May 1984, in *ACDP*, 08-001-1070/2.

[32] *Der Spiegel*, 7 May 1984, pp. 28–9.

[33] Gérard Bökenkamp, *Das Ende des Wirtschaftswunders. Geschichte der Sozial-, Wirtschafts- und Finanzpolitik in der Bundesrepublik 1969–1998* (Stuttgart: Lucius & Lucius, 2010), p. 256.

[34] *Bei der linearen Progression steigt der Grenzsteuersatz zwischen Eingangssteuersatz und Spitzensteuersatz geradlinig an. Dadurch werden die sprunghaften Übergänge der Steuerstufenmodelle vermieden.*

[35] Reimut Zohlnhöfer, *Die Wirtschaftspolitik der Ära Kohl* (Opladen: Leske & Budrich, 2001), pp. 85–7.

[36] *Die Zeit*, 13 February 1987, p. 22.

Kohl's unprecedented threat to resign worked and led to a breakthrough in early March. The CDU declared that it was now prepared to reduce the top income tax rate to 53 per cent.[37] The issue of corporate taxes sparked an equally heated debate. As a compromise, the coalition partners agreed to reduce the maximum corporate tax rate to 50 per cent.

The two reductions in the top income tax bracket were the most controversial aspects of the tax relief debate, although they amounted to only a small proportion of the cutbacks that were eventually agreed. The coalition agreed to a gross reduction of 44.4 billion DM, of which 19 billion DM was to be financed by reducing subsidies. The largest proportion of the reductions came from introducing the linear progressive tax rate. This amounted to 23.7 billion DM and primarily benefited middle-class wage earners. In an effort to maintain social symmetry, the coalition decided to compensate for the reduction in the top tax bracket by reducing the entry-level rate by 3 per cent.

The agreement was not well received by the general public, who were taken aback by the intense bickering within the coalition. To make matters worse, major challenges still lay ahead for the coalition. During negotiations, the coalition partners had carefully avoided the thorny issue of how exactly they planned to slash 19 billion DM in subsidies to finance their tax relief scheme. One of the finance minister's biggest accomplishments that summer was that no aspect of the negotiations over the subsidy cutbacks was leaked to the outside world. A group of five politicians from the coalition was charged with drawing up a list of subsidies to be considered for elimination. The list officially amounted to 17 billion DM in cutbacks to finance the tax reform. In early October 1987, the coalition partners largely approved the proposals. Although there were deep divisions over two of the approved financing measures – the withholding tax and a fuel tax for private aircraft – which eventually contributed to Stoltenberg's departure from the Finance Ministry in 1989, the proposals were ultimately largely implemented.

Sweden: A Social Democratic Paradise?

In the 1970s and 1980s Sweden, more than any other country, was seen by many as some sort of social democratic paradise. Even today, research on equality and satisfaction among the population gives the country top ranking. The Social Democratic Party governed Sweden without a break from the end of the Second World War to the 1970s. Until the middle of that decade, the government pushed to expand the social state, and as

[37] Wirsching, *Abschied*, p. 278; and Bökenkamp, *Ende*, pp. 273–4.

a result Swedish tax and expenditure ratios steadily increased.[38] In 1974 Sweden had a public expenditure ratio of 48.1 per cent and a tax rate of 48.8 per cent, both of which were the highest in the world.[39]

In 1976 the opposition won an election that led to the formation of a coalition government consisting of three conservative parties. During the election campaign, each of these parties had urged tax reductions, but these benefited different groups due to the diverse nature of the different parties' supporters. Subsequently, the coalition partners were unable to agree to comprehensive reforms and the existing system remained largely in place. Nevertheless, a variety of so-called tax loopholes were created for each group of political supporters and generous subsidies were distributed.[40] The rise in the tax rate due to bracket-creep and increases in VAT did nothing to diminish this. The exorbitant subsidies, however, caused the budget deficit to soar to 13 per cent of GDP during the coalition's last year in office.[41] Furthermore, the public expenditure ratio and the tax rate rose continuously and had reached 64.6 per cent and 58.3 per cent, respectively, by 1981. In both cases, these were again world record highs.[42]

In 1982 the Social Democrats returned to power. Confronted with widespread dissatisfaction over the tax loopholes, along with very high tax rates for average income earners, they established a tax reform commission whose work would extend over two legislative periods. In 1988 this led to a reform of the budget process and in 1992 a major tax reform, called the 'tax reform of the century'.[43] The Social Democrats and the Liberals reached an agreement on these finance policy amendments,

---

[38] Nils Elvander, *Svensk skattepolitik 1945–1970. En studie i partiers och organisationers funktioner* (Stockholm: Rabén & Sjögren, 1972). For an overview of the political development with a strong emphasis on budget policy, see Sven Steinmo, *The Evolution of Modern States: Sweden, Japan and the United States* (Cambridge: Cambridge University Press 2010), pp. 30–87.

[39] Organisation for Economic Cooperation and Development, *Historical Statistics 1960–1986* (Paris: OECD 1988), p. 64.

[40] Axel Hadenius, *Spelet om skatten. Rationalistisk analys av politiskt beslutsfattande* (Lund: Nordstedt & Söner 1981).

[41] Gary Burtless, 'Taxes, Transfers, and Swedish Labor Supply', in Barry P. Bosworth and Alice M. Rivlin, *The Swedish Economy* (Washington, DC: The Brookings Institution, 1987), pp. 185–239; and Hugh Heclo and Henrik Madsen, *Policy and Politics in Sweden: Principled Pragmatism* (Philadelphia: Temple University Press, 1987), pp. 62–79.

[42] Organisation for Economic Cooperation and Development, *Historical Statistics 1960–1986*, p. 64.

[43] Hakan Malmer, Annika Persson and Åke Tengblad (eds.), *Århundradets skattereform* (Stockholm: Fritzes, 1994); Jonas Agell, Peter Englund and Jan Södersten, *Svensk skattepolitik i teori och praktik: 1991 års skattereform* (Stockholm: Fritzes, 1995); Jonas Agell, Peter Englund and Jan Södersten, 'The Swedish Tax Reform', *Swedish Economic Policy Review*, 2 (1995), 219–28.

despite staunch resistance from many of the trade unions. During the course of these reforms, consumption taxes and social contributions were increased, the tax base was broadened and taxes on company earnings were reduced. Likewise, the highest rate for corporate taxes was cut from 52 per cent to 30 per cent. The reform amounted to a total of 97.3 billion crowns, of which 89.1 billion was used to reduce income taxes and corporate taxes and 8.2 billion for expenditures to balance out the resulting changes.

It was calculated that the reform would pay for itself, thanks to the expansion of the tax base and the increase in indirect taxes, but this assumption proved to be optimistic, for in 1991 the government faced a loss of 2.3 billion crowns. Of the 95.1 billion crowns collected to finance the tax reform, 38.6 billion came from expanding the tax base for capital income tax and property taxation, 28.4 billion from increasing indirect taxes and 12.7 billion from increasing the income tax base. The rest came from other, smaller-scale initiatives. The reform mainly benefited high-income earners, but proved highly disadvantageous for part-time workers, including a particularly large number of women. After all, they had little to gain from the tax reductions but had to pay their full share of the increase in indirect taxes.[44]

The reform was a response to Sweden's development, which since the 1970s had strongly relied on comprehensive taxation of the masses and kept corporate and capital taxes relatively low or provided them with considerable tax loopholes. The emphasis thus shifted from taxing labour to taxing consumption. Nevertheless, during the 1980s Sweden still ranked among those countries that collected the largest proportion of their total revenues from taxing labour, whereas its taxation of consumption tended to be lower than the European average. Hence, the reform moved the country closer to the European average. Since the 1980s, Sweden has been widely recognised as a country that combines high productivity and the welfare state, although the costs of the latter are primarily borne by the lower and middle classes.[45] However, it should be stressed to a greater degree than by the studies referred to here that Sweden is a country with a relatively high degree of inequality in terms of market income, which is strongly offset, particularly by social benefits, to make Sweden one of the most egalitarian countries in

---

[44] Leibfritz, Thornton and Bibbee, *Taxation*, pp. 122–4.
[45] Aaron Wildavsky and Carolyn Webber, *A History of Taxation and Expenditure in the Western World* (New York: Simon & Schuster, 1986); Kato, *Regressive Taxation*; and Peter H. Lindert, *Growing Public: Social Spending and Economic Growth since the 18th Century* (Cambridge: Cambridge University Press, 2004).

the world with regard to disposable income. This position, which had been achieved by the 1970s, was slightly eroded during the 1980s due to the tax reforms.[46]

France under François Mitterrand: '(Pseudo) Keynesianism in One Country'?

The countries in the tax group defined by Peters as southern European must have felt the least pressure to introduce changes, particularly since the shift introduced by Thatcher in Britain from income and property taxes to consumer taxes and social contributions had already been made in these countries many years before. France is a prime example. Due to its economic structure, which is characterised by many small companies and widespread tax evasion, the French government decided early on to approve many legal loopholes for wage and income taxes, combined with an extremely low entry-level tax rate. At the same time, in an effort to collect sufficient revenues, the French government significantly increased social contributions and sales taxes, which are much more difficult to evade.

As a result, there were hardly any tax protests in France during the 1970s.[47] When the Socialist François Mitterrand was elected president in 1981[48] after many years of conservative governments, he launched policies that in many areas stood in direct contrast to Reagan's and Thatcher's.[49] Faced with high inflation and rising unemployment, the French Socialists decided to boost the economy with state aid. In 1981 a solidarity tax for the wealthy was introduced. Furthermore, 100,000 new jobs were created in the public sector, and minimum wages, pensions, and allowances for children and housing were increased by 20–50 per cent.[50] At the same time, the government nationalised more companies, placing thirteen

---

[46] Chen Wang and Koen Caminada, 'Leiden LIS Budget Incidence Fiscal Redistribution Dataset' (2011), available online: www.lisdatacenter.org/resources/other-databases (accessed 11 June 2015).

[47] For more on the constant dwindling of tax protests from the 1950s to the 1980s in France, see Harold L. Wilensky, *Rich Democracies: Political Economy, Public Policy, and Performance* (Berkeley, CA: University of California Press, 2002), pp. 365–7.

[48] Pierre Favier and Michel Martin-Roland, *La Décennie Mitterrand*, vol. 1: *Les ruptures (1981–1984)* (Paris: Seuil, 1990).

[49] It should be stressed that the French system was also very state-centred under conservative governments.

[50] Mark I. Vail, *Recasting Welfare Capitalism: Economic Adjustment in Contemporary France and Germany* (Philadelphia: Temple University Press, 2010), pp. 60–1; Vivien A. Schmidt, *From State to Market: The Transformation of French Business and Government* (Cambridge: Cambridge University Press, 1996), pp. 107–8.

of the twenty largest French corporations in government hands.[51] The primary objective here was to use redistribution and the government's expenditure policy to boost consumption and economic growth and thus reduce unemployment. In view of the stark contrast between this and the trend in nearly all leading industrialised nations, Timothy B. Smith calls this '(Pseudo) Keynesianism in one country'.[52] Even with the new tax on the rich, the French tax system remained the most regressive in Europe. However, the proportion of social spending in government expenditures, which had already been relatively high, increased considerably with these policies. The public expenditure ratio in 1983 was 52 per cent, by far the highest among the G7 states.[53]

This course led to an increase in inflation and a rise in the government deficit. What is more, it sparked a flight of capital from France and resulted in three devaluations of the franc. The government introduced an initial cost-cutting programme in June 1982, but this could not stem the tide.[54] In March 1983, the French government had to choose whether to maintain its economic policies, which would have forced it to leave the European Monetary System, or to chart a new course.[55] Mitterrand decided in favour of the latter, a decision that resulted in the Communists leaving the government. The government then switched to a rigid policy of austerity. The Delors Plan, introduced in 1983, called for expenditure cutbacks amounting to 15 billion francs – the lion's share from the social budget – and the elimination of tax incentives to the tune of 11 billion francs, which primarily affected state-owned companies.[56] This radical turnaround from a state economic programme to a strict austerity course, with much greater cutbacks in social spending than in the United States or Britain, was possible in part because the French political system has few veto players. The government was thus able to push through changes without having to contend with strong institutional resistance in the state apparatus. The policy changes of 1983 are considered by some to mark

---

[51] Peter Hall, *Governing the Economy: The Politics of State Intervention in Britain and France* (Oxford: Oxford University Press, 1986), p. 194.

[52] Timothy B. Smith, *France in Crisis: Welfare, Inequality and Globalization since 1980* (Cambridge: Cambridge University Press, 2004), p. 97.

[53] Organisation for Economic Cooperation and Development, *Historical Statistics 1960–1986*, p. 64.

[54] Hall, *Governing*, pp. 199–200.

[55] David Cameron, 'Exchange Rate Politics in France: The Regime-Defining Choices of the Mitterrand Presidency', in Anthony Daley (ed.), *The Mitterrand Era: Policy Alternatives and Political Mobilization in France* (New York: New York University Press, 1996), pp. 56–82.

[56] Schmidt, *From State to Market*, pp. 110–13.

the collapse of the entire *dirigisme* system which constituted the foundation for the French post-war economy.[57]

In the literature, France's development in the years 1981–3 is often
cited as proof that a political policy that is strongly based on redistribution was hardly feasible after the collapse of Bretton Woods, due to the
growing tendency to lift restrictions on movement of capital, accompanied by increasing international interdependencies, because the risks of
the flight of capital posed too much of a threat.[58] The austerity programme was successful to the extent that it reduced inflation from 12
per cent (in 1982) to 6 per cent (in 1986), but unemployment continued to rise from 8 per cent (in 1982) to 10 per cent (in 1986).[59] This
did not do the Socialists much good at the next election, and in 1986
the balance of power changed in parliament, leading to the formation of
a new government. The incoming Prime Minister, Jacques Chirac,
abolished the tax on the rich, but the Socialists reintroduced it in 1988
and it is still in force today. Nonetheless, it has done little to alter the
rather unprogressive character of the French tax system. But it did
make some impact in one respect: Thomas Piketty and Emmanuel Saez
stress that the tax played a decisive role in ensuring that the assets of
the richest 1 per cent of the population in France have not increased as
massively in recent years as they have in Britain and, above all, in the
United States.[60] What is more, France was one of the few leading
OECD countries in which inequality in disposable income decreased
slightly during the 1980s.[61] Even today, though, the French tax system
has a very minimal redistributive impact compared to other countries.
France is thus to a much greater extent than Sweden a country that
finances its comprehensive welfare state primarily through indirect taxes
and social contributions, and enlists relatively little support in this
respect from its high-income earners.

[57] Jonah D. Levy, *Tocqueville's Revenge: State, Society and Economy in Contemporary France*
(Cambridge, MA: Harvard University Press, 1999), pp. 23–56; Vivien Schmidt,
'Running on Empty: The End of Dirigisme in French Economic Leadership', *Modern
& Contemporary France*, 5/2 (1997), 229–41. Arguing for survival, see Ben Clift, 'The
New Political Economy of Dirigisme', *British Journal of Politics and International
Relations*, 8/3 (2006), 388–409.
[58] Hall, *Governing*, p. 196.
[59] Jeffrey Sachs and Charles Wyplosz, 'The Economic Consequences of President
Mitterrand', *Economic Policy* 1/2 (1986), 264.
[60] Thomas Piketty and Emmanuel Saez, 'How Progressive is the U.S. Federal Tax
System? A Historical and International Comparison', *Economic Perspectives* 21/1
(2006), 19.
[61] Chen Wang and Koen Caminada, 'Leiden LIS Budget Incidence Fiscal Redistribution
Dataset' (2011), available online: www.lisdatacenter.org/resources/other-databases
(accessed 11 June 2015).

Convergence and Divergence in the Tax Systems of the 1980s

In contrast to the expectations and efforts of many European governments, the average tax rate in these countries did not fall. Instead, further expansion took place, but in a significantly slower form than before.

In the 1970s, the tax rate in the nine EEC countries rose by 5 per cent but in the 1980s by only 1.3 per cent. However, the four-country comparison in Table 5.1 shows the special position occupied by Sweden (which joined what then became the EU 15 in 1995): while Germany, France and Britain remained within a 5 per cent margin of the EU mean value, Sweden was 15 per cent above this in 1990. The 'reform of the century' in 1990/1 only briefly changed this pattern. The tax rate dropped in 1994 to just under 50 per cent, but by 1997 it was over 54 per cent again. It is also clear that Britain had a higher tax rate in 1970 than France and Germany, but that situation had reversed by 1980. The differences between the four countries increase considerably when one examines the tax structure.

Table 5.2 shows an extremely high degree of consistency with regard to the average distribution among the three main types of taxes in the

Table 5.1. *Total taxation as a percentage of GDP*[62]

	Germany	France	Sweden	UK	EU 15
1970	35.7	35.1	–	37.2	34.4
1980	41.6	41.7	49.1	36.6	38.3
1985	41.6	44.5	50.0	38.7	40.4
1990	39.5	43.8	55.8	38.0	40.6

Table 5.2. *Tax groups as a percentage of overall tax revenues*[63]

	Germany			France			Sweden			UK			EU 15		
	D	I	S	D	I	S	D	I	S	D	I	S	D	I	S
1970	31	37	32	21	43	36	–			47	38	15	31	39	30 (EU-9)
1980	31	32	38	21	37	43	44	27	29	44	38	18	33	33	34
1985	31	30	39	21	36	43	42	33	25	45	36	19	33	33	34
1990	29	32	40	21	35	44	42	31	27	46	36	18	33	33	34
1997	24	30	46	24	34	42	42	30	28	42	39	19	32	33	35

Note: D = direct taxes, I = indirect taxes, S = social contributions.

[62] Eurostat, *Structures of the Taxation Systems in the European Union 1970–1997* (Luxembourg: Eurostat, 2000), p. 68.
[63] Ibid., pp. 76, 94, 112.

fifteen EU countries. In the 1980s, direct taxes, indirect taxes and social contributions accounted for one-third of overall tax revenues. During this period, no trend can be observed in the direction of regressive indirect taxes and social contributions in the group of fifteen EU countries. It is apparent that the two countries that are the furthest apart in terms of their tax rates, Sweden and Britain, have great similarities in terms of the tax structure: an above-average proportion of revenues from direct taxes and a below-average proportion from social contributions. Judging from the mix of taxes, Britain and Sweden have comparatively progressive systems, whereas Germany has a slightly regressive and France a strongly regressive system.

At first glance, it is surprising that, despite the drastic increase in VAT introduced by Thatcher in the 1980s, the importance of indirect taxes in Britain has not increased, in contrast to what is suggested in most of the literature. The reason for this is that tax rates for individual goods (excise duties) were reduced.[64] The literature also pays little attention to the remarkable convergence between Germany and France with regard to the three main types of revenues, in particular with respect to the harmonisation in the percentage of direct taxes in 1997 after these figures were so clearly divergent in 1980. This is an impressive development, which can primarily be attributed to the harmonisation of income taxes. Their proportion of overall tax revenues rose in France between 1980 and 1997, from 13 per cent to 18 per cent, while it fell during the same period in Germany from 25 per cent to 19 per cent. This convergence can be dated to the introduction of the solidarity tax by the Mitterrand administration in France and the income tax reductions of the first two Kohl cabinets in Germany in the 1980s, although it accelerated in the 1990s.

This analysis provides a completely different picture from that suggested by Junko Kato. She merely notes that the proportion of indirect taxes in the 1980s and 1990s fell in France, while it rose in Sweden. Consequently, she presents Sweden as a country that primarily relies on revenues from VAT, while she presents France as a country that finances its expansion of the welfare state from social contributions.[65] Furthermore, France is presented as a country with a tax system that dramatically sets it apart from the other industrialised nations.[66]

That Kato overlooks the fact that France already relied more heavily on indirect taxes in 1970 than did Sweden means that her analysis is

[64] Paul Baker and Vanessa Brechling, 'The Impact of Excise Duty Changes on Retail Prices in the UK', *Fiscal Studies* 13/2 (1992), 48–65.
[65] Kato, *Regressive Taxation*, ch. 2.
[66] Ibid., p. 94.

distorted. In 1997 Sweden still had higher direct taxes than those in France, whereas its proportion of indirect taxes was lower. Hence, in the 1990s Sweden's highly extensive welfare state was more strongly financed by progressive income taxes than similar systems in most other western European countries. To confuse the picture further, Kato fails to take into account the marked process of harmonisation between France and Germany.

All in all, it appears that Kato's main hypothesis relies on a coincidental correlation between two factors rather than that a truly conclusive correlation proves there was path dependency. Her theory that those countries that introduced a VAT before 1973 were better able to expand the welfare state gives too much credit to VAT as a source of revenue for this expansion. In fact, the data for the nine EEC countries in 1970 indicate that the proportion of overall tax revenues that came from indirect taxes tended to decline in some of the western European countries between 1970 and 1990. The example of Britain also shows that the expansion of VAT was offset by reductions in other indirect taxes. The data for the nine EEC countries suggest that this same development also took place there during the first half of the 1970s.[67] A more consistent hypothesis would be that the expansion of the welfare state after the crisis was possible primarily due to a combination of regressive indirect taxes and social contributions. Nevertheless, it should not be forgotten that in Sweden and Denmark the expansion of the welfare state in the 1970s and 1980s was among the most comprehensive of its kind and both countries financed this, to a greater degree than most other countries, with revenues from progressive income taxes.

If one looks for some kind of neo-liberal convergence of the various tax systems, there is no recognisable shift towards regressive taxes, at least not for the European countries in the 1980s. A slightly different picture emerges when one examines in some depth the individual taxes. For instance, in the case of social contributions in Europe, the proportion paid by employees gradually increased, with a corresponding drop in the employers' share. This was particularly marked in Britain.[68] But changes to income tax were presumably of even greater importance to the overall impact of the tax system. The trend towards lowering the top tax rates in particular contributed to a reduction in the redistributive impact of the tax system.

Table 5.3 shows the importance of the struggles in which the CDU workers' wing was engaged. It was only in Germany that the entry-level

[67] Eurostat, *Structures*, pp. 80–8.
[68] Eurostat, *Structures*, pp. 114–21.

Table 5.3. *Changes in entry-level and top-level tax brackets, 1975–90*[69]

	1975		1985		1990		Change 1975–90	
	Entry	Highest	Entry	Highest	Entry	Highest	Entry	Highest
Germany	22	56	22	56	19	53	−3	−3
France	5	60	5	65	5	50	0	−10
United Kingdom	35	83	30	60	25	40	−10	−43
Sweden	32	85	35	80	30	50	−2	−35
United States	14	70	11	50	15	28	+1	−42
OECD	21	68	22	63	24	50	+3	−18

tax rate was cut as much as the top tax rate. This gives us one explanation of why in Germany inequality in post-tax income distribution rose moderately in comparison to that in the United States and Britain. Elsewhere, the top tax rate dropped more than the entry-level rate or, as in the United States and in the OECD average, the entry-level rate was even raised. In the OECD average, this meant that the difference between the entry-level and the top-level rates dropped by over 20 per cent, which considerably reduced the progressive impact of the income tax system. In Germany the situation was completely turned on its head within fifteen years. Although it had the lowest top income tax rate in 1975 among the countries examined here, in 1990 it had the highest. This runs counter to social science models that posit a high degree of static equilibrium with regard to the various tax systems in each country and tend to assess the transformation of tax systems as generally minimal in nature.

The main focus of political debates is the issue of the social impact of taxes and social contributions.

Table 5.4 perhaps best illustrates the differences between the countries. Whereas the difference in the Gini coefficient for market income is less than 50 points, and thus is relatively small, with regard to disposable income it exceeds 100 points between egalitarian Sweden (S 92) and far less egalitarian countries like Britain (UK 91) and the United States (US 91). In Sweden nearly half of the market income inequality is reduced by state action; in Germany (G 89) and France (F 89) it is reduced by roughly 40 per cent; and in the United States and the United Kingdom by less than 30 per cent.

---

[69] See Arnold Heidenheimer, Hugh Heclo and Carolyn Adams, *Comparative Public Policy* (New York: St Martin's Press, 1990), p. 211.

Table 5.4. *Fiscal redistribution in the five countries examined based on the Gini coefficient, 1989–92*[70]

	Market income	Disposable income	Total redistribution	Tax redistribution	Transfer redistribution	% Total redistribution	% Tax redistribution	Transfer redistribution	Tax	% Transfer
F 89	0.474	0.287	0.187	0.020	0.167	39	4	35	10	90
G 89	0.431	0.258	0.173	0.048	0.125	40	11	29	28	72
S 92	0.462	0.229	0.232	0.031	0.202	51	7	44	13	87
UK 91	0.475	0.336	0.139	0.030	0.109	29	6	23	21	79
US9 1	0.439	0.338	0.101	0.042	0.059	23	10	12	42	58

[70] Wang and Comida, 'Leiden LIS Budget Incidence Fiscal Redistribution Dataset'. See also the update on the LIS data in this volume, Chapter 8.

In Sweden, as in France, social transfers play a major role. This explains why taxes in France in particular have a negligible redistributive impact. Social transfers in the United States are much less pronounced – more than three times lower than in Sweden. Hence, taxes play a particularly important role in achieving a social balance in the United States. This impact was significantly curtailed by President Reagan, who introduced the largest inequality in terms of disposable income in the late 1980s. In the late 1980s, Germany's tax system had the greatest degree of redistribution. Since Germany also has the lowest Gini coefficient with regard to market income, it is (after Sweden in 1990) the country with the most egalitarian distribution of disposable income among the five countries studied.

Conclusion

In the 1970s, there were vehement tax protests in the liberal welfare states with highly progressive tax systems. Accordingly, the pressure to change was particularly strong there. The reforms to the tax system undertaken by Thatcher and Reagan were extensive and radiated out to countries with diverging tax systems. The pressure to change varies greatly, however, depending on individual national tax traditions. Nonetheless, there was a tendency in most western European countries to follow the trend and lower the top rates for income and corporate taxes, although this was rarely as comprehensive as it was in the United States or Britain. However, that is not to say that there was a clear shift towards particularly regressive taxes in the 1980s, as Kato and others maintain.

In effect, the changes in state financial policy, particularly in the United States and Britain, primarily benefited top earners and companies. By contrast, the gains made by the middle classes from tax reductions in many countries were offset by increases in sales taxes and VAT, as well as in social contributions. Nearly everywhere the reduction in the top tax rates ensured that society's most affluent members benefited the most. The governments thus fuelled the accumulation of large concentrations of wealth, which increased considerably during the 1990s and formed the basis for the rapid growth in the movement of speculative capital at the end of the twentieth century. In particular, the harmonisation of top tax rates led to a partial convergence of tax systems in the Western industrialised countries, and this process has continued since the 1990s. Yet even today it is possible to identify diverging tax systems, even if these differences are not as great as they were in the early 1970s.

6 The Swiss Tax Haven, the Bretton Woods System Crisis and the Globalisation of Offshore Finance

Christophe Farquet

Introduction

The late 1970s and early 1980s saw the simultaneous deregulation of international financial transactions, which followed the collapse of the Bretton Woods system, and the marked growth of banking activities linked to offshore finance. Following the first boom in the 1920s in reaction to the increase in taxation brought about by the First World War, the international tax evasion market contracted with the Great Depression of the 1930s, the Second World War and the post-war period of financial control. Cross-border wealth management expanded in conjunction with the liberalisation of economic flows and the rebuilding of savings in the West during the 1960s, a time characterised by heavy tax burdens on high incomes. However, the exponential growth of offshore finance really began with the transition to flexible exchange rates, the lifting of capital controls and the accelerated financialisation of the economy between the mid-1970s and the beginning of the 1980s. With the neo-liberal turn and the adoption of more relaxed policies on capital in Western countries, offshore finance became truly globalised in all the major financial centres. This globalisation brought with it an increased use of aggressive fiscal attraction practices, such as guaranteed banking secrecy, tax relief on non-resident investments and the granting of massive fiscal privileges to domicile companies, trusts and holding companies.

This chapter analyses the globalisation of offshore banking by examining the policies adopted in Switzerland. While the acceleration of capital movements stimulated, in the first instance, the influx of illegal foreign assets to the Swiss tax haven, the increase in offshore finance practices all over the world ultimately carried with it a double threat with regard to the nodal position Switzerland had acquired since the First World War as the world's leading cross-border asset manager. On the one hand, the fact that other financial centres had adopted similar or even more advantageous fiscal attraction practices than those in force in Switzerland reduced one of the key advantages that the Swiss banks

126

had in terms of attracting foreign assets. On the other, while both Western and developing countries faced an explosion in public debt and massive outflows of capital, more political demands for Switzerland not to accept tax-evading assets were voiced. However, and somewhat surprisingly, there was not a great deal of sustained pressure on the Swiss tax haven from the international community during the 1970s, with the most vociferous criticisms coming from within the Swiss Confederation itself. Even though domestic and international attacks on banking secrecy intensified from the end of the 1970s, the Swiss elites had succeeded in thwarting them all by the mid-1980s.

Based on a large sample of original archives, this chapter analyses the different initiatives deployed against the Swiss tax haven between 1971 and the beginning of the 1980s and shows how the main decision-making bodies in Switzerland – the government, the Swiss National Bank (SNB) and the Swiss Bankers Association (SBA) – managed, in the new economic environment, to secure a position for the Swiss financial industry in the vanguard of the international tax evasion market. It is worth highlighting the original contribution to research here. This defining moment in the construction of the Swiss tax haven, which probably represents, along with the two post-war periods, one of the most decisive stages in its evolution over the twentieth century, has never before been the subject of close study in Swiss banking historiography.[1] Indeed, the same is true for the history of offshore finance more generally: the study of its development and the attempts to regulate against it is still in its infancy.[2] However, the archives also provide fresh insight into the history of taxation from the 1970s onwards. This chapter shows that the well-known shift to the neo-liberal policies of international tax competition was simultaneously accelerated by the

---

[1] For the history of the Swiss tax haven and its banking secrecy until the end of the Second World War, see, for instance, C. Farquet, 'La Défense du paradis fiscal suisse avant la seconde guerre mondiale: une histoire internationale' (PhD thesis, Université de Lausanne, 2014); P. Hug, 'Steuerflucht und die Legende vom antinazistischen Ursprung des Bankgeheimnisses. Funktion und Risiko der moralischen Überhöhung des Finanzplatzes Schweiz', in J. Tanner and S. Weigel (eds.), *Gedächtnis, Geld und Gesetz: Vom Umgang mit der Vergangenheit des Zweiten Weltkrieges* (Zürich: vdf Hochschulverlag an der ETH Zürich, 2002), pp. 269–321; S. Guex, 'The Origins of the Swiss Banking Secrecy Law and its Repercussions for Swiss Federal Policy', *Business History Review* 74/2 (2000), 237–66.

[2] For a global view on the history of offshore finance, see R. Palan et al., *Tax Havens: How Globalization Really Works* (Ithaca, NY: Cornell University Press, 2010). For the history of regulation on international taxation, see T. Rixen, *The Political Economy of International Tax Governance* (Basingstoke: Palgrave Macmillan, 2008); T. Godefroy and P. Lascoumes, *Le Capitalisme clandestin. L'illusoire régulation des places* offshore (Paris: La Découverte, 2004); S. Picciotto, *International Business Taxation: A Study in the Internationalization of Business Regulation* (London: Weidenfeld and Nicolson, 1992).

globalisation of offshore finance and the leading Western governments' relative tolerance of it. In other words, fiscal competition took on a two-fold dimension after the Bretton Woods system collapsed. One aspect was the downward pressure on income tax rates with the so-called 'race to the bottom';[3] the other was the expansion of the international tax evasion market.

The Globalisation of Offshore Finance and the Swiss Tax Haven

The history of offshore finance, far from originating with the financial globalisation of the 1980s, is consubstantial with the history of taxation. From the beginning of the twentieth century, and particularly since the First World War, capital flight has sought to evade the progressive taxes that were introduced in the major European countries, by taking refuge in the financial centres of smaller countries. However, offshore finance began a new phase in its history following the collapse of the Bretton Woods system in around 1971 and reached a totally unprecedented level of expansion, particularly from the mid-1970s onwards. Despite the difficulty in quantifying illegal capital flows, there is a wealth of data that clearly support this observation. For example, between 1968 and 1978, the value of bank accounts held in tax havens increased from $10.6 billion to $384.9 billion, representing a twenty-fold growth in real terms.[4] This trend accelerated in the late 1970s and early 1980s and bank deposits from non-residents, other than banks, quintupled globally, rising from $149.1 billion to $796.1 billion between 1975 and 1985.[5]

This sharp acceleration in offshore activities during the 1970s and 1980s was conditioned by the fact that, with the end of the Bretton Woods system, where the guarantee of pegged exchange rates was supported by restrictions on financial movements,[6] the liberalisation of capital flows and financial markets facilitated offshore placements, while simultaneously pushing up the volume of mobile assets. The removal of capital controls by the United States in 1974 was followed by the progressive lifting of barriers to the expansion of international financial

---

[3] On tax competition during the 1980s, see A. J. Heidenheimer et al., *Comparative Public Policy: The Politics of Social Choice in America, Europe, and Japan* (New York: St Martin's Press, 1990), pp. 209–14; V. Tanzi, 'The Response of Other Industrial Countries to the U.S. Tax Reform Act', *National Tax Journal* 40/3 (1987), 339–55.

[4] *Tax Havens and Their Use by United States Taxpayers – An Overview*, Submitted by Richard Gordon, Special Counsel for International Taxation, 12 January 1981, p. 41.

[5] International Monetary Fund, *International Financial Statistics Yearbook* (Washington, DC: International Monetary Fund, 1986), pp. 78–81.

[6] B. Eichengreen, *Globalizing Capital: A History of the International Monetary System* (Princeton, NJ: Princeton University Press, 2008), pp. 91–133.

markets throughout Europe.[7] In the late 1970s and early 1980s two other factors were conducive to offshore finance. First, at the political level, the shift towards neo-liberalism in the West during this period was accompanied by a lenient attitude as far as international fiscal competition was concerned, since such competition helped to dismantle, or at least curb, funding for the welfare state. Between 1975 and 1990, while the top income tax rates were reduced by 42 and 43 per cent in the United States and Great Britain respectively, they decreased on average by 18 per cent in the OECD countries.[8] The loopholes offered by offshore finance, through the structural pressure that it exerted on tax systems, thus contributed to this programme of lowering the tax burden on capital. Second, on the demand side, the development of offshore markets was also influenced by an economic factor. The massive increase in oil revenues in the OPEC countries during the 1970s, on the one hand, and the untimely capital flows following the onset of the Latin America debt crisis in the early 1980s, on the other, both led to a massive amount of non-Western capital taking refuge in the principal financial centres, which stimulated their cross-border asset management activities.

As far as the international market for tax evasion was concerned, this new environment fuelled competition between banking centres to attract and retain capital. Alongside an increase in the use of the off-shore structures that were already operational (banking secrecy and holding companies in Switzerland, Eurodollars in the City of London and island tax havens) all banking centres promoted the globalisation of international tax evasion practices. This competition, which has received little attention in the history of taxation or finance, is found in different practices. First, banking secrecy – that is to say, very loosely, the confidentiality of bank accounts in response to the requests of tax administrations – was strengthened in a number of medium-sized centres. In 1979 and 1981, Austria and Luxembourg adopted relatively similar legislation to that in force in Switzerland by further strengthening bank account confidentiality against inspection by state bodies.[9] With the liberalisation of capital flows, the taxation at source of non-resident

---

[7] E. Helleiner, *States and the Reemergence of Global Finance: From Bretton Woods to the 1990s* (Ithaca, NY: Cornell University Press, 1994), pp. 123–68.

[8] M. Buggeln, 'Steuern nach dem Boom. Die Öffentlichen Finanzen in den westlichen Industrienationen und ihre gesellschaftliche Verteilungswirkung', *Archiv für Sozialgeschichte*, 52 (2012), 86.

[9] On Austrian legislation, see Swiss Federal Archives (SFA), E 2010(A), 1995/313, vol. 577, Report of the Austrian Minister of Finance, 27 June 1983. On Luxembourg, see C. Schmitt and M.-P. Weides-Schaeffer, *Le secret bancaire en droit luxembourgeois* (Luxembourg: Banque internationale à Luxembourg, 1984), pp. 38–47.

assets was then relaxed with the aim of both retaining and attracting new foreign investment. This movement led the United States, Germany and even France, under its Socialist government, to abandon withholding taxes on interests in 1984. Finally, many new fiscal benefits were granted to foreign assets with the same goal in mind. As a typical example of this deregulation, the United States introduced the International Banking Facilities in December 1981, which are a set of privileges for bank trans-actions made from outside the country, including the abolition or reduc-tion of local state taxes.[10]

How far was the Swiss banking centre's vanguard position in the inter-national tax evasion market directly threatened by this globalisation of offshore finance that had emerged in the 1970s? Various statistics indicate that the Swiss Confederation was still the leader in international asset management in the late 1970s and early 1980s. First, in the biggest finan-cial market in the world, namely that of the United States, the Swiss tax haven was by far the main holder of shares and bonds, bringing in 28.5 per cent of all US dividends and interests transferred abroad in 1978 against the United Kingdom's 13.4 per cent.[11] This situation came about as a direct result of the Swiss banks' management of securities owned by non-residents. Second, while the Swiss market's share for non-resident bank deposits fell slightly between 1975 and 1984 (from 17.1 per cent to 15.2 per cent), placing Switzerland quite clearly behind the United Kingdom (from 14 per cent to 21.2 per cent),[12] these figures do not take into account the off-balance-sheet securities that were managed by the Swiss banks for foreign clients. Going by the few statistics available, these securities had already reached around US$60–70 billion in the mid-1970s, that is almost half of all global offshore deposits listed by the International Monetary Fund. These deposits then grew exponen-tially at the beginning of the 1980s. Including assets in Swiss hands, they rose in 1986 to approximatively US$770 billion.[13] Third, Switzerland retained a hegemonic position – at least within Europe and as long as Liechtenstein, whose activities were closely intertwined with the those of the Swiss banks, was included – in the formation of domicile companies,

---

[10] M. Moffett and A. Stonehill, 'International Banking Facilities Revisited', *Journal of International Financial Management and Accounting* 1/1 (1989), 88–103.

[11] *Tax Havens and Their Use by United States Taxpayers*, 12 January 1981, p. 177.

[12] International Monetary Fund, *International Financial Statistics Yearbook* (Washington, DC: IMF, 1986), pp. 78–81.

[13] For the first figure, see *Notice économique de l'UBS*, November 1975. The securities under management are evaluated at 300–350 billion Swiss francs, half of them owned by foreign owners. For the second figure in 1986 (1387 billion Swiss francs): M. Mazbouri et al., 'Finanzplatz Schweiz', in P. Halbeisen et al. (eds.), *Wirtschaftsgeschichte der Schweiz im 20. Jahrhundert* (Basel: Schwabe, 2012), p. 477.

used by both the multinationals and the wealthy to hide or channel their incomes and capital. According to the OECD, in 1977, Switzerland had more than 17,000 holding companies, whereas the number of letterbox companies in Liechtenstein grew between 1972 and the beginning of the 1980s from 20,000 to 40,000. Their closest rival, Luxembourg, harboured only 5,000 holding companies in 1977, a figure that must certainly have doubled since 1970.[14]

However, the situation for the Swiss tax haven was becoming precarious in the face of the globalisation of offshore practices that had begun at the end of the 1970s. Contrary to popular belief, in terms of taxation the legendary Swiss banking secrecy was dependent not so much on Article 47 of the Banking Act of 1934 – which guaranteed the automatic application of penal sanctions in cases where employees of a financial institution breached confidentiality – as on a set of federal and cantonal legislations and on international law agreements, which ensured compliance with this article in cases of tax evasion.[15] While ostensibly iconoclastic, this interpretation was nevertheless supported at the time by members of both the SNB and the SBA,[16] as well as by a number of renowned banking secrecy legal specialists.[17] At the end of the 1970s and beginning of the 1980s, finance centres like Luxembourg had adopted banking legislation that provided a greater guarantee of banking secrecy than Article 47, and some countries even introduced laxer tax rules than those in force in Switzerland in terms of monitoring bank accounts. For example, according to a report from the OECD's Committee on Fiscal Affairs, the Portuguese and Irish administrations went as far as not infringing banking secrecy in cases of active tax fraud, whereas in Switzerland, with a few exceptions, only tax evasion by not disclosing liable assets to the tax authorities was covered by bank confidentiality.[18] Moreover, aside from the legal friability of banking secrecy,

---

[14] Archives of the OECD (AOECD), CFA/WP8/82.13, Note by the Secretariat, 24 May 1982.

[15] However, the historical debate concentrated on Article 47. See Robert U. Vogler, *Das Schweizer Bankgeheimnis: Entstehung, Bedeutung, Mythos* (Zürich: Verein für Finanzgeschichte, 2005); Hug, 'Steuerflucht und die Legende vom antinazistischen Ursprung des Bankgeheimnisses. Funktion und Risiko der moralischen Überhöhung des Finanzplatzes Schweiz'; Guex, 'The Origins of the Swiss Banking Secrecy Law and its Repercussions for Swiss Federal Policy'.

[16] Archives of the SBA (ASBA), Minutes of the *Verwaltungsrat*, 19 June 1977, p. 25, and 29 September 1977, pp. 7–8; Archives of the SNB (ASNB), 1241, Report of Ehrsam, Director of the SNB, 16 May 1975; Minutes of the Governing Board of the SNB, 91, 11 February 1982, p. 173.

[17] See, for instance, Maurice Aubert et al., *Le Secret bancaire suisse* (Berne: Ed. Stämpfli, 1982), pp. 445–8.

[18] AOECD, DAF/CFA/WP8/81.8, Note by the Secretariat, 4 September 1981.

the Swiss tax system became internationally uncompetitive as soon as the focus was directed away from the usual comparative taxation indices – the overall tax burden or theoretical tax rates – and towards taxes that squeezed offshore activities directly. Although these taxes might have been reduced by double taxation agreements, the rate of withholding tax on interests and dividends – which has remained at 35 per cent since 1976 – was one of the highest among the developed countries.[19] The same was also partly true for the system of tax privileges granted to holding companies with regard to the legislation of Liechtenstein, Luxembourg and even the Netherlands,[20] not to mention the total tax exemption granted to companies in certain large island tax havens, such as the Bahamas and Bermuda.

This situation should not be overstated, however. The fiscal attractiveness of the Swiss financial centre rested not so much on its domestic legislation as on two principles that secured a very large tax reduction on foreign clients' assets once these had passed into the hands of the Swiss bankers. First, stimulated by the highly decentralised tax system, a particularly relaxed interpretation of the rules of law was applied by the Swiss administration. This, coupled with the internationalisation of certain banking activities, left the Swiss banks with a lot of room for manoeuvre for tax evasion. For instance, in response to the increase in international fiscal competition, a very rapid, non-state-regulated development of typically Swiss accounts, the fiduciary deposits, followed in the 1970s. These were off-balance-sheet cash deposits, which the bank placed, with no guarantee to the client, in a foreign account in order to evade the withholding tax on interests in the Swiss Confederation.[21] They grew from 43,693 billion to 229,031 billion Swiss francs between 1974 and 1984.[22] A second comparative advantage for the financial centre was the corpus of double taxation agreements signed between the Swiss Confederation and twenty-two countries at the end of the 1970s.[23] These agreements

[19] B. Christensen, 'Switzerland's Role as an International Financial Centre', *IMF Occasional Paper* (1986), 37: in the mid-1980s tax rates on dividends and banking interests were respectively 25 per cent and 0 per cent in Germany; 20 per cent and 20 per cent in Japan; 5–15 per cent and 30 per cent in the United Kingdom; 30 per cent and 0 per cent in the United States.

[20] For the situation in the mid-1980s, see P. Hess, *Der Holding-Standort 'Schweiz': ein steuerlicher Vergleich mit dem Ausland* (Basel: Schweizerische Bankiervereinigung, 1987), p. 25.

[21] More than 90 per cent of these accounts were owned by foreign clients, and they were mainly denominated in US dollars. See ASNB, Minutes of the Governing Board of the SNB, 487, 21 July 1978.

[22] *Historical Time Series of the SNB*, Series 5: 'Banks in Switzerland'.

[23] G. Menétrey, 'Droit fiscal international 1968–1977', *Annuaire suisse de droit international* 34 (1978), 247–87.

offered tax relief at source on the foreign investments of Swiss banks and, with the exception of one ambiguous article in the 1951 agreement with the United States and a few cosmetic clauses, made no mention of any measures to assist foreign administrations tackling tax evasion. By assuring double tax relief on assets under management at the domicile of its owner and at the source of the income, Switzerland differentiated itself both from the smaller tax havens – which did not have such a vast network of agreements and whose external investments were consequently subject to taxation at source – and from other major financial centres, most of whose agreements were coupled with anti-avoidance measures that allowed the countries to identify and tax the holders of expatriate assets.[24]

Half-Hearted Attacks on the Swiss Tax Haven during the Bretton Woods Crisis

The competitiveness of Switzerland's tax system – its main attraction as far as capital flight was concerned, alongside its political stability, the strength of its currency and the deregulation of its banking sector – was thus founded on principles that were vulnerable to attack in the 1970s. At the international level, because of the determining role of the double taxation agreements in the protection of banking secrecy and fiscal attractiveness, Switzerland had made itself vulnerable to demands for renegotiation from foreign governments in the context of the Bretton Woods crisis and the disruptive capital movements that had come to the fore at this time. It is not surprising that the first real attack on Swiss banking secrecy should have come from the United States, the pillar of the monetary system and one of the main victims of capital flight. The US administration had been a repeated critic of the Swiss tax haven since the late 1950s, not only because of tax losses due to international tax evasion but also because the attractiveness of the Swiss financial centre fuelled the US balance-of-payments deficits. Following five years of negotiations, in 1973 the US government managed to sign a mutual legal assistance agreement with the Swiss Confederation. This agreement opened up the opportunity for limited cooperation between the courts in tax evasion cases related to organised crime in Switzerland. While the agreement was the first of its kind to include a clause linked to taxation, it nevertheless constituted, by virtue of its highly targeted nature, only a minor attack on the attractiveness of the Swiss offshore market.[25]

[24] AOECD, DAF/CFA/75.18, Note by the Secretariat, 1 October 1975.
[25] 'Message du Conseil fédéral à l'Assemblée fédérale … (du 28 août 1974)', *Feuille fédérale* 2/39 (1974), 582–631.

During the 1970s, negotiations on international taxation mainly took place multilaterally between Western countries under the auspices of the OECD's Committee on Fiscal Affairs. Created in 1956 by the Organisation for European Economic Cooperation (OEEC), and initially called the Fiscal Committee, this commission was holding discussions on international taxation for the Paris-based organisation with the fundamental aim of resolving the problem of double taxation of foreign investments. These debates resulted, most notably, in the creation of a model agreement on double taxation in 1963.[26] Integrating with the core vision of the OEEC's and subsequently the OECD's political agenda – that is, the liberalisation of economic flows within European countries – this programme was partly called into question in the context of the economic crisis and the collapse of the international monetary system from 1971 onwards. With the increase in public deficits in the 1970s, political pressure opposing practices that attracted illegal capital was brought to bear by a coalition, led by Germany and France and supported by the US Treasury, of heavily tax-burdened European governments. France's voice was all the more influential because, at the time, the Committee was chaired by one of its Finance Ministry's directors, Pierre Kerlan, who was a well-informed critic of tax havens. In June 1974, the OECD's Committee on Fiscal Affairs set up a subcommittee charged with the responsibility for launching a programme of discussions on international tax avoidance and evasion.[27] This initiative ultimately resulted, two and a half years later, in the creation of a permanent working group, named Working Party 8, which was wholly dedicated to investigating this topic.[28] Criticisms were also being repeatedly levelled at offshore centres by other working groups during this period, particularly on the subject of the taxation of multinational companies. The problem of transferring profits to low-tax zones through transfer price manipulations was hotly debated, and this discussion led to the issuing of a set of recommendations for governments to counter these practices.[29]

Nevertheless, the OECD discussions failed to produce a single outcome that was capable of challenging the expansion of offshore markets until, in 1977, the Committee on Fiscal Affairs finalised the revision of the 1963 double taxation model agreement. This had been given the

---

[26] AOECD, C(63)87, Report of the Fiscal Committee of the OECD, 6 July 1963.
[27] AOECD, CFA(74/15), Note by the Secretariat, 'L'évasion et la france fiscale [*sic*]', 13 December 1974.
[28] AOECD, CFA(76/10), Note by the Secretariat, 13 December 1976.
[29] AOECD, DAF/CFA/75.13, Note by the Secretariat, 12 June 1975. These discussions took place within Working Party 6.

highest priority because it influenced interstate negotiations. As far as tax evasion was concerned, however, the revision did not include a major overhaul of the only article addressing the exchange of information between national administrations, namely Article 26. This article offered, in compliance with domestic practices and legislation, an extensive guarantee to banking secrecy.[30] In other words, the post-war consensus among international organisations – according to which fiscal multilateralism was, above all, aimed at reducing tax charges on foreign investments – had remained only slightly ruffled in the period prior to 1977. Similarly, in bilateral relations before 1978, the Swiss tax haven had had to face no increase of international criticism of its banking secrecy. The Bretton Woods system crisis, far from leading to an orchestrated attack on the Swiss tax haven, did not even engender any strong tensions in external fiscal relations. European integration certainly acted to harmonise the tax systems, and this was accompanied by a denunciation of dumping by tax havens, both within and outside the Community. It was not only budgetary issues that were at play, but also monetary problems. In 1975, for example, during negotiations between the Swiss and French leaders concerning the Swiss Confederation's possible membership of the European system of monetary stabilisation (dubbed the 'monetary snake'), Pierre Kerlan made Switzerland's entry contingent on its participation in the fight against international tax evasion, 'since capital flight ... contributes to driving the Swiss franc upward'.[31] While the Swiss leaders chose to remain on the margins of the 'snake', the head of the Federal Finance Department, Georges-André Chevallaz, noted a year later that 'foreign pressures ... are still not very strong, and this is due to the fact that the member states of the European Communities have not yet succeeded in reaching an agreement among themselves'.[32]

International discussions remained, therefore, largely consonant with the defence of the fiscal attractiveness of Switzerland, solidly supported within the Confederation by the government, the federal administration and the major economic associations. During the 1970s,

---

[30] C. Farquet, 'Exploring the failure of International Tax Regulations throughout the Twentieth Century', Working Papers of the Paul Bairoch Institute of Economic History, University of Geneva, 2016.

[31] 'Note sur des pourparlers franco-suisses en liaison avec l'entrée de la Suisse dans le serpent monétaire européen', Bern, 19 September 1975, p. 2 (www.dodis.ch/39713). See also T. Straumann, *Fixed Ideas of Money. Small States and Exchange Rate Regimes in Twentieth-Century Europe* (Cambridge: Cambridge University Press, 2010), p. 295.

[32] SFA, E 2001 E, 1988/16, vol. 853, Minutes of the Commission of the *Conseil des Etats* 'chargée de l'examen des projets d'arrêtés fédéraux approuvant des accords italo-suisses ...', 13 August 1976, p. 3.

Swiss international fiscal policy thus focused on continuing the work of previous periods by expanding its network of double taxation agreements. Eleven new bilateral agreements were signed between 1971 and 1977, seven of which were with countries with no previous conventions. These agreements offered substantial tax relief on dividends, interest payments and royalties received abroad by Swiss banks and industries, without any compensatory incentives to combat tax evasion. They involved a greater loss of budgetary revenue for the foreign states than for Switzerland due to the latter's net external asset position. This aggressive strategy turned into a real show of strength when, in accordance with a programme developed at the beginning of the decade by the federal administration and the government,[33] Swiss leaders succeeded in implementing it for the first time with a series of non-Western countries in the midst of an economic crisis. In addition, in 1976, at the end of negotiations that had begun five decades earlier, the Swiss government signed a double taxation agreement with Italy, the only major European economic partner not yet in possession of a bilateral fiscal convention with the Swiss Confederation. Italy was not only one of the main importers of Swiss capital, it was also one of the Swiss banks' offshore services' principal clients.[34]

The facts are unequivocal. International negotiations on tax evasion evinced a remarkable lethargy in the context of the 1970s economic and monetary crisis. The only tangible progress made in this respect was the unilateral measures, set out in national legislations at the beginning of the 1970s, against tax havens and the illegal transfer of profits through domicile companies. On 8 September 1972 Germany passed a law, targeted particularly at Switzerland and Liechtenstein, preventing the domicile of German companies in such countries. The law considered certain types of income from letterbox companies as directly taxable sums for their German shareholders. Belgium and France subsequently adopted new legislation in 1973 and 1974 that automatically surcharged multinational groups that operated in tax havens.[35] Any attempts by poorer countries to stop the wealth haemorrhage came up against not only the federal authorities' determination not to cooperate in the identification of foreign Swiss bank account holders, but also difficulties in

---

[33] Report of the Federal Finance Department, 18 August 1971 (dodis.ch/35235). Pakistan was the only non-Western underdeveloped country with which Switzerland had signed before the 1970s a double taxation agreement.

[34] 'Message du Conseil fédéral concernant une convention de double imposition avec l'Italie (5 Mai 1976)', *Feuille fédérale* 2/20 (1976), 653–87.

[35] For a comparison between these laws, see AOECD, CFA(75)16, Note by the Secretariat, 15 December 1975.

equipping themselves with an arsenal of legislation akin to that of the wealthy countries. The issues associated with capital flight from non-Western countries, and particularly the concealment of potentates' and dictators' wealth, resulted in an increase on the previous decade in the number of legal cases. The biggest case was probably that relating to the significant assets of Emperor Haile Selassie, which had been deposited in Switzerland.[36] The Ethiopian government made an unsuccessful claim to recover this wealth when Selassie was deposed in 1974. Such international critics of banking secrecy, however, never made a big enough noise to have any real effect on the Swiss banks' asset management activities.[37]

Renewed Domestic Lobbying against Banking Secrecy in the Mid-1970s

While these international political pressures opposing banking secrecy continued, albeit half-heartedly, there was a revival of domestic criticism in the mid-1970s of the Swiss financial sector in general and of banking secrecy in particular. Within Switzerland, banking secrecy had met with broad approval from the main political forces since the beginning of the twentieth century, with the exception of the troubled world war and post-war periods. This assent was fundamentally based on a combination of three factors. First, in terms of political power relations, the structural weakness of the Swiss institutional left, whose Socialist Party had only ever received around a quarter of the votes at the federal elections for the lower house since the end of the First World War, meant it was unable to challenge one of the pillars of the Swiss economy. Second, at the financial level, because Switzerland was not a participant in the two world wars, the maintenance of what was a weak state by international standards stifled any desire to tax banking activities heavily. Third, the very broad consensus on the preservation of a strong currency within the Swiss Confederation – clearly influenced by the banking world's strength but also by the SNB's considerable autonomy and the export industry's preference for sophisticated, low-price-elasticity products – encouraged the adoption of policies that tended to increase the influx of foreign capital into Switzerland.

These factors, which were highly conducive to banking secrecy, were undermined from four quarters in the mid-1970s. First, increased

---

[36] SFA, E 2001E-01, 1987/78, vol. 265, Letters from Langenbacher, Swiss Ambassador in Addis Ababa, 7 October 1974 and 3 February 1975.

[37] For a survey on scandals linked to banking secrecy, see Vogler, *Das Schweizer Bankgeheimnis: Entstehung, Bedeutung*, pp. 80–96.

support for the Socialists in the 1974 federal elections, coupled with the growing influence of intellectuals from the new left, who focused on problems in the developing world, revived criticisms of the Swiss financial centre's welcoming of illegal capital. The leading figure in this movement, Jean Ziegler, a Genevan professor and parliamentarian, published *Une Suisse au-dessus de tout soupçon* (*Switzerland Exposed*) in 1976.[38] Written for a general audience, this book on the tax evasion and money laundering practices associated with the Swiss banks met with international success. Far from remaining merely an intellectual critic of these practices, however, Ziegler submitted a large number of parliamentary questions in the 1970s. Opposing banking secrecy, he called for statistics on the illegal inflows of capital into Switzerland, the Swiss Confederation's cooperation regarding requests from poor countries for the restitution of assets deposited in Swiss banks by their former leaders, and, more generally, the introduction of rules to identify account holders and for collaboration with other countries to combat tax evasion. These demands were supported on the political scene by the emergence of a number of militant, left-wing and religious non-governmental organisations, especially when they concerned North–South inequalities. In the post-1968 Swiss political context, it would be easy to see this strengthening of oppositional discourse as a strategy on the part of the Socialists to win over the far left. It is striking, however, how much the big players in the financial world, who were generally accustomed to having much greater deference shown to them, were unusually agitated at what the secretary of the SBA, Heinrich Schneider, called Ziegler's 'obscure theories', describing him as someone who 'enjoys his role of martyr and plays it well'.[39]

However, the anti-capitalist activism within the Socialist Party was not the most novel shift made during the 1970s. More unusual still was the partial erosion within the main economic decision-making circles in Switzerland of the previously unanimous consensus on the defence of banking secrecy. The second factor that prompted this revised position was linked to the budget deficits recorded by the Swiss Confederation during the 1970s economic crisis. As a consequence of the decrease in tax revenues, the deterioration in the public accounts served to revive the political debate on the taxation of assets held in banks. In the mid-1970s, therefore, the Swiss government included, by way of compensation for increased indirect taxes, a strengthening of measures against tax evasion in a package aimed at raising new income from taxation.

[38] J. Ziegler, *Une Suisse au-dessus de tout soupçon* (Paris: Seuil, 1976).
[39] ASBA, Minutes of the *Ausschuss* of the SBA, 5 November 1976, p. 17.

This package was initially made up of clauses intended to limit banking secrecy in relation to the federal tax administration. It was a remarkable manoeuvre on the whole, because it was the Federal Council's first real step in this direction since the publication of a report in 1962 by the Finance Department, the main practical outcome of which was the instigation of a tax amnesty in 1969.[40] The initial draft of the 'federal act instituting measures to combat tax evasion more effectively at the direct federal tax level', published on 8 January 1975, was certainly ambiguous. Although it guaranteed professional secrecy and therefore, by extension, banking secrecy, it would nevertheless allow the fiscal administration to ask asset managers for information about their clientele in cases where a taxpayer had not provided the exact information requested.[41]

Aside from the budgetary problem, a third factor contributed to this change in Swiss tax legislation on asset management activities. The government was seeking to anticipate future foreign political pressure by appearing to dissociate the protection of banking confidentiality from tax fraud practices. Its motive was explicitly expressed by Georges-André Chevallaz in a parliamentary committee in 1975. In a speech that was more reflective of the Swiss financial debate than of the federal councillor's actual intentions, Chevallaz, echoing Ziegler's rhetoric, condemned the banks' power: the 'banks have a tendency to believe they are a state within a state', he declared, and they did not deserve to be made 'objects of worship'. He added that, in spite of the 'envious gaze' of other countries, there was 'no point in becoming the "fiscal Rhodesia" of Europe'.[42] This slight incursion in the course of Swiss politics was also taken up by the Socialist Pierre Graber, who was the other main government official responsible for international tax matters and the head of the Political Federal Department. In a general appraisal of foreign policy before parliament in 1975, he condemned the Swiss government's poor reputation in its external relations, which he claimed was due to the financial world's abuse of banking secrecy.[43] Two years later, he envisaged a revision in the future of Switzerland's refusal to assist other countries in combating tax evasion.[44]

[40] 'Rapport du Conseil fédéral à l'Assemblée fédérale sur la motion Eggenberger (... 25 May 1962)', *Feuille fédérale* 1/23 (1962), 1097–159.

[41] 'Message du Conseil fédéral à l'Assemblée fédérale ... ', 8 January 1975, *Feuille fédérale* 1/4 (1975), 382–5.

[42] SFA, E 6801, 1985/125, vol. 87, Minutes on 'délibérations sur le projet de loi instituant des mesures propres à lutter efficacement contre la fraude fiscale', Bern, 29 May 1975.

[43] *Bulletin officiel de l'Assemblée fédérale*, Minutes of the *Conseil national*, 16 June 1975, p. 847.

[44] SFA, E 2001E, 1988/16, vol. 400, Report by Graber, 22 February 1977.

In addition to bolstering opposition, revising tax legislation and anticipating foreign attacks, the final factor fuelling the criticism of banking secrecy in Switzerland concerned monetary policy. The leaders of the highly orthodox SNB, spurred on by its president, Fritz Leutwiler, were relatively well disposed to imposing restrictions on cross-border asset management activities in 1975. Proposals were put forward, first, for a ban on some of the Swiss tax haven's most controversial practices, such as the infamous numbered bank accounts, and, second, for taxation of securities deposits and fiduciary accounts.[45] Without revising its fundamental support of banking secrecy, but urging people not to make it a 'taboo' subject,[46] the SNB's board of directors thereby clearly sought, in addition to restoring the Swiss financial centre's tarnished image, to combat the sudden rise of the Swiss franc on the exchange market by curbing foreign capital attraction. In July 1975, the bank's executive suggested that 'the aim of banning numbered accounts is, first, the guarantee of national prestige abroad and, second, the influence over the franc's exchange rate'.[47] The rise of the Swiss franc against the German Mark in the mid-1970s diminished the competitiveness of export industries with Switzerland's main trading partner. This programme of monetary stabilisation, through the moderation of international banking activities, continued the efforts of the SNB, which had been ongoing since the 1970s, to limit, via the banking sector's self-regulation, the possibilities of foreign investment in Swiss francs.[48] Although it faced an outcry from the large financial institutions, the SNB was able to benefit from the support of some export industries (such as watchmaking), which had suffered from a decline in foreign orders due to the strength of the Swiss currency.[49]

The Dynamics of Failure in International Tax Regulation: Failed Attempts to Challenge Banking Secrecy in the Late 1970s and early 1980s

It is clear that until the mid-1970s, while international initiatives against the Swiss tax haven had been somewhat half-hearted, domestic discussion had been a lot livelier, even if it had not yet led to any concrete resolutions. In 1977, there was a simultaneous eruption both domestically

---

[45] ASNB, Minutes of the Governing Board of the SNB, no. 555, 15 May, no. 608, 28 May, no. 789, 17 July and no. 957, 4 September 1975. For the second point, see ASNB, Minutes of the Governing Board of the SNB, no. 487, 21 July 1978.
[46] SNB, Minutes of the *Bankauschuss* of the SNB, 31 March 1977, p. 40.
[47] SNB, Minutes of the Governing Board of the SNB, 759, 4 July 1975.
[48] *Banque nationale suisse, 1907–2007* (Zurich, 2007), pp. 194–8.
[49] ASNB, Minutes of the Governing Board of the SNB, 698, 26 October 1978.

and abroad in political pressure against Swiss banking secrecy. Two discrete events contributed to an increase in attacks on the Swiss tax haven. At the domestic level, the biggest scandal in Swiss banking history, the Chiasso scandal, broke in the spring.[50] The affair, which was directly associated with the growth of Swiss banking's offshore practices, implicated a branch of the Crédit Suisse bank, located in the small town of Chiasso, in the canton of Ticino. This branch had specialised in welcoming Italian assets and re-exporting them to Italy via a holding company in Liechtenstein. The scandal, which involved a number of violations of both Swiss and Italian legislation (soliciting of clients on Italian territory, allowing contraband money to cross the border and fraud against Swiss withholding tax), came to light when Italian investments began to depreciate, mainly due to the devaluation of the Italian lira. This led to large-scale losses for the holding company and caused the whole tax evasion scheme to collapse. At the international level, the new working group at the OECD was beginning its study of tax evasion in the same period. Following the Community's administrative assistance directive of 19 December 1977, the debates were supplemented by European attempts to establish some standards for cooperation against tax evasion, which were destined to be extended beyond the member states. Over the next four years, both domestic and external measures against banking secrecy intensified, and far from evolving autonomously, they became intertwined in different ways.

In discussions within Switzerland the scale of the Chiasso scandal found an immediate resonance in political debates and drew criticism of Swiss banking offshore practices from all sides. At the beginning of May 1977, no fewer than nine interventions – motions, proposals and interpellations from all the main political factions – were presented to parliament. While only the left explicitly demanded an overhaul of banking secrecy, all sides were in favour of greater control of the financial world. In the wake of this, the Socialist Party raised the stakes by submitting a popular initiative. Launched on 20 May 1978, the text demanded, for the first time since a failed initiative in 1922, lifting banking secrecy for the Swiss tax authorities and an extension of cooperation with other countries.[51] This regulationist reaction was very quickly suppressed, however. In the face of this fresh outbreak of domestic and external criticism of banking secrecy, the Federal

---

[50] M. Mabillard and R. de Weck, *Scandale au Crédit Suisse* (Geneva: Tribune éditions, 1977).

[51] 'Message sur l'initiative populaire "contre les abus du secret bancaire et de la puissance des banques"', 18 August 1982, in *Feuille fédérale*, 2/36 (1982), 1237–78.

Council's strategy was set out quite clearly by Chevallaz before the National Council in June 1977. The Swiss government would attempt to rectify only the most unacceptable elements of international asset management. The government thus refused to enter into negotiations on banking secrecy with other countries while delegating a large proportion of Swiss decision-making power to the banks themselves. Chevallaz's discourse was revealing in terms of the freedom that the Federal Council intended to guarantee to the banks in the wake of the Chiasso scandal: 'As there is no question of suppressing banking secrecy, we must allow the banks to provide the safest means, within their internal organisations, of protecting the secrecy that they are entrusted with, since they are the ones who bear the responsibility.'[52]

This programme was carried out to the letter in the years that followed. Its implementation was admittedly facilitated by the stabilisation of the Swiss franc against other European currencies as well as the Socialists' prevarication caused by the contradictions between the political radicalisation expected by a sector of their electorate and the nomination in 1980 of one of their members, Willi Ritschard, as head of the Finance Ministry within a conservative-oriented government. These two factors served to reduce any lobbying against banking secrecy. Somewhat paradoxically, once the political world had moved on from expressing the appropriate indignation, the scale of the Chiasso scandal and the damage it was capable of inflicting on the Swiss financial centre actually prompted the conservative groups to close ranks in order to protect fiscal advantages. All the legislative processes that might have been able to retard the growth of the Swiss offshore market were then overturned. Once again defended by the SNB at the beginning of the 1980s, any plans to increase taxes on asset management, most notably through the taxation of securities deposits and fiduciary accounts, were suspended in the following years under strong pressure from the SBA, which brandished the threat of the tax attractiveness of other financial centres.[53] Simultaneously, the debate on the revision of banking legislation, within which the recasting of Article 47 on banking secrecy was envisaged, became sluggish.[54] Finally, the initiative on banking secrecy, having failed to arouse any serious concerns at the SBA,[55] met the usual

---

[52] *Bulletin officiel de l'Assemblée fédérale*, Minutes of the *Conseil national*, 22 June 1977, p. 841.
[53] SBA, 'Rapport sur le 68e exercice du 1er avril 1982 au 31 mars 1983', pp. 36–40.
[54] ASNB, Minutes of the Governing Board of the SNB, no. 270, 21 June 1984; K. Hauri, 'Ausblick auf das neue Bankengesetz', in U. Zulauf (ed.), *50 ans de surveillance fédérale des banques* (Zurich, 1985), pp. 177–90.
[55] ASBA, Minutes of the *Verwaltungsrat* of the SBA, 7 April 1978.

fate of popular initiatives introduced by the Socialists: it was rejected by 73 per cent of the electorate and by all the cantons on 20 May 1984.[56]

Instead of reshaping banking practices, Swiss leaders reacted to the Chiasso scandal by self-regulating the sector and introducing preventive legislation with regard to foreign measures against tax havens. In July 1977, a gentlemen's agreement came into force between the SNB and the SBA whereby financial institutions agreed to identify account holders and not to take any active steps to encourage tax evasion or welcome illegal capital.[57] In March 1981, a federal law was promulgated on international mutual assistance in criminal matters, which bound the Swiss authorities to assist their foreign counterparts in cases of tax fraud.[58] Swiss leaders thus defended banking secrecy from the point of view of taxation by crystallising a distinction that already existed in Switzerland. On the one hand, there was active fraud (*escroquerie fiscale*), for instance by means of false invoicing, which had to be stamped out; and on the other, there was tax evasion (*soustraction fiscale*) by not disclosing to the authorities the full income or wealth liable to tax, to which greater tolerance was to be shown. However, the federal administration had not acquired an effective means of distinguishing the litigious cases. This positioning was to remain the main line of defence of banking secrecy for the rest of the twentieth century.

While Swiss leaders were implementing the legislative measures aimed at deflecting foreign pressure, multilateral initiatives were also becoming, if not stagnant, then at least diluted between 1977 and the mid-1980s. The OECD's Working Party 8's decision-making process was marred by its slowness, which sometimes verged on immobility. The experts were very cautious in drawing up recommendations on tax evasion that were capable of contravening national legislation. Under cover of a technical discourse, tax administration representatives embarked on a large number of studies and surveys for each file before drawing up practical measures and having their decisions validated by the Committee on Fiscal Affairs. Moreover, the joint development by the OECD and the Council of Europe of a multilateral agreement on administrative aid against tax evasion, ostensibly a real innovation in terms of international regulation, contributed ultimately to bogging the debate down along three separate lines.

---

[56] 'Arrêté du Conseil fédéral constatant le résultat de la votation populaire du 20 mai 1984', 3 July 1984, *Feuille fédérale* 2/29 (1984), 1019–21.

[57] ASNB, Minutes of the Governing Board of the SNB, 438, 16 June 1977.

[58] 'Loi fédérale sur l'entraide internationale en matière pénale', *Feuille fédérale* 1/12 (1981), 807–38.

First, at the opening of the Council of Europe's proceedings, all the ministers' deputies from each of the major European countries expressed reservations about the opportunity to bring about a multilateral agreement and favoured holding talks at the OECD.[59] Second, the Committee on Fiscal Affairs from the Paris organisation, spurred on most notably by the principal financial powers – namely, the United States, Great Britain and Japan[60] – favoured a bilateral approach, prompting a shift towards recommendations of non-binding expertise, destined for implementation in interstate relations. Central to discussions at the beginning of the 1980s were all the studies that had been carried out on the abuse of banking secrecy, domicile companies and tax havens. However, these were merely filed away in a 1987 OECD publication entitled *International Tax Avoidance and Evasion*, which was an intellectual output with no real practical implications, save some vague recommendations on the strengthening of tax controls and international exchanges of fiscal information.[61] Third, although the multilateral approach was gradually appearing to be more feasible at the OECD from 1981 onwards through its pooling of studies on tax assistance with the Council of Europe, cooperation between the two organisations involved so many exchanges back and forth that it proved largely counterproductive. The multilateral agreement on tax evasion, which was open for ratification from 1988 onward, with no binding force for the member states, only entered into effect for the signatory countries in 1995.[62] In short, the 1980s saw no significant progress in the multilateral fight against tax havens.

How can we explain this sclerosis in international efforts against tax havens at the very moment offshore activities were soaring? Part of the explanation for this failure of international regulation on tax evasion lay in the ability of financial centres in the vanguard of the offshore market to obstruct measures against them. The Swiss leaders, following the same political line since the 1920s, positioned themselves at the head of this movement and of all multilateral discussions on tax evasion, at

---

[59] SFA, E 2210.6(B), 1993/29, vol. 54, 292nd Meeting of the Ministers' Deputy, 25–27 September 1978; 294th Meeting of the Ministers' Deputy, 24–26 October 1978.

[60] AOECD, CFA/79.5, Note by the Secretariat, 19 April 1979.

[61] Organisation for Economic Cooperation and Development, *International Tax Avoidance and Evasion: Four Related Studies* (Paris: OECD, 1987). The results had been the same, three years earlier, for the works on transfer pricing. Cf. Organisation for Economic Cooperation and Development, *Transfer Pricing and Multinational Enterprises: Three Taxation Issues* (Paris: OECD, 1984).

[62] Godefroy and Lascoumes, *Le capitalisme clandestin: L'illusoire régulation des places offshore*, p. 140; Picciotto, *International Business Taxation: A Study in the Internationalization of Business Regulation*, p. 256.

both the OECD and the Council of Europe. They were the only ones to have openly and systematically dissociated themselves from all major progress against tax evasion. For example, they tried to delay the studies of Working Group 6 in 1979 after recommendations were set out against transfer-pricing manipulation by the multinationals. They also abstained from supporting a standard agreement in 1980, developed for the recovery of unpaid tax debts, and they did the same two years later regarding a recommendation from the OECD Council in favour of the creation of an agreement on administrative assistance in 1982, as well as during its final development in 1986. Following the failure of the campaign for the Socialist initiative in May 1984 and the caution shown by the electorate on that occasion concerning banking secrecy, the Swiss delegates were finally able to reject in full the regulations against the abuse of banking secrecy and to oppose many recommendations made against the use of domicile companies and tax havens.[63] Nevertheless, it would be a mistake to overestimate the exceptional nature of the Swiss policies. By virtue of the globalisation of offshore finance, Switzerland's allies increased in number in the international arena. For example, Austria, Portugal and Luxembourg all voiced reservations on the subject of administrative assistance and the recommendations on banking secrecy.[64]

The second part of the explanation is, of course, linked to the remarkable tolerance shown by the powerful nations' elite groups towards tax havens. This tendency represented a structural trend throughout the twentieth century. It resulted, on the one hand, from the influence of the groups and individuals that used international tax evasion practices over governments and, on the other, from the relative dependence of states with regard to offshore centres, particularly concerning the financing of public debt and the guarantee of monetary stability. This tolerance was further accentuated with a neo-liberal turnaround at the time and the governments' determination to lower tax charges on capital incomes and capital gains.

The case of France's Mitterrand government provides a good illustration of how a Socialist executive gave way to the structural pressure exerted by offshore finance on national financial systems. Bilateral discussions were held with Switzerland from 1982 onward in response to France's request for an extension of the assistance clause in the 1966

---

[63] For more details on the Swiss policy, see the working paper related to this paper published by the Paul Bairoch Institute of Economic History.

[64] AOECD, CFA/WP8/82.3, A summary of discussions in the Committee on Fiscal Affairs on the Draft Multilateral Convention, 26 January 1982.

bilateral double taxation agreement.[65] In the midst of a generalised tendency to speculate against the French franc, capital flight in the direction of the Swiss tax haven was hastened by the arrival of a left-wing executive with a programme to nationalise the banks, enact so-called 'Keynesianism in one country' and increase taxes on the very rich. Negotiations quickly turned to the Swiss financial centre's advantage at the beginning of 1983 in conjunction with Mitterrand's austerity U-turn. The French government, unable to find any allies for its policies in Europe or to stop the flight from the franc, adopted an austerity plan on 16 March 1983, opening the floodgates to a large credit fund from the European Community.[66] Less than a month later, France's first step towards neo-liberalism translated directly into relations with the Swiss tax haven. On 11 April, an additional clause to the double taxation agreement was signed, which comprised, as the only clause linked to tax evasion, a purely formal note stipulating the existence of Swiss legislation on mutual legal assistance.[67] Three days later, during an official visit to Switzerland on 14 and 15 April, when Mitterrand met the directors of the major French banking institutions in the Swiss market, the French president chose to smooth relations with the Swiss financial centre – one of France's major creditors – by offering explicit guarantees on the subject of banking secrecy.[68]

The French example is in no way unique. A similar process can be observed, for example, at the end of the 1970s during the ratification of the double taxation agreement with Italy. Beyond the usual international noises denouncing tax evasion, it is doubtful, therefore, whether there was any real determination within international organisations to tackle the problem of tax havens head-on during the period in which we are interested. Multilateral negotiations on tax evasion have always been marred by considerable ambiguity. Given the difficulties of reaching a tangible agreement and of the very strong inclination within the most powerful spheres not to encourage such negotiations, these discussions can be seen as a convenient way for governments to appear to be dealing with the problem while fully anticipating that they will ultimately result in a stalemate. This was the dynamic at work from the

---

[65] SFA, E 2010(A), 1995/313, vol. 362, Letter from Ritschard, Swiss Federal Councillor, to Laurent Fabius, Ministre du Budget, 18 February 1982.

[66] Helleiner, *States and the Reemergence of Global Finance: From Bretton Woods to the 1990s*, pp. 140–4.

[67] SFA, E 7001 C, 1994/105, vol. 35, 'Avenant à la convention entre la Confédération suisse et la République française . . . ', 11 April 1983. However, the agreement would not be put into practice because of the Swiss parliament's opposition to this clause.

[68] Centre des archives économiques et financières (CAEF), B 0054306, 'Conférence de presse du Président de la République', 15 April 1983.

very start of the multilateral negotiations on tax evasion at the Genoa Conference in spring 1922. With the benefit of some perspective on the discussions held at the end of the 1970s and beginning of the 1980s and given the unproductive toing and froing between the various negotiation forums, the hypothesis that a similar dynamic occurred would not be an exaggerated one. A report by the OECD Secretariat, for example, noted in September 1983 that, within member countries, 'no clear trend towards a relaxing of bank secrecy seems to emerge, however undesirable, for tax and non-tax reasons, some effects of the situation may be'.[69]

Conclusion

The 1970s represents, in many respects, a paradoxical moment for the Swiss tax haven. While capital poured into the Swiss banking centre with financial liberalisation and the destabilisation of the international monetary system, the comparative advantages that Switzerland had enjoyed since the First World War, at least as far as taxation was concerned, tended to diminish simultaneously on account of medium-sized financial centres within Europe as well as the large British and US banking centres. Added to this, domestic challenges to banking secrecy were surfacing with the acuteness of both the monetary and financial crisis in Switzerland and the post-1968 political context. Thus, the late 1970s and early 1980s constitute, after the two post-war periods, a third nodal point in the history of the Swiss tax haven. Faced with a combination of international initiatives against tax evasion and domestic lobbying, Swiss leaders managed to fend off all the threats that hung over their financial centre, and this left the field open for three decades of exponential growth in its offshore market in an area that was becoming increasingly competitive. Coupled with some minor concessions in domestic legislation, the obstruction strategy that had led the elite bankers and federal authorities to work hand in glove in combating these international actions proved all the more effective because, given the globalisation of tax evasion practices in other financial centres, they had found a good number of allies. As for the major powers, in the context of the neoliberal turnaround at the time, not one of them seemed determined to prevent the expansion of the international tax evasion market.

In conclusion, it is probably not superfluous to express, in the guise of a research programme, a few historiographic reflections. In addition to encouraging the adoption of a broad vision of international fiscal

---

[69] AOECD, CFA/WP8/83.6, Note by the Secretariat, 5 September 1983.

competition, by fully taking into account the development of offshore finance and the tolerance of the great powers in that respect, this chapter also shows the need for a more complex analysis of the Swiss tax haven. This means making a break with a standardised, if not teleological, history of the development of this tax haven. The usual perspective is incorrect because it does not do justice to the different phases of acceleration and deceleration in the Swiss tax evasion market or to the equally non-linear evolution of Switzerland's international position in offshore markets. It would therefore be useful to identify much more clearly and over the long term the forms and degrees of fiscal attractiveness in Switzerland with regard to other countries. For too long now, the literature has considered the singular character of Swiss banking secrecy, understood as Article 47 of the law on banks, and its central role in the attractiveness of the Swiss financial centre as an established fact. As we have seen, this history is only partially admissible since it neglects to make a close analysis of both Swiss fiscal practices and the development of legislation in other countries. In other words, historians should move in the direction of an international approach to the history of the Swiss tax haven. In so doing, they would reflect all the ambiguities in the construction and modernisation of the progressive taxation systems in Europe, consubstantial with the creation of loopholes allowing the most wealthy to evade them.

7   Post-War Fiscal Traps

Peter H. Lindert

Introduction

Do redistributions last, and can they even become more extensive? Are there any obstacles to economic growth?

History shows us a multitude of cases where fiscal decisions have been locked into place, and some of these from the post-war period are examined in this chapter. Whether the redistributions are traps in the sense that they reduce the level and growth of real GDP per capita is something that must be judged from a variety of circumstantial data: theoretical intuition, the historical narrative and 'soft' econometric tests using relevant panel data. History does not supply randomised trials of a rigorous statistical standard. Accordingly, this chapter's argument about the causal influences on economic growth will be based on the soft support documented here, leaving sceptics considerable opportunity to harbour their doubts.

After introducing a simple political economy framework in the following section, we turn to the historical dynamics, mainly in the form of fluctuations in the size of the affected interest groups. We find cases where post-war fiscal redistributions have indeed proved to be long-lasting, featuring a great deal of path dependence. Perhaps the most clear-cut example of fiscal path dependence is the inability of the United States to adopt a value added tax.

The most common kinds of redistributions in favour of special interest groups are given to sectors in decline: the agricultural sector as a whole and failing industries. The continuing shrinkage of these sectors bolsters their lobbying success in defence of their state subsidies. Only in the twenty-first century, and only in Japan and the European Union, do we find clear evidence that their influence may have begun to decline. In the meantime, the prolonged shrinkage of these sectors has limited the negative impact that support for them has on GDP. Of the cases considered here, the only one in which redistribution appears to have an increasing cost is the employee protection laws, which remain strong in the Mediterranean countries and in Latin America.

The case of a redistribution in favour of a group destined to grow, as a proportion of both the electorate and the population, is that of rising post-war state pensions and health insurance for the elderly. Setting aside the vexed health insurance sector, we shall examine post-war state pension history, which shows that very few countries have ring-fenced pensions sufficiently to rein in the rising share of GDP they consume. As to whether or not state pensions stand in the way of economic growth, the answer depends on the choice of a counterfactual alternative. If the alternative is a private pension system, or one with mandatory individual savings, it is not clear that the continued prevalence of state pensions has any growth cost. If the alternative is to channel less towards state pensions by investing more in the young, then yes, pensions do have a growth cost. The countries most inclined to an apparent spending bias in favour of the elderly are Japan, Italy, Greece and the United States.

Pressure Groups and Redistribution: A Simple Framework

Comparative Statics of a One-off Fiscal Fight

Both fiscal and political history are dominated by struggles between competing pressure groups over the redistribution of power. Useful simple models of redistributive contests between pressure groups have emerged in the late twentieth century. Some are top-down models, which focus more on the decision-making of a self-interested autocrat or ruling clique, as in the McGuire–Olson model[1] of stationary versus roving bandits. Such top-down models deliver greater predictive power the greater is the power of the single autocrat, or competing warlords, over a cowed populace. Yet, for modern democracies, more power is gained from bottom-up models that take as their starting point interest groups competing for legislated power. In this approach subservient behaviour is found at the top, as the government carries out the will of the winning faction. This chapter adopts the bottom-up approach to arrive at predictions about the struggles of pressure groups in competitive democracies.

---

[1] Martin C. McGuire and Mancur Olson Jr, 'The Economics of Autocracy and Majority Rule: The Invisible Hand and the Use of Force', *Journal of Economic Literature* 34/1 (March 1996), 72–96; and Mancur Olson, *Power and Prosperity: Outgrowing Communist and Capitalist Dictatorships* (Oxford: Oxford University Press, 2000).

In the bottom-up pressure group approach, even more than in the top-down approach a pioneering role was played by Mancur Olson,[2] who focused on the difficulty of maintaining a large political group's cohesion in the face of individuals' incentive to free-ride and not be actively involved. Gary Becker[3] compressed similar reasoning into a powerful yet simple model of a redistributive contest between two camps. Kristov, Lindert and McClelland[4] extended Becker's framework to distinguish between the groups affected by the contested redistribution and the political camps themselves. Acemoglu and Robinson[5] have formalised important intuitions about how changes to the political rules affect the incentive to fight, incentives that again differ according to group size. This chapter adds predictive power by bringing out some historical dynamics omitted from the generally static models.

Consider a fight over whether or not a government will transfer income between two groups of economic agents, with possible side-costs. The ultimate size of the transfer depends on the pressure exerted by the pressure groups. This can take a variety of forms, among them voting to oust or re-elect incumbents, campaign contributions and violent protests or bribery. The key features of exerting political pressure are that it consumes resources and has an impact on the redistribution. For this reason, an individual must decide whether to join the political camp in favour of the redistribution (the F group), join those against it (the A group) or do nothing (the passive I group). The decision will be based on how strongly the individual feels about the economic stakes of the groups affected.

To define the groups and the disputed transfer, we shall use Kristov, Lindert and McClelland's symbols. Let G be the real value of a proposed transfer from N_T taxpayers (the T group), to N_S subsidised individuals (the S group). In simple terms, assume that the transfers are shared equally within each group so that everyone in S receives the per

[2] Mancur Olson, *The Logic of Collective Action: Public Goods and the Theory of Groups* (Cambridge, MA: Harvard University Press, 1965); *The Rise and Decline of Nations* (New Haven, CT: Yale University Press, 1982); and 'Space, Organization, and Agriculture', *American Journal of Agricultural Economics* 67 (December 1985), 928–37.

[3] Gary S. Becker, 'A Theory of Competition among Pressure Groups for Political Influence', *Quarterly Journal of Economics* 98/3 (August 1983), 371–400; and 'Public Policies, Pressure Groups, and Dead Weight Costs', *Journal of Public Economics* 28/3 (December 1985), 329–48.

[4] Lorenzo Kristov, Peter Lindert and Robert McClelland, 'Pressure Groups and Redistribution', *Journal of Public Economics* 48/2 (June 1992), 135–63.

[5] Daron Acemoglu and James A. Robinson, 'Economic Backwardness in Political Perspective', *American Political Science Review* 100/1 (February 2006), 115–31; and 'Persistence of Power, Elites, and Institutions', *American Economic Review* 98/1 (March 2008), 267–93.

capita subsidy s = G/N_S, and everyone in T pays the tax rate t = G/N_T. In addition to the direct effects, there are deadweight costs or benefits that will be distributed between the two groups. Let us focus on the case of net deadweight costs, D_S and D_T, rather than on net benefits. Each member of the subsidised group must bear costs D_S (G)/N_S as a subtraction from its gain of G/N_S, and each member of the taxed group must bear the combined cost (G + D_T)/N_T. The deadweight costs are increasing and accelerating functions of the amounts transferred.

The two pressure groups competing for the transfer do not necessarily correspond to the subsidised and taxed groups. In real life it is rarely the case that everyone votes for their wallet, as Becker implies. Introducing this generalising distinction into the simpler Becker model gains us a lot. We can directly model group sympathies and pave the way for estimates about the whole range of cases in which the taxed or subsidised group has no political voice. There are nine possible groups (see Table 7.1). Anticipating the direct and deadweight effects of a proposed tax and transfer, agents form two opposing pressure groups: the F group, size N_F, in favour of the proposal, and the A group, size N_A, against it. The familiar vote-for-your-wallet models admit groups S_F and T_A only. We include all nine groups, however, so that each group can include a mix of individuals to be subsidised, taxed or unaffected, even though we can imagine a correlation between the F group and S group membership and between the As and the Ts. The two opposing groups put pressure on the government, pressure that we imagine to be an increasing function of the time and money they spend. Let E_F and E_A be their expenditure in the struggle. The size of the redistribution is a response to the opposing pressures, with diminishing returns to each side's pressure. The groups' aggregate expenditure (E_F, E_A) determines the value of the transfer (G), which in turn determines the values of D_S and D_T, and the net effects on the S group and T group members.

Table 7.1. *Breakdown of population by affected group status and political pressure group status*

	Affected group status		
	To be		To be
Political camp	Subsidised (S)	Unaffected (U)	Taxed (T)
Actively in favour (F)	group S_F	group U_F	group T_F
Inactive (I)	group S_I	group U_I	group T_I
Actively against (A)	group S_A	group U_A	group T_A

Source: Kristov, Lindert and McClelland, 1992.

In a single redistributive fight, the positive and negative comparative-static influences on the outcome are set out in Table 7.2. Its 'caring coefficients' summarise some commonsense conclusions about personal values. To the extent that people are politically apathetic, caring more about their own direct consumption than about the possible gains that accrue from a political struggle, the side they might have favoured will tend to lose. If apathy grips those who might have sympathised with the group to be subsidised (taxed) by the redistribution, the amount redistributed will be reduced (raised). By contrast, the more deeply they care about the effects on one or the other affected group, the more resources they will contribute to its cause. Apathy is likely to be greater in a poor group, since they inevitably focus more on current private consumption than on the prospect of later gains from any redistribution. Thus the poor tend to drop out of political fights, resulting in redistributions that are less progressive and/or more regressive in poorer countries or countries with greater income inequality.

The size of the affected groups typically has negative effects that may be counter-intuitive. While one might think that a larger group has more political clout, this does not translate into its receiving bigger subsidies. As Olson, Becker and others have stated, larger group size erodes the average stake of each group member, reducing the subsidy rate $s = G/N_S$ or the tax rate $t = G/N_T$. The model generally assumes strong narrow interests and weak multitudes. This has some obvious limits, however. It is not true that redistribution favours the narrowest

Table 7.2. *Comparative static influences on a redistributive fight*

Effect of an increase in	On E_F effort for redist.	On E_A effort against	On G^* redist. result
Caring coefficients			
apathy: F-group focuses on its own private consumption	−	0	−
apathy: A-group focuses on its own private consumption	0	−	+
sympathy for subsidised group S	+	−	+
sympathy for taxed group T	−	+	−
Sizes of affected groups (concave, not monotonic; see text)			
subsidy coverage (N_S)	−	+	−
tax coverage (N_T)	+	−	+
Marginal deadweight costs from redistribution			
borne by subsidised group (D'_S)	−	+	−
borne by taxed group (D'_T)	−	+	−

Source: Kristov, Lindert and McClelland, 1992.

possible pressure group, namely a single individual. Equally obviously, the zero limit of having no political voice at all does not make for a powerful lobby. What the model predicts is not a monotonic negative effect of group size on redistributive success, but a 'concavity' that makes the effect of additional members more negative as group size increases. We shall apply this prediction several times in what follows.

Finally, at the bottom of Table 7.2, the marginal deadweight cost of any redistribution will tend to restrain it. This is not to say that the interplay of pressure groups in a democracy will rule out economically inefficient results, only that the negative side-effects will be considered automatically during the pressure group contest.

Long-Run Historical Drifts Recast in Terms of the Model

Let us now recast the final redistribute result (G) in a way that is statically equivalent, but reveals more about the historical dynamics.

As a first step note the starting point of the postulated fight. It does not start from zero government, but from a status quo equipped with legislation favouring the winners in previous fights over redistribution, in some cases with taxes and subsidies. Recognising this simple point adds realism at no cost in terms of model complexity. It also makes it easier to identify the role of inertial forces.

A second step is a minimal injection of reality about the form that a fight over redistributive budgetary changes will take. What the political fight fixes is not the aggregate amount of expenditure itself but the statutory tax rates and subsidy entitlement rates, subject to the estimated, but changeable, size of the groups. As noted, G is two products comprising rates and affected group population sizes: $G = t * N_T = s * N_S$. If those in favour of the change are successful, t and s are fixed, and the size of the affected groups may drift over time. Indeed, the advocacy groups also change in size in ways that historians have long emphasised.

A third step is to recognise that exogenous changes in the political voice can cut the costs of participation. The main candidate here is extension of the franchise in the nineteenth and twentieth centuries to the lower classes. Gaining political voice at a stroke is equivalent to having the cost of participation slashed relative to the price of ploughing one's own field and ignoring politics altogether.

A final step is to note a similar drop in the cost of participation for winners of past redistributive struggles. Once a victorious coalition has been formed, it tends to stay together to defend what it has gained. Its victory also tends to enshrine in law privileges that can also be viewed as a selective reduction in the cost of participation.

Having taken these simple steps, we can add historical movements to the static model of pressure groups' struggles over redistribution.

'You can't get there from here': Path Dependence and Budgetary History

In fiscal experience, history's greatest predictive power takes the form of path dependence. That is, history predicts best when it does no more than forecast that the next few years will be like the last few years in the same place, rather than trying to link behavioural variables. Redistributive fiscal outcomes are designed to have inertia; thus it takes sizeable subsequent shocks to change the rates of taxation and entitlement. The resulting random walks add permanence to international differences in fiscal approach. Those in favour of change must overcome major obstacles that favour the status quo. The two main obstacles to further redistributive change have been noted: the winners of redistributive struggles remain organised for future battles; and their victory typically ensures legislation designed to prevent any changes that could reverse their gains. Familiar examples are laws requiring a super-majority to overturn a redistributive mechanism, laws preventing review and reconsideration for several years, and the setting up of government agencies that are answerable to the newly empowered interest group.

Post-war Tax Mixes: Strong Path Dependence

The post-war era, despite the great expansion of government budgets, has shown remarkable stickiness in the differences among nations in the mix of taxes and in the levels of benefit entitlements. This section discusses some of the international stickiness of tax preferences, leaving differences in benefit entitlements to the next two sections.

While countries do adjust their tax rates and innovate by introducing new forms of taxation, there is remarkable stability to their chosen mix over time and across countries. One could forecast which OECD countries would derive a high share of total tax revenues from direct taxes on incomes, profits and capital gains in 2010, for example, by knowing which countries did so in 1965. Such direct taxes accounted for around half the total tax revenues of New Zealand, Australia, the United States and Denmark, whereas the Mediterranean countries collected only a quarter (or less) of their revenues from taxing income, profits and capital gains.[6] The tax mix stability itself does not allow us to distinguish

---

[6] Among twenty-three countries for which we have data, the correlations with the later 2010 shares of direct taxation in total tax revenues were 0.74 in 1965, 0.71 in 1978 and 0.86 in 1990.

between pure inertia and consistent responses to variables that happen to behave consistently. Yet it does suggest a low probability of a country's undertaking a radical tax reform.

History does not show us any correlation between the share of direct taxes in total taxes and big government. Europe's large-budget welfare states made no greater use of direct taxation than did the lower spenders of North America, Australasia and Japan. That is, the welfare states did not soak the rich.

Another path dependence, another fixity in countries' relative tax mixes, relates to the role of 'sin' taxes. For decades now, countries have been more or less uniform in their use of taxes on three products with harmful personal and environmental effects: tobacco, alcohol, and oil and petrol. The differences seem to reflect international differences in lobbying power rather than international differences in the economic or health effects of these products. This chapter uses the case of taxation on fuel, setting aside tobacco and alcohol. Figure 7.1 shows that tax differences drive the international differences in the price of petrol, and that relative prices (and taxes) tended to be similar in 1978 and 2007. The underlying reasons for the persistent differences in taxation may include transportation economics (big, low-density countries give more lobbying power to petrol consumers), the power of producer lobbies and attitudes to government. The point here is simply that the international differences in petrol tax rates have persisted throughout the post-war era.

Since the 1960s, OECD countries have also differed in their use of the value added tax (VAT) and related sales taxes on general consumption. As a share of GDP, the differences have been consistent and path dependent. The leaders here have been the Nordic welfare states, New Zealand and Israel. As a share of total tax revenue, reliance on VAT and general sales taxes has been through two phases. From the 1960s to the 1980s, heavy use of VAT emerged in the welfare state pioneers of northern Europe. In this period the share of tax revenues collected as VAT or general sales tax was highly correlated with the size of the social budget or total government budget. Then, as the use of VAT spread, the correlation with large welfare states diminished. The new fixity was of the kind also seen in this chapter's emphasis on path dependence; that is to say, since 1990 the countries have kept the same rankings in the share of their tax revenues derived from VAT and sales tax. Countries with consistently high shares of their tax revenues from general consumption taxes now include not just welfare states but such free-market reformers as Chile, New Zealand and Estonia.

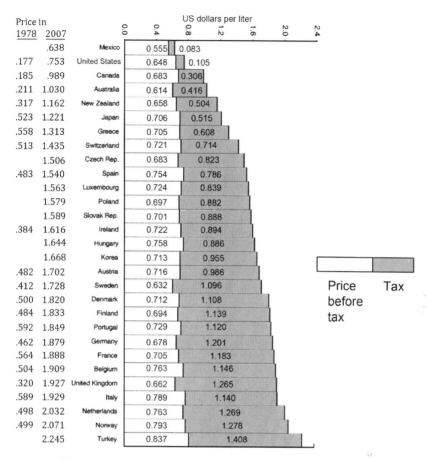

Price in 1978	2007	Country	Price before tax	Tax
	.638	Mexico	0.555	0.083
.177	.753	United States	0.648	0.105
.185	.989	Canada	0.683	0.306
.211	1.030	Australia	0.614	0.416
.317	1.162	New Zealand	0.658	0.504
.523	1.221	Japan	0.706	0.515
.558	1.313	Greece	0.705	0.608
.513	1.435	Switzerland	0.721	0.714
	1.506	Czech Rep.	0.683	0.823
.483	1.540	Spain	0.754	0.786
	1.563	Luxembourg	0.724	0.839
	1.579	Poland	0.697	0.882
	1.589	Slovak Rep.	0.701	0.888
.384	1.616	Ireland	0.722	0.894
	1.644	Hungary	0.758	0.886
	1.668	Korea	0.713	0.955
.482	1.702	Austria	0.716	0.986
.412	1.728	Sweden	0.632	1.096
.500	1.820	Denmark	0.712	1.108
.484	1.833	Finland	0.694	1.139
.592	1.849	Portugal	0.729	1.120
.462	1.879	Germany	0.678	1.201
.564	1.888	France	0.705	1.183
.504	1.909	Belgium	0.763	1.146
.320	1.927	United Kingdom	0.662	1.265
.589	1.929	Italy	0.789	1.140
.498	2.032	Netherlands	0.763	1.269
.499	2.071	Norway	0.793	1.278
	2.245	Turkey	0.837	1.408

Figure 7.1.   Price of petrol and taxes in OECD countries, late 2007. *Source:* Organisation for Economic Cooperation and Development (OECD), International Energy Agency. 2008. *Energy Prices and Taxes, Quarterly Statistics, Fourth Quarter 2007* (Paris: IEA). Record Number: 2008 IIS 2380-P2.

Why Is VAT Un-American?

The striking oddity, or trap, about VAT is this: conventional economics embraces it as a pro-growth device, yet the world capital of conventional economics, the United States, is the country among the thirty-five OECD nations that avoids it most resolutely. Even if we treat state-level sales taxes as equivalent to VAT, in 2010 they accounted for only 2 per cent of GDP in the United States and only 8.1 per cent of all government revenue, far below taxation of income, profits and capital gains, which accounted for 10.8 per cent of GDP and 43.6 per cent of tax revenue. This pattern pertains not just in the United States but in other relatively regressive countries as well: Japan (2.6 per cent of GDP), Australia (3.5 per cent), Switzerland (3.6 per cent), Mexico (3.9 per cent), Canada (4.3 per cent) and South Korea (4.4 per cent).

Conventional economics favours general consumption taxes as pro-growth because they have such low administrative costs and they exclude from taxation the key growth engine of private savings and investment. Indeed, contrary to popular belief, taxing consumption need not be, and often is not, regressive. It has emerged as a progressive tax in countries that use a flat percentage of consumption to pay for universal benefits such as health insurance, which are flatter in absolute magnitudes and are thus progressively redistributive. It was in fact to finance a comprehensive health insurance scheme and related universal benefits that Sweden's Social Democrats took a decisive political gamble on consumption taxes in the 1950s.[7]

Despite this, ever since the 1970s the United States has turned its back on VAT. That it could have acted otherwise if the issue had been given a different political spin is well captured by a statement attributed to Larry Summers. According to the conservative economist Bruce Bartlett:[8]

There is an oft-repeated saying about the VAT made by Larry Summers back in 1988. The reason the United States doesn't have one, he said, is because conservatives view it as a money machine [for big government] and liberals see it as a tax on the poor. We will have a VAT, Summers predicted, when liberals figure out that it is a money machine and conservatives see that it is a tax on the poor.

The anti-VAT path was taken because Republicans rejected any tax that would raise large revenues for social safety nets, and Democrats realised that the only reason a VAT was being discussed in Congress was as a regressive Republican device for replacing taxes on high incomes. The VAT, like any other programme for streamlining the country's complex income tax system, was dead on arrival in Congress.

Given this death by polarisation, a federal VAT will probably never be introduced in the United States.

---

[7] Sven Steinmo, *Taxation and Democracy: Swedish, British and American Approaches to Financing the Modern State* (New Haven, CT: Yale University Press, 1993).
[8] Summers has never acknowledged saying this, although Bartlett has attributed it to Summers on at least four occasions: see (1) www.ncpa.org/abo/quarterly/20043rd/clip/20040729lat.htm; (2) www.taxpolicycenter.org/publications/template.cfm?PubID=900684; (3) www.brookings.edu/comm/events/20040623.pdf; and (4) http://underbelly-buce .blogspot.com/2009/11/summers-on-vat.html.

My interpretation of the anti-VAT trap relates to countries' having different positions for the lower-income groups. In more conservative countries with larger income disparities between the middle-income earners and the poor, the poor have less political voice, and others feel less affinity with them. These are the countries where the survey question 'Why do you think some people are poor?' gets as its largest reply: 'Because they are lazy.' In these countries there is little pressure for universal entitlements. In the absence of such pressure, the only reason for proposing VAT would be to reduce income tax. That is met with such strong opposition from organised labour that the proposal to introduce VAT is killed off. The result is smaller government and a relatively greater proportion of government revenue being raised by direct taxes on income and wealth, which are seen as less of a 'money machine'. By contrast, welfare states tend to be countries where organised labour feels greater affinity with the poor and is less opposed to paying consumption taxes to fund progressive universal entitlements. The key is that middle-income earners must be willing to pay for entitlements enjoyed by the poor.

Once momentum builds for or against the combination of general consumption taxes and universal entitlements, path dependence takes over.

Historical Group-Sized Dynamics

If historical shocks cause redistributions with relatively fixed rates of real taxes and subsidies, what happens next? Does the redistribution itself grow or shrink, and do its effects on GDP expand or diminish?

If the results were dominated by endogenous responses to the new incentives, the redistribution could create an imbalance as more and more people try to join the subsidised group and avoid taxed status. In a hypothetical perfect storm, the deadweight cost of these responses could spiral if group size had a positive effect on lobbying power. That is, one can imagine a scenario in which the subsidised and growing 'parasite' lobbies for ever more redistribution until a point is reached where a highly exploitative equilibrium results in the heavily taxed host being barely able to survive.

Yet, such cumulative traps tend not to be set for two reasons. First, today's political processes tend to redistribute in favour of groups that have recently suffered economic decline; and second, history tends to continue its assault on the same groups so that they carry on shrinking, with the result that there is a diminishing economic cost of the redistribution to taxpayers and to the economy as a whole.

This section illustrates these general tendencies, and the next section considers today's principal potential exception to this rule.

That the political process tends to favour groups that have suffered decline has been emphasised by Richard Baldwin and Frédéric Robert-Nicoud in their model of the marriage of government and 'losers'.[9] Their motif fits quite easily into the pressure group model discussed above. As Baldwin and Robert-Nicoud rightly note, a sector threatened by a recent shock mobilises, resolving its internal organisational problems, such as free-riding incentives. Once its lobbying is rewarded by government, the cost of defending its rents drops permanently. Baldwin and Robert-Nicoud summarise it thus:

> [P]olicy is influenced by pressure groups that incur lobbying expenses to create rents. In expanding industries, entry tends to erode such rents, but in declining industries, sunk costs rule out entry as long as the rents are not too high. This asymmetric appropriability of rents means losers lobby harder. Thus it is not that government policy picks losers, it is that losers pick government policy.

History is replete with illustrations of this mechanism. We turn next to the pre-eminent case.

The Agricultural Support Trap

Government support for the declining agriculture sector is history's classic redistributive trap, one that visits all countries once their economies start to develop. The historical mechanism can be paraphrased as follows. For millennia, the agricultural sector has distributed a large share of any polity's population geographically. The population's dispersal and low-income per household are accompanied by political weakness, other than in those cases where the landed agricultural interest holds extreme political sway. As soon as the nation's average income expands, the agricultural sector shrinks, as dictated indirectly by Engel's law.[10] At that point a short-run shock, usually accompanied by plummeting prices for farm products, brings about a successful plea for government assistance. Once assistance is granted it proves to be highly durable thanks to features that the winning side has built into the supporting legislation. These typically include legislation offering

---

[9] Richard E. Baldwin and Frédéric Robert-Nicoud, 'Entry and Asymmetric Lobbying: Why Governments Pick Losers', *Journal of the European Economic Association* 5/5 (September 2007), 1064–93.

[10] Engel's law states that among individual households the share of expenditure going to food declines as their total expenditure rises. This translates indirectly into a declining share of total production going to agricultural producers, once one makes history's easy substitution of household with 'world' or 'nation', of food with 'agriculture' and of expenditure with 'production'.

protection against imports that extends over several years, and price-support policies rather than direct subsidies. The problem with direct subsidies is that they are visible to taxpayers and come up for renewal with each annual budget. Meanwhile, government agencies such as the Ministry (or Department) of Agriculture are given the task of furthering support for agriculture.

As the agricultural sector continues to shrink, its lobbying power persists. Its legislative voice is also protected by institutions preserving the shares going to areas that are losing population. Engel's law thus generates secular decline in the size of the subsidised group (N_S) and growth in the taxed group (N_T), shifting the intensity of lobbying effort in favour of the former. What tightens the noose is the group-size dynamic. Olson and others have noted the inverse relationship of group size to lobbying power.

Only when the sector is extremely small does it begin to lose power. The few countries that do not pass through such a cycle are those rare cases in which agriculture is unprotected because it hardly existed in the first place. Examples include the urban islands of Hong Kong and Singapore.

The vast literature on government protection of agriculture has clearly identified two reliable patterns, both over the course of history and around the world in any given year:

(1) *The developmental pattern:* Low-income countries generally burden farm producers with taxes and poor terms of trade, whereas high-income countries generally subsidise and protect their agriculture.
(2) *The anti-trade bias:* In all countries, policies tend to protect producers of importable agricultural products, but not producers of exportables, thus reducing trade and prejudicing overseas producers.

How this has played out in the post-war era is shown in Figure 7.2. The still developing countries are moving away from taxing agriculture and towards subsidising it. The bottom curve reveals the heavy tax burden they placed on their exportable farm products before the 1990s. A prototypical case is the exploitation of West African cocoa farmers by governments that paid them only half the world price, pocketing the difference as revenue to the advantage of the urban sector. This exploitation is now approaching zero, however, as incomes rise and the farming sector shrinks. Meanwhile, the developing countries protected their farmers who had to compete with imports, a politically easy solution when overseas suppliers lack the vote and can be attacked as unfairly competitive.

Among the more developed countries, the same difference holds between importable and exportable agricultural products, with the

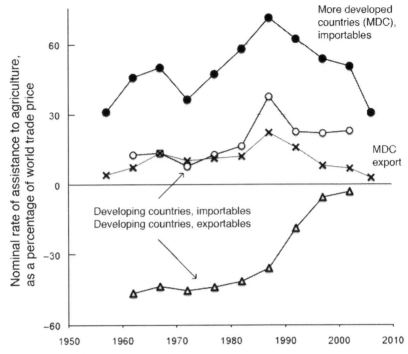

Figure 7.2.   Rate of assistance to agriculture, 1955–9 to 2005–7.
Source: Kym Anderson (ed.). 2009. *Distortions to Agricultural Incentives: A Global Perspective, 1955 to 2007* (Washington, DC: World Bank; Basingstoke and New York: Palgrave Macmillan).

former receiving far more income protection. This anti-trade pattern also holds across regions. The agriculture exporters of the Cairns Group of twenty countries[11] face near-free-trade conditions on world markets by comparison with the import-competing agriculture. At the most protectionist end of the spectrum are wealthy countries with high farming costs and tiny farming sectors, such as Japan, Korea, Norway and Switzerland.

What is true of the post-war era has also been true over the last couple of centuries as we can see in the case of Japan's rice policy. Throughout the twentieth century, as Japan became richer and less agricultural, its protection of agriculture, and especially of rice, soared (see Figure 7.3).

---

[11] Argentina, Australia, Bolivia, Brazil, Canada, Chile, Colombia, Costa Rica, Guatemala, Indonesia, Malaysia, New Zealand, Pakistan, Paraguay, Peru, the Philippines, South Africa, Thailand, Uruguay and Vietnam.

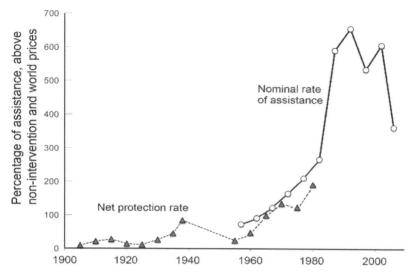

Figure 7.3. Rate of protection to Japanese rice, 1903–7 to 2005–7.
Source: Kym Anderson and Yujiro Hayami. 1986. *The Political Economy of Agricultural Protection: East Asia in International Perspective* (London: Allen and Unwin), pp. 20, 128–9.

For as long as the protection curves keep rising, and agriculture keeps shrinking as a share of the economically active population, one can imagine an approximate confirmation that a smaller affected group size goes hand in hand with more receiving generous subsidies. The actual pattern is more complex, of course, and one might question how one can explain the dip in protection in recent years. As Figure 7.3 shows, Japan cut its rice protection in 1999 to less astronomical heights in the wake of its liberalising Basic Law on Food, Agriculture and Rural Areas. The model sketched above sheds no light on this, but can offer a partial explanation for Figure 7.2's larger reduction in agricultural protection since the earlier 1990s. That reduction occurred mainly in western Europe, and within the European Union in particular. While much of this reduction was due to international pressures that are not captured by our simple pressure-group model, there is one influence the model does predict that helps to explain the European Union's reduction in subsidies and protection under the Common Agricultural Policy (CAP). It was in the 1990s that the European Union tackled the agricultural implications of its expansion into eastern Europe. The ten new member countries had sizeable agricultural populations, which threatened to break the CAP budget; this reality forced a scaling back of the rate of subsidy. For the earlier EU members this is equivalent to having the affected agricultural population (the S group in our simple model) suddenly expand, diluting its per capita benefits of redistribution and eroding its lobbying efforts.

Thus over the whole sweep of development, redistribution towards the agricultural sector becomes more generous, even as it shrinks in size. The rising redistribution implies welfare costs to society as a whole.[12] These costs do not spiral upwards, however, since the sector has continued to shrink following Engel's law.

Help for Declining Industrial Sectors

While agriculture is the most obvious case of a sectoral lobby that gains power and rents even as it shrinks, it is not the only case. Increasing protection has also been given to declining industrial sectors as well, as Baldwin and Robert-Nicoud have emphasised.

To underline this point, let us consider a post-war case in which the press and many scholars were most convinced that policy backed the most rising and expanding industries, contrary to our model's prediction. Many were convinced that Japan and Korea were to be congratulated for government policies fostering their export-oriented growth miracles through planning and targeting. In particular, during Japan's strong pre-1990 growth, it was believed that its Ministry of International Trade and Industry (MITI) worked intelligently with such export sectors as consumer electronics to foster their growth. Yet this was the MITI myth, given the sector patterns of government aid revealed by Richard Beason and David Weinstein.[13] Analysing Japan's policy between 1995 and 1990, Beason and Weinstein considered four forms of official aid: (1) subsidised Japan Development Bank loans; (2) direct government subsidies; (3) tariff protection; and (4) tax relief. The results show that the fastest-growing sectors – electronics, general machinery and transport equipment (cars, ships) – received the least support from government, including from MITI. The industries getting the most help were relatively slow-growing, such as textiles, mining and chemicals. Yet, even these were not as heavily protected, or as stagnant, as Japan's agricultural sector. Here again, the force preventing government redistribution from spiralling was simply that it was directed at declining sectors.

---

[12] Kym Anderson (ed.), *Distortions to Agricultural Incentives: A Global Perspective, 1955 to 2007* (Washington, DC: World Bank; Basingstoke and New York: Palgrave Macmillan, 2009).

[13] Richard Beason and David Weinstein, 'Growth, Economies of Scale, and Targeting in Japan (1955–1990)', *Review of Economics and Statistics* 78/2 (May 1996), 286–95, especially 288, 289.

Labour Protection and Lost Human Capital in the Mediterranean

Another post-war case in which governments redistributed in favour of a group destined to decline was the enactment of employee protection laws (EPLs) throughout western Europe in the late 1960s. These highly redistributive devices do not feature in government budgets. Rather, they take the form of legal restrictions on dismissing workers categorised as 'permanent'. These restrictions have remained in place ever since, though some countries have liberalised them. The general pattern is that northern European countries along with Italy relaxed their restrictions on worker dismissals in the 1990s. Yet they remain strong today throughout the Mediterranean (including France, but not Italy) and in Latin America, including Chile.[14]

As with the other redistributions to declining economic groups, this one favours a vested interest group that is declining as a share of the economy, namely senior, 'permanent' workers in long-established firms and sectors. There is a twist, however, which has raised their social cost over time. To use the terminology employed by Assar Lindbeck and Dennis Snower,[15] EPLs divide the workforce into a stagnant number of 'insiders' and a growing number of 'outsiders'. What is detrimental to the outsiders is that employers' 'firing problem' becomes a 'hiring problem'.[16] Unable to dismiss unproductive workers without great difficulty, employers avoid hiring young workers whose productivity they cannot be certain of. Econometric evidence[17] strongly suggests that the restrictions had little effect from the late 1960s to around 1980, but in the 1980s and 1990s the growing share of outsiders did considerable harm to human capital. The percentage of workers whose career development was delayed grew and grew. The symptoms appear most clearly in the reduction of employment, especially permanent employment,

---

[14] For indices of the strictness of EPLs, see Gayle J. Allard and Peter H. Lindert, 'Euro-Productivity and Euro-Jobs since the 1960s: Which Institutions Really Mattered?', in Timothy J. Hatton, Kevin H. O'Rourke and Alan M. Taylor (eds.), *The New Comparative Economic History: Essays in Honor of Jeffrey G. Williamson* (Cambridge, MA: MIT Press, 2007), pp. 365–94. Also available as NBER Working Paper 12460. See also OECD iLibrary Home/Statistics/OECD Employment and Labour Market Statistics/Employment Protection Legislation.

[15] Assar Lindbeck and Dennis Snower, *The Insider–Outsider Theory of Employment and Unemployment* (Cambridge, MA: MIT Press, 1988); and 'Insiders versus Outsiders', *Journal of Economic Perspectives* 15/1 (Winter 2001), 165–88.

[16] See Robert J. Flanagan, 'Unemployment as a Hiring Problem', *OECD Economic Studies* 11 (Autumn 1988), 123–54; and 'Macroeconomic Performance and Collective Bargaining: An International Perspective', *Journal of Economic Literature* 37/3 (September 1999), 1150–75.

[17] Allard and Lindert, 'Euro-Productivity and Euro-Jobs since the 1960s'.

among younger workers. There may even be a loss of productivity on the job, due to the resulting brake on in-house skills, but this cannot be shown econometrically. The tentative conclusion is that EPLs have redistributed in a way that has protected a declining group, but at a cost that has been growing rather than declining.

Aid to the Elderly: A Twenty-First-Century Trap?

Of all the distributions since the 1960s, the one that may have set the greatest fiscal trap of all is redistribution to the elderly, a group that will continue to grow in the twenty-first century. We are reminded every week that the world's population is ageing, and the most recent data suggest that the trend is accelerating faster than predicted.[18] We are warned that redistributions to the elderly will explode and trigger financial ruin before the century is out.[19] On the other hand, the pressure group model implies that the rise in the elderly proportion of the adult population will itself undermine 'grey power' by making advocates of generous pensions realise that their gains will be spread more thinly and by alienating younger taxpayers. Which view is the correct reading of twentieth-century history, and which offers the better forecast of inter-generational transfers in the twenty-first?

Historical Shocks Brought about Government Aid to the Elderly

The twentieth-century experience with support for the elderly was rich in a key ingredient for the pressure group model: shocks that explain when and where the political process took up the cause. One shock, already mentioned, was the extension of the franchise, which undermined the elitist presumption that insuring for one's old age was a private, individual matter. The other main shock was those global threats to our sense of security. The two world wars and their resulting price inflation gave rise to demands that all the elderly were entitled to income security and healthcare. This was stated most famously in William Beveridge's 'welfare state'. The Great Depression of the 1930s also convinced many that the elderly needed social insurance, most famously realised in the United States' Social Security Act of 1935.

---

[18] Karen N. Eggleston and Victor R. Fuchs, 'The New Demographic Transition: Most Gains in Life Expectancy Now Realized Late in Life', *Journal of Economic Perspectives* 26/3 (Summer 2012), 137–56.

[19] Laurence J. Kotlikoff and Scott Burns, *The Coming Generational Storm: What You Need to Know about America's Economic Future* (Cambridge, MA: MIT Press, 2005).

Once the safety nets were in place they were not to be removed, as our intuition about pressure group legislation tells us.[20]

A particularly powerful illustration of the role of shocks and institutional inertia in setting traps comes from the United States' experience with health insurance, which has a problematic historical link to the interests of the elderly. At the heart of the problem is a series of historical wrong turns. Employer-based plans gained popularity in the Second World War, when wage controls prevented employers' competing for scarce workers by offering higher wages, but allowed them to offer attractive fringe benefits. Then came a tax policy, enacted in 1943 and solidified in a 1954 Supreme Court ruling, that exempted employer contributions to employee health plans from taxation, either as corporate income or as employee income.[21] The tying of health insurance to employment, combined with the soaring costs and desirability of healthcare, frightened the elderly population. This in turn led to the introduction of Medicare in 1965, which insured the over-65s. The United States remained trapped in a system that under-insured dependants aged 64 and less and denied insurance to those who changed jobs. These omissions were finally addressed in the Affordable Care Act of 2010, though the special subsidies on employer-based health coverage continued to fund the anti-reform lobby.

To follow the political tug-of-war over the cost of supporting the elderly, however, let us concentrate on the case of pensions, setting aside the issue of health insurance, which is more complex and is not as closely tied to the elderly in countries other than the United States.

Divergent Trends in Public Pension Support

We can trace the cost, or generosity, of public pension transfers using one of two measures. The first takes state pensions as a share of GDP, giving us an implicit tax rate for society as a whole. The second takes the generosity of what each beneficiary receives relative to society's income-generating power:

pension support ratio, or 'replacement rate' = (public old-age, survivor, and disability payments per person over 65) divided by (GDP per person 15–64), or

---

[20] On the inflation and Depression shock origins of state-dominated pension solutions, see Enrico Perotti and Armin Schwienbacher, 'The Political Origin of Pension Funding', *Journal of Financial Intermediation* 18/3 (July 2009), 384–404.

[21] Melissa A. Thomasson, 'From Sickness to Health: The Twentieth-Century Development of U.S. Health Insurance', *Explorations in Economic History* 39/3 (2002), 233–53; and 'The Importance of Group Coverage: How Tax Policy Shaped U.S. Health Insurance', *American Economic Review* 93/4 (September 2003), 1373–84.

(public old-age, survivor, and disability payments per person over 65) as a share of GDP / (the share of persons over 65 in the population older than 15).[22]

It turns out that the two measures have behaved very similarly over the last half-century, since population ageing proceeds slowly and steadily. We can therefore gain a clear picture just from the first and more widely used measure, namely gross pension benefits as a percentage of GDP. We are warned repeatedly that this share of GDP, and the overall tax rate it implies, cannot be allowed to rise indefinitely. Given that an ever-greater proportion of the population will be aged sixty-five or more, holding down pensions as a share of GDP requires a downward drift in the pension support ratio.

Has the share of national product channelled into pensions continued to rise with the ageing of the population as inertia in the support ratio, or 'replacement rate', would imply? Or has its rise been checked by the weakness of ever-larger population groups? Remember that these shares of national product were near zero until the Second World War, so we pick up their long post-war rise at the year 1980, the starting point for the measures currently used by the OECD.[23] Figure 7.4 summarises how pensions as a share of GDP have behaved in the thirty-four countries now supplying consistent data series to the OECD. For these countries as a whole, the share crept up at 0.5 per cent of GDP per decade from 1980 to 2007, though it rose more rapidly in the recessions of 1991–3 and 2008–9 (the shaded areas in Figure 7.4). This suggests a slowly simmering crisis for the OECD as a whole. Why is the share continuing to creep up despite public warnings and despite our theoretical hunch that having a larger share of the population receiving benefits should weaken support for public pensions?

---

[22] Both measures here are based on the OECD's gross benefits data. These fail to distinguish between 'non-contributory' benefits paid by the rest of society and the 'contributory' benefits paid by the recipients themselves, either during their earlier careers or as clawback taxes on the retirement benefits received in the current year. The second measure invites the incorrect assumption that all pension recipients are aged over 65 and that all GDP is generated by persons aged 15–64 years. While neither is true, it is useful and convenient to relate pensions to the size of the over-65 age group which drives pension totals, and to relate GDP to the size of the age group that clearly generates most of it.

[23] The measure used for 1960–81 would be better for debating the rise in universal pensions such as US Social Security, since it sets aside the pensions paid to government employees themselves. The latter are part of the public sector's wage bargaining, just as private pensions are part of the wage bargaining of private industry, rather than being redistributions from the rest of society. See Organisation for Economic Cooperation and Development, *Social Expenditure 1960 –1990* (Paris: OECD, 1985). Yet, to follow the story since 1980, we must use the current OECD measures, which combine government benefit payments for both public sector and private sector workers.

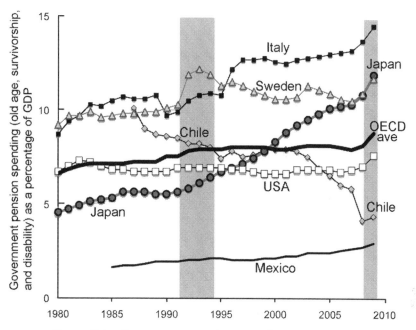

Figure 7.4. Government pension spending as a share of GDP, 1980–2009.
Source: OECD, 2011. Online at OECD iLibrary / Statistics / Social Expenditures.

Within the group of thirty-four countries there are sharp differences in pension trends, and these must be explained. Three of the countries – Chile, New Zealand and Luxembourg – have slashed their share of public pension benefits in the national product. The most publicised case is that of Chile, famous (or infamous) for the pension privatisation imposed by Augusto Pinochet in 1980.[24] As Figure 7.4 shows, Chile's pension expenditure has dropped by more than half since 1987. Three points should be emphasised to avoid misinterpretation of this long reduction to public pensions. First, it was not privatisation of a universal 'social security' pension, since Chile never had one before 1980. Rather, before 1980 Chile had a chaotic and regressive mix of occupation-specific pensions for those in the public sector and in privileged private formal sectors such as maritime trade and mining. Second, the Pinochet regime, despite its power, recognised that it had to cushion the impact of

[24] For a review of the first two decades of Chile's pension reform, see Rodrigo R. Acuña and Augusto P. Iglesias, 'Chile's Pension Reform after 20 Years', World Bank SP Discussion Paper 0129 (2001).

the new system. One such cushion was to exempt the military, which continues to receive the bulk of its funding from general taxpayers. Another cushion was the use of general funds to continue payments to retirees covered under the old system. Third, a remarkable feature of the Chilean system is that most of the reduction in the public pension share came after 1990, that is, after the restoration of democracy and the arrival of centre-left *concertación* governments. That is, despite the dramatic shift in regime, pensions policy remained locked into the system imposed by Pinochet, with the gradual phasing out of general government payments to civilian retirees – another illustration of path dependence.

Offsetting the shift away from state pensions in Chile, New Zealand and Luxembourg is the rise of pension shares in other countries. This rise is neither surprising nor alarming in the cases of still-developing countries with younger populations, such as Mexico and Turkey. More striking are the cases in which the pensions bill has risen above 10 per cent of national product over the last three decades, with no sign of abating in Japan and a Mediterranean group (France, Greece, Italy and Portugal). Aside from referring loosely to path dependence and inertia, it is not clear why these countries have still failed to check the rising cost of pensions. All five countries have certainly debated the issue of spiralling pensions, yet their reforms have been consistently tentative – until 2011 in Italy, that is. Taken at face value, Italy's recent pension reforms under the interim government of Mario Monti and the coalition government of Enrico Letta have been significant. The number of years of contributions from income has been increased, along with the statutory age to receive full benefits. In principle, this would seem to embody the realisation that the elderly are becoming so large a group that their pension benefits must be held in check. This conforms to the pressure group model's prediction of redistribution away from groups as they become larger. The jury is still out, however, on Italy's pension reforms of 2011–12. The reforms are on course to take effect in a few years, yet the ruling coalition is weak.

In contrast to Japan and the four troubled Mediterranean countries, the three countries whose pension policies are most debated – namely, the United States, the United Kingdom and Sweden – have experienced less ominous trends, or even stability. The furore over the future of Social Security in the United States fails to feature in Figure 7.4. United States pensions' share of national product remains stable and lower than the average for OECD countries. In part this is because the US population has not aged as fast as the populations of, say, Italy or Japan, thanks to more immigrant workers and to its higher fertility rate. In terms of the pressure group model, the elderly are still not a large enough share of the adult population to have their lobby weakened by dilution of benefits.[25] In the United Kingdom, Margaret Thatcher's drive to privatise pensions achieved only a modest reduction in state pension generosity by 1989, and since then the state pension share has risen above its 1980 level, though it remains below the OECD average.

Sweden's pension wars since 1980 have moved in the opposite direction. In the 1980s, while Thatcher was holding the line in Britain, Swedish pensions (and other government expenditures) were rising, and continued to do so until the general economic crisis of the early 1990s. Since then pensions in Sweden have been held down, with the help of the country's Notional Defined Contribution Plan set up in 1998. The country now automatically adjusts its annual pension benefits to reflect the rise in life expectancy. While the political system did bend the rules somewhat in favour of pensioners during the mild slump of 2008–9, Sweden is a country that has come to grips with population ageing. Its legislated pension formulas *automatically* reduce the average generosity of transfers to pensioners as their proportion of the adult population rises.[26] But even without this mechanism, the other three Nordic countries – Finland, Norway and Denmark – also slightly decreased their state pension share of GDP between 1997 and 2007. They too are countries with relatively old populations, further hinting that the increase in the elderly share of the adult population may produce less generous benefits.

Does Public Aid to the Elderly Reduce GDP?

Whether or not allowing support for the elderly to rise is a trap in terms of efficiency depends on the counterfactual alternative that one postulates.

The usual counterfactual, call it 'privatising pensions', is that we could have had lower taxes and payroll contributions and more private saving for retirement. In this standard counterfactual, it is not clear that there is much efficiency gain from privatisation; in other words, there is no clear loss from leaving state pensions unchanged. A country could meet any changes in conditions by adjusting the parameters of either a

---

[25] A smaller part of the credit for the stability in pension costs in the United States goes to the Greenspan Commission on Social Security Reform of 1983, which is gradually raising the full retirement age from 65 to 67 by the year 2027.

[26] On Sweden's pension reforms, see Peter H. Lindert, *Growing Public: Social Spending and Economic Growth since the Eighteenth Century*, 2 vols. (Cambridge: Cambridge University Press, 2004), ch. 11; Agneta Knuse, 'A Stable Pension System: The Eighth Wonder', in Tommy Bengtsson (ed.), *Population Ageing – A Threat to the Welfare State?* (Berlin and Heidelberg: Springer-Verlag, 2010), pp. 47–64.

private or a state system. In particular, the spectre of a longer life in retirement will similarly force any pension plan – even purely individual private savings – to adjust by lowering annual consumption relative to working-age earnings. The data are similarly neutral or non-existent regarding any GDP effects of privatisation.[27]

On the other hand, consider the counterfactual 'invest in the young'. With the same revenue, a government could shift some spending away from pension transfers and into such human capital investments as public education or public health. In general, the literature shows that there is a strongly positive rate of return on human investments.[28]

Yet since the 1960s the general drift has been *towards* support of the elderly and *away from* investing in the young. One sees a shift, away from targeting the disadvantaged and towards universalist transfer programmes appealing to middle-class as well as elderly voters.[29] As a result, since the 1960s, poverty rates have been reduced much more for the elderly than for children or persons of working age. Figure 7.5 shows this for the United States, and Table 7.3 shows the same for averages over groups of OECD countries. In the United States since the 1960s, poverty has declined dramatically for those aged over 65 but not for children. In larger groupings of OECD countries we see a clear divide around the age of 50. All age groups up to 50 years of age experienced an increase in their share of poverty relative to the population as a whole, while those above 50 moved out of poverty faster than the whole population.

The drift towards lowering the poverty rates more for the elderly than for children and those of working age is clearly tied to a bias in expenditure policy, particularly in certain countries. To show this, one needs to avoid examining social expenditures as a share of GDP alone, which can

---

[27] Two partial, and not decisive, factors pull in opposite directions regarding privatisation. A hypothetical factor in favour of privatisation might be that the political process is so trapped into running pension deficits that it will fail to adjust the pension parameters to balance the overall government budget, and may damage the country's borrowing ability.

A tangible factor against the privatisation alternative is that both British and Chilean experience have shown that the mandatory placement of savings into designated private investment management firms brings an unreasonable administrative expense on the order of 15 per cent of the amounts contributed under the mandated programmes. By contrast, Social Security now operates with an administrative cost share of only 0.5 per cent. See the IRS *Data Book*'s online archive at www.irs.gov/taxstats.

[28] George Psacharopoulos, 'Returns to Investment in Education: A Global Update', *World Development* 22/9 (September 1994), 1325–43; and 'Public Spending on Higher Education in Developing Countries: Too Much Rather than Too Little', *Economics of Education Review* 15/4 (October 1996), 421–2.

[29] Peter Baldwin, *The Politics of Social Solidarity and the Bourgeois Basis of the European Welfare State, 1875–1975* (Cambridge: Cambridge University Press, 1990).

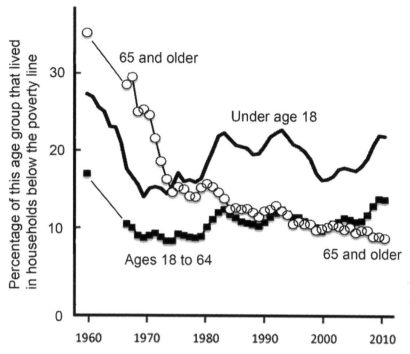

Figure 7.5.   US poverty rates by age group 1959–2011.
Source: www.census.gov/hhes/www/poverty/data/historical/people.html,
accessed 31 December 2011.

Table 7.3. *Relative risks of poverty, by age of individuals in the OECD, mid-1970s to mid-2000s (poverty rate of the entire population in each year = 100)*

	<18	18–25	26–40	41–50	51–65	66–75	>75
OECD-23	110	95	78	70	93	134	190
	116	112	83	69	83	115	169
Mid-2000s	119	127	85	77	80	99	144
OECD-7 mid-1970s	84	113	61	66	119	180	214
Mid-1980s	115	120	78	64	87	120	178
Mid-1990s	116	143	81	61	82	99	149
Mid-2000s	112	147	86	72	78	95	150

Source: OECD, *Growing Unequal* (Paris: OECD, 2008), chapter 5, figure 5.5, updated 12 September 2008.
Note: OECD-23 is the average of poverty rates across the OECD countries excluding Australia, Belgium, Iceland, Korea, Poland, the Slovak Republic and Switzerland.

OECD-7 is the average for Canada, Finland, Greece, the Netherlands, Sweden, the United Kingdom and the United States. Data for mid-1980s refer to around 1990 for the Czech Republic, Hungary and Portugal; those for the mid-2000s refer to 2000 for Austria, Belgium, the Czech Republic, Ireland, Portugal and Spain (where 2005 data are not comparable with those for earlier years). Data based on cash income.

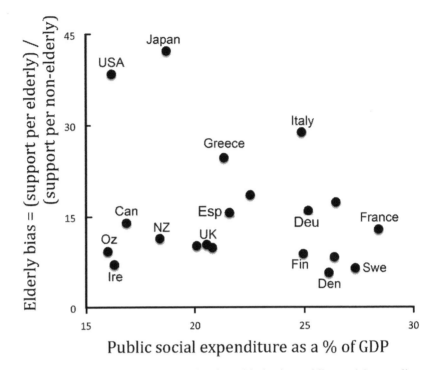

Figure 7.6. Bias towards the elderly in public social spending, 1985–2000.
Source: Lynch (2006). For similar figures covering 1980, 1985 and 1993, see Lynch (2001).

be driven by the age group shares of total population. A more telling kind of expenditure measure is a relative support ratio, dividing social expenditure on the elderly *per elderly person* by social expenditure on the young *per young person*. Such a ratio should be above unity, since the average dependency ratio is higher for those aged over 65 than for younger age groups. We can compare the same ratio across countries to detect outliers.

Calculating such ratios takes some work, but fortunately much of this has already been done for us. Figure 7.6 shows some of Julia Lynch's calculations of such an inter-age-group support ratio, against the overall social spending share.[30] The bulk of countries in Figure 7.6 have similar

---

[30] Julia Lynch, 'The Age-Orientation of Social Policy Regimes in OECD Countries', *Journal of Social Policy* 30/3 (2001), 411–36; and *Age in the Welfare State* (Cambridge: Cambridge University Press, 2006).

inter-age group ratios, whether they are high-budget welfare states like France and Sweden or lower-budget states like Australia, Ireland and Canada. There are four outliers, however, all of them having social expenditures biased heavily in favour of the elderly: these are Japan, the United States, Italy and Greece. For the United States one immediately thinks of the fact that Social Security and Medicare, both concentrating on Americans over 65 years of age, are more generous than public support for the poor of working age. Yet the outliers are not extreme in their generosity to the elderly themselves, as defined by social expenditures on the elderly per elderly person/GDP per capita. Rather, they stand out because they give so little to those of working age and to children. For those four countries their path-dependent history seems to have caught public finance in a trap that may be both anti-growth and inegalitarian.

Summary and Remaining Tasks

Adding history to a simple static model of struggles between pressure groups has provided an overview of how redistributions play out over the decades. Most fiscal redistributions prove to be durable, largely because they were designed to be as irreversible as the original legislation could make them: that is, path dependence dominates the history of fiscal redistribution. Once a country's political process has set up a particular approach to taxation and entitlements, that approach becomes a national fingerprint, which is not easily erased. From the 1970s to the 1990s, national fiscal paths diverged. The welfare states of the 1970s are today's welfare states; the countries that rely mainly on direct income taxation today are those that did so consistently over the last half-century. Countries also differ consistently in the share of revenue they derive from taxing harmful products (tobacco, alcohol and petrol).

Whether each of the distributive locks is a trap in the sense of dragging down economic growth depends on the dynamic of the sizes of the affected groups. Some redistribution, though permanently locked in, has the saving grace of affecting a smaller and smaller proportion of our economic life. So it is with the classic case of buying off a special interest, namely government support for agriculture. And so it is with support for declining industrial sectors. Such redistributions presumably reduce GDP and well-being, but only in dwindling degrees.

Other redistributions, however, may grow if they are not dismantled by new historical shocks. One trap in terms of economic growth took the form of the employee protection laws that continue to be strict in the Mediterranean countries and Latin America. These have gradually eroded the human capital of labour market outsiders.

The biggest case of a growing subsidised lobby is still in progress: state pensions and health insurance for the elderly threaten to spiral, because the elderly are surviving longer and longer in retirement. Granted, these benefits have not yet done any demonstrable damage to GDP, but their effects on government finances could lower GDP if they continue unchecked. Fortunately, some countries have already begun to take the precautionary step of reducing pension benefits as a share of GDP. This can improve growth prospects, particularly if the money saved on state pension growth is channelled into investment in the young, especially in the formative stages of education. Those for whom this task remains most seriously unfinished are Japan, Italy, Greece and the United States.

Some possible fiscal traps have not been considered here and remain to be addressed in a larger fiscal history. One is whether or not the entitlements of public sector employees have spiralled out of control. This remains underexplored, here and elsewhere, for want of reliable measures of whether public sector pay has really exceeded the market pay for persons of the same skills after one adds pension entitlements and other fringe benefits to the levels of pay alone. On the pension front, we do have evidence that public sector pension obligations are underfunded in many countries.[31] However, the current benefit part of this long-run threat is already built into this chapter's discussion of public pensions, since the post-1980 OECD data include the pension benefits of all public sector employees.

A second fiscal trap calling for ongoing research is the *potential healthcare crisis* that threatens all OECD countries. It is not first and foremost a fiscal crisis, but rather has its roots in the deviations of the healthcare sector from competitive, demand–supply economics.

Finally, a topic that by its nature can never fully disappear consists of the *recurring crises in the over- or under-provision of worker disability insurance*. What makes the issue recur is also what prevents my describing it as a trap: there are no easy rules to follow or violate, and governments keep adjusting their policy guidelines and enforcement procedures.

---

[31] Eduard Ponds, Clara Severinson and Juan Yermo, 'Funding in Public Sector Pension Plans – International Evidence', NBER Working Paper 17082 (2011).

8 Fiscal Redistribution in Comparative Perspective: Recent Evidence from the Luxembourg Income Study (LIS) Data Centre

David K. Jesuit and Vincent A. Mahler

The aim of this chapter is to present an overview of recent trends in income inequality and government redistribution in twenty developed countries, using data that have been computed from household-level income surveys available from the Luxembourg Income Study Database (LIS).[1] The central accomplishment of the LIS, which was established in 1983, has been to harmonise household-level income surveys produced by national statistical agencies and other authoritative bodies so that they conform to a common definitional framework. LIS micro-data are then made available to researchers, who can use them to calculate, among other things, the redistributive effect of direct taxes and various types of social transfer. LIS data are available for ten waves, centred on 1970, 1975, 1980, 1985, 1990, 1995, 2000, 2004, 2007 and 2010.[2] However, not every country is represented in every wave and some countries include more than one year in a single wave.

The LIS has compiled data on a wide variety of sources of private sector income, including wages and salaries, self-employment income, interest and dividends, and rental income and royalties. It also measures income from a large number of individual public social transfers, including pensions, unemployment benefits, child allowances and means-tested public assistance. Finally, most LIS surveys account for

---

[1] LIS Cross-National Data Centre in Luxembourg, *Luxembourg Income Study Database* (2015) www.lisdatacenter.org/our-data/lis-database.

[2] Technically, the datasets before 1980 are called 'historical', since they preceded the establishment of the LIS and initially were not fully harmonised. 'Wave I' thus refers to income surveys centred on 1980. However, historical datasets have recently been harmonised and are thus comparable to later sets, and we have employed them when available. For clarity, we use the generic term 'wave' in referring to LIS surveys in general, including historical surveys. However, we use the official LIS designation, in which Wave I centres on 1980 when referring to individual LIS waves.

the most important direct taxes, including income taxes and social insurance contributions.[3]

The data presented in this chapter update and extend our 'Fiscal Redistribution Dataset', which has provided information on a number of aspects of inequality reduction in developed countries by way of taxes and social transfers. The dataset was first compiled from LIS micro-data in 2005.[4] In 2008, it was updated to reflect changes in LIS methodology and to include several newly available income surveys.[5] Some of our measures were further extended and updated in 2011 by Koen Caminada and Chen Wang.[6] Our revised dataset, as well as Caminada and Wang's, are available on the LIS website and have been widely used by researchers interested in income inequality and government redistribution.

The purpose of this chapter is to describe the results of a thorough update of our data on fiscal redistribution which we have recently undertaken, an update in which we have not only added new figures but also recalculated earlier ones to reflect recent changes in LIS methodology. For a number of reasons, we believe this is an opportune time to update our dataset 'from the ground up'. First, in mid-2011 the LIS implemented a new data template. This made a number of changes to traditional LIS variables. One important revision was a new definition of post-government income, which is now called 'disposable household income' (DHI). The main change is that most non-cash income (but not imputed rent) is now included in market income. This is most important for developing countries, but it also has some effect on the developed countries that are our focus. Since this new DHI income concept has become the basis for the LIS's widely used 'Key Figures',[7] we believed that it was important for us to employ it as well.

Beyond this, there has been a broader effort in the new LIS template to improve standardisation of income definitions across countries, and

---

[3] Property taxes are not, however, included in LIS's coverage of direct taxes. Across our twenty countries these accounted for an average of 2.1 per cent of GDP in 2011, in comparison with 19.7 per cent for individual income taxes and social insurance contributions. Organisation for Economic Cooperation and Development, *Revenue Statistics – OECD Member Countries*. http://stats.oecd.org/Index.aspx?DataSetCode=REV (2015).

[4] V. A. Mahler and D. K. Jesuit, *Fiscal Redistribution Dataset*, version 1 (2005); and 'Fiscal Redistribution in the Developed Countries: New Insights from the Luxembourg Income Study', *Socio-Economic Review* 4 (2006), 483–511.

[5] D. K. Jesuit and V. A. Mahler, *Fiscal Redistribution Dataset*, www.lisdatacenter.org/wp-content/uploads/2011/02/fiscal-redistribution-details.pdf (2008).

[6] K. Caminada, and C. Wang, *Leiden LIS Budget Incidence Fiscal Redistribution Dataset*, www.lisdatacenter.org/wp-content/uploads/2011-Fiscal-Redistribution-Doc.pdf (2011); and K. Caminada, K. Goudswaard and C. Wang, 'Disentangling Income Inequality and the Redistributive Effect of Taxes and Transfers in 20 LIS Countries over Time', Luxembourg Income Study Working Paper 581 (Luxembourg, 2012).

[7] www.lisdatacenter.org/data-access/key-figures/download-key-figures.

numerous smaller revisions and corrections have been made to various datasets in recent years, some initiated by the LIS and others by the national statistical agencies that supply the original data. Finally, nearly all LIS variable names were changed in 2011 in an attempt to develop a consistent nomenclature. In this revision we use the new names, which should make it easier for others to replicate, update or extend our calculations.

Aside from the new template just described, the LIS database has grown considerably since our last calculations. While our original dataset included 59 country-years, the version described here includes 116. One reason for this is that LIS waves have become more frequent: they are now conducted approximately every three years instead of every five. Of special interest is the fact that wave VIII includes surveys conducted in 2010, after the onset of the 2008 global financial crisis. In addition, the figures described here include no fewer than seven countries that were not represented in earlier versions, either because the starting point of then available surveys measured income net of direct taxes or because they have recently joined the LIS project.

To be specific, this revision includes all currently available (as of June 2015) LIS 'gross income' datasets, that is, datasets whose starting point is pre-tax income.[8] It does not include 'net income' datasets, for which it is not possible to account for direct taxes, or 'mixed' datasets, for which coverage of direct taxes is incomplete.[9] Furthermore, our coverage is limited to the developed countries; it does not include LIS datasets for transitional or developing economies. In all, we include twenty countries for an average of 5.8 points in time, ranging from 1967 through to 2010. The countries and years, along with all data and details on household size equivalisation, household weighting, survey weighting, the treatment of zero income and top and bottom coding, are available in an online appendix.[10]

Measuring Income Inequality and Government Redistribution

The starting point in computing summary figures for income redistribution is to measure the distribution of private sector income. The most important source is earnings, which comprise wages, salaries and income

---

[8] The one exception is the 2013 US dataset, which is not included because it is, at present, the only available appropriate dataset from LIS Wave IX.
[9] The LIS characterises all three Italian datasets as 'mixed', but we have included them because they account for the most important direct taxes, income taxes and social insurance contributions.
[10] www.lisdatacenter.org/resources/other-databases.

from self-employment, including where possible non-cash compensation. To this figure are added income from property, such as interest and dividends, rental income, royalties, non-cash income where possible and pensions received by private and public sector employees. The total is defined as 'factor income'. Finally, we add to factor income three relatively minor sources of private but non-market income: merit-based educational transfers, transfers from non-profit institutions and inter-household transfers, such as alimony or child support.

In measuring the effect of direct state redistribution via taxes and transfers it is first necessary to add to private sector income a number of public sector social transfers. As has been indicated, the coverage of such transfers in LIS income surveys is quite extensive. The main benefits include retirement pensions, child and family allowances, unemployment benefit, sickness benefit, accident benefit, disability benefit, maternity benefit, 'other social insurance' and means-tested social assistance of various kinds. After summing private and public sector sources of income, we arrive at 'total gross income'. The final step is to deduct from total gross income the most important taxes that are paid directly by households: income taxes and social insurance contributions. When this is done, we arrive at our measure of post-tax and post-transfer income, which is called 'disposable household income'. This is the actual income households receive.

There is an additional measurement issue that must be taken into account. This is the inherent difficulty of separating public and private sector pensions in countries in which there is a substantial private pension system. In particular, in a number of countries supplementary private pensions are mandatory or strongly encouraged through various state incentives, but entirely financed and allocated by employers and employees. In these cases, the distinction between public and private pensions is somewhat artificial: in countries with closely linked supplementary private pensions one would not expect the state to provide the same level of public pension coverage as in countries in which the public system is more dominant, since part of the income needs of pensioners are already being met. Beyond this conceptual difficulty, for 27 of our 116 income surveys it is impossible to disaggregate income from public and linked private systems.

There is clearly no perfect solution to this problem, but for the conceptual reasons noted earlier, as well as a desire for consistency across countries and a reluctance to lose a fifth of our income surveys, our main measure of transfer redistribution considers the pension system as a whole. In addition to this broad measure of pensions, we have reported data for unambiguously public programmes for the smaller number of countries for which they are available.

Income Inequality and Government Redistribution: An Overview

We now describe our data, with a particular focus on changes since our dataset was last updated. As we have indicated, our complete 116-case dataset is available in an online appendix to our chapter.[11] For ease of exposition, we begin our summary by focusing on national averages over multiple LIS waves for each of our twenty countries.

We begin with pre-tax and pre-transfer inequality.[12] As can be seen in the first column of Table 8.1, countries vary quite widely in the extent of income inequality generated by the market and, to a much lesser extent, private transfers: pre-tax and pre-transfer inequality ranges by 164 Gini points across our twenty countries, from a high of 0.542 in Greece to a low of 0.378 in Iceland.[13] The large countries of the developed world fall between these extremes: Italy reports the third highest level, followed by the United Kingdom in fourth, the United States in

---

[11] www.lisdatacenter.org/resources/other-databases.

[12] Many readers will be interested in the highest income groups, those above the 95th or 99th percentile. These are an important focus of T. Piketty, *Capital in the Twenty-First Century* (Cambridge, MA: Harvard University Press, 2014), among others. However, LIS data are not well suited to focusing on these groups because of top-coding issues. For those interested in cross-national data on top incomes, see F. Facundo Alvaredo, T. Atkinson, T. Piketty and E. Saez, *The World Top Incomes Database* (2015), http://topincomes.g-mond.parisschoolofeconomics.eu. See also LIS Cross-National Data Centre in Luxembourg, *The Luxembourg Wealth Study* (2015), www.lisdatacenter.org/our-data/lws-database, a companion to the LIS that measures accumulated wealth, but whose data are available for many fewer countries and years.

[13] In measuring inequality we have employed the Gini index, which ranges from 0 (all households receive the same income) to 1 (one household receives all income). Gini coefficients can be measured on either a 0–1.000 scale or a 0–100 scale; we use the former. By 'Gini point' we mean an increment of 0.001. As to redistribution, we have reported the absolute rather than the relative change in the Gini index as a result of redistribution, a measure that is not only more straightforward but also has the benefit of allowing one to compare the extent of state redistribution in a way that is not affected by levels or trends in market income inequality. In practice, these variables are strongly positively related, with a bivariate r of +0.930 across our 116 country-years. For those who prefer them, relative-change figures can easily be calculated from our pre- and post-tax/transfer figures. In calculating redistribution, we employ the approach often attributed to M. Reynolds and E. Smolensky, *Public Expenditures, Taxes and the Distribution of Income: The U.S, 1950, 1961, 1970* (New York: Academic Press, 1977), which re-ranks households after public social transfers have been added and direct taxes deducted from private sector income when calculating the Gini coefficient (see also Caminada and Wang, *Leiden LIS Budget Incidence Fiscal Redistribution Dataset*; and Caminada et al., 'Disentangling Income Inequality and the Redistributive Effect of Taxes and Transfers in 20 LIS Countries over Time'). This is termed 'net redistribution'; it is computed using the 'SGINI' Stata module (P. van Kerm, 'SGINI: Generalized Gini and Concentration Coefficients (with Factor Decomposition) in Stata', www.researchgate.net/publication/255589700_Generalized_Gini_and_Concentration_coecients_%28with_factor_decomposition%29_in_Stata (2010)).

Table 8.1. Aspects of fiscal redistribution: averages by country

	A			B				C				
	Gini coefficient			Relative shares		Fiscal redistribution from		Redistribution from				
Country[1]	Private	Dispos.	Fiscal redist.	Tax	Transfers	Taxes	Transfers	Country[2]	Pensions	Working aged	Public pensions	Public pensions/ pension[3]
Belgium	0.466	0.236	0.229	29.8	70.2	0.068	0.161	Austria	0.122	0.033	–	–
Finland	0.466	0.238	0.228	20.9	79.1	0.047	0.181	Belgium	0.115	0.046	0.115	100%
Greece	0.542	0.326	0.216	16.9	83.1	0.035	0.181	Netherlands	0.115	0.050	0.090	78%
Sweden	0.439	0.228	0.212	21.9	78.1	0.043	0.168	Luxembourg	0.112	0.039	0.113	100%
Ireland	0.518	0.309	0.209	25.4	74.6	0.053	0.156	Germany	0.110	0.031	0.119	90%
Netherlands	0.462	0.255	0.207	20.5	79.5	0.043	0.165	Italy	0.110	0.004	0.109	99%
Denmark	0.440	0.236	0.205	19.5	80.5	0.040	0.165	Spain	0.109	0.022	0.103	95%
Austria	0.458	0.269	0.189	18.0	82.0	0.034	0.155	Sweden	0.108	0.060	0.104	100%
Luxembourg	0.458	0.271	0.187	18.9	81.1	0.035	0.152	Denmark	0.107	0.057	0.095	84%
Germany	0.450	0.268	0.181	21.5	78.5	0.040	0.141	Finland	0.107	0.074	0.088	82%
Norway	0.415	0.240	0.175	23.4	76.6	0.040	0.134	Greece	0.107	0.073	0.105	98%
UK	0.485	0.317	0.168	19.2	80.8	0.030	0.138	Switzerland	0.088	0.014	0.069	79%
Italy	0.493	0.330	0.163	30.0	70.0	0.049	0.114	Norway	0.083	0.051	–	–
Spain	0.472	0.320	0.152	14.2	85.8	0.021	0.131	UK	0.079	0.059	0.062	79%
Australia	0.457	0.309	0.148	31.8	68.2	0.047	0.101	Ireland	0.067	0.089	0.056	84%
Canada	0.435	0.300	0.134	28.3	71.7	0.037	0.097	Iceland	0.063	0.023	–	–
Iceland	0.378	0.259	0.119	27.3	72.7	0.033	0.086	Australia	0.060	0.041	0.051	85%
USA	0.467	0.349	0.118	36.7	63.3	0.043	0.075	Canada	0.058	0.039	0.032	56%
Switzerland	0.396	0.287	0.108	7.6	92.4	0.007	0.102	USA	0.055	0.020	0.050	90%
Japan	0.382	0.302	0.080	25.0	75.0	0.020	0.060	Japan	0.051	0.009	–	–
MEAN	0.454	0.282	0.171	22.8	77.2	0.038	0.137	MEAN	0.091	0.042	0.085	88%

[1] Listed in descending order of total fiscal redistribution.
[2] Listed in descending order of pension redistribution.
[3] Ratio computed using only those datasets where public pensions are reported.

sixth and Germany in thirteenth place. All the Nordic countries, with the exception of Finland, are in the lower part of this spectrum, along with Canada, Switzerland and Japan.

Pre-tax and pre-transfer inequality bears only a limited resemblance to inequality of disposable income in our countries, since in every case the state plays an important role in redistributing income by way of taxes and social transfers. That said, there is considerable variation in the extent of redistribution, as is evidenced by comparing the distribution of pre-tax and pre-transfer inequality to that of disposable income, which is listed in section A of Table 8.1. The country with the highest level of disposable income inequality, the United States, is separated by 121 Gini points from the country with the lowest level of disposable income inequality, Sweden. With respect to rankings, one of the most dramatic changes is the rise of the United States from being the sixth most inegalitarian of our countries in terms of pre-tax and pre-transfer inequality to the most inegalitarian in terms of disposable income. Switzerland, for its part, moves from the third most egalitarian pre-tax and pre-transfer distribution to the middle of the pack when taxes and social transfers are taken into account. In the lower part of the disposable income spectrum are the Nordic countries, Belgium and the Netherlands. As to the remaining countries, only Germany and Luxembourg are in the lower half. Italy and Greece have the second and third highest levels of disposable income inequality, followed by Spain, the United Kingdom, Australia and Ireland.

The cause of these shifts is the extent to which pre-tax and pre-transfer inequality is reduced by the redistributive effect of direct taxes and social transfers. The third column of section A of Table 8.1 shows redistribution for our twenty countries. (Countries in this part of the table are listed in descending order on this measure.) At the top of the scale are Belgium, Finland and Greece, in which pre-tax and pre-transfer inequality are reduced by 229, 228 and 216 Gini points respectively. Next come Sweden, Ireland, the Netherlands and Denmark, for which pre-tax and pre-transfer Gini coefficients are reduced by 205 or more points. At the bottom are the United States, Switzerland and Japan, with Gini reductions of 118, 108 and 80 points respectively. As has been noted, these three countries are ranked very differently in terms of pre-tax/transfer inequality. Switzerland and Japan rose considerably in the inequality rankings because of limited redistribution, but remained in the middle of the spectrum in terms of disposable income inequality because of their relatively egalitarian distribution of private sector income. The United States, for its part, started in the upper third of the inequality spectrum, but well below the top. It ended at the top in terms of inequality of disposable income not so much because of an exceptionally high level of pre-tax and pre-transfer inequality but because of limited redistribution in comparison to the other countries we examine.

Disaggregating Taxes and Transfers

Fiscal redistribution by the state is, of course, not of one piece. In particular, it is possible that different trends will be in evidence for the two main modes of direct redistribution: taxes and social transfers. To explore this, we have partitioned the total Gini reduction accomplished by the state into two components: the part achieved by direct taxes and the part achieved by social transfers. We have further disaggregated the Gini reduction as a result of transfers into programmes aimed primarily at the elderly and those aimed primarily at working-age persons.

We begin with taxes. Unfortunately, there is a limitation in using LIS data to explore tax redistribution. The problem is that the national income surveys from which the LIS derives its data do not measure indirect taxes, such as sales, value added and excise taxes, whose precise amount is rarely known even by those paying them and whose incidence is thus very difficult to determine. For this reason, we consider Gini reduction by way of direct taxes only, the primary components of which are income taxes and mandatory employee social insurance contributions. The omission of indirect taxes is important because the countries we examine vary greatly in the share of revenue raised by such taxes, from a low in 2011 of 4.4 per cent of GDP in the United States to a high of 15.2 per cent in Denmark.[14] Some scholars have argued that, even though indirect taxes are not themselves redistributive – in fact, are commonly regressive (although this is usually reduced by lower rates on food, medicine and other essentials) – they nonetheless play a critical role in raising the revenue that funds redistributive social benefits.[15] Is there empirical evidence for such a relationship? One way of exploring this, at least in a preliminary way, is to relate the share of indirect taxes in a country's GDP to the extent to which inequality of private sector

---

[14] Data are from Organisation for Economic Cooperation and Development (OECD), *Revenue Statistics – OECD Member Countries*. http://stats.oecd.org/Index.aspx?DataSet Code=REV (2015).

[15] See, for example, P. Beramendi, and D. Rueda, 'Social Democracy Constrained: Indirect Taxation in Industrialized Democracies', *British Journal of Political Science* 37 (2007), 619–41; J. Kato, *Regressive Taxation and the Welfare State: Path Dependence and Policy Diffusion* (New York: Cambridge University Press, 2003); and P. H. Lindert, *Growing Public: Social Spending and Economic Growth since the Eighteenth Century*, vol. I: *The Story* (New York: Oxford University Press, 2004).

income there is reduced by social transfers. When these variables are related we find that the magnitude of indirect taxes is strongly positively related to the degree to which public social transfers reduce private sector inequality; the bivariate correlation is +0.62. This is not to say that consumption taxes directly finance social transfers in the same way that social security contributions do; with that exception, taxes are fungible. It does, however, offer evidence that indirect taxes on consumption represent a powerful revenue-raising vehicle that supports an array of social transfers, which in turn substantially ameliorate market inequality. Having said that, we note that any transfer redistribution financed, directly or indirectly, by indirect taxes is captured in LIS figures for social transfers, for which we do have data.

With these qualifications, we report the shares of total redistribution accounted for by direct taxes and social transfers in the first column of Table 8.1, section B. In describing the results, we begin with the observation that overall government redistribution in our countries is much more a product of the redistributive effect of social transfers than of direct taxes: across our twenty countries the average share of Gini reduction accomplished by direct taxes is 22.9 per cent while that accomplished by transfers is 77.1 per cent. There is, however, considerable variation about these averages. In particular, the United States and Australia top the list of our countries in the share of fiscal redistribution achieved by taxes: in these countries 36.7 and 32.0 per cent respectively of all redistribution is achieved by direct taxes, well above the twenty-country average. Because total redistribution in these countries is below average, they do not rank quite as high in absolute tax redistribution (see Table 8.1, section B, column 3), although both are in the upper third of that spectrum as well. Other countries are lower on the absolute redistribution list, with Spain, Japan and Switzerland at the bottom.

We now turn to redistribution by way of social transfers. We start with a Gini reduction as a result of social transfers as a whole. As can be seen in the final column of Table 8.1, section B, our countries vary considerably on this measure. At the top of the scale are Finland and Greece, whose pre-tax and pre-transfer Gini coefficient is reduced by 181 Gini points by transfers alone. Most of the Nordic countries are in the upper third of the list, as are the Netherlands and Belgium. The large transfer reduction value for Greece was unexpected. Recall, however, that this country began with a much more inegalitarian distribution of pre-tax and pre-transfer income than our other countries; and even after extensive redistribution it remained among the most inegalitarian of our twenty countries. (Obviously, the Greek situation with respect to this has changed dramatically since the last available income survey in 2010.) At the low end in terms of transfer reduction are Switzerland, Australia, Canada, Iceland, the United States and Japan. These countries differ greatly in the pre-tax and pre-transfer starting point; in particular, Switzerland, Iceland and Japan have relatively low levels of private sector inequality.

Total fiscal redistribution by way of public social transfers encompasses a number of distinct programmes. The most basic breakdown is between pensions, which are aimed primarily at the elderly, and transfers aimed mainly at the working-age population – a category that includes a wide variety of individual programmes, including unemployment benefits, child allowances and means-tested social assistance.[16]

We begin with pensions, which not only constitute the largest social benefit programme in the developed world but also produce the most redistribution, at least in absolute terms. These figures are reported in Table 8.1, section C. On average, across our twenty countries pensions alone reduced private sector inequality by 91 Gini points, more than twice as much as all other transfer programmes combined and just over half of the total reduction in inequality achieved by taxes and transfers together. At the top of the list for pension redistribution were Austria, Belgium and the Netherlands, in which pensions reduced the private sector Gini coefficient by 115 points or more. In the bottom part were Australia, Canada, the United States and Japan, in which pensions reduced the pre-tax and pre-transfer Gini by at most 60 points.

Part of the explanation for the wide cross-country divergence in the redistributive effect of pensions is cross-national variation in the proportion of the elderly in the population. However, the size of public programmes and their internal progressivity also matter: the R^2 of a regression across our 116 LIS datasets that uses the share of the population aged sixty-five or older to explain variation in our pension reduction variable is 0.38, indicating that less than half of the variation in this mode of redistribution across countries and years is explained by demographics.[17]

What of programmes aimed mainly at the working-age population? To start, it should be noted that these programmes accomplish a good deal less inequality reduction than do pensions: as shown in the third column of Table 8.1, section C, on average they result in a reduction of income inequality of 42 Gini points, less than half that for pensions. Even so, the extent of redistribution is substantial – in fact, on average,

---

[16] For most countries it is not possible to distinguish between pensions for the elderly and the (much smaller) coverage of survivors (that is, widows, widowers and minor children of those who died) and the disabled.

[17] K. Armingeon, L. Knöpfel, D. Weisstanner and S. Engler, *Comparative Political Data Set I 1960–2012* (Bern: Institute of Political Science, University of Bern, 2014).

greater than that of tax redistribution. It should be noted that, although all these programmes are aimed primarily at the working-age population, they are quite mixed in other respects. Some – particularly child and family allowances – typically offer flat-rate benefits; some offer means-tested public assistance; and some – particularly unemployment benefits – are commonly tied to the income of recipients when they were working. It is possible to disaggregate these programmes further using LIS data, but only at the expense of comparability. LIS harmonisation, which entails converting national definitions into a common framework, tends to become more difficult as the scope of programmes becomes narrower – something that is exacerbated by the fact that programmes sometimes supplement or substitute for one another. In particular, although we would have liked to, we were unable to separate unemployment benefits from other work-related social insurance transfers for many of our datasets.

The penultimate column of Table 8.1 reports the national averages of our estimates of redistribution from pensions that are unambiguously public. Unfortunately, our data are, for the first time so far, incomplete. The reason for this is that the LIS does not allow us to distinguish purely public pensions from closely linked private pension programmes for twenty-seven of our datasets, including several datasets for Denmark, Germany, Luxembourg, the Netherlands and Sweden, as well as all available datasets for Austria, Iceland, Japan and Norway. As a result of these missing data, this series is not strictly comparable to our mean national estimates for redistribution from public pensions. In order to make meaningful comparisons, we recomputed national means for pension redistribution using only those datasets that also reported our measure of public pensions alone and report these values in the final column of Table 8.1, section C. As this section of the table shows, unambiguously public pensions reduce inequality by an average of 85 Gini points, which comprises nearly 90 per cent of pension redistribution in the countries we examine. However, the mix between public and linked private pensions varies widely. For example, nearly half of pension redistribution in Canada can be attributed to linked private pensions, while in Belgium all redistribution is due to public pensions.[18] Although not shown in the table, the online appendix reveals that redistribution by way of public pensions has declined over time,

---

[18] The LIS does offer data on 'voluntary individual pensions', which are completely separate from the public system, but data are unavailable for a large number of datasets and these figures are not reported.

while the redistributive role of linked occupational and other individual pension plans has increased, as one would expect given the pension reforms of the last decade.[19]

Second-Order Effects

So far we have measured government redistribution in the conventional way by comparing income inequality before and after taking into account taxes and social transfers. However, like all measures of direct redistribution, this conventional measure has one potentially serious limitation. The problem is that, although Gini-change measures like those described in this chapter capture first-order effects whereby taxes and social transfers directly affect the extent of income inequality in a country, they do not capture any second-order feedback effects whereby taxes and social transfers affect private sector income. Specifically, it is often claimed that any direct redistributive effect of taxes and transfers will be wholly or partly undermined if it dampens the incentives of households to increase their earnings or accumulate savings.[20]

Discussions of second-order effects have been especially heated in the field of tax policy, with critics of progressive tax systems arguing that the high marginal income tax rates that prevailed in many developed countries until the 1980s created disincentives for earners.[21] However, high marginal rates have declined sharply in many countries in more recent decades; as will be seen in the discussion of trends in redistribution that follows, the absolute amount of Gini reduction accomplished by direct taxes in our twenty countries has changed little over the last four decades, despite a marked increase in private sector inequality.

---

[19] www.lisdatacenter.org/resources/other-databases. See also Organisation for Economic Cooperation and Development, *OECD Principles of Occupational Pension Regulation: Methodology for Assessment and Implementation* (Paris: OECD, 2010), http://browse. oecdbookshop.org/oecd/pdfs/free/2110031e.pdf.

[20] P. Beramendi, 'The Politics of Income Inequality in the OECD: The Role of Second Order Effects', Working Paper 284 (Luxembourg: Luxembourg Income Study, 2001); A. Bergh, 'On the Counterfactual Problem of Welfare State Research: How Can We Measure Redistribution?', *European Sociological Review* 21 (2005), 345–57; S. Pressman, 'Income Guarantees and the Equality–Efficiency Tradeoff', *Journal of Socio-Economics* 34 (2005), 83–100; N. Lupu and J. Pontusson, 'The Structure of Inequality and the Politics of Redistribution', *American Political Science Review* 105 (2011), 316–36; and K. Van Kersbergen and B. Vis, *Comparative Welfare State Politics: Development, Opportunities and Reform* (Cambridge: Cambridge University Press, 2014).

[21] C. J. Katz, V. A. Mahler and M. G. Franz, 'The Impact of Taxes on Growth and Distribution in the Developed Capitalist Countries: A Cross-National Study', *American Political Science Review* 77 (1983), 871–86; and P. Diamond and E. Saez, 'The Case for a Progressive Tax: From Basic Research to Policy Recommendations', *Journal of Economic Perspectives* 25 (2011), 165–90.

Another potential second-order effect that has received a good deal of attention has been associated with public sector pensions.[22] The basic concern is that in countries that maintain generous and predominantly public pension coverage, workers will have little incentive to save for their retirement, since they enjoy guarantees of adequate retirement income from the state. When they do retire, their private sector income is likely to be low, but these retirees are poor only in a nominal sense, since they benefit from guarantees of future income throughout their retirement.

In a recent article, we discussed in some detail the problem of second-order effects as they apply to pensions.[23] This is thus not the place for a full-scale discussion of this topic, for which we refer readers to our earlier piece. However, we have extended and updated the data we used in that article and recalculated the figures presented there using the new LIS template. Country averages are reported in Table 8.2.

As described in our earlier article, a frequently used alternative to the conventional measure of pension redistribution is to exclude the elderly from consideration by focusing inequality comparisons only on households headed by persons of 'prime age'.[24] In this context, 'prime age' household heads are defined as persons between the ages of 25 and 59, who are very likely to be either full-time members of the workforce or involuntarily unemployed or underemployed, rather than retired or still in education. One problem with this approach is that it is a blunt instrument: it simply excludes from consideration not only a large part of the contemporary welfare state, but also a potent political actor, the elderly. Nonetheless, since focusing on 'prime age' household heads is common and useful for some purposes, we have calculated basic redistribution statistics covering only households headed by persons between the ages of 25 and 59.

There is another way of measuring redistribution that may help account for the second-order effects associated with pensions.[25] Our approach thus far has been to measure the net redistributive effect

[22] D. Bradley, E. Huber, S. Moller, F. Nielsen and J. D. Stephens, 'Distribution and Redistribution in Postindustrial Democracies', *World Politics* 55 (2003), 193–228.

[23] D. K. Jesuit and V. A. Mahler, 'Comparing Government Redistribution across Countries: The Problem of Second-Order Effects', *Social Science Quarterly* 91 (2010), 1391–404.

[24] Bradley et al., 'Distribution and Redistribution'; and L. Kenworthy and J. Pontusson, 'Rising Inequality and the Politics of Redistribution in Affluent Countries', *Perspectives on Politics* 3 (2005), 449–71.

[25] I. Joumard, M. Pisu and D. Bloch, 'Income Redistribution via Taxes and Transfers', in P. Hoeller, I. Joumard and I. Koske, *Income Inequality in OECD Countries: What Are the Drivers and Policy Options?* (Hackensack, NJ: World Scientific, 2014), pp. 85–134; and S. Jenkins and P. Van Kerm, 'Trends in Income Inequality, Pro-Poor Income Growth and Income Mobility', *Oxford Economic Papers* 58 (2006), 531–48. We use the 'INEQDECO' Stata module to compute the Gini coefficients. See S. Jenkins, 'INEQDECO: Stata Module to Calculate Inequality Indices with Decomposition by Subgroup', http://EconPapers.repec.org/RePEc:boc:bocode:s366002 (2015).

Table 8.2. *Alternative measures of redistribution: averages by country*

	A				B				
	Prime-age				Ranked by disposable household income (no re-ranking)				
Country[1]	Private	Disposable	Fiscal redist.	Country[1]	Fiscal redist.	Pensions	Working aged	Public pensions	Public pensions/pension[2]
Ireland	0.470	0.303	0.167	Ireland	0.165	0.043	0.074	0.044	100%
Finland	0.373	0.220	0.153	Belgium	0.162	0.064	0.037	0.064	100%
Belgium	0.361	0.224	0.137	Denmark	0.152	0.080	0.037	0.076	90%
Greece	0.462	0.330	0.132	Finland	0.152	0.067	0.042	0.056	84%
Sweden	0.333	0.205	0.127	Sweden	0.137	0.066	0.037	0.063	100%
Denmark	0.335	0.211	0.125	Australia	0.129	0.049	0.036	0.044	90%
Netherlands	0.363	0.246	0.117	Norway	0.125	0.052	0.037	0.049	100%
Luxembourg	0.377	0.275	0.103	UK	0.121	0.049	0.048	0.044	90%
Australia	0.397	0.297	0.100	Netherlands	0.110	0.047	0.030	–	–
Norway	0.322	0.223	0.099	Canada	0.097	0.029	0.034	0.018	62%
Austria	0.363	0.265	0.098	Germany	0.095	0.043	0.023	0.056	100%
UK	0.408	0.312	0.096	Luxembourg	0.094	0.034	0.031	0.032	100%
Canada	0.376	0.294	0.083	Italy	0.093	0.043	0.004	0.042	98%
Germany	0.334	0.257	0.076	USA	0.085	0.028	0.017	0.027	96%
USA	0.415	0.339	0.076	Spain	0.084	0.050	0.015	0.048	96%
Iceland	0.323	0.250	0.074	Iceland	0.083	0.034	0.020	–	–
Italy	0.405	0.331	0.074	Austria	0.082	0.026	0.027	–	–
Spain	0.384	0.320	0.064	Switzerland	0.048	0.038	0.010	0.037	97%
Switzerland	0.310	0.278	0.033	Greece	0.044	0.033	−0.017	0.014	42%
Japan	0.309	0.281	0.027	Japan	0.041	0.018	0.005	–	–
MEAN	0.371	0.273	0.098	MEAN	0.105	0.045	0.027	0.045	91%

[1] Listed in descending order of total fiscal redistribution.
[2] Ratio computed using only those datasets where public pensions are reported.

of taxes and transfers, following Reynolds and Smolensky.[26] In this approach, households are first ranked by private sector income and then re-ranked when transfers are added and direct taxes deducted from household income. However, it is also possible to compute a 'pre-government' Gini that maintains the disposable income ranking. This results in an index that focuses on the movement of income across income groups. Such an approach is particularly helpful in addressing second-order effects associated with pensions, since when households are not re-ranked their disposable income ranking, rather than their private sector ranking, is the starting point. We have computed redistribution figures employing this approach for all of our countries, which are available in our online appendix.[27]

As can be seen in Table 8.2, section B, there are some differences in the figures. As we would expect, the extent of Gini reduction is, on average, smaller when examining this component of net redistribution: the average Gini change across our countries due to movement of income across groups is 105 points, as opposed to 171 points when mobility (re-ranking) is taken into account. However, in most cases the relative position of countries does not change greatly; the major exception is Greece, which moves sharply down on the redistribution scale. The reason is the unusually large share (37 per cent) of the population in that country whose only income was from public pensions, a share that is substantially higher than in any other country. This is consistent with the observation that 'The difference [in measures] is most pronounced for countries ... which are characterized by a large share of pensions paid to the working-age population due to a low effective retirement age.'[28] (As has been indicated, the Greek pension system has been drastically curtailed since 2010, the most recent available LIS income survey.) Even including Greece, the two measures are fairly strongly positively correlated: $r = 0.743$ across our 116 country-years. Without Greece the figure increases to $r = 0.812$.

As is probably evident from the discussion so far, the second-order effects problems that affect the measurement of income redistribution entail some difficult and imperfect choices. Moreover, while counterfactual concerns have been raised primarily in the context of taxes and pensions, there is no reason why they would not also affect programmes aimed at those of working age: indeed, the conservative critique of such programmes emphasises the disincentives to earn and save that

---

[26] Reynolds and Smolensky, *Public Expenditures*.
[27] www.lisdatacenter.org/resources/other-databases.
[28] Joumard et al., 'Income Redistribution', 90.

they are said to impose on the unemployed and poor.[29] For that matter, incentives associated with social insurance need not necessarily be negative; one of the basic justifications for the welfare state is that offering a measure of income security to workers across their lifetime contributes to their productivity in a manner similar to insurance in other contexts.

In the final analysis, any 'pre-government' counterfactual at all is ultimately artificial; in Esping-Andersen and Myles' words, 'To really estimate redistribution we would need to invent a counterfactual "virgin" distribution that was unaffected by social policy altogether. No such distribution exists in the real world.'[30] Similarly, Lindert compares the 'distortion-filled world of the "second best" [that exists in the real world to] the first-best Garden of Eden so often portrayed in textbooks and in classrooms. To get reliable estimates of welfare states versus free-market economies, one must wander through this second-best world.'[31] In conclusion, we agree with McCarty and Pontusson that 'second-order effects represent a difficult theoretical as well as empirical problem that the existing literature on the politics of redistribution has yet to tackle in a comprehensive way'.[32] This discussion is intended to contribute to a better understanding of this difficult problem and to offer data that may shed some light on it.

The Temporal Dimension of Fiscal Redistribution

Our discussion thus far has neglected changes over time in order to focus on cross-country comparisons. At this point, it is useful to turn to the temporal dimension of taxation and transfer redistribution. This discussion speaks to the extensive literature on welfare state retrenchment of the last decade, with some scholars emphasising the constraints on long-standing benefit programmes and others stressing their resilience.[33]

---

[29] S. Danziger and E. Smolensky, 'Income Transfer Policies and the Poor: A Cross-National Perspective', *Journal of Social Policy* 14 (1985), 257–62; and H. Kim, 'Anti-Poverty Effectiveness of Taxes and Transfers in Welfare States', *International Social Security Review* 53 (2000), 105–29.

[30] G. Esping-Andersen and J. Myles, 'Economic Inequality and the Welfare State', in W. Salverda, B. Nolan and T. M. Smeeding (eds.), *The Oxford Handbook of Economic Inequality* (Oxford: Oxford University Press, 2009), p. 641.

[31] Lindert, *Growing Public*, p. 31.

[32] N. McCarty and J. Pontusson, 'The Political Economy of Inequality and Redistribution', in Salverda et al., *The Oxford Handbook*, pp. 665–92.

[33] Among the former, see R. Clayton and J. Pontusson, 'Welfare State Retrenchment Revisited: Entitlement Cuts, Public Sector Restructuring and Inegalitarian Trends in Advanced Capitalist Societies', *World Politics* 51 (1998), 67–98; and W. Korpi and J. Palme, 'New Politics and Class Politics in the Context of Austerity and Globalization: Welfare State Regress in 18 Countries, 1975–95', *American Political Science Review* 97 (2003), 425–46. Among the latter, see P. Pierson, 'The New Politics of the Welfare State', *World Politics* 48 (1996), 143–79; and D. Swank, 'Globalisation, Domestic Politics, and Welfare State Retrenchment in Capitalist Democracies', *Social Policy and Society* 4 (2006), 183–95. For a comprehensive review of the large literature on this topic, see P. Starke, 'The Politics of Welfare State Retrenchment: A Literature Review', *Social Policy and Administration* 40 (2006), 104–20.

As noted previously, it is possible to group LIS surveys not by country but by wave, comparing fiscal redistribution over the ten LIS waves: 1970, 1975, 1980, 1985, 1990, 1995, 2000, 2004, 2007 and 2010. In this section we first discuss results in which we compute wave averages. It should be noted that in these comparisons the number and composition of countries included in each wave varies, so that average wave values to some extent reflect the countries for which data are available at various points in time. (Unfortunately, only three countries have data for all ten time points.) Below we report results for several individual countries with relatively long time-series.

Figure 8.1 reports mean pre- and post-tax and post-transfer Gini coefficients for each wave. As is evident, the last four decades have witnessed considerable growth in income inequality on both these measures. The greatest increase was in pre-government inequality, which increased by 110 Gini points between about 1970 and 2010. Inequality of disposable income also grew over the same period, but by only 18 points. This provides further evidence that redistribution has continued to play an important role in moderating market-driven growth in inequality, but has not entirely kept pace with large increases in private sector inequality.

Although the increase in income inequality over the last four decades was fairly steady, there were several notable fluctuations in this period. In particular, the mid-1990s saw a spike in private sector income

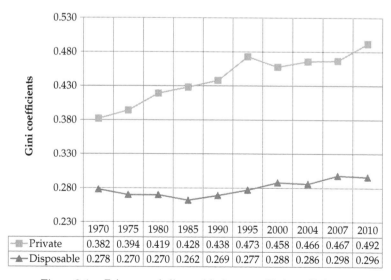

	1970	1975	1980	1985	1990	1995	2000	2004	2007	2010
Private	0.382	0.394	0.419	0.428	0.438	0.473	0.458	0.466	0.467	0.492
Disposable	0.278	0.270	0.270	0.262	0.269	0.277	0.288	0.286	0.298	0.296

Figure 8.1. Private and disposable income Gini coefficients: mean by LIS wave.

inequality, which also increased between 2007 and 2010, a trend no doubt associated with the economic crisis in the period after 2008.

Figure 8.2 disaggregates the overall redistribution picture shown in Figure 8.1, reporting not only redistribution as a whole but also, separately, redistribution by way of pensions, transfers aimed primarily at the working-age population and taxes. The first trend of note is in total redistribution. In accordance with the steady growth in income inequality reported in the previous figure, redistribution grew fairly steadily until about 1995 and then alternated between decreases and increases over the four remaining LIS waves. The largest component, pension redistribution, grew steadily over the entire period, accounting for a good deal of the growth in overall fiscal redistribution. Transfers aimed at those of working age, including unemployment benefit, child allowances and means-tested social assistance, also grew, but here the growth was more uneven; clearly, these benefits are more susceptible to short-term market forces than are pensions. As to direct taxes, this mode of redistribution remained almost flat over the entire period, at a time when other modes of redistribution were growing in many countries. This trend was noted by Esping-Andersen more than two decades ago: 'The role of tax systems is

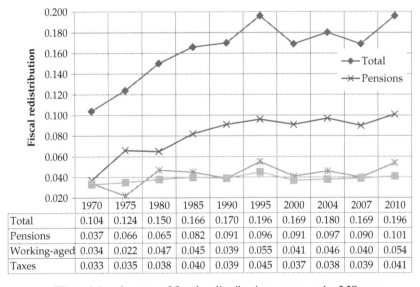

	1970	1975	1980	1985	1990	1995	2000	2004	2007	2010
Total	0.104	0.124	0.150	0.166	0.170	0.196	0.169	0.180	0.169	0.196
Pensions	0.037	0.066	0.065	0.082	0.091	0.096	0.091	0.097	0.090	0.101
Working-aged	0.034	0.022	0.047	0.045	0.039	0.055	0.041	0.046	0.040	0.054
Taxes	0.033	0.035	0.038	0.040	0.039	0.045	0.037	0.038	0.039	0.041

Figure 8.2.   Aspects of fiscal redistribution: averages by LIS wave.

gradually [being] replaced by social transfers as the major weapon for redistribution.'[34]

Although the wave-averaged results reported here provide important insights into general trends over the last four decades, our conclusions are limited by the fact that somewhat different numbers and types of countries are included in each wave. Figures 8.3 and 8.4 report private sector and disposable income Gini coefficients for six countries represented by relatively long and continuous time-series; these are Australia, Canada, Germany, Norway, the United Kingdom and the United States.

As Figure 8.3 shows, although there is some national variation in the rate of growth, private sector income inequality in the developed world grew steadily in all six countries. The single greatest increase was in the United Kingdom, where the Gini coefficient grew by 190 points over the period (albeit from a relatively egalitarian starting point). Pre-tax and pre-transfer inequality in Germany and the United States also grew significantly, by 135 and 95 Gini points respectively. In most cases the increase in inequality began in around 1980, which has been said to

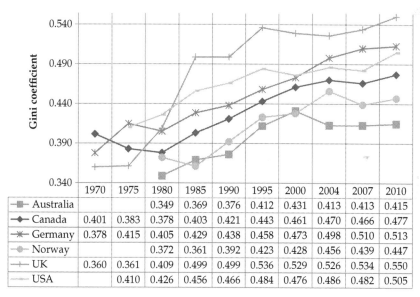

	1970	1975	1980	1985	1990	1995	2000	2004	2007	2010
Australia			0.349	0.369	0.376	0.412	0.431	0.413	0.413	0.415
Canada	0.401	0.383	0.378	0.403	0.421	0.443	0.461	0.470	0.466	0.477
Germany	0.378	0.415	0.405	0.429	0.438	0.458	0.473	0.498	0.510	0.513
Norway			0.372	0.361	0.392	0.423	0.428	0.456	0.439	0.447
UK	0.360	0.361	0.409	0.499	0.499	0.536	0.529	0.526	0.534	0.550
USA		0.410	0.426	0.456	0.466	0.484	0.476	0.486	0.482	0.505

Figure 8.3.   Pre-government Gini coefficients by LIS wave for selected countries.

[34] G. Esping-Andersen, *The Three Worlds of Welfare Capitalism* (Princeton, NJ: Princeton University Press, 1990), p. 56. Recall, however, our earlier discussion of indirect taxes, which, while regressive, have helped to finance the growth of redistributive transfers.

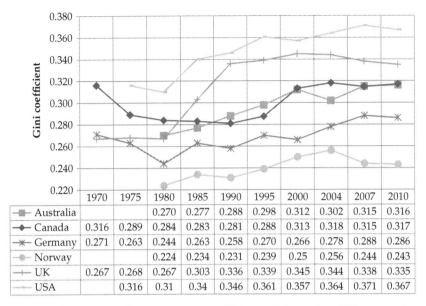

	1970	1975	1980	1985	1990	1995	2000	2004	2007	2010
Australia			0.270	0.277	0.288	0.298	0.312	0.302	0.315	0.316
Canada	0.316	0.289	0.284	0.283	0.281	0.288	0.313	0.318	0.315	0.317
Germany	0.271	0.263	0.244	0.263	0.258	0.270	0.266	0.278	0.288	0.286
Norway			0.224	0.234	0.231	0.239	0.25	0.256	0.244	0.243
UK	0.267	0.268	0.267	0.303	0.336	0.339	0.345	0.344	0.338	0.335
USA			0.316	0.31	0.34	0.346	0.361	0.357	0.364	0.371	0.367

Figure 8.4. Post-government Gini coefficients by LIS wave for selected countries.

mark the start of a 'great U-turn' in inequality, reversing the egalitarian trend of the preceding three decades.[35] In sum, on the basis of an analysis of a number of individual countries over several decades, we conclude that the growth of pre-government income inequality in the developed world was both steady and considerable.

As to post-tax and post-transfer inequality, depicted in Figure 8.4, it is clear that this too has grown over time, although the growth is less pronounced and more variable than is the case for private sector inequality. The United Kingdom is a good example. Over four decades its disposable income Gini coefficient rose by 68 points – among the highest of any country, but only half the growth of private sector inequality. Broadly similar trends were in evidence for the other countries.

Finally, levels of overall redistribution for these six countries are reported in Figure 8.5. As can be seen, there are a number of spikes and troughs during this period. Overall, though, it is clear that all of the redistributive regimes for which we have long time-series grew over the last four decades, although at different rates and from different starting points.

---

[35] A. S. Alderson and F. Nielsen, 'Globalization and the Great U-Turn: Income Inequality Trends in 16 OECD Countries', *American Journal of Sociology* 107 (2002), 1244–99.

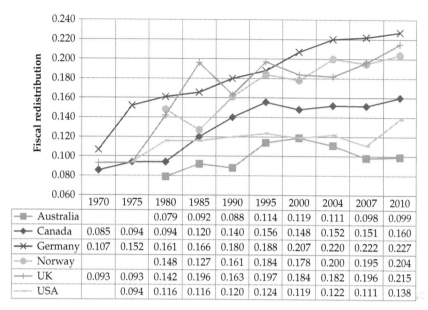

	1970	1975	1980	1985	1990	1995	2000	2004	2007	2010
Australia			0.079	0.092	0.088	0.114	0.119	0.111	0.098	0.099
Canada	0.085	0.094	0.094	0.120	0.140	0.156	0.148	0.152	0.151	0.160
Germany	0.107	0.152	0.161	0.166	0.180	0.188	0.207	0.220	0.222	0.227
Norway			0.148	0.127	0.161	0.184	0.178	0.200	0.195	0.204
UK	0.093	0.093	0.142	0.196	0.163	0.197	0.184	0.182	0.196	0.215
USA			0.094	0.116	0.116	0.120	0.124	0.119	0.122	0.111	0.138

Figure 8.5. Overall fiscal redistribution by LIS wave for selected countries.

Conclusion

The purpose of this chapter has been to measure and describe overall fiscal redistribution and its major components using comparative data from the Luxembourg Income Study (LIS). In so doing, we have also computed and reported pre- and post-tax and post-transfer inequality measures. We provide these data for twenty countries for all available LIS waves, resulting in a total of 116 observations made between 1967 and 2010.

In describing our results, we began by reporting average national values over all available time points. We observed substantial cross-national variation in the degree and nature of redistribution. In particular, liberal market economy countries consistently report the lowest levels of redistribution and the highest levels of disposable income inequality. In addition, in disaggregating overall fiscal redistribution into its major components we noted that most fiscal redistribution is accomplished by transfers rather than by taxes. More than half occurs as a result of a single benefit: pensions. Next, we presented a discussion of second-order feedback effects whereby taxes and social transfers are said to affect pre-government income by offering incentives or disincentives to households to earn and save. We proposed alternative measures that addressed this problem with respect to pensions, but also defended the value of traditional measures.

With respect to changes in redistribution over time, we found that overall redistribution by way of taxes and social transfers has increased steadily since 1970. Much of this growth was due to an increase in redistribution resulting from pensions. Redistribution resulting from direct taxes, in contrast, remained flat over the four decades we have examined. Finally, redistribution by way of transfers aimed primarily at the working-age population fluctuated over this period to a greater degree than redistribution by pensions or by taxes.

When we turn to the broader implications of our analysis, we find it is clear that the steady increase in market income inequality over the last thirty-five years, which sharply reversed the egalitarian trend of the previous three decades, poses a very serious challenge to the social compact that emerged in the post-war period. Until this point, taxes and public social transfers have substantially, but not completely, kept pace with the increase in market inequality. Whether this will continue, or whether government efforts to reduce inequality will run up against increasing fiscal and political constraints, is one of the central political questions facing the contemporary developed world.

9   The State, Public Finance and the Changing
     Response to Investing in the Future: The
     Case of the United Kingdom since the 1970s

Martin Chick

Introduction

In the golden age of low unemployment, low inflation and historically high economic growth rates in the United Kingdom, there were periodic public expenditure crises. One occurred in 1958 when Peter Thorneycroft, the Chancellor of the Exchequer, resigned after objecting to the government's increased expenditure plans. Another occurred in 1967 following the devaluation of sterling, when the chancellor, Roy Jenkins, began implementing the largest deflationary package of cuts in the post-war era. Biennially, usually in an odd-numbered year, the UK economy could almost be expected to experience some sort of balance-of-payments problem. Yet, it was not until the 1970s that the state of the public finances and the contribution of, and consequences for, public expenditure became an issue of persistent central political concern. Against a background of rising inflation, slowing economic growth, OPEC oil price hikes and rising unemployment, political concern with public finance and expenditure grew and was linked to worries that the limits to taxable capacity had been reached, while the structure and level of taxation reduced incentives to work and to take risks.

The main argument of this chapter is that, from the mid-1970s, not only was public expenditure and its related financial borrowing requirement assigned a more prominent role than previously in government economic policy, but there also began a marked withdrawal of government from publicly financed fixed capital investment. This marked a break with the central concerns of Keynes' *General Theory*, not in the withdrawal of government from direct involvement in fixed capital investment, but rather in its reduced concern to influence expectations of the returns likely on future fixed capital investment. This striking change in public fixed capital investment activity is not only of interest in itself, but also inasmuch as it was associated with successive governments' approach to the financing and appraisal of fixed capital investment.

Running through this chapter is an argument that behind the data on public fixed capital investment lay an altered temporal approach by government to the appraisal of proposed investment projects. Where once provisionist governments had considered the financial costs of funding investment, increasingly UK governments emphasised the future returns on proposed fixed capital investment. In a shift from an ex post to an ex ante social cost–benefit analysis of proposed investment, not only was it the temporal stance that shifted, there was also a tendency to move away from thinking in terms of existing and previously incurred average costs and prices, to considering the future marginal costs and benefits of the project. The development of such a systems-based, marginalist approach introduced a more individualistic approach to investment appraisal, and, in thinking of the future marginal benefits, the economic benefits expressed not only in future per capita income, but also in terms of individual human lives and/or of time-savings for individuals, became more prominent. Over the final quarter of the twentieth century in the United Kingdom, there was a distinct shift away from the post-war collectivist pooled provisionist approach, whether in nationalisation, the construction of council houses or the provision of national education and health services, to an approach that found increasing expression in terms of the social cost–benefits accruing on a marginal systems basis to individuals whose own economic value and derived utilities varied. This was some way from Keynes' concerns with expectations of marginal returns on potential fixed capital investment, and as such, a close study of fixed capital investment activity in the United Kingdom provides one means of analysing wider changes in the role of the state in the United Kingdom since the 1970s.

Public Expenditure

These developments in the character of public expenditure occurred within a framework of increasing, if fluctuating, public expenditure.[1] The broad details are set out in Table 9.1. While the cyclical nature of

[1] Various measures of categories of public expenditure are used in this chapter. Total managed expenditure (TME) comprises expenditure by the entire public sector, namely the central government, local authorities and public corporations. General government expenditure (GGE) is a narrower measure of government spending than TME, because the former excludes spending by public non-financial corporations, such as the formerly nationalised utilities. See R. Crawford, C., Emmerson and G. Tetlow, *A Survey of Public Spending in the UK*, Institute for Fiscal Studies, Briefing Note 43 (London: Institute for Fiscal Studies 2009), p. 4.

Table 9.1. *Public sector expenditure, investment and depreciation: £ billion (2012/13 prices) and as percentage of national income*

	Total managed expenditure £ billion	per cent GDP	Current spending £ billion	per cent GDP	Public sector net investment £ billion	per cent GDP	Depreciation £ billion	per cent GDP
1949/50	119.9	37.2	102.6	31.8	6.4	2.0	11.0	3.4
1954/5	139.8	37.8	112.3	30.4	14.8	4.0	12.7	3.4
1959/60	154.0	36.7	125.1	29.9	14.5	3.4	14.4	3.4
1964/5	193.4	38.1	149.8	29.6	26.3	5.2	17.2	3.4
1969/70	247.5	42.5	191.4	32.9	35.4	6.1	20.7	3.6
1974/5	328.3	48.6	261.4	38.7	38.3	5.7	29.3	4.3
1979/80	335.3	44.6	286.3	38.1	17.2	2.3	31.9	4.2
1984/5	377.8	47.5	335.3	42.2	12.5	1.6	30.0	3.8
1989/90	382.3	38.9	344.3	35.1	12.0	1.2	26.0	2.6
1994/5	450.4	42.1	415.9	38.9	14.8	1.4	19.7	1.8
1999/2000	460.0	36.3	436.1	34.4	7.2	0.6	16.6	1.3
2004/5	597.8	40.6	554.4	37.6	25.0	1.7	18.5	1.3
2009/10	724.9	47.4	651.5	42.6	52.4	3.4	20.9	1.4

Source: Institute for Fiscal Studies.

total managed expenditure as a percentage of GDP is clear, the data on public sector net investment show both a steady rise from 2 per cent of GDP in 1949/50 to a peak of 6.1 per cent in 1969/70, and then a fall to 0.6 per cent of GDP in 1999/2000. The sharp drop from 1974/5 to 1979/80 is particularly striking. What is also evident, but perhaps needs emphasising, is that, for all the political rhetoric, the share of public sector expenditure (allowing for cycles) stayed more or less constant over time. The main changes have been in the composition of public sector expenditure, which is the focus of this chapter.

In the early post-war decades, while there were periodic public expenditure crises, essentially economic growth, low unemployment and a favourable shift of the revenue/expenditure ratio oiled the wheels of public finances. While it is true that there was a ratchet effect on public expenditure throughout the Second World War, the ratcheting up of public revenue was even greater. During the war there was a substantial increase in the rate and incidence of taxation, and government revenue absorbed 23.4 per cent of GDP in 1939 and 37.6 per cent in 1945, compared with 9 per cent in 1900 and 40.2 per cent in 2000.[2] In general, the public sector financial deficit settled at 2–3 per cent of GDP between 1953 and 1967, and while it rose to 4 per cent in 1968, fiscal tightening produced surpluses in 1969 and 1970.[3]

It was from the mid-1970s that public finance difficulties became more persistent and that the size of public expenditure and public finance deficits became a persistent feature of political rhetoric. Particular political importance was assigned to the government's own borrowing as both an indicator and a means of achieving its economic aim of reducing inflation. In March 1980, *The Government's Expenditure Plan* stated that in order to reduce inflation it was 'essential to contain and reduce progressively the growth of the money supply', which meant that 'government borrowing must, in turn, be controlled. It is a main determinant of monetary growth.'[4]

The identification of the public sector borrowing requirement (PSBR), a cash measure of the annual borrowing required to bridge the gap between expenditure and receipts, as an instrument of monetary policy had gained momentum from the IMF's increasing influence on

---

[2] T. Clark and A. Dilnot, *Long-Term Trends in British Taxation and Spending*, Briefing Note 25 (London: Institute for Fiscal Studies, 2002).

[3] T. Clark and A. Dilnot, *Measuring the UK Fiscal Stance since the Second World War*, Briefing Note 26 (London: Institute for Fiscal Studies, 2002), p. 2. Clark and Dilnot, *Long-Term Trends in British Taxation and Spending*.

[4] P. M. Jackson, 'The Public Expenditure Cuts: Rationale and Consequences', *Fiscal Studies* 1/2 (March 1980), 66–82.

economic policy in the wake of the decision to devalue sterling in 1967. The danger was that targeting both the money supply and the PSBR would intensify downturns in the cycle and would be pro-cyclical rather than counter-cyclical. To monetary purists, it also meant that fiscal policy became geared in part to meeting monetary targets, which, as Milton Friedman told the Treasury and Civil Service Committee in 1980, was not a sensible way to conduct either fiscal or monetary policy.[5] That the political highlighting of the PSBR was favoured reflected a good housekeeping wish to be seen to be bearing down on public expenditure and a desire to find one indicator that was neither unhelpful (inflation and unemployment both rose) nor erratic (the exchange rate) in the early years of the first Thatcher administration. Given the leap in the PSBR (in current prices) from £9,932 million in 1979/80 to £13,173 million in 1980/1, even this indicator proved disappointing, and that was before consideration was given to the impact of signalling restrictive policies in *The Government's Expenditure Plan* of 1980 on the stock-building, fixed capital investment and use of existing capacity within the economy.[6]

Of the components of public expenditure, the largest was social security and the fastest growing was health (see Table 9.2).

As a share of total public spending at the beginning of the post-war period, around 15 per cent of total public spending went on social security and, despite a significant growth in the value of benefits and the number of those entitled to claim, social security's share of total public spending was only 20 per cent in 1975. From the mid-1970s, with changes in the demographic and family structure, including the increase in low-income, lone-parent families and the rise in unemployment and non-employment, social security's share of total public spending approached 30 per cent in 1986, after which it remained fairly stable.[7]

As Table 9.2 makes clear, between 1969/70 and 2009/10, social security expenditure as a share of national income increased by about 70 per cent. From 1979, the largest proportionate increase in total public sector expenditure was in health, which grew both as a share of public expenditure and as a share of national income. This rate of increase rose over time. From April 1979 to March 1997 spending on the National Health Service (NHS) rose at an annual average real rate

[5] M. Friedman, Memorandum of Evidence. Treasury and Civil Services Committee, House of Commons (London: HMSO, 1980).
[6] 'Funding the Public Sector Borrowing Requirement: 1952–1983', *Bank of England Quarterly Bulletin* (December 1984), 482–92.
[7] Clark and Dilnot, *Long-Term Trends*, p. 10.

Table 9.2. Public sector expenditure on social security, health, education, defence, public order and safety, and transport: £ billion (2012/13 prices) and as percentage of national income

	Social security	per cent	Health	per cent	Education	per cent	Defence*	per cent	Public order and safety	per cent	Transport	per cent
1949/50	16.6	5.1			10.3	2.8						
1954/5	18.8	5.1			14.7	3.5	30.4	8.2				
1959/60	25.0	6.0			21.8	4.3	25.8	6.1				
1964/5	31.5	6.2			28.4	4.9	28.8	5.7				
1969/70	45.6	7.8			38.8	5.7	27.3	4.7				
1974/5	55.2	8.2			39.3	5.2	31.3	4.6				
1979/80	74.7	9.9	33.0	4.4	40.3	5.1	34.4	4.6	11.5	1.5		
1984/5	98.5	12.4	38.6	4.9	47.1	4.8	41.5	5.2	15.1	1.9		
1989/90	101.3	10.3	44.0	4.5	54.5	5.1	38.2	3.9	18.7	1.9	13.3	1.4
1994/5	147.2	13.7	59.3	5.5	61.2	4.5	35.1	3.3	23.5	2.2	17.3	1.6
1999/2000	143.3	11.3	72.3	5.2	79.0	5.4	34.3	2.7	27.2	1.9	12.0	0.8
2004/5	166.1	11.3	100.6	6.8	95.6	6.2	36.2	2.5	34.6	2.3	19.4	1.3
2009/10	204.0	13.3	127.8	8.3			40.8	2.7	37.0	2.4	24.5	1.6

Source: Institute for Fiscal Studies.

Note: Defence data 1954/5 to 1994/5 excluding non-cash; 1999/2000 to 2009/10 including non-cash.

of 3.2 per cent. Between April 1999 and March 2008 spending on the NHS grew by an average of 6.3 per cent annually in real terms.[8] Over the entire post-war period, health expenditure increased from 9.3 per cent of TME in 1949/50 to 18.3 per cent in 2007/8. This reflected demographic change as the population aged, although ageing per se was not tightly correlated with health expenditure. Most such expenditure continued to fall in the final year of life, almost irrespective of age. Nonetheless changes in the demand for healthcare and treatment did outweigh countervailing pressure from technological improvements and the expiry of patents, which would reduce the cost of treatments over time.[9] More broadly, the financing of old age in state pensions, some healthcare and health treatment combined was likely to account for an increasing proportion of public expenditure. In 1990/1 health spending accounted for 12.2 per cent of total public spending, but by 2010/11 its share had grown to 17.5 per cent. Over the same twenty-year period, spending on pensions increased from 10.6 per cent of the total to 12.6 per cent.[10]

Such proportionate increases necessarily came at the expense of other programmes, notably defence. Defence's share was almost halved between the mid-1980s and 2009/10. Education expenditure followed a more fluctuating path. Within education, since 1996/7 further education and spending on pre-school have benefited from relatively large increases, with higher education receiving much smaller increases.[11]

Public Fixed Capital Investment

In addition to concern with the total and component shares of national income accounted for by public expenditure, a third area of interest was the shifting ratio within public investment between current and investment expenditure. Between 1958/9 and 2007/8, the ratio of current to investment spending increased from 10:1 to 19:1 in 2007/8, hitting peaks of 118:1 in 1988/9 and 70:1 in 2000/1.[12] The public sector net investment data shown in Table 9.1 have been mentioned. The trend of gross public investment as a percentage of GDP similarly fell almost continuously from the mid-1970s, from 8.9 per cent of GDP in 1975 to

---

[8] Crawford, Emmerson and Tetlow, *A Survey of Public Spending*, p. 19.
[9] Ibid., p. 18.
[10] R. Crawford and P. Johnson, 'The Changing Composition of Public Spending', IFS Briefing Note 119 (London: Institute for Fiscal Studies, 2011).
[11] R. Chote, R. Crawford, C. Emmerson and G. Tetlow, 'Public Spending under Labour', IFS, 2010 Election Briefing Note 5 (IFS BN 92), 7–8.
[12] Crawford, Emmerson and Tetlow, *Survey of Public Spending*, p. 16.

1.7 per cent in 2000. This decline of 7.2 per cent of GDP stood at £67 billion in 2000.[13] In the 1990s, public investment in the United Kingdom declined at an average annual rate of 0.8 per cent, from 1.3 per cent in 1988 to 0.98 per cent in 1997, perhaps the lowest level of all the OECD countries.[14] There was a decreasing willingness to provide for the upfront financing of capital investment projects. Where the government was largely responsible for the provision of services (as in health, education and prisons), from the 1990s it sometimes abandoned such financing completely, preferring instead to buy a stream of services by means of the private finance initiative (PFI) announced by Chancellor Norman Lamont in his autumn statement of 1992. The PFI allowed infrastructure projects not to feature in the PSBR, highlighting the income and expenditure flow account basis of the national accounts rather than any basis in an asset and liability stock account.[15] Whereas the public sector had traditionally contracted for and financed in advance (quite possibly adding to PSBR) the construction of an asset which it then owned, controlled and used, in the PFI model the private sector would fund, build and own the asset, from which the public sector would then purchase services. What was notable about PFI contracts was that different risks were bundled and priced together.

Although overrunning construction times were a long-standing concern to the Treasury, penalty clauses in construction contracts were a well-established means of addressing this problem. The construction of schools and hospitals was broadly a familiar task, which, since the finance and construction of such projects resulted in a tangible asset, could be considered a low risk. What was less certain was for how long clients would continue to buy services. The political hue of governments could change and governments in western Europe had walked away from such large sunk investments as nuclear power. Such risks and the difficulties of specifying service requirements made these incomplete contracts of higher risk, this being bundled up in the total risk pricing assessment for the whole project.[16]

[13] T. Clark, M. Elsby and S. Love, 'Twenty-Five Years of Falling Investment? Trends in Capital Spending on Public Services', Briefing Note 20 (London: Institute for Fiscal Studies, 2001), p. 2.

[14] M. Florio, *The Great Divestiture: Evaluating the Welfare Impact of the British Privatizations, 1979–1997* (Cambridge, MA: MIT Press, 2004), p. 93.

[15] D. Helm, oral evidence to the House of Commons Treasury Committee on the Private Finance Initiative, 14 June 2011.

[16] Jackson, 'The Private Finance Initiative', 16–17; O. Hart, 'Incomplete Contracts and Public Ownership: Remarks and an Application to Public–Private Partnerships', *The Economic Journal* 113/486 (March 2003), Conference papers, C69–76.

It was not the source of funding, but the location of risk, which was a key PFI issue. This was understated in value-for-money (VFM) comparisons.[17] Given the difference in risk of the various phases (finance, construction and use) of each project, the application of a 6 per cent VFM, which was estimated to be the social rate of time preference, was inappropriate. In 2003 the Treasury reduced this to 3.5 per cent, which was significantly lower than any discount rate used when appraising private sector projects. Where it was ultimately the demand for the output of the fixed capital investment that was the main source of risk rather than its construction, then these risks should be kept separate and not allowed to be bundled together and covered by a single risk rating. If risks were not high, then the question arose why it was of benefit to finance the project at a higher private, rather than a lower public, cost of borrowing. This was, of course, to ignore the fact that the PFI marked a departure from the previous Ryrie Rules under which private finance could only be a substitute for, and not an addition to, public expenditure.

However, the impact of PFI should not be overstated. Following a slow initial take-up, it was decided in November 1994 that the PFI should become the preferred option for capital projects.[18] During 2000, the inclusion of PFI investments would have raised gross public investment from 1.7 per cent to just 2.1 per cent of GDP, still leaving it at about half its 1985 level. Between 1997 and 2002, over 500 PFI project contracts were signed. The total value of these contracts was £22 billion. As such, PFI spending was about 10 per cent of public sector gross capital spending. In terms of its impact on net public sector debt it was even less significant. For example, if PFI expenditure had been incurred by the public sector through traditional public sector procurement, then net public sector debt as a proportion of GDP would have been only 1 per cent higher in 2001/2, that is, 37.9 per cent instead of 36.8 per cent.[19]

Privatisation

Accompanying the decline in public fixed capital formation were periodic transfers of stock. Notable among such transfers were the privatisation of nationalised industries and the sale of council houses.

[17] P. A. Grout, 'The Economics of the Private Finance Initiative', *Oxford Review of Economic Policy* 13/4 (1997), 53–66.

[18] HM Treasury, *Treasury Committee, Sixth Report, The Private Finance Initiative* (London, 1996).

[19] P. Jackson, 'The Private Finance Initiative, From the Foundations up – A Primer', Hume Occasional Paper 64 (Edinburgh: The David Hume Institute, February 2004), 5.

Programmes such as the privatisation of nationalised industries represented efforts both to earn a one-off payment from the sale of assets and to free the public finances from future obligations to the former nationalised industries. While the transfer of assets might at times be under-priced, there need be no net loss in the quantity of capital investment. However, the proceeds from privatising the nationalised industries were not reinvested in fixed capital. As Newbery observed, 'if we ask what happened to privatisation proceeds ... the implication is that Britain has eaten the capital that was in the public sector'.[20]

More problematic in terms of the economic and political issues involved was the sale of council houses. This was a more significant transfer of capital stock than that of the privatisation of nationalised utilities. The social consequences of the privatisation of social housing were greater than those of the privatisation of nationalised industries, not least as it reduced the ability of the public sector to provide a source of affordable accommodation to low-income groups.[21]

The interest in selling council houses to private buyers derived in part from Treasury concerns with the low rate of return earned on the stock of capital assets that council houses represented. The concern gained political teeth in the 1970s owing to public finance pressures on the one hand, and increasing political interest in the electoral gain of selling council houses to their occupants on the other. By the mid-1970s, that rents were too low and too uniform was acknowledged. Yet even to have earned a 3 per cent real return on council house stock would have required a 50 per cent increase in rent. Earning a real return of 10 per cent would have made council rents more expensive than privately built houses financed by mortgages.[22]

Alongside the pressure to raise the rate of return on the stock of council houses was a more general concern to improve the efficiency with which the entire national housing stock was used.[23] Low rents could be seen to be encouraging over-consumption of housing and hence an over-commitment of investment resources to housing. As a share of national income, investment in housing was 3.7 per cent in 1978 compared with the 4.1 per cent share of manufacturing investment. Rent did have an allocative function, and the view could be taken that if

---

[20] Florio, *Great Divestiture*, p. 295. D. M. Newbery, 'Che cosa puó imparare l'Europa dalle privatizzasioni britanniche' [What Europe Can Learn from British Privatisations], *Economia Pubblica* XXXIII/2 (2003), 63–76.

[21] Florio, *Great Divestiture*, p. 276.

[22] TNA T379/23; J. L. Carr, 'Calculation of Unsubsidised Rents', 10 May 1976, para. 3.

[23] TNA T386/595; Mr O'Donnell, Mr King and Mrs S. P. B. Walker, 'The Effects of Housing Subsidies on the PSBR and the Economy', 20 June 1980, para. 6.

low-income groups could not afford the rent, then this was an income problem rather than a price subsidy one.

Yet arguments to improve the use of the existing housing stock, and possibly to reduce the flow of investment into housing by emphasising the allocative function of council rents, sat uneasily alongside the absence of any taxation of the imputed rental income enjoyed by those living in a property they had purchased. The taxation of the imputed (rental) income from home ownership had ended following the abolition of Schedule A in 1963. Not only was the use of the home not taxed, but tax relief was offered on the mortgage used to buy the house. In 1977 Peter Shore, minister for the environment, wanted to offset an increase in council house rents against the abolition of higher-rate mortgage tax relief for nearly one million taxpayers; above the 50 per cent rate the number came down to about 150,000 actual mortgagors (worth about £20 million).[24] A combination of increasing council house rents by 50 per cent to earn a 3 per cent real return, allied to a complete scrapping of higher-rate mortgage tax relief, was estimated to be worth about £1.25 billion in revenue. The total abolition of mortgage tax relief would bring in a further £2 billion and, taken together, these increased revenues would form about one-quarter of the current PSBR.[25]

Discussion of council house rents, mortgage tax relief to house purchasers and the possible sale of council houses was further complicated by wider political considerations. Although the Thatcher government was to give impetus to the sale of council houses by the introduction of the Right to Buy programme, arguments for the sale of council housing stock were being made within the Labour government in the mid-1970s. In August 1976, it was Shore, newly appointed Secretary of State for the Environment, who wrote to the Chancellor of the Exchequer, Denis Healey, saying that one of the policy objectives of the Housing Finance Review

should be to give strong encouragement for home ownership. The gains from this would be enormous – not only is it what most people want but they are prepared to pay more for it out of their own pockets. We should of course match the encouragement of home ownership with steps to improve the status of council tenants, and we should also do more to encourage the new forms of tenure

---

[24] TNA T364/102; A. H. Lovell, Draft Note for the Chancellor, 'Housing Policy Review and Mortgage Tax Relief', 22 April 1977, paras. 2, 10.

[25] TNA T386/595, 'The Effects of Housing Subsidies', paras. 2, 6, 24. The estimated cost to the government of mortgage tax relief in 1980–1 was about £2 billion.

which are now being discussed. But if we are to come out more strongly in favour of home ownership, our policy will be crucially dependent upon the consistent and adequate supply of house purchase finance.[26]

On the Conservative side in the mid-1970s there was the traditional political interest in encouraging a property-owning democracy, allied to a deep concern to do more to protect capital assets of all types from taxation. In the context of the debate, which occurred in Britain in the mid-1970s and later concerning the importance of incentives to work, one defence of providing tax relief on mortgages was that it offered the further incentive of enhancing the ability to purchase capital stock. In the Treasury, suggestions for the abolition of higher-rate mortgage tax relief were opposed by the Permanent Secretary Douglas Wass, who claimed that 'It deals a pretty severe blow at the man who is on higher-rate and who has no capital.'[27] Wass argued that the withdrawal of higher-rate mortgage tax relief worked against easing the tax burden on and increasing the incentives for the highly skilled and managers, which had been one of the concerns of the recent budget. Middle-income earners would be adversely affected, as a married man with a £10,000 mortgage would move into the first higher-rate band on a gross annual income of about £8,000, and would begin to pay a marginal rate of tax of 50 per cent at an annual income of around £10,000.[28] An emerging feature of the Conservative Party's political thinking from the mid-1970s was a determination to reduce the taxation of capital. Elsewhere, when the economist James Meade reported on the recommendations of the Institute for Fiscal Studies committee on the structure and reform of direct taxation, he was bluntly informed by Geoffrey Howe, Mrs Thatcher's future first Chancellor of the Exchequer, that taxes on capital would not be tolerated. Access to capital stock by means of earning income was to be encouraged, not least on the grounds of reward and desert. This was at odds with the economist Friedrich Hayek's view, in which the role of luck was emphasised and any positive correlation between income and social value was disputed. This aspect of Hayek's writings tended to be overlooked by the Conservatives in their selective use of his writings.[29]

---

[26] TNA T364/54; Letter, Peter Shore (Department of the Environment) to Denis Healey (Chancellor of the Exchequer), 2 August 1976.

[27] TNA T364/102, 'Housing Policy Review', note by Douglas Wass, 25 April 1977, para. 5.

[28] TNA T364/102, A. H. Lovell, Draft note for the Chancellor, 'Housing Policy Review and Mortgage Tax Relief', 22 April 1977, paras. 5, 6.

[29] F. A. Hayek, *Law, Legislation and Liberty*, vol. 2: *The Mirage of Social Justice* (London and Henley: Routledge & Kegan Paul, 1976), pp. 80–1.

Reflecting its concern to reduce the size of the PSBR and to encourage the private ownership of the capital stock, the Thatcher government's Right to Buy programme gave a strong fillip to the sale of council houses to their tenants. The programme differed from previous approaches to the sale of council house stock as it reduced the ability of local authorities to decide which houses could and which could not be sold. Council house sales averaged 130,000 a year between 1980 and 1990, compared with 3,000–5,000 a year in 1960–7, 8,000 in 1968–70 and 100,000 in 1970–3, before slowing to 4,000 in 1974–6. Whereas in the mid-1970s slightly more than half of all dwellings were occupied by their owners, by the mid-1990s the proportion had increased to more than two-thirds.[30]

While council house sales would produce a one-off lump sum contribution to the public finances, as with the privatisation of nationalised industries this was at the cost of forgoing future rental incomes. As with the privatisation of nationalised industries, the proceeds of the sale of council houses were not invested in new social housing. Local councils could spend only one-fifth of the monies raised from the sale of council houses; the rest had to go towards paying off their debts.[31] Some council houses were sold to non-governmental 'social landlords' whose aim was to provide affordable housing to the low-paid. While in 1972 social landlords had produced only 9,750 new dwellings, this had increased to 39,328 by 1995.[32] However, this did not offset the fall in new local authority housing. Government-financed housing investment, which had fluctuated at around a rate of 2 per cent of GDP and at around 5.5 per cent of general government expenditure (GGE) in the two decades after 1956, effectively came to a halt between 1976 and 1982 and it was not significantly to exceed 1 per cent thereafter. In 2000 it stood at –0.1 per cent. From a peak of 151,824 new dwellings completed in 1976, the number fell to 39,960 in 1982 and to a mere 1,058 by 1998, less than 1 per cent of the 1976 level.[33] Publicly financed housebuilding was slashed and private and housing association-financed building failed to make good the shortfall. Expressed as units of housing, Tables 9.3 and 9.4 record the extent and trend of the withdrawal of the local authorities, New Towns and government departments from initiating the construction of housing.

---

[30] Florio, *Great Divestiture*, p. 276.
[31] Ibid.
[32] Clark, Elsby and Love, 'Twenty-Five Years of Falling Investment?', p. 12.
[33] T. Clark, M. Elsby and S. Love, 'Trends in British Public Investment', *Fiscal Studies* 23/3 (2002), 319, 322; Clark and Dilnot, *Long-Term Trends*, p. 15.

Table 9.3. *Housing completions, 1950–94 (Great Britain, thousands)*

	Private enterprise	Housing associations	Local authorities, New Towns and government departments
1950	27.4	1.6	169.2
1955	113.5	4.6	199.4
1960	168.6	1.8	127.4
1965	213.8	4.0	164.5
1970	170.3	8.5	171.6
1975	150.8	14.7	147.6
1980	128.4	21.1	86.0
1985	156.5	13.1	27.2
1990	160.7	17.0	16.6
1994	146.0	34.3	1.9

Source: Economic Trends, Annual Supplement, 1996, table 4.5.

Table 9.4. *Housing starts: local authorities, New Towns and government departments, 1974–88 (Great Britain, thousands)*

1974	1975	1976	1977	1978	1979	1980	1981	1982	1983	1984	1985	1986	1987	1988
134.3	154.1	141.6	103.9	86.9	65.3	41.5	26.0	34.9	34.6	27.3	22.0	20.4	19.9	16.4

Source: Economic Trends, Annual Supplement, 1996, table 4.5.

As is evident from the fixed capital investment formation data shown in Table 9.5, while the share of total investment in housing remained remarkably constant, during the second half of the twentieth century the private and public sources of that investment were effectively reversed.

This decline in local authority house building coincided with an increase in the total number of households, from 18.6 million in 1971 to 24.1 million in 2001. Housing costs rose throughout the 1980s, promoting greater inequality.[34] This overshadowed the progressive element to the sale of council houses as this sale of over 1.5 million family units between 1979 and 1997 at a discount often in excess of 30 per cent of the value of the assets represented a progressive transfer between the average taxpayer with a higher income to the average council house buyer.[35] In general, as stock was sold, so the asset valuation of the public sector fell. Estimates of the public sector net worth declined from 77.1 per cent of GDP in 1980/1 to 15.6 per cent by 1999/2000[36] (see Table 9.6).

[34] A. Goodman and S. Webb, *For Richer, For Poorer: The Changing Distribution of Income in the UK, 1961–91*, Commentary 42 (London: Institute for Fiscal Studies, 1994).
[35] Florio, *Great Divestiture*, p. 277.
[36] Ibid., p. 279.

Table 9.5. *Gross domestic fixed capital formation by sector and by dwellings*

	Analysed by sector as a percentage of total GDFCF			Dwellings as percentage of total GDFCF		
	Private sector	General government	Public corporations	Private	Public	Total
1950	52.3	30.9	16.6	3.4	16.3	19.7
1955	54.4	25.9	19.6	10.1	12.8	22.9
1960	61.1	20.3	18.6	11.6	6.4	18.0
1965	58.0	22.5	19.5	12.5	8.4	20.1
1970	57.7	25.1	17.2	11.0	8.2	19.2
1975	57.6	23.7	18.6	13.0	9.3	22.3
1980	70.0	13.6	16.4	14.7	6.2	20.9
1985	78.9	11.3	9.8	15.9	4.2	20.1
1990	83.6	11.8	4.6	16.0	3.9	19.9
1994	82.6	12.6	4.8	18.2	2.7	20.9

Source: Economic Trends, Annual Supplement 1996, table 1.8.

Table 9.6. *UK public finances, 1970/1 to 1999/2000 (five-year intervals, and 1999/2000)*

	Public sector current expenditure £ million (1998/9)	Public sector net capital expenditure £ million (1998/9)	General government expenditure £ million (1998/9)	Public sector current receipts £ million (1998/9)	Public sector net debt per cent of GDP	Public sector net worth per cent of GDP
1970/1	143.5	29.0	183.3	42.7	69.6	41.7
1975/6	196.3	28.5	238.1	42.7	54.2	66.5
1980/1	217.7	10.6	245.4	42.6	46.2	77.1
1985/6	246.6	8.0	261.8	43.2	43.6	61.0
1990/1	250.3	10.5	268.8	39.0	26.3	62.8
1995/6	311.3	10.5	331.0	37.9	43.2	21.6
1999/2000	321.6	6.2	340.8	39.6	38.2	15.6

Source: Florio, *The Great Divestiture*, table 8.3, p. 279.

Investment Appraisal

In addition to the shifts in expenditure between current and capital expenditure, within government there were also important shifts in how the cost of capital expenditure was perceived. This partly invoked a widening interest in the use of cost–benefit analysis (CBA) to evaluate the social and economic aspects of capital investment projects, but it also involved a shift in the temporal perspective from which proposed projects were viewed. One instance of this was in the appraisal of fixed capital investment in the nationalised industries. From the initial position at the moment of nationalisation in the 1940s that industries should cover costs taking one year with another, on the back of the 1958 public expenditure crisis there was a move in 1961 to prescribing that a required rate of return (RRR) should be earned on existing assets. This was an ex post judgement in that it sought to earn higher financial returns from assets that already existed, that is to say somebody else had previously decided to build them. This ex post judgement of the capital stock was superseded in 1967 by the ex ante application of a test discount rate, which required proposed fixed capital investment projects to clear the set hurdle.[37] The ex ante approach did not ask how to increase returns on existing assets, but asked instead what those returns would be were the asset to be built. Since these prospective returns would come in the future, the practice was to discount them back to a present-day value and then compare the present value of the costs and benefits. Crucial to this assessment was the choice of the level of discount rate to use when bringing prospective future returns back to a present-day value. Inasmuch as this was done for individual projects which might be added to an existing system, this formed a forward-looking, marginal and system-based analysis of proposed investment.

Beyond the nationalised industries, similar approaches to public sector investment and expenditure were being developed. In healthcare the development of QALY (quality-adjusted life year) measures was one instance, as also was the pressure in higher education to make students pay fees for what were seen as the increasingly private benefits of attending university.[38] Less well known was the tendency towards the individualisation of benefits in the assessment of road traffic accidents and the related issue of when and where improvements were made to roads and traffic systems. From the interwar period until the 1960s the main approach used by the Road Research Laboratory adopted an ex post approach to calculating the monetary cost to society of an 'average' accident.[39] The alternative was an ex ante approach, which took into account the benefit to society, including the individual concerned when a death was prevented. In the ex post approach the individual

---

[37] M. Chick, *Industrial Policy in Britain, 1945–1951* (Cambridge: Cambridge University Press, 1998), ch. 5; and *Electricity and Energy Policy in Britain, France and the United States since 1945* (Cheltenham: Edward Elgar, 2007), ch. 5.

[38] One accessible route into the large literature on the allocation of health resources is R. Cookson and K. Claxton (eds.), *The Humble Economist: Tony Culyer on Health, Health Care and Social Decision Making* (London: Office of Health Economics, 2012).

[39] D. J. Reynolds, 'The Costs of Road Accidents', *Journal of Royal Statistical Society*, Series A, 119, Part IV (1956).

concerned was excluded from the society being considered. In the ex ante approach he or she was included. On an ex-post basis when an individual was killed, it was agreed that society lost the present value of that person's future output, but at the same time gained to the extent that it no longer had to provide for his or her future consumption. The measure of lost output was therefore taken net of consumption. On the ex ante basis, which measured the benefit of keeping an individual alive who, but for the introduction of some safety measure, would have died, it was agreed that the measure of output should be gross and not net of consumption. On this basis, since the individual was alive and able to enjoy his or her consumption, this consumption was a benefit to him or her and, since the individual was a member of society, a benefit to society. Consumption therefore was not netted out of output. Where an individual enjoyed a higher utility than that reflected in measured consumption, this formed his or her consumer surplus.[40]

The impact of this changed approach to the evaluation of the living over the dead, allied to increases in economic growth and rising productivity, was to increase the value placed on human life. In 1970, the valuation of a life saved was almost doubled, with the valuations in 1970 prices being £17,000 for a fatality, £900 for a serious injury and £30 for a minor injury.[41] Expressed in 2004 prices, the value of a prevented fatality (VPF) of a road fatality rose from £37,500 in 1952 to £1,384,500 in 2004, a 37-fold increase (see Table 9.7).

As an ex ante approach to preventing fatalities was adopted, so it became tempting to distinguish between the economic value of the individual lives that were being saved. This value was calculated from their annual output and the number of expected future years of work. It became possible to differentiate the value of prevented fatalities by age, income and gender. So, for example, motorcyclists tended to be young men, whereas pedestrian casualties were weighted towards the elderly and children. In economic terms, the young and employed were worth more than the old and retired; the individual motorcyclist or car occupant was worth more than the individual pedestrian.[42] The economic value of the retired was treated as nil since retired people had no present output and consumed out of past earnings (savings) or from

[40] TNA MT 120/186; R. H. Bird, 'The Prediction and Evaluation of Road Accidents', 16 August 1965, para. 11; TNA MT 92/40, J. Jukes, Note on 'Accident Costs', 19 August 1970, para. 10; TNA, MT92/481, Paper on 'Accident Cost Valuation', n.d. and unsigned, paras. 9, 12.

[41] TNA MT 120/186, E. Dale, 'Differentiation of Road Casualty Costs', 3 December 1970.

[42] TNA MT 92/404, L. E. Dale, 'Differentiation of Road Casualty Costs', memorandum, 30 December 1970, paras. 4, 6.

Table 9.7. *Value of preventing a UK road fatality: selected years, 1952–2004*

Year	Value at current prices	Value at 2004 prices	Value at 2004 prices (2004 = 100)	Value at 2004 prices (1952 = 1)	Value relative to real household disposable income (1952 = 1)
1952	£2,000	£37,500	2.7	1.0	1.0
1963	£7,880	£107,500	7.8	2.9	2.0
1971	£18,420	£169,700	12.3	4.6	2.6
1978	£89,300	£333,400	24.1	8.9	4.2
1987	£500,000	£916,100	66.2	24.5	9.1
2004	£1,384,500	£1,384,500	100.0	37.0	8.3

Source: NERA Economic Consulting, *Human Costs of a Nuclear Accident: Final Report*, 3 July 2007, cols. 1–4: A. Evans, 'Evidence to the House of Lords Economics Affairs Committee Inquiry into the Government's Policy on the Management of Risk', *Economic Trends Annual Supplement 2005* (2006), table 1.6.

transfer payments (e.g. old age pensions). However, the fact that the rest of society was prepared to forgo some consumption to allow non-producers to consume suggested that this provided a minimum estimate of the value of life of these non-producers, which was how the £5,000 non-economic (or subjective) cost value was derived. Thus, the consumption stream of retired people was used as a basis for calculating the subjective cost.[43]

Back to Keynes?

Given the long-run interest in the use of public fixed capital investment projects in the form of public works, and Keynes' emphasis in *The General Theory* on the expected marginal efficiency of investment in encouraging private investment, it is perhaps of interest to consider how the significant withdrawal of the state from fixed capital investment subsequently affected its response to the economic consequences of the financial implosions of 2008. After that crisis there was renewed interest in Keynes' writings of the 1930s and, in part, in his focus on fixed capital investment.[44] If we take chapter 11 (on the marginal efficiency of investment) of *The General Theory* to be its central chapter, then it is interesting to compare how its advocacy sits alongside UK government economic policy from 2008 onwards. Since Keynes prioritised the

[43] TNA MT 92/404, Note by G. Mooney, 13 October 1970, para. 4.
[44] G. A. Akerlof and R. J. Shiller, *Animal Spirits: How Human Psychology Drives the Economy and Why it Matters for Global Competition* (Princeton, NJ: Princeton University Press, 2009); and R. Skidelsky, *Keynes: The Return of the Master* (London: Allen Lane, 2009).

marginal efficiency of investment and argued sequentially that it preceded an ability to influence liquidity preference and the multiplier
effects of the consumption function (and need not require that there be
a *unique* rate of interest), then he was drawn towards a more active
approach to economic management. Indeed, in *The General Theory*
Keynes wrote of the 'socialisation' of investment, but made it clear that
by socialisation he did not mean nationalisation:

> The State will have to exercise a guiding influence on the propensity to con-
> sume partly through its scheme of taxation, partly by fixing the rate of interest,
> and partly, perhaps, in other ways. Furthermore, it seems unlikely that the
> influence of banking policy on the rate of interest will be sufficient by itself to
> determine an optimum rate of investment. I conceive, therefore, that a some-
> what comprehensive socialisation of investment will prove the only means of
> securing an approximation to full employment; though this need not exclude
> all manner of compromises and devices by which the public authority will
> co-operate with private initiative. But beyond this no obvious case is made out
> for a system of State Socialism which would embrace most of the economic life
> of the community. It is not the ownership of the instruments of production
> which it is important for the State to assume. If the State is able to determine
> the aggregate amount of resources devoted to augmenting the instruments and
> the basic rate of reward to those who own them, it will have accomplished all
> that is necessary. Moreover, the necessary measures of socialisation can be
> introduced gradually and without a break in the general traditions of society.[45]

More generally, as in his 1933 *The Means to Prosperity* newspaper
articles published in *The Times*, Keynes argued that as a first step to
recovery, bank credit should be made cheap and abundant, and, as a
second step, the long-term rate of interest should be low for all reasonably financially sound borrowers. However, he then went on to argue
that 'even when we have reached the second stage, it is very unlikely
that private enterprise will, on its own initiative, undertake new loan-
expenditure on a sufficient scale'. The reluctance of business to expand
until *after* profits begin to recover, and the fact that increased working
capital would not be required until *after* output began to increase,
meant in Keynes' view that an important role fell to those public and
semi-public bodies that undertook 'a very large proportion of our *normal* programmes of loan-expenditure'. In contrast to the 'comparatively
small' new loan expenditure required in any year by trade and industry,
Keynes emphasised how 'building, transport and public utilities are
responsible at all times for a very large proportion of current loan

---

[45] J. M. Keynes, *The General Theory of Employment, Interest and Money* (London:
Macmillan for The Royal Economic Society, 1973), p. 378; and P. Davidson, *John
Maynard Keynes* (Basingstoke: Macmillan, 2007), p. 67.

Table 9.8. *Public sector, debt interest payments in £ billion (2012/13 prices) and as a percentage of national income*

	Public sector net debt interest payments £ billion	per cent GDP	PG gross debt interest payments	per cent GDP	GDP £ billion	TME less social security less gross debt	per cent GDP
1949/50	9.3	2.9	15.8	4.9	322.2	87.5	27.2
1954/5	8.9	2.4	16.5	4.5	369.7	104.5	28.3
1959/60	15.8	3.8	18.6	4.4	419.2	110.4	26.3
1964/5	17.7	3.5	22.0	4.3	506.9	139.9	27.6
1969/70	21.2	3.6	26.8	4.6	582.1	175.1	30.1
1974/5	25.1	3.7	32.6	4.8	675.3	240.5	35.6
1979/80	30.0	4.0	37.9	5.0	751.1	222.8	29.7
1984/5	33.0	4.1	41.3	5.2	795.2	238.0	29.9
1989/90	25.9	2.6	38.1	3.9	982.1	243.0	24.7
1994/5	29.2	2.7	35.4	3.3	1070.4	267.9	25.0
1999/2000	28.2	2.2	34.1	2.7	1267.0	282.6	2.3
2004/5	22.9	1.6	30.3	2.1	1474.1	401.4	27.2
2009/10	29.9	2.0	33.5	2.2	1530.8	487.4	31.8

Source: Institute for Fiscal Studies.

expenditure'. Therefore, in leading off an attempted recovery, 'the first step has to be taken on the initiative of public authority' and organised 'on a large scale and organised with determination'.[46]

During the eighty years between Keynes' *The Means to Prosperity* and the present, the UK state increasingly intervened and then steadily withdrew from capital investment. In the wake of the 2008 financial collapse, the government appeared reluctant to tackle the first of Keynes' triumvirate of building, utilities and transport targets, namely financing the construction of new, low-rent housing. As these social rents would be low they would not earn a 'market' rate of return on capital investment, but so long as net rental income exceeded the costs of borrowing, revenue would go into the state coffers and improve the structural deficit. While debt would increase, the deficit would reduce; such trading of debt against deficit arguably being attractive. Net debt interest payments were not high by historical standards (see Table 9.8).

As for public utilities, the second of Keynes' targeted areas for loan-financed investment, there remained a clear role for the state in easing anxieties concerning the risk of making large sunk capital investments.

[46] J. M. Keynes, *The Means to Prosperity* (London: Macmillan, 1933), ch. 3.

In the privatised electricity industry, where EDF and other generators were negotiating to supply new nuclear and conventional generating capacity, investors of sunk capital looked for assurances that adequate returns on this fixed capital investment would be reasonably assured. The risks of such investment arose from uncertainty as to the future relative price of competing sources of electricity which would influence the market price, and hence the rate of return.[47] The state could reduce the risk by effectively offering some form of guaranteed return on the asset base. It seemed willing to do this for some energy projects, notably wind power, through the use of the Renewable Obligation, which required suppliers to purchase a proportion of wind turbine output. It seemed less willing to do this for potential investors in new conventional generating capacity, presumably as it feared they would not appear to be operating in a competitive market. Although competitive pool trading arrangements can be designed, the very gaming activity within them, which benefited nuclear suppliers, caused such pooling arrangements to be scrapped. Outside of such pools, it is far from clear how much scope there is for competition in a very high sunk cost industry like electricity, especially, ex ante, in terms of encouraging fresh investment.

Conclusion

This chapter has surveyed the share, composition and, unusually perhaps, the tendency to 'individualisation' of assessments of public fixed capital investment projects since 1970. This last development can be seen more widely beyond public fixed capital investment, notably in expenditure in the health and education programmes. The public finance pressures underlying such developments arose from the increasing demands placed on public finances at a time of lower rates of economic growth, rising unemployment and the ever-increasing cost of financing pensions and health. This combination of pressures on public finance became evident in the 1970s. It was from that decade that UK governments began to withdraw from fixed capital investment and shifted to a greater role as a transfer-payment state. As the subsequent privatisation programme of the 1980s indicated, emerging from the 1970s was a debate not simply about public finance, but about the role of the state. This found particular and clear expression from the 1970s in successive governments' approach to public fixed capital investment

---

[47] D. Helm, 'Infrastructure Investment, the Cost of Capital, and Regulation: An Assessment', *Oxford Review of Economic Policy* 25/3 (2009), 314–15.

in the United Kingdom, both in the aggregate and in the specific character of the fixed capital investments, which they were, and were not, willing to undertake. By 2010 the role of the state had changed substantially from that exemplified by the Attlee governments with their programmes of nationalisation and the provision of public housing. In effecting this change, recourse was made to an altered temporal stance (from ex post to ex ante) and to a more systems-based, marginal approach to fixed capital investment, which emphasised the future discounted benefits for individuals. Individuals in turn had their own future value, and therefore derived benefit, related to their future economic value. A growing tendency developed to distinguish between public and private benefit. The state moved to concentrating on conditions in which investment might flourish, rather than undertaking the investment itself. Yet it fought shy of providing the type of 'socialised' return on potential investment of which Keynes had written, even in the case of durable, necessary investments such as in housing and utilities. Such a shift in the role of the state occurred as much for reasons of public finance as because of any major changes in economic theory. It points to the vulnerability of any post-war Keynesian revolution, which practically had its roots in improved public finances in the golden age. For, as public finances faltered and political emphasis switched to the cash PSBR measure, the post-war Keynesian revolution was challenged by an approach that shared Keynes' interest in future returns, but was disinclined to act to reduce the uncertainty and risks affecting expectations of returns on future fixed capital investment projects.

10 From 'Brink of the Abyss' to 'Miracle'? Public Spending in Denmark and the Netherlands since 1980

Reimut Zohlnhöfer[1]

Introduction

Denmark and the Netherlands shared a similar fiscal policy trajectory in the last quarter of the twentieth century. For both countries, the golden post-war years came to a halt with the first oil price shock of 1973 and the economic turmoil that followed. While both countries at first adopted a Keynesian approach to their economic difficulties,[2] this strategy proved highly ineffective and the situation in both countries worsened by the end of the decade. In the Netherlands, the term 'Dutch disease' – originally coined to describe the negative effect of gas exports on the domestic industry[3] – gained currency as a description of the wider economic situation,[4] while in Denmark the Social Democratic Minister of Finance, Knud Heinesen, argued in 1979 that the country's economy stood at the 'brink of the abyss'[5] – again, a judgement that was widely shared in the country. Moreover, public spending was perceived to lie at the heart of the problem in both

[1] Funding for research by the German Research Foundation is gratefully acknowledged (ZO 126/2-1 and ZO 126/2-2). I would also like to thank Franz-Xaver Kaufmann, the editors and the participants in the workshop 'Leviathan after the Boom' for helpful comments and Fabian Engler for research assistance.

[2] For Denmark, see P. Nannestad, *Danish Design or British Disease? Danish Economic Crisis Policy 1974–1979 in Comparative Perspective* (Aarhus: Aarhus University Press, 1991), pp. 141–84. For the Netherlands, see A. Knoester, *Economische politiek in Nederland* (Leiden: Stenfert Kroese B.V., 1989); B. Snels, *Politics in the Dutch Economy: The Economics of Institutional Interaction* (Aldershot: Ashgate, 1999); and J. Toirkens, *Schijn en werkelijkheid van het bezuinigsbeleid 1975–1986* (Deventer: Kluwer, 1988).

[3] R. Lubbers and C. Lemckert, 'The Influence of Natural Gas on the Dutch Economy', in R. T. Griffiths (ed.), *The Economy and Politics of the Netherlands since 1945* (The Hague: Martinus Nijhoff, 1980), pp. 87–113.

[4] See K. van Paridon, 'Wiederaufbau – Krise – Erholung. Die niederländische Wirtschaft seit 1945', in F. Wielenga and I. Taute (eds.), *Länderbericht Niederlande. Geschichte – Wirtschaft – Gesellschaft* (Bonn: Bundeszentrale für politische Bildung, 2004), pp. 363–422.

[5] P. Nannestad and C. Green-Pedersen, 'Keeping the Bumblebee Flying: Economic Policy in the Welfare State of Denmark, 1973–99', in E. Albæk, L. C. Eliason, A. S. Nørgaard and H. S. Schwartz (eds.), *Crisis, Miracles, and Beyond: Negotiated Adaptation of the Danish Welfare State* (Aarhus: Aarhus University Press, 2008), pp. 33–74.

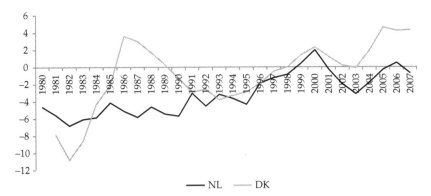

Figure 10.1. General government financial balances as a percentage of nominal GDP, Denmark and the Netherlands, 1980–2007.
Source: OECD Economic Outlook 81.

countries. Finally, the deteriorating economic situation in both countries and the decreasing effectiveness of traditional fiscal policy responses to these problems brought bourgeois[6] governments to power in 1982 which aimed at, and eventually implemented, a break with traditional economic policies.

Twenty years later, around the turn of the century, both Denmark and the Netherlands were being described as 'miracle' countries[7] – that is, highly successful in economic policy – or even as exemplary cases. This is true not least in respect of public finances as both countries had substantially reduced their budget deficits in the 1980s and had even run surpluses in the 2000s (see Figure 10.1).

Nonetheless, the two countries' route to budget consolidation differed substantially. While in 1980, before the changes in fiscal policy were introduced in earnest, both countries were very similar in terms of

---

[6] I use the term 'bourgeois' rather than conservative for the parties of the centre-right in both countries for two reasons. First, the Dutch CDA is a Christian Democratic party and research has repeatedly shown that Christian Democrats have pursued social policies that were quite different from those of conservative parties for much of the post-war era. Second, while the Danish bourgeois coalitions comprised the Conservative People's Party, they were four-party coalitions and the label conservative does not do all of them justice (particularly because the Conservatives were not always the leading party of the coalition).

[7] For Denmark, see H. M. Schwartz, 'The Danish "Miracle". Luck, Pluck, or Stuck?', *Comparative Political Studies* 34 (2001), 131–55; for the Netherlands, see J. Visser and A. Hemerijck, *Ein holländisches Wunder? Reform des Sozialstaates und Beschäftigungswachstum in den Niederlanden* (Frankfurt and New York: Campus, 1998).

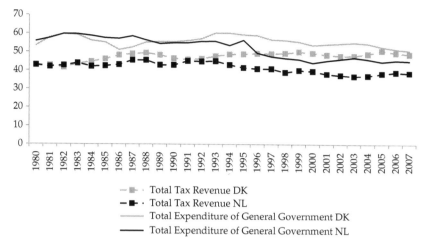

Figure 10.2. Total tax revenues and total expenditure of general government as a percentage of nominal GDP, Denmark and the Netherlands, 1980–2007.
Source: OECD Economic Outlook 91 (Government Expenditure); OECD Revenue Statistics.

total government expenditure as well as the tax ratio (at around 55 and 43 per cent of GDP respectively), they diverged markedly through the 1980s and the divergence was even more pronounced after 1990. While Denmark's total governmental outlays remained steady for the most part after 1990, and fell only moderately over the whole period, between 1983 and 2007 the Netherlands experienced a substantial reduction in its government spending of around 25 per cent (i.e. 15 percentage points) (see Figure 10.2). Similarly, while the tax ratio increased moderately in Denmark, particularly in the 1980s, taxation fell slightly in the Netherlands.

Moreover, if we follow Francis Castles' distinction between social spending and core spending (total spending less social spending),[8] we find another surprising difference between the two countries (see Figure 10.3). While social expenditure in Denmark remained more or less constant, with a slight overall increase over the twenty-eight years under review, Danish core expenditure fell by around 10 percentage points after 1983. In contrast, social and core expenditure in the Netherlands moved

[8] F. G. Castles, 'Introduction', in F. G. Castles (ed.), *The Disappearing State? Retrenchment Realities in an Age of Globalisation* (Cheltenham and Northampton: Edward Elgar, 2007), pp. 1–18.

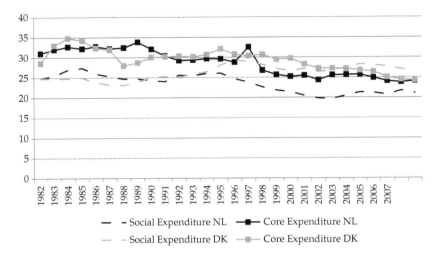

Figure 10.3. Social and core expenditure as a percentage of GDP, Denmark and the Netherlands, 1980–2007.
Source: OECD Economic Outlook 91; OECD Social Expenditure Database.

more or less in tandem, that is to say, both expenditures were cut quite significantly, by 6 and 8 percentage points between 1983 and 2007.

This is significant because it means not only that the difference in overall public spending between Denmark and the Netherlands can be explained essentially by the differences in changes in social spending, but also that while Denmark – like most other advanced democracies – was not able to reduce its social expenditure significantly and over a longer period of time, the Netherlands did succeed in this respect.

The question I shall address in this chapter follows directly from these data: What accounts for the different public (and social) spending trajectories in the Netherlands and Denmark between 1982 and 2007? A comparison of the two countries is pertinent because, as we have seen, we find very different spending patterns despite their many similarities. Denmark and the Netherlands are both comparatively small, economically open and affluent western European countries and were members of the European Community (EC)/EU during the whole period under discussion here; both are parliamentary democracies, which can be characterised as consensus democracies according to Lijphart;[9]

---

[9] A. Lijphart, *Patterns of Democracy. Government Forms and Performance in Thirty-Six Countries*, 2nd edn (New Haven, CT, and London: Yale University Press, 2012).

and the system of interest group intermediation in both countries is consistently classified as corporatist in the literature.[10] Thus, if the spending trajectories in Denmark and the Netherlands differ despite these similarities, the reasons may well lie in the few remaining differences. The most likely candidates explaining the differences in public (and social) spending over the period seem to be the current account situation, membership of the European Monetary Union (EMU) and the patterns of party competition. In this chapter, I shall discuss these three possible explanations in turn.

The period of observation covers the years between 1982 and 2007. The post-war boom had come to an end before 1982 in both countries; and indeed it was the first oil price shock of 1973 that marks the end of the golden age. Nonetheless, as we shall see in the next section, it took policy-makers some years to come to grips with the new economic situation. Thus, in both countries the government initially tried to tackle the crisis in a traditional, Keynesian way. It was not until the early 1980s and the respective changes of government that took place in both countries in 1982, and that brought new bourgeois governments under Ruud Lubbers in the Netherlands and Poul Schlüter in Denmark to power, that more supply-side-oriented (neo-liberal) thinking began to inform government policy to any appreciable degree. Thus, the literature on both countries agrees that the change of government in 1982 marked the main turning point in the economic policy development of both countries after the boom.[11] As the financial crisis of 2007/8 and the Great Recession that followed it had a tremendous impact on public finances and may indeed mark another turning point, the years after 2007 are not discussed here. Thus, the period of observation ends on the eve of the financial crisis.

In addition to the secondary literature, the case studies presented here are based on a variety of original sources and around twenty

---

[10] A. Siaroff, 'Corporatism in 24 Industrial Democracies: Meaning and Measurement', *European Journal of Political Research* 36 (1999), 175–205; and D. Jahn, 'Changing of the Guard: Trends in Corporatist Arrangements in 42 Highly Industrialized Societies from 1960 to 2010', *Socio-Economic Review* (first published online, 26 August 2014), doi: 10.1093/ser/mwu028.

[11] For Denmark, see E. Damgaard, 'Crisis Politics in Denmark 1974–1987', in E. Damgaard, P. Gerlich and J. J. Richardson (eds.), *The Politics of Economic Crisis: Lessons from Western Europe* (Aldershot: Avebury, 1989), pp. 70–88; and Nannestad and Green-Pedersen, 'Keeping the Bumblebee Flying', 33–74. For the Netherlands, see Knoester, 'Economische politiek in Nederland', 159–62; T. Reininga, 'Coalition Governments and Fiscal Policy in the Netherlands', in Banca d'Italia (ed.), *Fiscal Rules* (Rome: Banca d'Italia, 2002), pp. 555–75; and E. Seils, *Finanzpolitik und Arbeitsmarkt in den Niederlanden. Haushaltsinstitutionen, Koalitionsverträge und die Beschäftigungswirkung von Abgaben* (Wiesbaden: Verlag für Sozialwissenschaften, 2004).

interviews, most with experts directly involved in fiscal policy-making in the two countries during the period under review. Among those interviewed were ten former members of government (finance or tax ministers and prime ministers).

In the next two sections, I discuss the effects of differences in the two countries' current account position and the Maastricht convergence criteria on public spending developments in Denmark and the Netherlands. While the Netherlands historically ran current account surpluses and sought entry into the European Monetary Union (EMU), Denmark ran current account deficits until around 1990 and secured an opt-out regarding EMU. Nevertheless, I shall show that neither difference can explain the spending patterns in the two countries. Next, I discuss the politics of reining in public and particularly social spending and show that the party system constellations were key factors facilitating or hindering spending restraint.

The Current Account Position and Public Spending Patterns in Denmark and the Netherlands

As we have seen, both Denmark and the Netherlands faced profound economic problems at the beginning of the 1980s. Unemployment was very high, inflation was rising and the budget deficit was approaching record levels.[12] What is more, in both countries the bourgeois parties that came to power in 1982 believed that consolidation of the budget was necessary in order to solve the countries' respective problems, as many of the policy-makers I interviewed confirmed. Nonetheless, the problems Denmark and the Netherlands faced in the early 1980s, although apparently similar, were not identical and thus the policy mix, of which a reduction in public spending and the budget deficit were a part, differed in some respects.

The most important difference concerns the current account position. The Dutch economy has traditionally been dominated by a number of huge multinational enterprises. This comparatively favourable situation, together with the revenues from the sales of natural gas, resulted in a current account surplus.[13] Due to the current account surpluses (which were in large part linked to gas sales after 1973) the guilder appreciated continuously. This meant that exports became more expensive abroad, which in turn meant a loss of competitiveness

---

[12] See R. Zohlnhöfer, *Globalisierung der Wirtschaft und finanzpolitische Anpassungsreaktionen in Westeuropa* (Baden-Baden: Nomos, 2009).
[13] Lubbers and Lemckert, 'The Influence of Natural Gas', pp. 87–113.

in international markets. Thus, Dutch industry was priced out of the market through the exchange rate effect of the gas sales – what economists termed the 'Dutch disease'.[14] One of the consequences was a massive loss of jobs as the gas industry was unable to create enough new jobs to compensate for the contraction in the industrial sector. This set up a vicious circle as the rise in unemployment, as well as the indexation of benefits to increasing wages, resulted in higher social security contributions, which in turn led to higher labour costs, which again reduced the competitiveness of the Dutch economy, resulting in even higher rates of unemployment.[15]

Governments' response in the 1970s to the economic and budgetary problems that were increasingly apparent in the Netherlands initially was not informed by these considerations.[16] The leftist den Uyl government (1973–7) first attempted a reflationary policy to overcome the oil price shock during the first part of its term in office, but moderated its stance later without conceding to a neo-liberal explanation of the economic problems the Netherlands was experiencing. In contrast, the van Agt government of Christian Democrats and liberals that replaced the den Uyl coalition in 1977 accepted the neo-liberal argument that labour costs were at the heart of the problem, but failed to act accordingly and thus contributed to a further deterioration of the economy and the budget situation.

After two short-lived coalitions of Christian Democrats, left-liberals and (initially) Social Democrats led by Dries van Agt, a coalition government of Christian Democrats (CDA) and market liberals (VVD) led by Prime Minister Ruud Lubbers came to power in 1982. This new government agreed that labour costs in the Netherlands were too high and that this was impairing the competitiveness of Dutch industry and thereby leading to rising unemployment.[17] As increases in public spending led to higher taxes and, above all, higher social security contributions, which in turn further increased labour costs, the government's goal was to reduce public spending, not least on welfare, to cure the Dutch disease. Similarly, the Lubbers government (as well as its

---

[14] See, for example, P. R. Krugman, *Rethinking International Trade* (Cambridge, MA: MIT Press, 2000), p. 114.

[15] See F. Bos, 'The Dutch Fiscal Framework: History, Current Practice and the Role of the Central Planning Bureau', *OECD Journal on Budgeting* 8 (2008), 16.

[16] D. Braun, *Grenzen politischer Regulierung: Der Weg in die Massenarbeitslosigkeit am Beispiel der Niederlande* (Wiesbaden: DUV, 1989); Knoester, *Economische politiek in Nederland*; Seils, *Finanzpolitik und Arbeitsmarkt in den Niederlanden*; Snels, *Politics in the Dutch Economy*; and Toirkens, *Schijn en werkelijheid*.

[17] Braun, *Grenzen politischer Regulierung*, pp. 233ff.; and Seils, *Finanzpolitik und Arbeitsmarkt in den Niederlanden*, p. 76.

successors) was keen to make tax cuts which would pave the way to wage moderation. This was the second cornerstone of the new government's economic policy strategy.

The situation in Denmark was very different. Here the agricultural sector was comparatively important and there were very few multinational enterprises. Even in the 1980s, the OECD noted that 'the tradable goods sector is small and appears to suffer from a certain backwardness in technological adaptation and development'.[18] As a consequence, one of the main problems for the Danish economy for virtually the whole post-war period until 1990 was a substantial current account deficit.[19] One of the consequences was that interest rates had to be comparatively high in order to attract sufficient capital imports to finance the current account deficit. Moreover, due to the current account problems, Danish economic policy in the Keynesian era was characterised by stop–go patterns, similar to what could be observed in the United Kingdom until the 1970s.[20]

The restrictions that the current account situation imposed on counter-cyclical fiscal policy in Denmark can also be seen in its response to the first oil crisis.[21] The reflationary policy initially adopted relied heavily on tax cuts. This led to a substantial deterioration in the current account. Therefore, from 1976 onwards, the government adopted a 'demand twist' policy: while private consumption was taxed more heavily, public spending expanded, not least with an increase in public sector employment. Essentially, this meant that the government actively sought to improve the current account by substituting private consumption with public consumption because the latter, it was hoped, would have a less negative impact on the current account. We can thus conclude that, at least in the 1970s, the current account problems induced governments to favour public over private spending, which increased public expenditure. So, was the current account situation also the reason why Denmark did not adopt spending restraint after 1982, in contrast to the Netherlands, which was not constrained by current account considerations?

---

[18] Organisation for Economic Cooperation and Development, *OECD Economic Survey Denmark* (Paris: OECD, 1986), p. 52.

[19] Nannestad and Green-Pedersen, 'Keeping the Bumblebee Flying'.

[20] P. S. Andersen and J. Åkerholm, 'Scandinavia', in A. Boltho (ed.), *The European Economy: Growth and Crisis* (Oxford: Oxford University Press, 1982), pp. 615, 629; L. Mjøset, 'Nordic Economic Policies in the 1970s and 1980s', *International Organization* 41 (1987), 428; and P. Nannestad, *Danish Design or British Disease? Danish Economic Crisis Policy 1974–1979 in Comparative Perspective* (Aarhus: Aarhus University Press, 1991), p. 136.

[21] Nannestad and Green-Pedersen, 'Keeping the Bumblebee Flying', 38–40.

The bourgeois government under Prime Minister Poul Schlüter initially relied on a policy mix that was not so very dissimilar to the economic policies adopted by the Dutch government under Lubbers. Like its Dutch counterpart, the Schlüter government abandoned Keynesianism and sought to improve the competitiveness of the Danish export sector. Thus, the government adopted a restrictive fiscal policy which, it hoped, would help cut interest rates. Budget consolidation was to be brought about via expenditure cuts, including limited welfare retrenchment, rather than by tax increases, for two reasons. First, the government hoped to improve the current account situation by reducing its demand for imports. Thus it adopted something like a reverse demand twist policy. Second, by avoiding tax increases the government hoped to support a policy of wage moderation.

If there ever was a policy that was too successful, the economic policy of the Schlüter governments between 1982 and 1985 is a case in point. The budget deficit was cut substantially, as were interest rates. This led to an increase in domestic demand, which in turn resulted in higher growth rates and increasing employment. This again led to an improvement in government finances.[22] The disadvantage was that the current account deficit continued to grow, reaching 5.2 per cent of GDP in 1986. The government reacted to this further deterioration with a programme commonly known as the 'potato diet'. The programme consisted of a number of tax increases, which were intended to reduce private (import) demand.[23] Although the programme and the tax reform of 1987 resulted in a substantial and prolonged slowdown of growth and a large increase in unemployment between 1987 and 1993, the main aim of the 'potato diet' was achieved as the deficit in the current account was reversed and a surplus was recorded in 1990 for the first time in living memory; the current account then remained positive for most of the following two decades.

So it turned out that Denmark could not follow the Dutch path of budget consolidation via expenditure cuts because the improving economic climate, as well as the associated interest rate cuts, led to an increase in private demand that drove the current account further into the red. Nonetheless, while it is important to keep in mind that the current account situation differed markedly in Denmark and the Netherlands in the 1980s, this can explain only a limited part of the differences in the spending trajectory of the two countries. For one thing,

---

[22] Organisation for Economic Cooperation and Development, *OECD Economic Survey Denmark* (Paris: OECD, 1988), pp. 10ff.

[23] Nannestad and Green-Pedersen, 'Keeping the Bumblebee Flying', 50.

although the tax increases of the mid-1980s were certainly not negligible, the 'potato diet' did not actively increase public spending, unlike the 'demand twist' policies of the 1970s. Thus, they had no direct impact on spending in Denmark. On the other hand, the current account deficit limited the Danish government's room for manoeuvre in fiscal policy only for a limited period. Indeed, after 1990, Denmark ran stable current account surpluses, not least thanks to the country's increasing oil and natural gas production. Thus, the current account situation would have allowed Denmark to adopt policies similar to those pursued in the Netherlands from the 1990s onwards – that is, it could have reduced its spending in order to enable tax cuts.[24] This, however, is not what happened. On the contrary, the real differences only started to emerge after 1990. So the question remains why the Dutch substantially reduced public – and in particular social – spending after 1990 while the Danes did not.

The Maastricht Convergence Criteria

Another possible explanation for the diverging public spending trajectories in the two countries concerns membership of the EMU. The Netherlands was not only a founding member of the EC, but essentially all established political actors in the country continued to consider Dutch participation in the process of European integration, including the EMU, as lying at the core of the national interest. Writing in 2005, Andeweg and Irwin pointed out that 'no major political party questions EU membership, and until very recently it was hard to find any differences in their views with regard to European integration'.[25] Thus, Dutch public finance had to meet the convergence criteria for entry into monetary union, the most important of which stipulated that the budget deficit should not exceed 3 per cent of GDP in the reference year: 1997. Indeed, this criterion served as the most important policy target for Dutch governments, particularly in the 1990s, and might therefore have induced them to cut spending in order to rein in the deficit. The Danish government, on the other hand, had negotiated an opt-out clause. This meant that Denmark was not obliged to join the euro and would thus have had fewer incentives to meet the convergence criteria. This in turn might have led to fewer restrictive policies.

---

[24] Zohlnhöfer, *Globalisierung der Wirtschaft*, p. 266.
[25] R. B. Andeweg and G. Irwin, *Governance and Politics of the Netherlands*, 2nd edn (Basingstoke: Palgrave Macmillan, 2005), p. 210.

At first sight, this seems plausible, particularly given the fact that the differences in the spending trajectories only began to emerge in the 1990s, precisely during the run-up to the Maastricht reference year. What is more, the Maastricht criteria did play an important role in the Dutch discourse on public finances – both before the reference year but also afterwards – while they scarcely featured in Danish policy.[26]

Nonetheless, EMU membership does not explain the differences in the spending trajectories between Denmark and the Netherlands. As is well known, the Maastricht criteria dealt with the level of public deficits and public debt, but not with the level of spending. Thus, public spending could only be affected indirectly by the convergence criteria, namely when government expenditure had to be curtailed in order not to produce a deficit of more than 3 per cent of GDP. In other words, if we were to explain the different spending trajectories after 1990 by the Netherlands' attempt to join the EMU and Denmark's decision not to do so, we should see the following pattern. The Netherlands would need to cut spending until it reached the 3 per cent threshold after which point no further spending cuts should be observed, whereas Denmark did not need to reduce its deficit as it did not have to take the convergence criteria seriously and, as a consequence, it could leave its spending unchanged. This is not what happened, however. On the one hand, Danish governments reduced their deficit despite the opt-out and would easily have met the Maastricht criteria without any need to reduce (social) spending. On the other hand, Dutch governments continued to curb spending even when the deficit was way below the 3 per cent threshold. In particular, both the coalition of Social Democrats and two liberal parties under Wim Kok (1994–2002) and the first Balkenende government of Christian Democrats and liberals (2002–6) adhered to the so-called 'Zalm norm', named after Gerrit Zalm, the liberal minister of finance in both governments. Accordingly, maximum levels of expenditure were stipulated in the respective coalition agreements irrespective of what happened to government revenues; revenues in excess of what had been planned and laid down in the coalition agreements could be used only to reduce government debt, but could not finance additional spending.[27] As revenues were substantially higher than anticipated during most of that period, this fiscal norm led to a substantial reduction of government expenditure relative to GDP – something that was unnecessary for meeting the Maastricht criteria.

---

[26] Zohlnhöfer, *Globalisierung der Wirtschaft*.

[27] Bos, 'The Dutch Fiscal Framework'; and M. Hallerberg, *Domestic Budgets in a United Europe* (Ithaca, NY, and London: Cornell University Press, 2004).

Thus, we can conclude that neither the different current account situations until around 1990 nor the Netherlands' desire to join the EMU can explain the divergence in spending patterns between these two countries. Rather, as I shall argue in the next section, it was the constellation of electoral competition which emerged from the respective party systems that made welfare retrenchment electorally much more risky in Denmark, where governments consequently refrained from making such decisions, than in the Netherlands, where cuts to the welfare state were feasible given certain conditions.

The Politics of Social Spending Restraint and the Effects of the Party System Constellation

When discussing the role of the party system constellations in public spending in Denmark and the Netherlands it is important to keep in mind that the different public spending patterns were mainly driven by changes in welfare spending, while core spending developed along more or less similar lines. Thus, the pertinent question to ask is why the Dutch were able to reduce their social spending substantially and sustainably while the Danes were not.

When we turn to the mainstream social policy literature led by the research of Paul Pierson, the Danish case is not difficult to explain. According to Pierson, welfare state retrenchment is an exercise in avoiding blame because the welfare state is popular with the electorate, and any party in power that cuts entitlements to benefits fears that it will lose out at the next election.[28] Therefore, it is argued, parties avoid welfare retrenchment unless they are confident that voters will not be aware of the cuts, or extraordinary circumstances, such as an economic crisis, open a 'window of opportunity' for them.

The Danish case in many ways is an exemplary corroboration of this argument. When the Social Democratic minority government resigned in 1982, the economic situation was extremely bleak – the country stood at the brink of the abyss, to use that well-worn expression again. The OECD, in its *Economic Survey of Denmark*, described the situation as follows:

in August [1982] it was clearly recognized that the budget deficit would attain an unacceptable level and that severe spending cuts would need to be implemented. At the same time, both the short-term outlook and the medium-term

---

[28] P. Pierson, *Dismantling the Welfare State? Reagan, Thatcher, and the Politics of Retrenchment* (Cambridge: Cambridge University Press, 1994); and P. Pierson, 'The New Politics of the Welfare State', *World Politics* 48 (1996), 143–79.

scenarios pointed to a further aggravation of the already severe disequilibria characterising the Danish economy ... As noted, medium-term scenarios also suggested that, in the absence of a marked change in policies, the scope for achieving more balanced economic developments was virtually non-existent.[29]

Moreover, in early 1983 Denmark's credit rating was downgraded from AAA to AA+. The incoming bourgeois government, led by Prime Minister Schlüter, was thus able to introduce a number of cuts to welfare programmes for which the outgoing Social Democratic government could be blamed. Moreover, the government was able to create a '"rally around the flag" sentiment ... among the public by pointing to the serious nature of the challenges facing the country'.[30] For a short period, budget consolidation, including limited cuts to the welfare state, even proved to be a vote winner, as the success of the bourgeois coalition in the 1984 elections confirms.[31]

But as the voters' perception of the crisis abated in the mid-1980s and the Social Democrats came to be seen as a credible defender of the welfare state the window of opportunity for welfare retrenchment closed. From that point onwards, the bourgeois government rescinded some of the earlier cuts and even expanded a few programmes. What is more, they would not retrench or restructure the welfare state further as long as the Social Democrats remained unwilling to back the reforms, because they feared that welfare retrenchment would be politicised by the Social Democratic opposition and would cost them decisive votes. As they did not receive the Social Democrats' backing, the bourgeois government refrained from making any more cuts to the welfare budget. Instead, it turned its attention to less politically sensitive ways to reduce the budget deficit. Therefore, apart from raising taxes, the government put pressure on local governments to restrict spending.[32] Thus, the central government passed the buck for spending cuts to the local governments – a policy that turned out to be a quite effective blame-avoidance strategy. However, it was an ineffective means to reduce overall, let alone social, spending.

In sum, the bourgeois government in Denmark in the 1980s was unwilling to implement welfare retrenchment during most of its time in office because it feared that the policy would be punished by the voters

---

[29] Organisation for Economic Cooperation and Development, *OECD Economic Survey Denmark* (Paris: OECD, 1983), p. 23.

[30] Nannestad and Green-Pedersen, 'Keeping the Bumblebee Flying', 47–8.

[31] See Hallerberg, *Domestic Budgets in a United Europe*, p. 179.

[32] Damgaard, 'Crisis Politics in Denmark 1974–1987', 78; P. M. Christiansen, 'Public Expenditures: Is the Welfare State Manageable?' in E. Albæk, L. C. Eliason, A. S. Nørgaard and H. S. Schwartz (eds.), *Crisis, Miracles, and Beyond: Negotiated Adaptation of the Danish Welfare State* (Aarhus: Aarhus University Press, 2008), p. 157.

at the next election. Instead, it concentrated on raising taxes and making cuts in core expenditure. This, however, was not sufficient to reduce overall spending substantially.

What happened under the bourgeois government of the 2000s, led by Prime Minister Anders Fogh Rasmussen, is very similar in most respects. Again, the government failed to introduce welfare reforms that were not backed by the Social Democrats and again it tried – with some success – to make local governments cut their spending.[33] Nonetheless, in contrast to the late 1980s and early 1990s, the Fogh Rasmussen government was able to negotiate welfare reforms with the Social Democrats, though this did not include immediate cuts to benefits, with the result that the impact on public spending in the short term was negligible.

The Social Democrat-led governments of the 1990s, in contrast, were in a better position to make retrenchments in the welfare state because the electorate saw the Social Democrats as the natural defenders of the welfare state. Moreover, any voters who were opposed to the welfare cuts introduced by the Social Democrats had no other party to turn to because the bourgeois parties could be expected to pursue similar policies and the parties on the left had little option other than to support a Social Democrat government. Thus, the Social Democrats implemented a number of moderate cuts to the welfare state while at the same time overall spending increased in real terms.[34]

In sum, insofar as total government expenditure has been reduced in Denmark, this is largely accounted for by a reduction in core expenditure and some windfall savings due to lower interest rates from the 1990s onwards and a significant reduction in the rate of unemployment since 1993. In contrast, social spending – and transfers in particular – has not been cut to any significant degree. While the bourgeois parties believed that, with the exception of the very first years after the change of government in 1982, the electoral risks of this kind of policy were too great, the Social Democrats had more room for manoeuvre with regard to welfare retrenchment, but were unwilling to take advantage of this.

Events in the Netherlands look decidedly different. All governments between 1982 and 2007 adopted sweeping welfare state reform; there the cuts were made in essentially all welfare programmes and all elements of the individual programmes: the level of replacement rates,

---

[33] Zohlnhöfer, *Globalisierung der Wirtschaft.*
[34] See C. Henkes, 'Dänemark', in W. Merkel, C. Egle, C. Henkes, T. Ostheim and A. Petring, *Die Reformfähigkeit der Sozialdemokratie. Herausforderungen und Bilanz der Regierungspolitik in Westeuropa* (Wiesbaden: Verlag für Sozialwissenschaften, 2006), pp. 315–50.

qualifying criteria, the entitlement period and the financing of some programmes. So, it is no coincidence that the Netherlands was among the most successful of the advanced democracies during 1980–2007 with regard to curbing social expenditure. The important question is why Dutch governments were willing to risk making cuts in the welfare state while governments in most other countries, including Denmark, were not – or at least not to the same extent. The reason is *not* that the Dutch electorate supported the welfare state less than voters elsewhere or did not punish retrenching governments at the polls. On the contrary, various surveys show that the Netherlands 'remained highly egalitarian' in the 1980s and 1990s,[35] and voters turned against governing parties that had retrenched quite heavily. For example, the Christian Democrats and Social Democrats who in 1993 made substantial reforms to the disability pension scheme (WAO) lost 21 percentage points of the vote, resulting in a loss of 32 of their 103 parliamentary seats, in the 1994 election.

This makes the fact that all Dutch governments have nevertheless retrenched even more puzzling. As Christoffer Green-Pedersen has shown, the answer lies in the configuration of party competition in the Netherlands.[36] Unlike bipolar party systems (Denmark among them) where essentially two party blocs compete and the one that wins the most votes forms the next government, the Dutch party system used to be 'pivotal'. (This has not been the case since the middle of the first decade of the twenty-first century at the latest.) That is to say, the Christian Democrats (CDA) were always in power and could select the party with which to form a coalition. The reason for this is that the labour party (PvdA) and the liberals (VVD) had rejected each other as coalition partners since the 1950s. Once a coalition between the VVD and PvdA was impossible, every government needed to include the Christian Democrats to make up the numbers. That meant that if the labour party and the liberals wanted to exercise political power, they had to ensure that the Christian Democrats thought of them as a reliable coalition partner. Therefore, the election results were far less important for government formation than the coalition game. Thus, in the early 1980s, when the Christian Democrats started to think of

[35] V. A. Schmidt, 'Values and Discourse in the Politics of Adjustment', in F. W. Scharpf and V. Schmidt (eds.), *Welfare and Work in the Open Economy*, vol. 1: *From Vulnerability to Competitiveness* (Oxford: Oxford University Press, 2000), p. 285.

[36] C. Green-Pedersen, 'Welfare-State Retrenchment in Denmark and the Netherlands, 1982–1998: The Role of Party Competition and Party Consensus', *Comparative Political Studies* 34 (2001), 963–85; and C. Green-Pedersen, *The Politics of Justification: Party Competition and Welfare-State Retrenchment in Denmark and the Netherlands from 1982 to 1998* (Amsterdam: Amsterdam University Press, 2002).

welfare retrenchment as a necessity if they were to cure the Dutch disease, they were able to implement a number of cuts with the VVD's support. The Social Democrats might have voiced harsh criticism of these cuts and expected electoral support as a result, but it was quite clear that the additional votes the party could win would not be enough to form a coalition without both the Christian Democrats and liberals. Consequently, the best bet for returning to power was to turn again to the Christian Democrats. As the Christian Democrats made 'responsible' fiscal policy, including a willingness to reduce welfare spending, a precondition for joining a coalition, the Social Democrats moderated their opposition to welfare cuts. Thus, they sacrificed the possibility of a much better election result, but were returned to government in 1989.

Once in power the party had to accept deep welfare retrenchment. A particularly important case in point was the reform of the disability pension scheme in 1993.[37] Although this led to plummeting support for the labour party in the opinion polls and to a substantial loss of membership, the party nonetheless backed the reform. The principal reason for this was that failure to do so would have put its ability to govern in jeopardy and would thus in all likelihood have meant exclusion from government for the foreseeable future. Therefore, even though the reform was highly controversial within the party and threatened to lose them support at the next election (which is indeed what happened), the labour party supported the reform in order to make sure that the other parties, particularly the CDA, would see them as a party that took sound and responsible fiscal policy positions – a precondition for remaining a participant in any coalition.

Even after the Christian Democrats had been relegated to the opposition benches for the first time since 1917, a similar logic applied because the PvdA–VVD coalition that was eventually formed in 1994 had become possible only because both parties had moved to the centre in their attempt to woo the Christian Democrats; thus sustainable public finances and further structural reforms of the welfare state remained on the agenda. Finally, in 2002, the Christian Democrats returned to government and temporarily regained their position as the pivotal player in the party system. As they still – or, to be more precise, again – believed further welfare reforms were necessary, they were able to see them through under Prime Minister Balkenende.

---

[37] For the following, see R. Hillebrand and G. A. Irwin, 'Changing Strategies: The Dilemma of the Dutch Labour Party', in W. C. Müller and K. Strøm (eds.), *Policy, Office, or Vote? How Political Parties in Western Europe Make Hard Decisions* (Cambridge: Cambridge University Press, 1999), pp. 130–3.

The bottom line is this: coalition formation in the Netherlands is not determined by election results and consequently the political parties are to some extent shielded from voter wrath when retrenchments to welfare are made. Therefore, as long as there was a pivotal party and as long as that party's aim was to reduce social expenditure, the other parties had an incentive to accept the cuts because it was more important for them to be seen as a reliable partner by the Christian Democrats than to maximise their vote at the polls. Thus, the constellation of electoral (non-)competition made far-reaching and lasting reductions to social expenditure possible in the Netherlands, while in most other countries, including Denmark, that lack a similar party system constellation, parties shy away from making such cuts as they fear losing votes, and consequently office, at the next election.

Conclusion

This chapter has discussed public spending patterns in two small, open, consociational democracies 'after the boom'. With regard to the overarching questions that this volume addresses it is evident from the case studies presented here that while the boom had come to an end in 1973 (if not earlier), the extensive policy changes needed time to materialise. In both countries, policy-makers, and the Social Democrats in particular, needed some time to adapt to what turned out to be an era of extensive economic change. Thus, the turning point regarding economic policies in both countries was a change of government in 1982, which brought bourgeois governments to power. The incoming governments started to implement some aspects of liberal supply-side policies (or neo-liberalism) in earnest. From the 1980s onwards, their macroeconomic framework can be regarded as neo-liberal, as combating inflation (including the rejection of competitive depreciations in the case of Denmark) and reducing the government deficit formed the cornerstones of economic policy for all parties in both countries. While this can be seen as a substantial policy change, particularly in Denmark, the repercussions for government expenditures were limited. Certainly, a reduction of public debt was afforded high priority in both countries. In this regard, one could speak of neo-liberal convergence, but that is as far as convergence went as the two countries chose decidedly divergent paths to reduce their deficits. While the Netherlands curbed government expenditure significantly, not least spending on welfare, public spending hardly changed in Denmark. Instead, the relative weight of different spending items there changed, as core spending was reduced while social spending increased.

So, despite any claims about neo-liberal convergence in the literature, I find marked differences between seemingly similar countries which need to be explained. Why did the Netherlands reduce public, and particularly social, spending substantially more than Denmark in the past thirty years? I have discussed three potential explanations. First, one might have expected that Danish governments would prefer higher taxation and more public spending in order to reduce export demand in a country that was experiencing notorious current account deficits – a policy that would have followed the 'demand twist' policies of the 1970s. This explanation is not entirely convincing, however, primarily because the Danish current account deficit disappeared from around 1990, and that was precisely when the divergence in the spending patterns between the two countries really started to become relevant. Nor can the Dutch willingness to enter the EMU, which was not the case in Denmark, serve as an explanation for the different spending trajectories. On the one hand, Denmark also reduced its public deficit substantially in the 1990s, despite not seeking EMU entry, and the country did not significantly curb spending in the process. On the other hand, successive Dutch governments continued to rein in government expenditure even when the deficit was way below the reference value of the Maastricht treaty. In other words, the convergence criteria did not determine spending decisions in the two countries in any meaningful way.

Rather, it turned out that the different party system constellations were important for any government's room for manoeuvre when it came to welfare retrenchment. The Danish two-bloc system in which government formation is closely linked to the results of general elections meant that the political parties did not make unpopular welfare cuts unless the country was in a deep economic crisis. Instead, for the most part, core expenditure was cut and taxes were increased in order to reduce the budget deficit. In contrast, the Dutch pivotal party system meant that government formation was detached from electoral results. When the CDA, for a long time the pivotal party in the Netherlands, deemed welfare cuts necessary, it could push them through with little partisan opposition because the principal opposition parties could not oppose these policies too openly if they wanted to remain players in the coalition game. Thus shielded from potential voter discontent over welfare cuts, the parties could risk retrenching and restructuring the welfare state quite drastically. This explains why the Netherlands was much more successful than Denmark and many other advanced democracies with regard to welfare state retrenchment.

Nonetheless, it must be emphasised that the specific constellation of electoral competition that was predominant in the Netherlands during the study period (but which no longer characterises the Dutch party system) is not a sufficient condition for implementing successful retrenchment of the welfare state. Rather, what is necessary in such a party system is a pivotal party that is willing to implement spending restraint. If, in contrast, a pivotal party is reluctant to endorse these policies, it is impossible to get them adopted even in a pivotal party system. This conclusion is confirmed if we turn to the so-called first Italian republic up to 1992 when the pivotal Christian Democrats were unwilling to reduce government deficits and rein in public spending, and these changes consequently failed to materialise.[38]

---

[38] The answer to the question why the pivotal Christian Democrats in the Netherlands and Italy followed these diverging paths is beyond the scope of this chapter, but in brief three factors could be relevant in this regard: (1) The existence of anti-system parties: As the centre parties in Italy agreed that Communists and Neo-Fascists were anti-system parties and should therefore be excluded from government, the possibility of the Christian Democrats' losing office was even less likely in Italy than in the Netherlands. (2) Patronage: While Dutch parties mainly competed on policies, an important factor when it came to winning votes in Italy was patronage (*voto di scambio*). (3) Factionalism: At least from 1982 onwards, the CDA in the Netherlands was comparatively congruent in questions of fiscal policy and loyal to its party leader; in contrast, the Italian DC was highly faction-ridden, which led to government instability and policy gridlock, not least in fiscal policy. For an accessible interpretation of the first Italian republic, see J. LaPalombara, *Democracy, Italian Style* (New Haven, CT, and London: Yale University Press, 1987).

11 The Politics of Public Debt Financialisation: (Re)Inventing the Market for French Sovereign Bonds and Shaping the Public Debt Problem (1966–2012)

Benjamin Lemoine

In June 2012, at the annual forum of the International Monetary Fund (IMF), Benoit Cœuré, former head of the French Ministry of Finance's debt agency and a member of the European Central Bank's (ECB) Executive Board, warned EU governments not to dispense with the 'disciplining role of financial markets'.[1] With the European sovereign debt crisis still unfolding, the French government and senior European authorities continued to view the financing of government deficit through financial markets as a 'disciplinary', and therefore healthy, way to manage public finance. The European Constitutional Treaties prohibit EU countries from financing their debts through the ECB and imply that they rely on the international financial markets.

Financing the state exclusively through market mechanisms limits economic policy options, and makes states' futures dependent on private financial actors: banks, private creditors and credit-rating agencies. Yet this approach to public finance is rarely challenged, even in times of crisis. In France, orthodox historical accounts and public finance textbooks[2] describe the commodification of public debt as a logical consequence of states' necessary modernisation and adaptation to global circumstances (i.e. financialisation, internationalisation and Europeanisation).

---

[1] Benoit Coeuré, 'The Euro Area Sovereign Debt Market: Lessons from the Crisis. Managing Sovereign Risk and Public Debt: A Seismic Shift in Demand and Supply Dynamics?', 12th annual meeting of the International Monetary Fund, Rio de Janeiro (28–29 June 2012).

[2] Laure Quennouëlle-Corre does not question the consequences, whether political or economic, of formalising the history of debt in 'modernisation' terms. Furthermore, some public finance specialists consider that the contest between 'political' and 'economic' power in France before the Second World War belongs to an 'era that is past' and is 'outdated'. L. Quennouëlle-Corre, *La Direction du Trésor, l'État banquier et la croissance (1947–1967)* (Paris: CHEFF, 2000); M. Bouvier et al., *Finances publiques* (Paris: LGDJ, 2011).

In contrast to these accounts, this chapter critically questions the 'naturalisation' of recourse to the market, namely, the process by which market devices and financial techniques were established and became unchallenged and uncontroversial technical issues.[3] The management of public debt in financial markets was initially one among many strategies, and market devices became a naturalised way of financing the state only after long ideological struggles and administrative change.

Drawing on sociological studies of the long-term effects that the development and legitimisation of technical instruments have on public policy,[4] I analyse state financing techniques as the products of a historical process, which varies across countries and institutional contexts. The apprehension of the sovereign debt problem cannot be reduced to measures such as debt-to-GDP ratios;[5] for political and institutional constellations do matter. Throughout history, there have been multiple, non-market, professional tools and administrative apparatuses, which financed public spending and deficits. As I show, in post-war France the interest rates of sovereign bonds were set administratively and not as the product of market supply and demand. Similarly, central banks in comparable countries could finance the government either by purchasing government bonds or by lending directly to the government.[6] This was the case in France, where the Banque de France lent money to the Treasury through a policy called *avances réglementées de la Banque centrale*. But this chapter shows how, at least from 1944 to 1967, alongside the central bank's direct financing approach, France turned to non-market debt financing. French politicians and civil servants called this system the 'Treasury Circuit' (*Circuit du Trésor*): the state required

---

[3] For an elaboration of the interest in studying the naturalisation process in economics, see T. Piketty, *Le capital au XXIème siècle* (Paris: Seuil, 2013) [*Capital in the Twenty-First Century* (Cambridge, MA: Harvard University Press, 2014)].

[4] Science and technology studies analyse how artefacts, instruments and devices can make politics. L. Winner, 'Do Artefacts Have Politics?', *Modern Technology: Problem or Opportunity?* 109/1 (Winter 1980), 121–36. P. Lascoumes and P. Le Galès, 'L'action publique saisie par ses instruments', *Gouverner par les instruments* (Paris: Presses de Sciences Po, 2004).

[5] For a perspective focused on debt-to-GDP ratios, see K. S. Rogoff and C. M. Reinhart, 'Growth in a Time of Debt', *American Economic Review: Papers and Proceedings* 100 (May 2010), 573–8.

[6] Eric Monnet, a French economic historian, explains that 'two polar cases can be considered: the Bank of England, which issued Treasury bills for the government and purchased them on the market, and, on the other hand, the Bank of France, which lent direct advances to the government but could not purchase or rediscount government bonds (and usually did not conduct open market operations with Treasury bills)'. Eric Monnet, 'Blurring the Lines between Monetary and Fiscal Financing of Public Debt: The French Case after World War II (1945–1973)'. Preliminary notes prepared for the workshop on History and Political Economy of Public Debt (Cambridge, 10–12 June 2015).

many public banks and financial institutions to deposit monies with the Treasury Department, which provided it with resources for public spending and Treasury management. In addition, beginning in 1948, a legal provision known as the 'Treasury bills floor' (*Bons Planchers du Trésor*) required banks to purchase and hold short- and medium-term Treasury bonds in their portfolios, allowing administrative decision-making to determine rates and prices for debt and Treasuries. Dismantling these instruments was a necessary condition for introducing and legitimising new market devices.

France's current dependence on financial markets can be analysed as a product of the accumulation of technical market devices. The French government adopted these devices in order to 'discipline' the state monetarily with the intention of creating non-inflationary growth.

In the years that followed, the political character of these market instruments gradually disappeared. Market policies and techniques changed the general view of public indebtedness, giving rise to a very particular framing of the problem of public debt. Public debts were now discussed exclusively in fiscal terms, as signifying excessive public spending. Within this new framework the state had to live as a borrower, not as an economic sovereign. The state was now subject to the market and was required to balance its budget and maintain a sustainable level of indebtedness.[7]

Market Framing Democracy

The institutionalisation of market techniques made it difficult to reverse[8] how public finance was problematised.[9] Indeed, market instruments stabilise the fiscal diagnosis of the debt problem and define who are the legitimate actors who can address its causes and effect its solutions. They do this by dividing the public debt problem into distinct components and marking the boundaries between the different sectors of public policy charged with tackling public debt. The creation of the

---

[7] What Wolfgang Streck would call the 'consolidation State'. W. Streck, *Du temps acheté. La crise sans cesse ajournée du capitalisme démocratique* (Paris: Gallimard, 2014).

[8] R. Boyer, B. Chavance and O. Godard, *Les Figures de l'irréversibilité en économie* (Paris: Éditions de l'EHESS, 1991).

[9] Problematisation, for Michel Foucault, points to the processes by which acceptable public problems and a range of expected solutions are defined. M. Foucault, *L'Usage des plaisirs* (Paris: Gallimard, 1984). As the sociologist Brice Laurent asserts, 'These processes pertain to the manufacturing of individuals, collectives and concerns solidified in various instruments and discourses.' B. Laurent, 'Perfecting European Democracy. Science as a Problem of Technological and Political Progress', in Benjamin Hurlbut and Hava Tirosh-Samuelson (eds.), *Perfecting Human Futures: Technology, Secularization and Eschatology* (Dordrecht: Springer, 2016).

Agence France Trésor in 2001 is an example of this sort of division of labour. This public debt office is now dedicated to issuing and managing French sovereign bonds by virtue of specific market codes, as a distinct professional jurisdiction. It enjoys autonomy from public debate and political decision-making, and is run by senior civil servants in partnership with banks and private financiers, who in turn became the 'owners of the technical problem of the State Treasury'.[10]

Looking at another side of the problem, the French Budget Office (Direction du budget), part of the Ministry of Finance, drafts the Budget Act and fiscal policy, so these can satisfy market expectations and be discussed by both politicians and the wider public. Dividing how debt is managed into sectors has had the effect of refocusing disagreement over how the state's budget is assessed – at the European level, between the national government and the European Commission services[11] – and how the government should reduce it. Limiting political opposition to a strictly fiscal framework that excludes debt management techniques from the debate is no longer challenged. The silencing of public debate on questions relating to debt issuance can thus be explained by the dismantling of state-administered Treasury mechanisms from the mid-1960s, and the piecemeal introduction of capital market organisations, systematised and intensified in the 1980s with the liberalisation of the financial markets.

This chapter looks first at analyses of the institutional changes to economic policies from the perspective of state financing methods. It then describes two controversies over Treasury instruments to illustrate how state financing through the markets, along with the budgetary framing of the public finance problem, has been naturalised. The first controversy relates to the market instrument that was imposed on the state for financing the Treasury in the late 1960s, with the shift from state-administered debt issuance to marketed debt. The second pertains to debates in the late 1990s on a particular financial innovation: inflation-indexed Treasury bonds. This highlights the naturalised status of the current configuration, which was inherited from previous market devices. This new government bond has both defined and imposed the negation of the monetary role of the Treasury and the state.

---

[10] J. Gusfield, *La Culture des problèmes publics. L'alcool au volant: la production d'un ordre symbolique* (Paris: Economica, 2009).

[11] B. Lemoine, 'Résister aux mesures européennes. Les États à l'épreuve de la surveillance statistique des finances publiques', *Quaderni* 20/80, 61–81 (Winter 2013).

Treasury Devices Shaping Economic Policies

A wealth of literature has studied economic change and the evolution of French public institutions. Scholars have identified the Keynesian economic policy regime, which extended from the end of the Second World War to the late 1970s/mid-1980s. Interventionist modes of economic governance – planning, controlling the banking system, intervening in the financial markets and national accounting – marked a departure from the long period that had preceded the war, known as the 'great liberal nineteenth century'[12] (1815–1935). These economic administrative devices encouraged public investment and allowed the authorities to determine what was productive and what was not.

The staff of the General Planning Commission (Commissariat general au plan, CGP), within the Economic and Financial Studies Service (Service d'études économiques et financières, SEEF) and the National Institute of Statistics and Economic Surveys (Institut national de la statistique et des études économiques, INSEE) devised national accounting, a tool used to steer the national economy.[13] Economic policy-making during the period following the Second World War until the mid-1960s has been studied by economic and political historians. A number of scholars have discussed the Keynesian moment as an ambiguous configuration and identified coexistence between economic interventionism, economic planning and monetary and financial orthodoxy. From the end of the Second World War, the new monetarist approach, grounded in the doctrine of quantitative monetary control, as prized by the Treasury Department, coexisted in the state apparatus with modernisers and CGP officials who were pushing for active state intervention in the economy.[14] The various state sectors were torn between the objective of economic expansion (the so-called spendthrift ministries and the CGP) and anticipation of the inflationist threat

---

[12] B. Théret, 'Apogée et déclin du rentier de la dette publique dans le "grand" XIXe siècle libéral (1815–1935). Éléments pour une réévaluation du développement historique du capitalisme en longue période', *Économies et Sociétés*, série *Œconomia*, 14 (January 1991), 87–136.

[13] T. Mitchell, *Rules of Experts : Egypt, Techno-Politics and Modernity* (Berkeley, CA: University of California, 2002); A. Vanoli, *Une Histoire de la comptabilité nationale* (Paris: La Découverte, 2002); F. Fourquet, *Les Comptes de la puissance* (Paris: Encres, 1980).

[14] F. Denord, *Néo-libéralisme version française. Histoire d'une idéologie politique* (Paris: Démopolis, 2007). Antoine Pinay's coming to power in 1952 led to François Bloch-Lainé leaving his eminently strategic position as director of the Treasury, even though he was one of the pillars of the modernisation networks. Valéry Giscard d'Estaing's appointment at the Ministry of Finance in 1962 also marked a reorientation in favour of that ministry. V. Spenlehauer, 'Intelligence gouvernementale et sciences sociales', *Politix*, 12/48 (1999), 95–128.

ambivalently highlighted by the Treasury Department during this period. Meanwhile, the Bank of France (a nationalised body and at the time called the *Institut d'émission*) saw the containment of inflation as structural and a sine qua non of economic growth and credit allocation.[15]

This historical review reveals how criticism arose early on from within the state apparatus regarding economic interventionism and the administration's ubiquitous presence in the allocation of credit and the financing of the economy. The first cracks in the post-war institutional configuration began showing in the mid-1960s. While all monetary functions (control of credit allocation and monetary policy), financial functions (control and regulation of banks, financing the state Treasury) and budgetary functions (public investment in the economy) were integrated into the state in 1946, these public policies were gradually separated into sectors or branched off. In his economic history research, Éric Monnet discusses the gradual rupture within the executive teams of the Bank of France, between credit policy (banking regulation, selectiveness in credit allocation and financing choices) and monetary policy (control over the rate of inflation). Monnet explains how, through the interest rate mechanism, the market replacing the administrative management of credit played a decisive role in the transformation of the institutions in charge of credit and money, thereby creating a new definition of what was in the general interest.[16]

This separation of the monetary, financial and budgetary functions within the public administration – which divided the public finance problem into discrete sectors – was largely achieved by reforming the state's Treasury instruments. This transformation is studied mainly as changes in the reference system, as ideological shifts or as the result of a departure from a belief in a Keynesian model (strong growth, aiming at full employment) to a monetarist model geared towards quantitative monetary control, in which any trade-off between inflation and unemployment no longer made sense.

The focus on instruments provides an opportunity to review analyses of institutional change in economic policy. It allows us to identify the paths followed by the actors themselves over the course of history between reforms all too readily discounted in the literature as technical or nugatory, and macroscopic transformations associated with paradigm

---

[15] M. Margairaz, *L'État, les finances et l'économie (1932–1952). Histoire d'une conversion* (Paris: CHEFF, 1991).

[16] E. Monnet, 'Politique monétaire et politique du crédit en France pendant les Trente Glorieuses (1945–1973)' (thesis, l'EHESS and l'École d'économie de Paris, 2012, supervisor, Pierre-Cyrille Hautcœur).

shifts in public policy.[17] Reform limited to the finance administration and implemented in an eminently technical sphere, in the name of immediate practical objectives, succeeded in transforming the economic and political order as a whole. This becomes apparent when one looks at how a macroeconomic form of government is manifested through its instruments' evolution. Indicators, national accounting aggregates, calculation methods and macroeconomic modelling slowly but surely redrew the boundaries between the different domains of public policy and set the limits of intervention between the public authorities and private economic and financial actors.[18]

By studying the stabilisation of the economic order through such instruments it is possible to analyse the ways in which institutional change is achieved, in other words, to describe which aspects of an institutional configuration are challenged and rendered negotiable and debatable, and which facets of public finance are excluded from the debate. In short, it makes it possible to map political conflict. Kathleen Thelen highlighted a mechanism of historical change, which she termed 'layering': the fundamental aspects of any institutional configuration prevail and history alters them only marginally.[19] In the mid-1960s liberal reformers and policy experts undertook the commodification of public debt at the Ministry of Finance for both ideological and pragmatic reasons: to fight inflation, which became a national priority for policy-makers, and to demonstrate the state's ability to act and overcome this risk.

Relying on the market to finance the Treasury thus remained unchallenged for over forty years, and subsequent changes were designed primarily with two intentions in mind. These were, first, to develop further those debt-issuing techniques that were considered to be noninflationary; and, second, to organise public finance policies according to the financial market's requirements, specifically through employing accounting techniques that were similar to private companies' requirements, and by making public spending more efficient.[20] The political

---

[17] P. Hall, *Governing the Economy: The Politics of State Intervention in Britain and France* (New York: Oxford University Press, 1987), pp. 172–3; P. Hall, 'Policy Paradigms, Social Learning, and the State. The Case of Economic Policymaking in Britain', *Comparative Politics* 25/3 (April 1993), 279.

[18] A. Desrosières, 'L'État, le marché et les statistiques: cinq façons d'agir sur l'économie', *Courrier des statistiques* 95–6 (December 2000).

[19] K. Thelen, 'How Institutions Evolve. Insights from Comparative Historical Analysis', in J. Mahoney and D. Rueschemeyer (eds.), *Comparative Historical Analysis in the Social Sciences* (Cambridge: Cambridge University Press, 2003).

[20] Y. Le Lann and B. Lemoine, 'Les comptes des générations. Les valeurs du futur et la transformation de l'État social', *Actes de la recherche en sciences sociales* 4/194 (2012), 62–77.

properties of the techniques, such as the rationale underpinning the market devices, thus constrained political actors in the long term: they imposed lock-in effects on economic institutions and established path dependence for policy-makers.[21] Explaining institutional transformations through instruments is, however, incompatible with a teleological perspective that posits the commodification of debt as the end-goal of a purposeful project, even if the final product – the 'market' configuration of public debt – resembles the vision initially shared by some senior state officials. In France, market devices prevailed after a series of intra-administrative controversies and gradually became part of the administrative and political landscape, to the point where they became seen as natural and hence were unchallenged.

A Disciplinary Solution

After the Second World War, during the reconstruction of the French economy, a very particular state financing system, called the Treasury Circuit, enabled the Treasury to bypass the market to finance public spending.[22] The state was partly self-financed: the Treasury Department, part of the Ministry of Finance, was able to finance it by mobilising a network of banking and financial institutions and collecting available savings.

Borrowing – or more precisely, appealing for funds outside of the monetary deposit circuits controlled by the finance administration – was one among many financing practices. Financing devices in this period were primarily geared towards ensuring a steady source of finance for public spending considered necessary for economic expansion and achieving full employment. The state financed an important part of its temporary overdrafts by gathering deposits and savings from its own financial public circuit, composed of private individuals and banking institutions. Money for the state coffers came from various sources, known as 'Treasury correspondents', and the Treasury in effect operated as a bank. Deposits provided it with ad hoc resources, which it then centralised passively, since it received liquid assets directly. The resources evolved with inflation: the greater the amount of money, the more liquid assets Treasury correspondents had to deposit at the

---

[21] Y. Barthe, 'Nuclear Waste: The Meaning of Decision-Making', in L. Aparicio (ed.), *Making Nuclear Waste Governable: Deep Underground Disposal and the Challenge of Reversibility* (Andra: Springer, 2010), pp. 9–27.

[22] For details of these non-market mechanisms, see B. Lemoine, 'Les Valeurs de la dette. L'État à l'épreuve de la dette publique' (PhD thesis, Centre de sociologie de l'innovation, Mines ParisTech, supervisor Michel Callon, presented 21 December 2011).

Treasury. The Treasury Circuit was a technical and political arrangement that allowed the state to finance itself from outside the markets: deficits could automatically be covered, making medium- and long-term state borrowing secondary and enabling the authorities to avoid advances from the Bank of France, the cap on which could be raised only by a parliamentary vote.[23]

The Treasury correspondents' cash deposits in the state accounts and savings collected through public channels – part of the Treasury Circuit – were supplemented by forcing the banking system to take out Treasury bonds. Under the 1948 'floor' system, banks were required to hold a sizeable proportion of government bonds and maintain the compulsory subscription above the floor (a kind of threshold). This state-administered management of short-term debt (also called the floating debt) enabled the Treasury to benefit from resources whose price it set unilaterally, without worrying about the free play of supply and demand. Furthermore, it allowed the Treasury to control the money supply by controlling bank deposits. By instating centralised control of the money supply at the Treasury level, as well as banks' use of monies, these financing instruments produced a state that both invests and controls its investments in the economy.

Debt Commodification as a Factor Driving the Separation of the State's Monetary, Financial and Budgetary Functions

Over the course of this period, monetary and financial functions were closely integrated into the state apparatus, so that the Treasury could at the same time control banks, orchestrate the circulation of money and finance its budget deficits. Laure Quennouëlle-Corre shows that 1948–52 was a period of the 'articulation between the monetary, the financial and the economic, effected in the assignments devolved to the Treasury'.[24] This integration of functions within the Treasury – and therefore the state – reached crisis point when reducing inflation became a government priority, at the expense of growth and full employment.

Inflation ceased to be seen as an inevitable outcome, one that was tacitly accepted by the administration as a necessary consequence of its

---

[23] J.-P. Patat and M. Lutfallah, *Histoire monétaire de la France au XXe siècle* (Paris: Economica, 1986), p. 121.
[24] L. Quennouëlle-Corre, *La Direction du Trésor, l'État banquier et la croissance (1947–1967)*.

legitimate policies. Instead, it started to be viewed as a matter of urgency, which governments needed to resolve. This change in the attitude to inflation overturned the state's reliance on funding outside the market. The shift to market loans could, according to officials, free the government to borrow without being concerned about inflation.

The Treasury's liberal reformers identified state-administered Treasury instruments as a cause of inflation that could be overcome, and argued that these instruments led to monetary and budgetary chaos. During the early years of the Fifth Republic, the Treasury bill floor system was gradually abandoned. For the issuance of Treasury bills, it was replaced by the auction system, which was based on the British model. The auction device gave rise to one-off and programmed sessions for debt issuance, which forced the Treasury Department to assess the demand for its bills and bonds and adjust its offered interest rate accordingly. It was a sharp break with the Treasury bills floor process, which allowed permanent and streaming purchase by banks.

General Charles de Gaulle also accused the Treasury facilities of encouraging inflation, writing about 'the commodities offered by inflation' in his *Memoirs*.[25] Similarly, Jean-Maxime Lévêque, presidential adviser from 1960 to 1964 and general secretary of the National Credit Council (*Conseil national du credit*, CNC), pointed out that the 1963 stabilisation plan 'did not tamper with the inflationist mechanisms so dear to the Finance Ministry'.[26] When Valéry Giscard d'Estaing moved to the Ministry of Economy and Finance, the government's ability to combat inflation was demonstrated by innovations in which it partly relinquished the Treasury's state-administered financing mechanisms. In March 1963, the controversy surrounding the reintroduction, at Giscard d'Estaing's insistence, of a market device to issue short-term public debt, intensified at the Treasury. Maurice Pérouse, Director of the Treasury at the time, voiced strong reservations, arguing that Treasury and state financing would be 'endlessly jeopardised'.[27] The government decision to abandon non-market financing devices even met some resistance within the finance services themselves. For example, for the Economic and Financial Studies Service (*Service des Études économiques et financières*, SEEF, precursor of the Forecasting Office), not only was inflation 'just one of a number of risks' (others being the public deficit and an economic downturn), more importantly this was

[25] Charles de Gaulle, *Mémoires d'espoir*, vol. II (Paris: Plon, 1971), p. 20, quoted in ibid.

[26] Quoted in ibid.

[27] Archives of the Ministry of Finance and Maurice Pérouse's personal archives, consulted by L. Quennouëlle-Corre, *La Direction du Trésor, l'État banquier et la croissance (1947–1967)*.

not entirely due to the Treasury's financing techniques.[28] From 1966 to 1968 the Debré–Haberer reforms[29] were the *coup de grâce* to the Treasury bill floor.[30]

The introduction of auctions and the discontinuation of the floor went against the Treasury Department agents' position. Jean-Yves Haberer, a thirty-five-year-old graduate of the École Nationale d'Administration and a finance inspector, was back from a work placement in the United States, where he had become 'fascinated with the vitality of the markets'.[31] Taking up the issue of Treasury reform again, he explicitly stated the objective of 'dismantling the Circuit [and] all these automatic mechanisms, which meant that without lifting a finger, the Treasury received liquid assets from all the French financial channels'.[32]

Turning the State into a Regular Borrower

Haberer, the transformation's main instigator, became director of the Treasury in 1978. He saw these reforms as a way of forcing the state to 'live like a borrower, in other words, to ask itself the questions a borrower would regarding the cost of borrowing and debt servicing'.[33] Treasury officials' inspiration came from the US and British systems, which they saw as models of market management of the state and the economy. The re-emergence of a market device, allowing the public borrowing supply and demand to be compared, clarified the very notion of Treasury debt to the outside world. From it emerged a state concerned with the cost of its financing and vigilant about the size of its budget and its monetary weight:

The day the Treasury bill floor was removed, Maurice Pérouse, the director of the Treasury, said: 'But how are we going to finance the Treasury now? With rates! You'll pay the rate it takes!' … But that would be more expensive.

---

[28] The service pointed out that the burdens that the Treasury had to bear, that is, the deficits, were the main reason for excessive monetary creation. The financing instrument was not responsible. Ibid.

[29] Michel Debré was the Minister for the Economy and Finance, and Jean-Yves Haberer was his cabinet adviser.

[30] Michel Debré's move to the rue de Rivoli (where the Ministry of Economy and Finance was located) was marked by many reforms giving greater autonomy to banks in their allocation of credit to the administrative authorities. It further challenged the Treasury Circuit. A final blow was dealt to the floor and they were definitively discontinued in 1967 when Maurice Pérouse resigned as director of the Treasury.

[31] Interview by the author with Jean-Yves Haberer, 2011.

[32] Interviews with Jean-Yves Haberer, carried out by Laure Quennoüelle-Corre in 1995. Audio archives of the CHEFF.

[33] Ibid.

So instead of thinking, 'I'll do whatever I want', the state is going to have to be a little more careful when it gets into debt, since public debt, that's a glass house, it's right in front of parliament.[34]

The idea that the Treasury's finance had a 'cost', revealed through market rates, was thus a market requirement that had to be imposed. The market rate, delivered through auctions, was considered to be a fair price (the authorities would pay 'the rate it takes!') that should allow the state to adopt sound monetary, budgetary and financial policies, which would both attract and assure market players. It was seen as a set of norms that had to be imposed on the administrative apparatus. Replacing a state-administered mechanism with a market-based Treasury instrument contributed to separating the monetary and financial functions within the state. Little by little, control over the money supply, bank deposits and credit in general was externalised, conferring greater autonomy on commercial banks and a more important role on the Bank of France.

Market Transparency against Administration Authority and Powers

Auctions, according to Haberer and other French reformers, also allow market democracy and transparency to emerge against excessive bureaucratic power and *dirigisme*. Market devices reconstruct the interest rate level as a constraint; it is no longer a state decision, as it was under the floor system. The gradual dismantling of the Circuit was therefore not only motivated by its internal dysfunctions; it was also part of a project for the monetary and budgetary disciplining of the state, particularly in the 1970s, when the country was experiencing double-digit inflation. However, this discipline prevailed only after the gradual withdrawal from certain practices, disparagingly called interventionist at the time. The measures of the 1960s–70s, which 'consisted in putting an end to the prerogatives that the Treasury granted itself', were designed, in Haberer's words, to 'introduce a little liberalism'[35] and to fight inflation and return to strong money. Thus the decision to resort systematically to the market was not merely a technical change; it was a real political objective, which aimed both to curb inflation and to develop liquid capital markets.

Yet while the 'commodification' dynamic was set in motion during those years, to some extent intentionally, the process became robust

---

[34] Ibid.
[35] Interview by the author with Jean-Yves Haberer, in 2011.

and indisputable only after various controversies had been resolved and thanks to the nature of subsequent interactions between banks, finance professionals and the authorities.

The state-administered and monetary Treasury financing technique thus became discredited. It was described as archaic and was ruled out as an interventionist procedure that could be justified only during the reconstruction of the economy after the Second World War.[36] The only solution for the public authorities was to pursue the commodification of state financing instruments in the hope of becoming competitive in the international capital market that was opening up at the time.[37] The state thus shaped the private money markets and developed a senior bureaucracy devoted to the market,[38] which encouraged and authorised financial innovations and the development of Paris's financial centre and stock exchange. Subsequent public support of the finance industry had the effect of making its regulation and control more complex, and making the state dependent on the markets and their rating agencies, as soon as its financing needs became systematic.

Circumscribing Political Will: Support for Financial Innovation

The trend towards the commodification of debt and the separation of public finance management from monetary policy which had started in the mid-1960s was intensified, extended and systematised during the 1970s. As oil crises broke and public deficits became entrenched, the government, and particularly the Treasury administration, set its sights on fully appropriating competitive borrowing technologies. The new version of the Treasury theory – in other words, all the monetary, financial and economic instruments and doctrines deployed by the Treasury Department – eventually prevailed in all the administrations and political decision-making bodies, legitimising the construction of a bond market designed to ensure non-monetary Treasury financing. From this new point of view, reducing the cost of the debt issued on the financial markets and achieving economies of scale necessitated commodifying the government debt, liquidating it and issuing large volumes of exchangeable bonds. Thus, beyond the grand narratives describing the

---

[36] In 1975, Jean-Yves Haberer described the Treasury to his students as a 'lord' that was beginning to have serious 'reservations' about its exorbitant powers (*Le Trésor et la politique financière, cours aux élèves de l'IEP Paris, 1975–1976*).

[37] In the 1980s, with financial liberalisation, the technical changes introduced in the late 1960s were taken further and implemented more fully.

[38] B. Hibou, *La Bureaucratisation à l'ère néolibérale* (Paris: La Découverte, 2012).

rise of a neo-liberal state, the public authorities thought they were pragmatically achieving their objectives and envisaged public policy performance exclusively with the help of market devices and rules.[39] Far from
being the result of a natural development,[40] financialisation of the
French government's public debt came about by abandoning the state-
administered strategies, which were now considered to be inflationary
and lax. Former non-market instruments were gradually buried, as
Kathleen Thelen would put it, under the 'strata' of the debt problem,
where they remained invisible and were never discussed.

The development of a full-fledged financial market for public debt
was instrumental in building a monetary discipline policy. The French
state became a debt issuer among others and began competing with
other states to finance itself in the markets. Starting in the mid-1970s
France embarked on the project of making its debt liquid and building
an innovative and 'attractive' bond market. Marketisation, therefore,
did not mean diluting political activity, but on the contrary reorienting
and transforming it. Successive finance ministers, both left-wing and
right-wing, turned away from control of the financial market and
planned management of the economy, and towards supporting innovation in public bonds and developing the sovereign bond market. Market
policies and promoting the Paris financial centre became uncontested
matters. Working for private financial firms seemed ideologically neutral or potentially convertible into political capital, even for a socialist: it
was considered to be a reflection of 'modernity', 'budgetary seriousness'
and economic 'competence'. The ministers in charge of public finance
saw the financial innovation race as a way to assert Paris's strength as a
financial centre. Meanwhile, senior Treasury officials put themselves at
the service of cabinet ministers from parties across the political spectrum, making state finance available by means of stable and low interest
rates for sovereign bonds issuance and sparing the French government
from abrupt cuts in public spending.

The debate triggered by the introduction of a financial innovation at
the Treasury reflects how combating inflation as a monetary policy
became a 'given' – one that was external to governments' political
orientation, devolved to the central bank and was naturally integrated
into the administrative and economic landscape. The new inflation-
indexed bond technique, introduced in the late 1990s, was a signal to

[39] G. R. Krippner, 'The Making of US Monetary Policy: Central Bank Transparency and
the Neoliberal Dilemma', *Theory and Society*, 36 (2007), 477–513.
[40] B. Carruthers, 'The Social Structure of Liquidity: Flexibility, Markets and States',
Theory and Society 28 (1999), 353–82.

investors of the Treasury's monetary neutrality and of its commitment to financial and budgetary discipline.

DSK Bonds and the Treasury's Natural Monetary Neutrality

In 1998, a new form of inflation-indexed government bond was issued: the DSK bond, named after the minister of economy and finance, Dominique Strauss-Kahn. DSK bonds were an unusual debt security: in exchange for inflation-proofing – the interest rate was tied to inflation – the creditor subscribing to this security agreed to a lower interest rate that offered a lower return and therefore was less costly to the state. At the time of the sale of the security, the Treasury gained by pocketing what is called a 'risk premium'. In a sense, the instrument benefited both parties: it was a win–win situation according to the economist Robert J. Barro.[41] Bond buyers were protected from the risk of their security's value depreciating, while the state reduced the amount of interest it paid, provided price stability was maintained (otherwise, the borrowing cost would increase steeply). The state was therefore gambling on price stability.

This new device protected the rentier from economic 'euthanasia' (erosion of its bond value) by means of inflation. Clients most interested in this type of bond were pension funds managing investors' money: insurance companies, state pension schemes and the Deposits and Consignments Fund (*Caisse des dépôts et des consignations*).

However, the introduction of the indexed bond also prompted a critical discussion within the Treasury Department. The civil servants who promoted it wanted to rein in the state and avoid the risk of inflation. Administration officials opposed to it claimed that any sort of indexation is a problem and a risk factor for inflation. Thanks to a high level of political support – specifically from the minister of finance and top bureaucrats – it was finally adopted after a heated debate with central bank officials.

---

[41] Robert Barro, an American neoclassical economist, uses this expression in his discussion of indexed bonds. See R. Barro, *Getting it Right: Markets and Choices in a Free Society* (Cambridge, MA: MIT Press, 1996), p. 100. He further developed rational expectations theory in the field of public finance, showing that stimulating budget spending has no effect, as households anticipate a rise in taxation to finance public debt and therefore do not consume or contribute to boosting economic activity as hoped. R. Barro, 'Are Government Bonds Net Wealth?', *Journal of Political Economy* 6/82 (1974), 1095–117.

'Being the First' State: Mimetism and the Spread of Financial Products

The United Kingdom under Prime Minister Margaret Thatcher had begun using this type of bond in 1981 (the UK Treasury called them indexed-linked gilts, or linkers). In fact, it was Barclays Bank that first created this product in the United Kingdom and was then mandated to prepare this new issue in close collaboration with the French state, after exporting it to Canada in 1991 and to the United States in 1997.[42] Although senior officials of the debt issuance office (the A1 office, which became France Trésor, then Agence France Trésor in 2001) generally enjoyed significant autonomy in the daily management of government debt, when it came to this kind of operation the minister of finance's staff was directly involved. As *Le Monde* pointed out, the stakes were high: the minister wanted to leave his stamp on a government debt security and the bond was inextricably tied to the minister's image, his credibility and the trust investors and market professionals had in him.[43] Moreover, arguing in favour of the bond was a way of embracing the trend in the bond market and possibly being ahead of the competition, and in particular ahead of France's main competitor, Germany. With indexation, France was to be the first country in what would become the Eurozone to issue this kind of product. In its basket of bonds, the state introduced products that were being demanded by investors worldwide. By scrupulously selecting the products, it built up a subscriber client base:

> There can be a need for investors. This was starting to be the case and, since the other states are doing it, if one state does not do it, investors will buy the Germans' inflation paper or some other state bonds. They will stop looking at French Treasury bonds. Then again, there is a need for a state to offer investors a range of products, across the whole yield curve.[44]

Developing these products put into effect a deflationary monetary policy. As the economist Michel Aglietta explains, 'When governments sought non-monetary means of financing, faced with rapidly growing deficits, rising social welfare and debt servicing costs, they turned to promoting attractive government papers (bonds) for investors. The government bond markets became the foundation of the financial markets.'[45] By structuring a market for indexed bonds on the assumption of stable

---

[42] In the United Kingdom, indexed bonds represented 20 per cent of the total public debt.

[43] *Le Monde*, 13 December 1997.

[44] Interview by the author with Jean-Pierre Mustier, former Société Générale manager, in 2010.

[45] M. Aglietta, 'La globalisation financière', *L'Économie mondiale*, CEPII (Paris: La Découverte, 1999), p. 54.

inflation, the Treasury provided financial markets with their 'bread and butter', while leaving itself room to make gains on the risk premiums linked to investors' desire for inflation-proofing. Sylvain Lemoyne de Forges, a central figure in the French Treasury from the mid-1980s (and director of the Agence France Trésor in 2001), described how this all took place in collaboration with the staff and services of the Bank of France, which had been in control of the core of monetary policy since the law establishing the bank's independence was enacted in 1993:

> The Americans had tested it, so we thought: 'Let's do that in France!' There had been the inflation-indexed bond in the United Kingdom for quite a while, but those bonds weren't well designed. We thought: 'Let's do the market!' still with the idea of being the first, because there's always an advantage to being the first with that kind of thing. So we worked on it and worked on it ... I took all precautions possible and imaginable to manage it. We were having loads of fun. We'd offered it to Minister Alphandéry's staff: No way! We'd offered it to Minister Jean Arthuis's staff: No way! But we carried on working at it relentlessly ... And then François Villeroy de Galhau became Dominique Strauss-Kahn's chief of staff in May 1997. We thought: 'Yummy!' François worked discretely; and I helped him. What's more, Strauss-Kahn liked the idea. Once the minister had agreed, it went ahead very fast.

Political and operational circumstances had both changed. A generation in favour of indexed bonds, both as technical instruments and ideologically, was now at the head of public administration. Yet, while the Ministry of Finance and part of the Treasury services rallied behind this innovation, others did not. The central bank governor and certain executives at the Treasury were wary of bond indexation. Observers at the time explained this as a generation gap. Senior officials who expressed reservations about the innovation were the same ones who fought, from the vantage point of the highest positions of the administration, against indexation mechanisms – particularly in wages – which they saw as inflationary.[46] The leaders of this anti-inflation generation would have instinctively reacted against this innovation, in a sort of 'Pavlovian reflex', in the words of a senior official who did back it:

> In the 1990s, we had the trauma of the 1970s and hyperinflation, and that was a difficult one to get rid of. We were struggling to move away from this kind of problem and everyone in the economy was aware of it. No corporate CEO was unaware of it. No financier was unaware of it. No civil servant was unaware of it. High inflation is volatile, unpredictable. It's a vortex nobody can control: that's remained a real trauma.[47]

---

[46] For example, Jean-Claude Trichet, who was governor of the Bank of France at the time of the discussions on inflation-indexed Treasury bonds.

[47] Interview by the author with a former senior Treasury official, in 2011.

The Self-Disciplining of the State

Indexing could be risky if it blunted public awareness, but on the other hand, indexed bonds should increase the state's desire to control inflation. The issue then was whether the state had a credible means of controlling inflation. The older monetarist generation saw any form of indexation, even just of sovereign bonds, as opening Pandora's box:

At the time, the Bank of France was reluctant, saying: 'But any indexation of inflation is by definition very bad: we mustn't fall back into indexation.' There's still a lot of fear in this institution [the Bank of France], rightly so in fact, of indexation mechanisms, even if we've now largely weaned ourselves. Well, it's still normal to be wary of them.[48]

There was therefore a tangible risk for the Treasury managers who were now in charge: proving that indexing Treasury bonds would not pave the way to what the Bank of France saw as an inflationary contagion. Senior officials had to convince the bank that indexing sovereign bonds and financial securities did not pose the same political risk – namely, a social demand for indexation, and therefore for maintaining purchasing power, extended to all social classes – as indexing wages or pensions:

The fight [against inflation] had to be led on all fronts, including health insurance, old age pensions. One can't imagine the number of things that had to be changed to get to the situation we have today. I spent twenty years contributing to the dismantling of indexation. So, the idea of reintroducing indexation at the very heart of the matter, public debt itself ... that is political: 'If we start re-indexing public debt: tomorrow it'll be civil servants' wages. The day after tomorrow, the minimum wage! In three days, pensions!' It's clear just how Pavlovian it was. Now it's disconnected, a number of things can be developed, without necessarily seeing these dreaded contagion effects ... [But] it was a gamble.[49]

This wariness was even more of a Pavlovian reflex and was difficult for the new Treasury agents to comprehend; for them, indexing public debt was counter-inflationary, because it was underpinned by an anti-inflationist rationale. They argued that this new product would contribute to stabilising inflation by creating strong incentives for the state not to allow public deficits to get out of control and not to intervene in monetary policy, at the risk of making the burden of its debt repayments soar.

---

[48] Interview by the author with Christian Noyer, Treasury director in 1993–5 and current governor of the Bank of France, in 2011.

[49] Interview by the author with Sylvain Lemoyne de Forges, in 2008.

The issue eventually made its way to the Ministry of Finance, which decided in favour of the innovation. During the 1997 annual conference on Treasury bonds organised by the primary dealers' organisation, the Association des spécialistes en valeurs du Trésor, Strauss-Kahn announced the introduction of inflation-indexed bonds. The first *Obligation du Trésor indexée sur l'inflation* (OATi), or DSK bond, was issued on 15 September 1998.

In the 1980s, senior officials had been eager to put an end to the indexing of wages, which they claimed only fuelled inflation. By contrast, the adoption of government bond indexing meant that the state now had a clear motive to protect savings through the control of inflation in order to prevent an increase in the cost of debt servicing. OATis, the indexing of public bonds in the vanguard of financial innovation, gave concrete form to the central bank's monetary independence from the Treasury and encouraged the state not to interfere with monetary policy by disciplining itself. The political will to control inflation was embedded in these financial products, which cemented interdependence between the Treasury, the Bank of France and later the ECB: managing the debt without breaking the bank was connected to a non-inflationary monetary policy. The inflation-indexed bond defined the fight against inflation, which from then on was understood as self-evident and made real in financial products. For the new generation of Treasury managers, while there was no question of extending indexation to other variables in the economy, the price stability objective was taken as read. It was simply a matter of how to take advantage of it. The struggles around the choice of Treasury instruments thus represented a tipping point from one economic and monetary order to another. They marked the shift from 'a regime of financial repression', of domestication and control of capital movements by states, to a regime of public 'monetary repression', to borrow Bruno Théret's term, within which inflation and public monetary creation were seen as the main drawbacks.[50]

***

The shift from financial repression to monetary control by market devices occurred in similar fashion in other leading nations, but at different times. In this regard, both Israel and India have been studied in the same terms of deliberately reintroducing market devices and

---

[50] B. Théret, 'Du keynésianisme au libertarianisme. La place de la monnaie dans les transformations du savoir économique autorisé', *Revue de la régulation* (online) 10/2 (2011).

market discipline.[51] In Germany and Belgium, among others, this rupture occurred at the end of central bank direct financing. During the 1990s, debt management professionalisation and autonomy from political decision-making became the norm and the standard promoted by international organisations, such as the International Monetary Fund, the World Bank and the Organisation for Economic Cooperation and Development. A number of countries, among them Austria, Belgium, Ireland, New Zealand, Portugal and Sweden, concluded that it was necessary to set up debt management agencies which enjoyed some autonomy from the political sphere.[52]

This chapter has shown how the commodification of public debt became naturalised after technical and political struggles and controversies. The self-administered structures of state financing and of the economy set up in 1945 first had to be dismantled. Then separation between the monetary and financial functions had to be firmly established within the bureaucratic apparatus; the entire political class had to rally behind the development of international bond markets; and finally, political confrontation and the desire for reform of public finance matters had to be confined to a debate formulated exclusively in budgetary terms.

The compartmentalised treatment of the debt problem has been realised through the division of labour between public and private organisations and the ensuing spatialisation of power, distributed into different, relatively discrete spheres of action. Each institution has its own role: monetary policy and price control are the remit of Bank of France experts; the budget and reducing the public deficit by cutting expenses goes to the Budget Department; and financial policy is determined by the Treasury Department, which ensures the competitive management of debt with the sound understanding of both investors and the financial market. Far from signalling the supposed end of state power, the commodification of public debt has allowed senior officials to claim new strategic domains – the development of financial innovation and the conquest of liquid debt – so that they now carry more

---

[51] R. Livne and Y. P. Yonay, 'Performing Neoliberal Governmentality: An Ethnography of Financialised Sovereign Debt Management Practices', *Socio-Economic Review* 13/4 (October 2015), 339–62; A. Kapadia, 'India's Fiscal–Monetary Machine: Construction and Overheating, 1966–1991', paper for the 'Global Politics of Public Debt, from the Late Eighteenth Century' conference, Centre for History and Economics, Cambridge, 11–12 June 2015; S. M. Ali Abbas, Laura Blattner, Mark De Broeck, Asmaa El-Ganainy and Malin Hu, 'Sovereign Debt Composition in Advanced Economies: A Historical Perspective', Working Paper 14/162 (Washington, DC: Fiscal Affairs Department, International Monetary Fund, September 2014).

[52] M. Cassard and D. Folkerts-Landau, 'Risk Management of Sovereign Assets and Liabilities', International Monetary Fund, Working Paper 97/166 (9 December 1997).

weight in a reorganised international world. The 'strategic state'[53] was redeployed around the challenges of international financial competition and efficient public debt issuance on financial markets.

While opening the financing of the state to the market was initially driven by the idea of introducing a 'dose of liberalism', these early intentions, shared by senior Treasury officials, political representatives, governments and banks, were subsequently exceeded and buried under the effect of the naturalisation process. The principle of the commodification of public debt was taken for granted by policy-makers and it efficiently constrained public policy levers in the long term. More significantly, debt issuing and trading instruments ultimately set the terms of public debate and political confrontation.

The lack of debate related to state financing correlates with the rise of the budgetary version of the public debt problem, that is, the emphasis on structural public deficits and public spending excesses, understood as an unsustainable and intractable burden. Treasury techniques are no longer matters of dispute, controlled as they are by senior officials, who themselves have become expert negotiators with banks and investors, but are legitimised in a state agency – the Agence France Trésor from 2001 – with little government intervention.[54] At the same time, measuring the public deficit and quantifying and controlling public spending pervades the public sphere. The concern with evaluating the size and limits of public debt – that is, the debt problem framed exclusively in accounting terms – came to the fore with its financialisation. This is because, in order to maintain the value of state financial securities and continue to issue them at a good price, it has become necessary to fully take stock of the debt, to anticipate how it will develop and to involve policy-makers in this type of measurement and in mastering it. This debt, with the financial liabilities it comprises, has become a focus of public attention: it is discussed in books by experts, non-professionals and economists, who consider its trajectory and worry about its evolution and persistence. But controversies surrounding state financing instruments have been excluded from such political and public discussions. Financing the state in the capital markets has become a buried stratum of the public finance problem. Deficits are considered to be the sole cause of public debt racing out of control, and the spectrum of solutions envisaged by politicians, at both the national and EU levels,

---

[53] P. Bezes, 'Le modèle de "l'État-stratège": genèse d'une forme organisationnelle dans l'administration française', *Sociologie du travail*, 4 (2005), 431–50.

[54] B. Coeuré, 'L'agence de la dette quatre ans après', *Revue française de finances publiques* 89 (2005).

has been reduced to decreasing the structural deficit and strictly monitoring public spending.

While the state was monetarily active from 1946 until the end of the 1960s, starting in the late 1970s its liabilities and budgets slowly came under close scrutiny. The situation described in this chapter, in which public finance problems were framed through the lens of Treasury instruments, redefined what constitutes the state. In other words, it redefined the state's limits and legitimate sphere of action.[55] The analysis of the commodification of public debt thus offers an illustration of the possibilities of extending the programme opened up by the sociology of economic performativity to institutional objects and to the construction of macroeconomic assemblages.[56] It was only after a series of technical devices were slotted together that the commodification of public debt proved to be a key element of a neo-liberal project that turned the state into a microeconomic agent, a borrower like any other. Its main concern now is to limit the size of its budget and how much it spends, and it must repeatedly prove its ability to honour its debt to financiers.

[55] T. Mitchell, 'The Limits of State: Beyond Statists' Approaches and their Critics', *American Political Science Review* 85/1 (March 1991), 77–96.

[56] M. Callon, 'What Does it Mean to Say that Economics is Performative?', in D. McKenzie, F. Muniesa and L. Siu (eds.), *Do Economists Make Markets? On the Performativity of Economics* (Princeton, NJ: Princeton University Press, 2007), pp. 311–57.

12 Structural Fiscal Imbalances, Financial Repression and Sovereign Debt Sustainability in Southern Europe, 1970s–1990s

Stefano Battilossi

Introduction

The second half of the twentieth century witnessed the fastest peacetime fiscal expansion ever experienced by the advanced economies. It had taken almost fifty years, from the early years of the century to the end of the 1950s, to double the average size of total public spending from 13 to 26 per cent of GDP. The acceleration that started in the 1960s, driven by the creation of mature welfare states, brought the average for OECD economies to 45 per cent in around 1990, a level that would have been inconceivable a few decades earlier.[1] Over the same period, the average size of social transfers (i.e. spending on welfare, unemployment, pensions, health and housing subsidies) more than doubled from 10 to 24 per cent of GDP.[2] This chapter examines how the southern European periphery participated in this secular take-off. More specifically, it focuses on how their governments used implicit tax revenues in the form of seigniorage and financial repression to accommodate structural fiscal shocks and improve debt sustainability.

'Southern Europe' is used here not as a merely geographic grouping but as a consistent regional concept. Comparative studies of welfare state institutions have identified a coherent southern European model that is profoundly different from that of the other corporatist and Catholic countries of northern Europe. This 'southern welfare syndrome' is defined, among other characteristics, by a fragmented income maintenance system skewed in favour of privileged groups, the construction of universal health systems and the extensive use of patronage

---

[1] V. Tanzi, 'The Economic Role of the State in the 21st Century', *Cato Journal* 25/3 (2005), 618–23.

[2] P. Lindert, *Growing Public: Social Spending and Economic Growth since the Eighteenth Century*, vol. 1 (Cambridge: Cambridge University Press, 2004), pp. 12–13.

to transfer resources to political client groups.[3] In turn, the roots of those common traits lay in the particularities of southern European countries' recent trajectory of economic development and real convergence: greater social heterogeneity, profound regional disparities in income and work opportunities, and the existence of large black economies. Combined with other political and institutional characteristics, such as the absence of a strong state technocracy and the prominent role played by political parties in the aggregation of social interests, these factors created a specific context for the development of welfare states, and this in turn led to both uncontrolled spending and less effective policy-making.[4]

A related common feature of southern Europe was the use of fiscal policy and, more generally, the public sector as an instrument of democratic consolidation.[5] In Italy, the expansion of the public sector, with the intervention of political parties and their strong links with interest and socio-economic groups, had played a key role in stabilising postwar democratic institutions by the early 1960s. Owing to strong ideological polarisation and absence of legitimacy among the main political forces, however, this early phase had led to a situation of exclusive legitimacy in which anti-regime forces at the extreme wings of the party system and their constituencies were excluded from central government. Full democratic consolidation, therefore, was achieved only in the 1960s–70s when a political compromise was reached between the parties, which included a further massive expansion of welfare spending, especially on pensions and healthcare.[6] In Spain, Portugal and Greece, which embarked on their political transitions in 1974–5,

[3] M. Ferrera, 'The "Southern Model" of Welfare in Social Europe', *Journal of European Social Policy* 6/1 (1996), 17–37.

[4] M. Rhodes, 'Southern European Welfare States: Identity, Problems and Prospects for Reform', in M. Rhodes (ed.), *Southern European Welfare States: Between Crisis and Reform* (London and New York: Routledge, 1997), pp. 4–11.

[5] See L. Morlino, *Democracy between Consolidation and Crisis: Parties, Groups and Citizens in Southern Europe* (Oxford: Oxford University Press, 1998); and R. Gunther, H.-J. Puhle and P. N. Diamandouros, 'Introduction', in R. Gunther, P. Nikiforos Diamandouros and Hans-Jürgen Puhle (eds.), *The Politics of Democratic Consolidation: Southern Europe in Comparative Perspective* (Baltimore, MD: Johns Hopkins University Press, 1995), pp. 1–32.

[6] See D. Hine, 'The Consolidation of Democracy in Post-War Italy', in G. Pridham (ed.), *Securing Democracy. Political Parties and Democratic Consolidation in Southern Europe* (London: Routledge, 1990), pp. 62–83; L. Morlino, 'Political Parties and Democratic Consolidation in Southern Europe', in Gunther et al. (eds.), *The Politics of Democratic Consolidation*, pp. 315–88; and L. McLaren, *Constructing Democracy in Southern Europe* (London: Routledge, 2008), pp. 115–19. On the expansion of the Italian welfare state in the 1970s and 1980s, see M. Ferrera, 'Italy', in P. Flora (ed.), *Growth to Limits: European Welfare States since World War II* (Berlin and New York: De Gruyter, 1986), pp. 385–482.

democratic consolidation was characterised by inclusive (quasi-inclusive for Portugal, due to the presence of an anti-regime Communist Party) legitimacy and alternation between the parties in office, and was completed only in the 1980s. Different political trajectories also help explain dissimilar patterns of fiscal convergence. As Table 12.1 shows, by 1970 both total and social spending in Italy were in line with western European norms. In Spain, Portugal and Greece, by contrast, autocratic regimes had allowed a huge gap in social spending to accrue and had relatively small governments (approximately 60 per cent of the median European economy). The strong demand for social welfare that accompanied democratisation led to a rapid increase in both social and total spending. By 1990 the size of government was only slightly below European standards, while in Italy total spending now exceeded the European average by 20 per cent and was scarcely kept in check by sporadic retrenchment efforts.[7]

Convergence in tax revenues was significantly slower, as governments adjusted their tax policy to structural shifts in spending patterns only after a considerable delay. In 1970 total tax revenue as a share of GDP ranged from 49 per cent of the western European average in Spain to 79 per cent in Italy (see Table 12.1).[8] Both direct and indirect tax revenues also fell short of their potential because of widespread evasion, lax enforcement and large black economies, which significantly reduced the tax base. Over time, the modernisation of indirect taxation, with the general adoption of VAT, income tax reform and the expansion of social security contributions, narrowed the gap, which was especially large with regard to revenues from household income in the four countries.[9] Nevertheless, in 1990 total tax revenues in Spain, Portugal and Greece were still 15–25 per cent lower than European standards; gaps in revenues from household income remained sizeable and, with the exception of Spain, social security was only partly offset by a higher tax burden on goods and services.

---

[7] M. Ferrera, 'Targeting Welfare in a "Soft" State: Italy's Winding Road to Selectivity', in N. Gilbert (ed.), *Targeting Social Benefits: International Perspectives and Trends* (New Brunswick, NJ, and London: Transaction Books, 2001), pp. 157–86.

[8] On the legacy of Franco's outdated and inefficient tax system and resistance to tax reform after the Spanish transition to democracy, see F. Comín, 'Reaching a Political Consensus for Tax Reform in Spain', in J. Martinez-Vazquez and J. F. Sanz-Sanz (eds.), *Fiscal Reform in Spain: Accomplishments and Challenges* (Cheltenham: Edward Elgar, 2007), pp. 8–58. For a comprehensive chronology of fiscal reforms in Spain, see I. Argimón et al., 'El sector de las administraciones públicas en España', *Banco de España-Estudios Económicos* 68 (1999). On post-war tax reforms in Italy, see P. Bosi, *I Tributi nell' Economia Italiana* (Bologna: Il Mulino, 1988).

[9] K. Messere, F. De Kam and C. Heady, *Tax Policy: Theory and Practice in OECD Countries* (Oxford: Oxford University Press, 2003), offers a general picture of the trends found in the tax burden and its structure in the OECD countries.

Table 12.1. *Comparative fiscal performance of the southern European countries*

	1970			1980			1990		
	Tax revenues	Total spending	Social transfers	Tax revenues	Total spending	Social transfers	Tax revenues	Total spending	Social transfers
European median (GDP %)	33.2	33.8	16.4	36.9	42.6	18.6	39.7	44.6	23.7
				ratio to European median					
Italy	0.79	1.00	1.03	0.82	0.99	1.00	0.98	1.20	0.98
Spain	0.49	0.62	0.35	0.63	0.83	0.86	0.84	0.96	0.83
Portugal	0.58	0.59	0.39	0.65	0.86	0.68	0.74	0.92	0.59
Greece	0.67	0.63	0.55	0.66	0.58	0.62	0.74	0.86	0.88

Source: IMF, *International Financial Statistics* and *Government Finance Statistics*; OECD data from Allard-Lindert dataset, available online at http://economics.ucdavis.edu/people/fzlinder/peter-linderts-webpage/data-and-estimates.

Note: Europe includes Austria, Belgium, Denmark, Finland, France, West Germany, Greece, Ireland, Italy, Netherlands, Norway, Portugal, Spain, Sweden, Switzerland and the United Kingdom.

By this time Italy's tax revenues, now in line with, or even above, European averages, still fell short of the spending of the 1980s.

Of course, growing fiscal imbalances, far from being the exclusive prerogative of southern Europe, were common in industrialised economies as governments slashed spending in response to an unprecedented increase in unemployment and a growth slowdown, followed in the 1980s by unusually high real interest rates.[10] As a consequence, fiscal sustainability worsened globally and the average debt-to-GDP ratio escalated from 20 to 60 per cent over the course of the 'Great Accumulation' of the last quarter of the twentieth century.[11]

Table 12.2 puts the deficit and debt performance of southern Europe in a European perspective. All the southern countries accumulated overall budget deficits that were significantly larger than the median European country. Lack of fiscal discipline was especially pronounced in Italy and Greece, which had deficits twice as large as the European median compared to the Iberian economies.[12] Larger deficits, combined with higher debt levels at the outset, explain why their debt followed much more explosive paths, peaking at 121 and 100 per cent of GDP in 1994 and 1993 respectively. By contrast, Spain's and Portugal's debts started from significantly lower levels and converged over time towards European median values. Relatively moderate inflation in Spain explains why governments there, with fiscal imbalances just above the median and an average GDP growth equal to that of Portugal, ended up with a debt ratio significantly higher than its neighbour. In fact, as the bottom part of Table 12.2 illustrates, inflation offset more than 70 per cent of the cumulative contribution of deficits to the increase of the debt ratio in Portugal, but only 44 per cent in Spain. In Italy and Greece, inflation was equally critical to moderating debt accumulation, absorbing between 60 and 70 per cent of the impact of cumulative deficits on the debt ratio.

[10] N. Roubini and J. Sachs, 'Political and Economic Determinants of Budget Deficits in the Industrial Democracies', *European Economic Review* 33 (1989), 903–38; and P. Ciocca and G. Nardozzi, *The High Price of Money: An Interpretation of International Interest Rates* (Oxford: Clarendon Press, 1996).

[11] A. Abbas, L. Blattner, M. De Broeck, A. El-Ganainy and M. Hu, 'Sovereign Debt Composition in Advanced Economies: A Historical Perspective', IMF Working Paper 162 (2014).

[12] An extensive theoretical and empirical literature explores the political and institutional determinants of fiscal outcomes in industrial economies, such as ideology, polarisation, government instability, power diffusion within ruling coalitions, fractionalisation of the decision-making process and lax budgetary rules. For a summary, see A. Alesina and R. Perotti, 'Budget Deficits and Budget Institutions', in J. M. Poterba and J. von Hagen (eds.), *Fiscal Institutions and Fiscal Performance* (Chicago and London: The University of Chicago Press, 1999), pp. 8–36; and R. Perotti and Y. Kontopoulos, 'Fragmented Fiscal Policy', *Journal of Public Economics* 86 (2002), 191–222.

Table 12.2. *Debt accumulation in southern Europe, 1970–98*

	Initial debt ratio (1970)	Peak debt ratio (year)	Final debt ratio (1998)	Average overall budget balance (% of GDP)	Real GDP growth (mean annual rate)	Inflation (mean annual rate)
Italy	0.371	1.212 (1994)	1.143	−11.5	2.1	10.8
Spain	0.115	0.675 (1996)	0.642	−5.1	3.1	9.4
Portugal	0.165	0.591 (1995)	0.503	−7.8	3.0	14.5
Greece	0.247	1.005 (1993)	0.945	−9.7	2.2	15.7
European median	*0.242*	*0.680*	*0.621*	*−4.8*	*2.2*	*7.0*
			ratio to European median			
Italy	1.50	1.78	1.84	2.40	0.95	1.54
Spain	0.48	0.99	1.03	1.06	1.41	1.34
Portugal	0.68	0.87	0.81	1.63	1.36	2.07
Greece	1.02	1.48	1.52	2.02	1.00	2.24

	Change in debt ratio	Cumulative contribution of:			Share of deficit offset by:	
		deficit	growth	inflation	growth	inflation
Italy	+0.772	+2.943	−0.492	−1.833	16.7%	62.3%
Spain	+0.526	+1.355	−0.284	−0.594	21.0%	43.8%
Portugal	+0.338	+1.962	−0.384	−1.403	19.6%	71.5%
Greece	+0.698	+2.670	−0.331	−1.823	12.4%	68.3%

Source: Debt ratio: IMF Historical Public Debt database, available online at: www .imf.org/external/pubs/cat/longres.aspx?sk=24332.0; see A. Abbas et al., 'A Historical Public Debt Database', IMF Working Paper 10/245 (2010). Nominal GDP: IMF International Financial Statistics. Real GDP (1990, Geary-Khamis, US$): The Conference Board Total Economy Database, available online at www.conference-board .org/data/economydatabase.

Note: Average overall budget balances are based on debt changes. Inflation is based on the GDP deflator. Growth rates are average annual compounded rates. Europe includes Austria, Belgium, Denmark, Finland, France, West Germany, Greece, Ireland, Italy, Netherlands, Norway, Portugal, Spain, Sweden, Switzerland and the United Kingdom. The decomposition of the change in debt ratio is not exact.

In fact, in the 1970s and 1980s the southern European economies all followed a monetary policy regime of inflationary finance. As a rising share of budget deficits was monetised (i.e. funded directly by central banks that were still strongly dependent on the government), money growth and inflation remained persistently higher than in the rest of Europe, as Table 12.1 shows. Inflationary finance allowed governments to exact significant seigniorage (revenues appropriated by the consolidated government thanks to its monopoly over the issue of zero-interest base money) from the private sector, which in turn contributed to improving debt sustainability.[13] Economic theory suggests that governments resort to seigniorage when the tax system is inefficient, that is to say, tax evasion is widespread and collection costs are high – a feature consistent with the situation in southern Europe in the 1970s and 1980s, as mentioned earlier.[14] In line with theory, central banks' dependence explains the positive correlation between budget deficits, inflation and seigniorage found in the southern European economies – a feature that was absent in the rest of western Europe, even in countries with similar or longer patterns of debt accumulation.[15]

This chapter sheds light on a related dimension of the inflationary finance policy regime of southern Europe and shows that seigniorage was neither the only nor (in some cases) the most important source of implicit revenue that governments used to improve the sustainability of their debt. In fact, they also managed to exact sizeable implicit resources from regulatory distortions imposed on their financial sectors. It was a combination of seigniorage and 'financial repression' – another unique feature of southern Europe in the 1970s and 1980s – that contributed to slow the rate of debt accumulation and postpone the need for real fiscal reform. This finding is consistent with the association between financial repression and inflation, as suggested by theory and documented for western European countries.[16] Although the use of financial repression for fiscal purposes in southern Europe during the 1980s has been explored by earlier country studies,[17] this chapter covers

---

[13] V. Grilli, 'Seigniorage in Europe', in M. De Cecco and A. Giovannini (eds.), *A European Central Bank?* (Cambridge: Cambridge University Press, 1989), pp. 53–79; and D. Gros, 'Seigniorage in the EC: The Implications of the EMS and Financial Market Integration', IMF Working Paper 7 (1989).

[14] A. Cukierman, S. Edwards and G. Tabellini, 'Seigniorage and Political Instability', *American Economic Review* 82 (1992), 537–55, find that not only economic determinants such as lower GDP per capita and trade openness, but also political instability (the frequency of government changes), led to a more intensive use of seigniorage as a source of government revenue in a sample of industrialised, middle-income and developing economies in the period 1971–82.

[15] V. Grilli, D. Masciandaro and G. Tabellini, 'Political and Monetary Institutions and Public Financial Policies in the Industrial Countries', *Economic Policy* 13 (1991), 361–2.

[16] C. Wyplosz, 'Financial Restraint and Liberalization in Postwar Europe', in G. Caprio, P. Honohan and J. E. Stiglitz (eds.), *Financial Liberalization: How Fast, How Far?* (Cambridge: Cambridge University Press, 2001), pp. 145–9.

[17] F. Bruni, A. Penati and A. Porta, 'Financial Regulation, Implicit Taxes, and Fiscal Adjustment in Italy', in M. Monti (ed.), *Fiscal Policy, Economic Adjustment, and Financial Markets* (Washington, DC: International Monetary Fund, 1989), pp. 197–230; R. Repullo, 'Financing Budget Deficits by Seigniorage and Implicit Taxation: The Cases of Spain and Portugal', CEPR Discussion Paper 583 (1991); and J. Braga de Macedo and M. Sebastiao, 'Public Debt and Implicit Taxes: The Portuguese Experience', *European Economic Review* 33 (1989), 573–9.

new ground in that it provides for the first time a comparative assessment of the size of aggregate implicit revenues, based on a consistent methodology and covering the period from the 1970s to the 1990s. The chapter also highlights important inter-country differences in governments' use of implicit revenues, the relative magnitude of seigniorage and financial repression, and the time-varying relationship between them.

The chapter is structured as follows. The first section summarises the key elements of a public finance approach to the political economy of financial repression: why governments use it as a source of implicit fiscal revenues and how it can complement seigniorage in an inflationary finance regime. Next, the chapter offers both qualitative and quantitative evidence of deferred financial liberalisation in southern Europe. It then presents a quantitative assessment of aggregate implicit revenues generated by the combination of seigniorage and financial repression in the four southern economies, while the penultimate section assesses their implications for fiscal fragility and debt sustainability by estimating counterfactual scenarios in the absence of financial repression. The chapter is summarised in the concluding section.

Why do Governments Repress the Financial Sector?

Financial repression can be defined as a set of policies, laws, regulations, taxes, distortions and qualitative and quantitative restrictions that prevent banks and other financial intermediaries from operating at their full technological potential.[18] Over the second half of the twentieth century financial repression was widely used in both developed and developing countries. The instruments employed included price and quantity restrictions, either domestic (such as credit ceilings, control of domestic interest rates, compulsory credit allocation, high reserve requirements, liquidity ratios and asset portfolio constraints) or external (such as the regulation of banks' external transactions and a ban or quantitative controls on, and tax discrimination against residents' holdings of foreign financial assets).

In the case of western Europe, a 'trilemma'-based interpretation argues that restrictions on domestic and external financial intermediation enabled governments to reconcile their strong preference for pegged exchange rates – under the Bretton Woods system of adjustable pegs and, after its demise, under the 'monetary snake' and the 'soft'

---

[18] N. Roubini and X. Sala-i-Martin, 'A Growth Model of Inflation, Tax Evasion and Financial Repression', *Journal of Monetary Economics* 35 (1995), 277.

European monetary system of the 1970s and early 1980s – while maintaining a degree of independence in monetary policy.[19] This interpretation emphasises the functional link between financial regulation and macroeconomic stabilisation as a means of insulating the economy from external shocks. At the same time, however, the empirical evidence suggests that financial restrictions did not improve the effectiveness of controls over monetary aggregates or succeed in reducing the volatility of nominal interest rates, whereas a delayed transition to full convertibility significantly increased the cost of capital.[20]

An alternative explanation, conventionally advanced for developing economies, suggests that financial distortions are instrumental to government debt sustainability, rather than monetary control. In the public finance approach, financial repression is basically explained as a means of keeping nominal interest rates for public debt artificially low, thus allowing the government to exact implicit fiscal revenues (the difference between the 'repressed' rate and the rate that would prevail in an undistorted market) from domestic holders of its liabilities. Like seigniorage, revenues from financial repression are particularly attractive to governments that are faced with uneven effective income tax rates due to systemic corruption, considerable disparity in their ability to verify social groups' incomes or large black economies.[21]

The public finance literature also emphasises the role of financial repression as a complement to inflationary finance.[22] An increase in the rate of monetary expansion, increases the seigniorage tax rate, but also raises the equilibrium rate of inflation and the nominal interest rate, thus reducing the inflation tax base as it results in falling demand for real money balances.[23] In fact, seigniorage is levied not only on cash held by the public, but also indirectly on borrowers and lenders when governments borrow from commercial banks at zero or very low costs by

[19] C. Wyplosz, 'Exchange Rate Regimes: Some Lessons from Post-War Europe', CEPR Discussion Paper 2723 (2001). On the EMS, see D. Gros and N. Thygesen, *European Monetary Integration. From the EMS to EMU* (London: Longman, 1998).

[20] Wyplosz, 'Financial Restraint', 153–7; H.-J. Voth, 'Convertibility, Currency Controls and the Cost of Capital in Western Europe, 1950–1999', *International Journal of Finance and Economics* 8/3 (2003), 255–76.

[21] P. Honohan, 'The Fiscal Approach to Financial Intermediation Policy', ESRI Working Paper 49 (1994). For a formal model, see J. P. Nicolini, 'Tax Evasion and the Optimal Inflation Tax', *Journal of Development Economics* 55/1 (1998), 215–32; and R. Gupta, 'Tax Evasion and Financial Repression', *Journal of Economics and Business* 60 (2008), 517–35.

[22] D. Romer, 'Financial Intermediation, Reserve Requirements, and Inside Money: A General Equilibrium Analysis', *Journal of Monetary Economics* 16 (1985), 175–94.

[23] T. Sargent, 'A Primer on Monetary and Fiscal Policy', *Journal of Banking and Finance* 23 (1999), 1463–82; see also Roubini and Sala-i-Martin, 'A Growth Model', 289–90.

setting high reserve requirements, by imposing portfolio constraints in the form of high liquid asset ratios or by making government securities the only asset eligible for meeting the requirements alternative to cash.[24] In particular, reserve requirements and liquid asset ratios can be used to raise the demand for money artificially.[25]

Governments can also deploy a variety of regulatory constraints to keep the yield of public debt denominated in the domestic currency below the level that would prevail in a free market. Interest rate ceilings impose a tax on financial intermediaries and reduce borrowing costs for the government and associated borrowers.[26] Credit ceilings ration domestic credit in favour of the latter, thus forcing private borrowers to resort to international credit and financial markets. Credit ceilings can also increase banks' excess liquidity and channel it towards the bond market, thus driving the market rate of public debt below its equilibrium level. Interest rate and credit controls keep the actual rate paid by governments on domestic debt below the rate paid in world capital markets. This differential represents an implicit tax rate imposed on the existing stock of domestic debt (the tax base) and can generate implicit revenues that are comparable to the size of seigniorage in many countries.[27] Governments can impose additional distortions on the financial system by regulating the composition of banks' asset portfolios. Compulsory liquidity and investment requirements in government or public sector bonds artificially increase the demand for public debt, while regulating the securities markets, combined with tax discrimination in favour of public debt, gives the government preferential access to capital markets. Finally, governments can skew the composition of their debt in favour of non-marketable instruments (bank loans, overdraft facilities, saving bonds and certificates) which

---

[24] P. Brock, 'Inflationary Finance in an Open Economy', *Journal of Monetary Economics* 14 (1984), 37–53; P. Brock, 'Reserve Requirements and the Inflation Tax', *Journal of Money Credit and Banking* 21 (1989), 106–21; and M. Fry, *Emancipating the Banking System and Developing Markets for Government Debt* (London: Routledge, 1997), pp. 69–76. By regulating interest rates, governments can also limit competition for loanable funds from the private sector.

[25] An additional nexus between seigniorage and financial repression stems from the limited number of financial instruments available in repressed systems, generally with very low, or even negative, interest rates. Other things being equal, this also tends to increase the demand for money: see R. Dornbusch and A. Giovannini, 'Monetary Policy in the Open Economy', in B. M. Friedman and F. H. Hahn (eds.), *Handbook of Monetary Economics*, vol. 2 (Amsterdam: North-Holland, 1990), pp. 1231–303.

[26] C. Chamley and P. Honohan, 'Taxation of Financial Intermediation', World Bank PRE Working Paper 421 (1990).

[27] A. Giovannini and M. De Melo, 'Government Revenues from Financial Repression', *American Economic Review* 83/4 (1993), 953–63.

are subjected to interest rate regulation – an unorthodox policy that became normal practice after the Second World War.[28]

Both seigniorage and domestic financial repression would be unenforceable without capital controls. These are essential to limit investors' and banks' ability to circumvent domestic regulation and avoid seigniorage by turning to offshore intermediaries or international money, capital and foreign exchange markets. By segregating domestic intermediaries from competition, governments also enhance the imposition of high reserve requirements and other distortionary regulations on the financial system.[29] There is widespread consensus that 'fiscal considerations are the most important determinants of the use of capital controls and that the controls, or some other factor highly correlated with the use of controls, have measurable effects on government revenues'.[30] The evidence of the determinants of capital controls in a sample of twenty OECD countries in the 1970s and 1980s is consistent with an inflation tax explanation.[31] Capital controls were also found to be closely associated with higher inflation, greater reliance on seigniorage and lower real interest rates in a separate sample of nineteen industrialised and forty-two developing countries in the period 1966–89.[32]

The public finance approach to monetary policy emphasises the fiscal implications of seigniorage and financial repression. In the absence of deficit monetisation by the central bank, the government's debt follows the dynamic:

$$\Delta d_t = d_{t-1}(r-g) - \mathrm{pb}_t \qquad (12.1)$$

where d is the debt-to-GDP ratio, r is the real interest rate on government debt (the nominal rate adjusted to inflation), g is the growth rate of real

---

[28] C. M. Reinhart and B. Sbrancia, 'The Liquidation of Government Debt', NBER Working Paper 16893 (2011). Abbas et al., 'Sovereign Debt Composition', find that, for a sample of advanced economies, the share of marketable over total sovereign debt fell from 85 per cent before the Second World War to about 50 per cent in the late 1970s.

[29] A. Drazen, 'Monetary Policy, Capital Controls and Seigniorage in an Open Economy', in M. De Cecco and A. Giovannini (eds.), *A European Central Bank?* (Cambridge: Cambridge University Press, 1989), pp. 13–32.

[30] M. Dooley, 'A Survey of Academic Literature on Controls over International Capital Transactions', *IMF Staff Papers* 43/4 (1996), 677.

[31] A. Alesina, V. Grilli and G. M. Milesi-Ferretti, 'The Political Economy of Capital Controls', in L. Leiderman and A. Razin (eds.), *Capital Mobility: The Impact on Consumption, Investment and Growth* (Cambridge: Cambridge University Press, 1994), pp. 289–321.

[32] V. Grilli and G. M. Milesi-Ferretti, 'Economic Effects and Structural Determinants of Capital Controls', *IMF Staff Papers* 42 (1995), 517–51.

output, and pb is the GDP ratio of the primary balance (the difference between total tax revenues and grants, and expenditures net of interest payments). With a primary balance equal to zero, d grows at a rate equal to the differential $(r - g)$, which is referred to as the flow cost of sovereign debt. For any given level of d_{t-1}, the fiscal burden, $d_{t-1}(r - g)$, determines the primary balance that a government must run in order to stabilise the outstanding debt-to-GDP ratio:

$$\Delta d_t = 0 \quad \text{if} \quad d_{t-1}(r - g) = \text{pb}_t \qquad (12.2)$$

Thus, the cost of borrowing, the state of the economy and the level of outstanding debt together determine the government's fiscal fragility and its incentive to pursue fiscal discipline.[33] The path of debt accumulation is essentially determined by how much the primary balance deviates from the fiscal burden, that is, how strong the government's preference for debt sustainability (i.e. stabilisation) is as a policy goal.[34] For $r > g$ (a positive fiscal burden), the debt ratio is bound to increase over time unless the government is able to run a primary surplus (pb > 0). A negative fiscal burden $(r < g)$, on the contrary, gives the government more fiscal leeway, since a primary deficit (pb < 0) is compatible with a stable, or even a decreasing, debt ratio. As more debt increases solvency risk and borrowing costs, the urgency of fiscal adjustment (via spending cuts, increased tax revenues, or both) increases with the debt ratio. At high levels of public debt, positive shocks to nominal interest rates, as well as negative shocks to inflation, real growth and the primary balance, tend to add to fiscal fragility and worsen debt sustainability.

Since changing the tax system has very high political and administrative costs[35] and real fiscal adjustments have complex distributional consequences, the inflationary finance with financial repression mix may be attractive to governments with persistent fiscal imbalances, rising debt and slow growth – a situation akin to that experienced by southern European countries since the mid-1970s. On one side, seigniorage $\left(s = \frac{S}{\text{GDP}}\right)$ provides additional resources that, by partly absorbing a primary balance shock (e.g. a large, permanent increase in spending

[33] J. Aizenmann and G. K. Pasricha, 'Fiscal Fragility: What the Past May Say about the Future', NBER Working Paper 16478 (2010).

[34] C. Wyplosz, 'Debt Sustainability Assessment: Mission Impossible', *Review of Economics and Institutions* 2/3 (2011), 2–37.

[35] See W. Hettich and S. Winer, *Democratic Choice and Taxation: A Theoretical and Empirical Analysis* (Cambridge: Cambridge University Press, 1999).

commitments not matched by an increase in tax revenues), help moderate debt accumulation:

$$\Delta d_t = d_{t-1}(r - g) - \mathrm{pb}_t - \mathrm{s}_t \tag{12.3}$$

On the other side, a combination of low and inflexible nominal interest rates[36] and high inflation can be used to obtain low, or even negative, real interest rates, r, which decrease flow costs and improve debt sustainability.[37] In an inflationary finance regime, financial repression allows policy-makers to gain time and shift the political pain of real fiscal adjustment on to future governments.

This also explains why financial repression can become especially resilient. Having grown accustomed to relying on large, implicit taxation, policy-makers who rationally anticipate the consequences of reforms may attempt to delay or even withdraw them if they expect to suffer significant fiscal losses.[38] In fact, macroeconomic stabilisation (central bank independence, falling inflationary expectations, high interest rates) and financial liberalisation (allowing nominal rates to rise to market level) are policy shocks that, by drying up the sources of implicit revenues, make real fiscal adjustment imperative, as existing spending commitments must be cut and the tax effort intensified in order to guarantee debt sustainability under the new, non-inflationary macroeconomic regime. If governments expect reforms to be exogenously imposed and anticipate the consequences of financial liberalisation, they have an incentive to maximise the exaction of revenues from implicit taxation in the short run in order to offset future debt problems. This is what southern European governments did, some studies contend, after the launch of the Single Market and the EMU in the late 1980s, in order to enter the new macroeconomic regime with a lower public debt and interest burden.[39]

---

[36] Interest rate regulation inhibits the Fisher effect (i.e. prevents nominal rates from adjusting to changes in the expected rate of inflation) and suppresses the impact of increasing solvency risk on the risk premium.

[37] Reinhart and Sbrancia, 'The Liquidation', show that a mix of inflation, interest rate regulation and the extensive use of non-marketable debt allowed the US and UK governments to liquidate the huge debt burden inherited from the Second World War. On the critical contribution of inflation to the reduction of the debt ratio in the United Kingdom from 1948 to 1984, see W. H. Buiter, 'A Guide to Public Debts and Deficits', *Economic Policy* 1/1 (1985), 15–21.

[38] D. P. Quinn and C. Inclán, 'The Origins of Financial Openness: A Study of Current and Capital Account Liberalization', *American Journal of Political Science* 41/3 (1997), 771–813.

[39] F. Giavazzi, 'The Exchange Rate Question in Europe', in R. C. Bryant, D. A. Currie, J. A. Frenkel, P. R. Masson and R. Portes (eds.), *Macroeconomic Policies in an Interdependent World* (Washington, DC: International Monetary Fund, 1989), pp. 283–304; and P. Bacchetta and R. Caminal, 'Optimal Seigniorage and Financial Liberalization', *Journal of International Money and Finance* 11 (1992), 518–38.

Financial Repression in Western Europe: Was the South Different?

Financial repression was a persistent characteristic of many western European economies. Starting in the 1950s, European governments subjected their banking systems to a wide array of monetary policy-oriented controls on financial prices and quantities (interest rate controls, bank-by-bank credit ceilings, regulated credit schemes, liquidity ratios, restrictions on banks' foreign borrowing and lending) in order to influence the cost, aggregate volume and allocation of domestic credit. While their intervention was typically based on moral suasion and bank cartelisation in the Nordic countries, command-and-control administrative regulations were more intensely used in countries with a stronger 'statist' tradition, such as France and the southern periphery.[40]

As financial openness gathered pace in the industrial economies during the inflationary cycle from the 1970s to the early 1980s,[41] the distortionary impact of direct instruments on credit allocation and bank competition, as well as their rigidity and increasing ineffectiveness for monetary control due to circumvention and bank disintermediation, became widely recognised. In an attempt to reduce excess liquidity and check inflationary pressures, monetary authorities gradually replaced direct controls with indirect instruments, among which central bank lending facilities, open market operations on government securities and changes in bank reserve requirements[42] were prominent. The prerequisites for the effective enforcement of this new, market-based approach to monetary policy were the elimination of interest rate controls, the liberalisation of capital flows, the deregulation of the banking system, and the development of money markets for short-term government securities.[43] For this reason, central banks – especially those that enjoyed a greater degree of autonomy from governments and pursued more vigorously the goal of monetary stabilisation

---

[40] T. R. G. Bingham, *Banking and Monetary Policy* (Paris: OECD, 1985), pp. 15–21.

[41] The United States, West Germany and Switzerland had fully liberalised their capital account transactions from the 1950s. Temporary restrictions on capital inflows were enforced in West Germany in the early 1970s, but removed in 1973–4. Capital flows were fully liberalised in the United Kingdom and Japan between 1979 and 1982. On the European experience, see A. F. P. Bakker, *The Liberalization of Capital Movements in Europe: The Monetary Committee and Financial Integration, 1958–1994* (Dordrecht, Boston, MA, and London: Kluwer Academic, 1996).

[42] Reserve requirements are a hybrid instrument. Although they are administered through regulation, their monetary effect is achieved through their impact on banks' demand for reserve money, while reserve money creation is controlled through the central bank's balance sheet. For this reason they are usually classified as indirect instruments.

[43] W. Alexander, T. Baliño and C. Enoch, 'The Adoption of Indirect Instruments of Monetary Policy', IMF Occasional Paper 126 (1995).

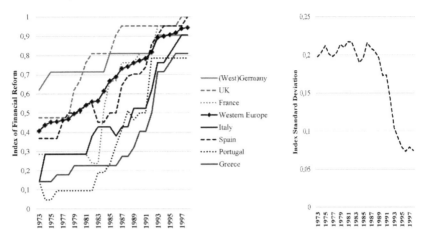

Figure 12.1. ADT Index of financial reform in western Europe, 1973–98.

Note: The Index ranges from 0 (full financial repression) to 1 (full financial liberalisation). Western Europe is a weighted average of sixteen European countries (Austria, Belium, Denmark, Finland, France, West Germany, Greece, Ireland, Italy, Netherlands, Norway, Portugal, Spain, Sweden, Switzerland and the United Kingdom) based on real GDP shares.

Source: Financial Reform Database, available online at www.imf.org/ external/pubs/cat/longres.aspx?sk=22485.0; see A. Abiad et al., 'A New Database of Financial Reforms', *IMF Staff Papers*, 57/2 (2010), 281–302.

(disinflation) – were active promoters of financial reforms.[44] However, the institutional balance of power between fiscal and monetary authorities was not the only force behind the transition to a market-oriented financial system. After the Single European Act of 1986 laid the foundation for the European single financial market and the European Monetary Union, financial reforms became institutional obligations that member governments had to meet, and all the more urgently so as the deadline of 1992 was approaching.[45]

European governments responded very differently to this combination of domestic and external constraints. Their paths to financial liberalisation are summarised in the left-hand panel of Figure 12.1, based on an Index of Financial Reform compiled by Abiad, Detragiache

[44] G. Pagoulatos, 'Financial Interventionism and Liberalization in Southern Europe: State, Bankers and the Politics of Disinflation', *Journal of Public Policy* 23/2 (2003), 171–99.
[45] W. Werner, 'Financial Market Integration: An Insurmountable Challenge to Modern Trade Policy?', in P. Clement, H. James and H. Van der Wee (eds.), *Financial Innovation, Regulation and Crises in History* (London: Pickering & Chatto, 2014), pp. 107–26.

and Tressel (ADT).[46] Using a de jure approach, the ADT Index scores countries on various dimensions related to financial repression: directed credit schemes in favour of priority sectors; reserve requirements; aggregate credit controls; interest rate regulation; entry barriers and extensive state ownership in the banking sector; capital controls; the quality of prudential regulation and supervision; and restrictions on the development of security markets. The Index, normalised to range from 0 (fully repressed) to 1 (fully liberalised), allows a cross-country comparison of the transition to a market-oriented financial system. In fact, the within-Europe variance of financial liberalisation remained high and stable until the late 1980s, followed by a rapid convergence in the following decade (Figure 12.1, right-hand panel). On the one hand, West Germany had already achieved a very high score in the early 1970s and progressed gradually towards a fully liberalised system in the following decades. On the other hand, countries such as the United Kingdom and France forced through drastic reforms – in 1979–82 and in 1983–7 respectively – moving quickly from a heavily regulated to a highly liberalised system.

At the opposite end of the spectrum, southern countries caught up after a significant delay. Spain was the country that followed most closely the western European experience. State ownership of the banks was not extensive and governments had lifted interest rate controls and relaxed entry barriers in the late 1970s.[47] After a short-lived reversal due to tightened interest rate controls, the policy of financial reforms gained renewed momentum in the late 1980s after the country's accession to the EEC, so that in 1991, at the time of the final negotiations on the Maastricht Treaty, the financial system in Spain was almost fully liberalised, with just a few restrictions on directed credit and aggregate credit ceilings.

In the rest of the south, liberalisation proved much more controversial. In Italy, in spite of an early deregulation of interest rates and liberalisation of capital controls, the financial system remained partly repressed well into the early 1990s, with pervasive state ownership, high entry barriers and large directed credit schemes.[48] Financial repression was even harsher and more persistent in Portugal and Greece, with extensive state ownership, regulated interest rates, directed credit

---

[46] A. Abiad, E. Detragiache and T. Tressel, 'A New Database of Financial Reforms', *IMF Staff Papers* 57/2 (2010), 281–302.

[47] S. A. Perez, *Banking on Privilege: The Politics of Spanish Financial Reform* (Ithaca, NY: Cornell University Press, 1997); and A. J. Lukauskas, *Regulating Finance: The Political Economy of Spanish Financial Policy from Franco to Democracy* (Ann Arbor, MI: University of Michigan Press, 1997).

[48] S. Battilossi, A. Gigliobianco and G. Marinelli, 'Resource Allocation by the Banking System', in G. Toniolo (ed.), *Oxford Handbook of the Italian Economy since Unification* (Oxford: Oxford University Press, 2013), pp. 485–515.

schemes, binding aggregate credit ceilings and a weak capital market.[49] Unlike the Spanish authorities, whose commitment to market-oriented financial reforms appeared to be less dependent on external institutional constraints, governments in Italy, Portugal and Greece attempted to retain a semi-repressed financial regime as long as possible and submitted reluctantly only in 1991–2, compelled by EEC obligations.

Figure 12.2 confirms a positive correlation between central bank independence and financial reforms in sixteen European countries. In the south, and especially in Italy, Greece and Portugal (although not exclusively there), highly dependent central banks, which were scarcely in a position to oppose deficit monetisation, refrained from promoting the liberalisation of financial systems. Again, among the four southern countries, the stance of the Spanish authorities stands out as most sympathetic to market-oriented reforms.

While a de jure approach provides a measure of the government's policy position, the intensity of financial repression to which a financial system is exposed can be gauged only de facto, by looking at quantitative indicators such as commercial banks' assets. From this perspective, it is important to note that the transition from direct to indirect monetary policy instruments did not necessarily erode governments' ability to distort their domestic financial systems. The greater use of reserve requirements is one example. By the mid-1980s the OECD recorded that the level of reserve requirements had declined or remained stable over time in the majority of western European countries, but had escalated in the countries of the southern periphery.[50] This is confirmed by Figure 12.3. Whereas there was a slight increase in reserve ratios at the European level, they reached exceedingly high levels in the four southern countries, with peaks above 15 per cent in Italy and even 20 per cent in Spain, Portugal and Greece. In the case of the latter three, levels remained very high into the 1990s, against a generalised convergence towards European levels. Their distortionary impact was further magnified by the fact that bank reserves in southern Europe were generally earning no interest or were remunerated at fixed, artificially low nominal rates.[51]

---

[49] A. Mendonça Pinto, 'Changing Financial Systems in Small Open Economies: The Portuguese Case', *BIS Policy Papers* 1 (1996), 96–113; G. Pagoulatos, 'Strength without Independence: Central Bank and the Politics of Greek Financial Deregulation', *Current Politics and Economics of Europe* 9/3 (2000), 330–59.

[50] Bacchetta and Caminal, 'Optimal Seigniorage', 518–19.

[51] In Italy, the interest rate on reserves deposited with the central bank remained fixed at 5.5 per cent from 1970 until the mid-1990s. In Spain, it remained at around 3 per cent until the early 1980s, when it was raised to approximately 7 per cent. In Portugal, reserves were not remunerated throughout the period. In Greece, reserves were not remunerated in the 1970s and 1980s; in the 1990s 50 per cent of outstanding reserves yielded a nominal rate of 12.5 per cent.

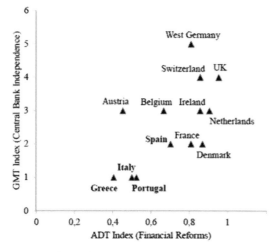

Figure 12.2.   Central bank independence and financial reforms in 1990.
Note: The GMT Index scores countries on a scale from 0 (maximum
dependence) to 15 (maximum independence) and includes both political
independence (the capacity to choose the final goal of monetary policy,
i.e. autonomy to pursue low inflation) and economic independence (the
capacity to choose the instruments of monetary policy, i.e. to set autonomously the terms and volume of the goverment's borrowing from the
central bank). Here I use only the five attributes that define a central
bank's economic independence with respect to monetary financing
of budget deficits: whether the direct credit to the government is non-
automatic, at market rates, explicitly stated as temporary and in limited
amounts; and whether the central bank does not purchase government.
Source: Index of Financial Reform, see Figure 12.1; Index of Central
Bank Independence: V. Grilli, D. Masciandaro and G. Tabellini,
'Political and Monetary Instituions and Public Financial Policies in
the Industrial Countries', *Economic Policy*, 13 (1996), 361–2.

Beyond reserve requirements, governments in the southern countries
demanded that banks and other financial institutions invest part of their
asset portfolio in bonds and paper issued by the Treasury or public
sector companies. However, as securitisation gained momentum in
the 1980s, the effectiveness of such requirements gradually declined.
Nevertheless, they were dismantled only slowly and selectively in Italy,
whereas in Spain, Portugal and Greece their use even increased in the
first half of the 1980s.[52] This is confirmed by Figure 12.4, which shows
the ratio of commercial banks' claims on government to their claims on
the private sector. Again, the four southern European economies were

[52] Bingham, 'Banking and Monetary Policy', 33–7.

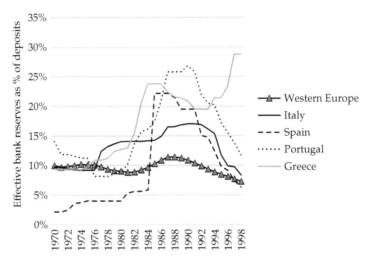

Figure 12.3.   Commercial banks' reserves with central banks.
Note: Five-year moving average of commercial banks' reserves with their central bank as a percentage of total deposits. Western Europe is a weighted average of sixteen European countries based on shares of GDP.
Source: IMF *International Financial Statistics.*

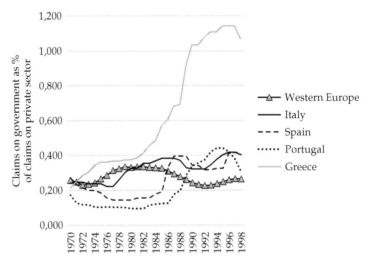

Figure 12.4.   Commercial banks' claims on government.
Note: Five-year moving average of commercial banks' claims on government as a percentage of claims on the private sector. Western Europe is a weighted average of sixteen European countries based on GDP shares.
Source: IMF *International Financial Statistics.*

characterised by a marked departure from the European experience in the 1980s – a divergence that reached unprecedented levels in Greece in the 1990s.

To sum up, both de jure and de facto indicators suggest that financial repression was a distinctive feature of the southern European economies in the 1970s and 1980s. As the other European countries moved towards financial deregulation and liberalisation, they delayed financial reforms and stepped up financial repression. Whereas Italy, Spain and Portugal finally converged towards European standards in the course of the 1990s, Greece retained the characteristics of a financially repressed economy for significantly longer. In the Greek case, delayed financial reforms accompanied slow macroeconomic stabilisation, which prevented the government from meeting the Maastricht convergence criteria in 1998 and led to its temporary exclusion from the euro.

How Large Were Implicit Revenues?

How large was the flow of implicit resources generated by financial repression in southern European economies and how did they compare with seigniorage? From the 1970s, the four governments resorted systematically to monetisation of the budget deficit, as the increasing share of government debt in the hands of monetary authorities confirms. Fiscal imbalances became an increasingly important motor of base money growth for all four countries, which maintained a large inflation differential compared to European countries with stronger macroeconomic stability and fiscal discipline.

Table 12.3 shows the average annual revenues from seigniorage (expressed as a percentage of GDP and tax revenues) from the 1970s to the 1990s estimated on the basis of alternative approaches.[53] The data reveal significant differences among the southern European countries in terms of their magnitude and time patterns. Monetary seigniorage peaked in Italy in the 1970s, reaching a maximum of 2.4 per cent of

---

[53] Different methods for measuring revenues from seigniorage exist; see P. Honohan, 'Does it Matter How Seigniorage is Measured?', *Applied Financial Economics* 6/3 (1996), 293–300. Monetary seigniorage measures government revenues from money creation (the ratio of the net change in base money to GDP or total tax revenues) and is equal to the increase in public debt that would generate any fiscal deficit in the absence of debt monetisation. An alternative approach is opportunity cost seigniorage, which captures the implicit current revenue in the form of interest savings, which arises from the government's exploitation of its monopoly power to issue currency (a zero-interest liability), as well as to oblige banks to keep reserves remunerated at a rate below the market rate. A third approach focuses on the inflation tax, which measures the capital loss caused by inflation to money holders.

Table 12.3. *Revenues from seigniorage*

	S_M/GDP	S_M/TAX	S_{OC}/GDP	S_{OC}/TAX	S_{INF}/GDP	S_{INF}/TAX
			Italy			
1970s	2.4%	9.4%	1.4%	5.3%	1.4%	5.5%
1980s	1.2%	3.6%	1.8%	5.3%	1.0%	3.0%
1990s	−0.5%	−1.2%	1.0%	2.4%	0.2%	0.5%
			Spain			
1970s	2.0%	10.4%	1.3%	7.0%	1.4%	7.4%
1980s	2.3%	8.5%	2.0%	7.2%	1.0%	3.6%
1990s	0.2%	0.5%	1.5%	4.4%	0.6%	1.8%
			Portugal			
1970s	3.5%	17.3%	1.9%	8.9%	3.0%	14.4%
1980s	6.0%	22.3%	4.8%	18.0%	3.9%	14.6%
1990s	0.0%	0.0%	2.3%	7.2%	1.3%	4.1%
			Greece			
1970s	2.7%	12.0%	1.8%	7.7%	1.8%	8.0%
1980s	3.3%	12.1%	3.8%	14.0%	3.0%	10.9%
1990s	1.6%	5.1%	2.1%	6.6%	1.0%	3.3%

Source: IMF *International Financial Statistics.*
Note: Each column reports the range of estimates of annual revenues for alternative measures of seigniorage: monetary seigniorage (S_M), opportunity cost seigniorage (S_{oc}) and the inflation tax (S_{INF}). Seigniorage from bank reserves held with the central bank is adjusted to take into account their remuneration. Data are averaged by decades and expressed alternatively as a percentage of GDP and total tax revenues.

GDP (9.4 per cent of tax revenues), but declined dramatically in the 1980s. By contrast, revenues from seigniorage increased over time in the other southern economies. In the 1980s seigniorage peaked at 2.3, 5.1 and 2.9 per cent of GDP in Spain, Portugal and Greece respectively, although the increase was less pronounced – or even turned into a slight decline – in terms of tax revenues, reflecting the intensification of their tax effort. In the 1990s seigniorage turned negative in Italy, Spain and Portugal, with Greece the only country that managed to sustain a significant flow of revenues. Figure 12.5 also shows that seigniorage was increasingly levied on the banking sector in the 1970s and 1980s.

Like seigniorage, financial repression allows the government to exact implicit revenues from the private sector. As previous studies suggest,[54] the differential between the shadow cost of borrowing in unregulated financial markets and the artificially low effective cost of borrowing from domestic banks and investors represents an implicit interest saving for the government. The nominal effective cost of borrowing for the

---

[54] Giovannini and De Melo, 'Government Revenues', 958.

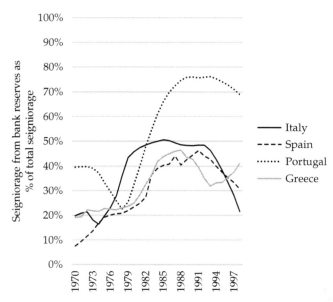

Figure 12.5.   Seigniorage revenues from bank reserves.
Source: IMF *International Financial Statistics.*

government (NEFFINT) is estimated ex post by dividing interest outlays by the average stock of government debt.[55] One should bear in
mind that the latter includes non-marketable debt (e.g. bank loans,
savings bonds and overdraft facilities with the Treasury, all subjected to
regulated nominal rates), which still accounted for a very substantial
share of southern governments' overall indebtedness.[56] As a first proxy

[55] In principle, the difference between effective borrowing costs on foreign currency-
denominated debt and domestic debt could be used as a proxy for the implicit interest
saving generated by financial repression. Unfortunately, data on interest payments
available for Italy, Spain, Portugal and Greece do not differentiate between outlays on
domestic and foreign currency debt. As a consequence, only an average effective borrowing cost of overall government debt can be calculated. Giovannini and De Melo
also suggest that the foreign borrowing cost should include an exchange rate component – namely, the realised depreciation of the domestic currency relative to the US
dollar or a weighted basket of international currencies, which would provide a proxy
for the change in domestic currency value of the stock of external currency-
denominated debt. However, in both cases the distortion is minimal, as the average
share of foreign debt over total debt was negligible: 5 per cent in Italy (1982–98) and
2.3 per cent in Spain (1989–98); no data are available for Portugal and Greece. See
OECD Statistics, *Central Government Debt*, available online at http://stats.oecd.org.

[56] The share of total government debt accounted for by non-marketable instruments was
quite large until the early 1980s (30, 70 and 75 per cent in Italy, Spain and Portugal
respectively) and declined gradually over the rest of the period. Data from OECD
Statistics, *Central Government Debt.*

of the government's shadow cost of borrowing, I use the yield on long-term government bonds traded in domestic secondary markets (YIELD).[57] This is a conservative measure as it can be affected by domestic financial repression.[58] As a consequence, their differential (YIELD – NEFFINT) should be considered as a lower bound for the estimate of revenues from financial repression. As an alternative, I proxy the government shadow price of funds by estimating its foreign borrowing cost (FOBC) in international markets. FOBC is calculated using the average yield on secondary markets of US$- and DM-denominated long-term government bonds, to which I add a three-year moving average of the annual realised depreciation of the Italian lira, Spanish peseta, Portuguese escudo and Greek drachma, measured as the annual change in their Nominal Effective Exchange Rate Index. The fact that YIELD and FOBC display similar patterns is reassuring.

Figures 12.6 and 12.7 show that the nominal effective interest cost of debt of the four governments remained consistently below our proxies for market rates until the 1980s. The savings for the governments peaked in the early 1980s, but fell rapidly in the middle of the decade, coinciding with the completion of financial liberalisation. Again, Greece was an exception, as its government continued to benefit from a substantial differential until the mid-1990s.

Following Giovannini and De Melo, I calculate implicit revenues from financial repression by multiplying the estimated borrowing cost differential by the stock of outstanding government debt, D, net of government debt held by the central bank, D_{CB}:

$$FR = \frac{(YIELD - NEFFINT) \times (D - D_{CB})}{GDP} \qquad (12.4)$$

The results are presented in Table 12.4 and expressed as a share of GDP and total tax revenues.

The data show that regulating the financial sector enabled governments to exact substantial resources in the 1970s and 1980s. As Figure 12.8 illustrates, this was especially the case for Italy and Greece, where implicit resources generated by financial repression were comparable to, or even higher than, seigniorage. This also suggests that in their case financial

---

[57] Only occasional data on Greek government bond yields are reported by the IMF; the series of nominal rates of Treasury bills starts only in 1986 and tracks closely the reported central bank discount rate. For this reason, I use the latter as a proxy, since it is available for the whole period of this study.

[58] In financially repressed systems, liquid asset ratios imposed on commercial banks and the limited availability of alternative private securities to investors tend artificially to increase market demand for government securities, thus exerting downward pressure on their nominal rates.

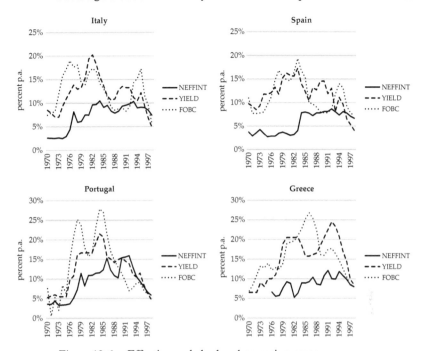

Figure 12.6.   Effective and shadow borrowing costs.

Note: NEFFINT: Nominal effective interest rate on government debt (interest Outlays/debt outstanding); YIELD: government bonds' yield in domestic secondary markets (for Greece, the central bank discount rate); FOBC: shadow foreign borrowing cost.

Source: IMF, *International Financial Statistics* and *Government Finance Statistics*; OECD Statistics, Central Government Debt (online); M. Francese and A. Pace, 'Il debito pubblico italiano dall'Unità a oggi. Una ricostruzione della serie storica', Banca d'Italia Occasional Paper 31 (2008); A. Carreras and X. Tafunell (eds.), *Estadísticas Históricas de España*, vol. II (2005), ch. 12; N. Valerio (ed.), *Estadísticas Históricas Portuguesas*, Vol. I (2001), ch. 9; Banco de Portugal, *Séries Longas para a Economia Portuguesa.*

repression was used as a substitute for declining seigniorage during the period of disinflation. On the other hand, seigniorage remained the most important source of implicit revenues for the two Iberian economies, although financial repression became a significant complement in Spain in the 1980s. Overall, aggregate implicit revenues, including both seigniorage and financial repression, were a permanent and significant component of southern European fiscal regimes throughout the second half of the twentieth century. They generated an annual volume of resources in

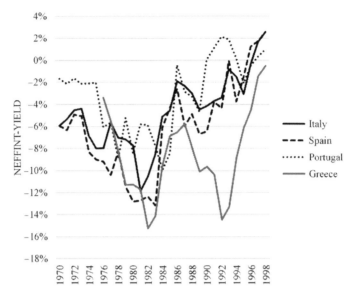

Figure 12.7.   Realised shadow borrowing cost differential.

Source: IMF, *International Financial Statistics* and *Government Finance Statistics*; OECD Statistics, *Central Government Debt* (online); M. Francese and A. Pace, 'Il debito pubblico italiano dall'Unità a oggi. Una ricostruzione della serie storica', Banca d'Italia Occasional Paper 31 (2008); A. Carreras and X. Tafunell (eds.), *Estadísticas Históricas de España*, vol. II (2005), ch. 12; N. Valerio (ed.), *Estatísticas Históricas Portuguesas*, vol. I (2001), ch. 9; Banco de Portugal, *Séries Longas para a Economia Portuguesa*.

Table 12.4. *Revenues from financial repression*

	Italy		Spain		Portugal		Greece	
	fr/gdp	fr/tax	fr/gdp	fr/tax	fr/gdp	fr/tax	fr/gdp	fr/tax
1970s	1.9	*7.2*	0.6	*3.2*	0.5	*2.3*	1.2	*4.9*
1980s	2.9	*8.7*	1.3	*4.4*	1.5	*5.6*	2.7	*9.7*
1990s	1.2	*3.1*	0.5	*1.4*	−0.2	*−0.7*	5.0	*15.8*

Source: IMF, *International Financial Statistics* and *Government Finance Statistics*; OECD Statistics, Central Government Debt (online); M. Francese and A. Pace, 'Il debito pubblico italiano dall'Unità a oggi. Una ricostruzione della serie storica', Banca d'Italia Occasional Paper 31 (2008); A. Carreras and X. Tafunell (eds.), *Estadísticas Históricas de España* vol. II (2005), ch. 12; N. Valerio (ed.), *Estatísticas Históricas Portuguesas*, vol. I, (2001), ch. 9; and Banco de Portugal, *Séries Longas para a Economia Portuguesa*.

Note: Estimates of annual revenues from financial repression are measured on the basis of the differential between shadow borrowing costs (YIELD) and nominal effective borrowing cost (NEFFINT). Data are averaged by decades and expressed alternatively as a percentage of GDP and total tax revenues.

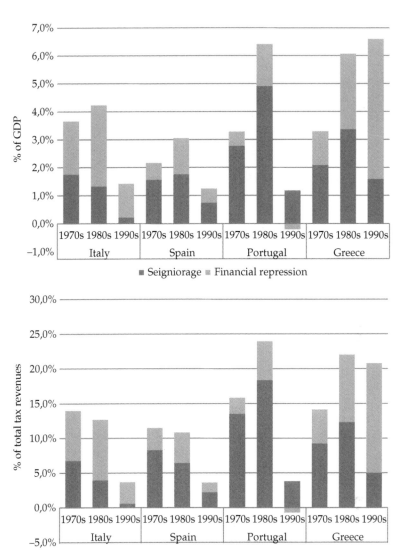

Figure 12.8. Total implicit revenues.

Note: Total implicit revenues are the sum of average seigniorage (mean of cash flow, opportunity cost and inflation tax) and revenues from financial repression.

Source: IMF, *International Financial Statistics* and *Government Finance Statistics*; OECD Statistics, Central Government Debt (online); M. Francese and A. Pace, 'Il debito pubblico italiano dall'Unità a oggi. Una ricostruzione della serie storica', Banca d'Italia Occasional Paper 31 (2008); A. Carreras and X. Tafunell (eds.), *Estadísticas Históricas de España* vol. II (2005), ch. 12; N. Valerio (ed.), *Estatísticas Históricas Portuguesas,* vol. I (2001), ch. 9; Banco de Portugal, *Séries Longas para a Economia Portuguesa.*

the range of 4 percentage points of GDP (13–14 per cent of tax revenues) in Italy in the 1970s and 1980s. In the other southern economies they peaked in the 1980s, although their magnitude was much lower in Spain (3 percentage points of GDP and 10 per cent of tax revenues) than in Portugal and Greece (6 percentage points of GDP and above 20 per cent of tax revenues). While implicit revenues declined dramatically in the 1990s in Italy, Spain and Portugal as a consequence of macroeconomic stabilisation and financial reforms, Greek governments continued to resort to them heavily even in the 1990s.

These data confirm the public finance interpretation presented in the opening section of this chapter. After the mid-1970s, southern European governments became especially dependent on seigniorage and financial repression as fiscal shock absorbers. By exploiting the opportunity allowed by faster money growth, higher inflation and delayed reforms in the financial sector, they maximised the exaction of implicit revenues during the 1980s in order to cushion the impact of persistent budget deficits and rising interest burdens on their debt. The scale of their dependence on seigniorage and financial repression also indicates the magnitude of the real fiscal adjustment that full financial liberalisation would have imposed. Turning away from implicit resources in the 1980s would have required structural spending cuts and increased tax revenues by introducing higher tax rates and more strenuous means of combating tax evasion of between 3 and 7 per cent of annual GDP.

The magnitude of the implied fiscal adjustment helps explain why financial sector reforms were implemented not only half-heartedly but also belatedly. In a comparative perspective, the protracted and intensive reliance on implicit resources by Greek governments during the 1990s, and their use of financial repression as an alternative to now declining seigniorage, emerges as a special case that runs counter to the experience of the other southern countries, which were unquestionably converging with the rest of Europe.

How Much Did Financial Repression Improve Fiscal Fragility and Contribute to Debt Sustainability?

As the preceding sections have shown, since the mid-1970s delayed financial reforms allowed southern European governments to keep the nominal effective interest rate on their debt persistently below their borrowing shadow costs. At the same time, systematic monetisation of the budget deficit gave rise to inflation rates that were significantly higher than those in the rest of western Europe. By combining a relatively high degree of financial repression with an inflationary regime in respect to monetary policy, governments created conditions that were conducive to negative real borrowing costs. To what extent did this policy moderate their fiscal fragility and improve the sustainability of their debt? To answer this question, I return to the debt accumulation identity presented in the opening section, in which the debt path is determined by how much the primary balance deviates from the debt-stabilising target (the fiscal burden, $d_{t-1}(r-g)$). In turn, the latter is determined by the interaction of three variables: the real rate on government debt (r, the nominal effective rate on government debt adjusted to the inflation rate), the growth rate of the real economy (g) and the lagged level of the debt-to-GDP ratio (d).

The left panel of Figure 12.9 shows that a combination of low nominal effective rates and high inflation produced persistently negative real rates on the debt of the four southern European governments from the early 1970s. As financial liberalisation brought nominal effective rates closer to market levels and macroeconomic stabilisation reduced inflation, real borrowing costs turned positive and increased in Italy, Spain and Portugal until the late 1990s. By contrast, delayed liberalisation and stabilisation allowed Greek governments to continue with negative real borrowing costs for a decade, that is, until the mid-1990s. At the same time, the four economies experienced a marked slowdown in their real output growth rate after the mid-1970s (see Figure 12.9, right panel).

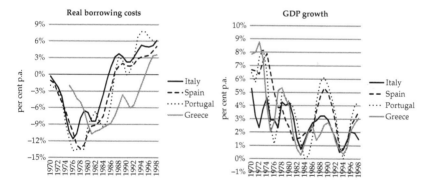

Figure 12.9. Real borrowing costs and GDP growth rates.

Note: Real borrowing costs are nominal effective interest rates on government debt (NEFFINT) minus a three-year moving average of consumer price inflation. GDP growth is a three-year moving average of annual growth measured at 1990 Geary-Khamis US$.

Source: Real borrowing costs: see Figure 12.8; Real GDP growth: The Conference Board Total Economy Database, available online at www.conference-board.org/data/economydatabase.

The end of the 'golden age' of growth came as a negative shock that, by increasing governments' exposure to positive flow costs and fiscal burdens, increased fiscal fragility and threatened debt sustainability.

How would their situation have changed if they had brought in financial reforms much earlier? To answer this, I estimate counterfactual series of flow costs, fiscal burdens and debt ratios, and compare them with realised data. As a proxy of the counterfactual real borrowing cost, $r^\star$, that would have prevailed under financial liberalisation, I use the secondary market yield of government bonds (a conservative proxy of the shadow nominal borrowing costs)[59] less expected inflation, that is, an inflation rate equal to the growth rate of its trend, estimated on the base of a Hodrick–Prescott filter. I also assume a growth rate of real output, $g^\star$, in line with its trend, and a fiscal policy equal to the realised primary balance. The counterfactual exercise addresses the question: Given the realised structural shocks to the government's primary balance and to the trend growth rate of real output, what would the debt path have been if early financial liberalisation had obliged them to fund budget deficits by issuing only marketable debt at market rates?

Figure 12.10 summarises the main findings. It shows that realised flow costs remained negative until 1992/3 in Italy, Spain and Portugal (a situation Greece managed to maintain until 1997). Counterfactual flow costs suggest that under full financial liberalisation the four governments would have experienced much less favourable conditions. The counterfactual scenario would have been especially adverse for Italy and Spain, whose flow costs would have turned positive (up to +5 per cent) by 1982. Due to delayed stabilisation, Portugal and Greece still would have faced negative (although much less favourable than realised) flow costs until the late 1980s. The 1990s scenario would have been extremely onerous for the Greek government, with very high flow

---

[59] We assume that governments adjusted their nominal interest payments to market-determined yields annually, which is plausible given the composition and average maturity of their debt, especially until the early 1990s. For instance, in the 1980s more than 80 per cent of the Italian government's outstanding marketable debt was represented by Treasury bills (BOT) with maturities varying between three and twelve months, and Variable Rate Notes (CCTs) with floating rates indexed to BOTs. Similarly, in the second half of the 1980s, 70 per cent of the Spanish government's marketable debt was accounted for by Treasury bills (*Letras del Tesoro*) and other money market instruments. In the same period, 66 per cent of marketable debt in Portugal was in Treasury bills and Variable Rate Notes. Data for Greece are available only since the early 1990s, when Treasury bills and Variable Rate Notes accounted for 75 per cent of outstanding marketable debt. In the 1980s, the weighted average maturity of Italy's and Spain's debt was 2.6 and 2 years respectively, and occasionally fell to just 1 year during periods of very high inflation. No maturity information is available for Portugal and Greece. See OECD Statistics, *Central Government Debt*.

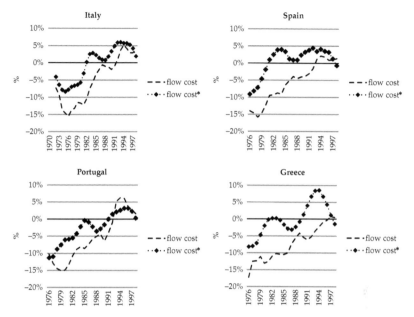

Figure 12.10.   Realised vs. counterfactual flow costs.
Note: The series are based on a three-year moving average.
Counterfactual series are indicated by an asterisk*.
Source: Real borrowing costs: see Figure 12.8; Real GDP growth:
The Conference Board Total Economy Database, available online at
www.conference-board.org/data/economydatabase.

costs (up to +9 per cent) during most of the decade. By delaying full
financial liberalisation, governments in all four countries managed to
postpone shocks to debt flow costs, thereby reducing fiscal fragility.

How much did they benefit from this policy? Gains from financial
repression can be measured in terms of flow cost savings (i.e. the average
gap between realised and counterfactual flow costs; see Table 12.5, a).
The ratio of flow cost savings to revenues from financial repression[60] also
gives a measure of the efficient use of financial repression across countries
and over time, in other words, how great the improvement in fiscal fragility
associated with revenues from financial repression equal to 1 per cent
GDP unit was. As Table 12.5 shows, the Greek and Spanish governments
were the main beneficiaries of financial repression throughout the period.
Italian governments saw their gains steadily decline over time, whereas the
governments in Portugal maximised their flow cost savings in the 1980s.

[60] For revenues from financial repression (FR), see Table 12.3.

Table 12.5. *Fiscal fragility gains*

	Average flow cost savings			Efficiency		
	(a)			(b)		
	Overall	1970s	1980s	1990s	1970s	1980s	1990s
Italy	4.7	**6.5**	5.9	2.4	3.4	2.0	2.0
Spain	6.4	7.5	**9.1**	3.0	12.5	7.0	6.0
Portugal	2.9	3.6	**5.3**	0.0	7.2	3.5	0.0
Greece	7.4	6.3	**8.2**	6.9	5.3	3.0	1.4

Source: Real borrowing costs, see Tables 12.3 and 12.4; and IMF, *International Financial Statistics*; Real GDP growth, The Conference Board Total Economy Database, available online at www.conference-board.org/data/economydatabase.
Note: Average flow cost savings are measured as the mean gap between realised and counterfactual flow costs. Efficiency is average flow cost savings divided by revenues from financial repression (expressed as a percentage of GDP; see Table 12.3).

Savings for Greek governments were even higher in the 1990s than in the 1970s. Spanish governments in general made more efficient use of financial repression (in the 1980s 1 per cent of GDP in revenues from financial repression reduced their flow cost by 7 percentage points), although financial repression was characterised by decreasing returns in terms of flow cost savings in all four countries (see Table 12.5, b).[61]

How would an early shock to flow costs caused by full financial liberalisation have affected their debt accumulation? For each country, Figure 12.11 presents five series: the realised primary balance; the realised and the counterfactual fiscal burdens; and their corresponding two debt paths. A common feature of the four southern European countries was a persistently negative fiscal burden until the early 1990s. However, Spain and Portugal, with values hovering at around −2 and −3 per cent of GDP respectively, were subjected to relatively stronger fiscal discipline than Italy, which had values of around −6 per cent of GDP from the mid-1970s to the early 1980s, although it decreased gradually in the second half of that decade, and Greece, which had values of −3 to −6 per cent of GDP. In the early 1990s Italy, Spain and Portugal entered a period of increasing fiscal fragility, signalled by positive fiscal burdens.

[61] A Spearman rank correlation shows that the reduction in fiscal fragility was not a side-effect of relative macroeconomic performance in terms of growth or inflation, but a direct effect of the government's ability to hold down nominal effective rates on its debt. Correlation of efficiency with: mean nominal effective interest rates on government debt, −0.727*** (*p*-value 0.007); mean inflation rate, 0.315 (*p*-value 0.318); and mean trend growth rate, 0.294 (*p*-value 0.353).

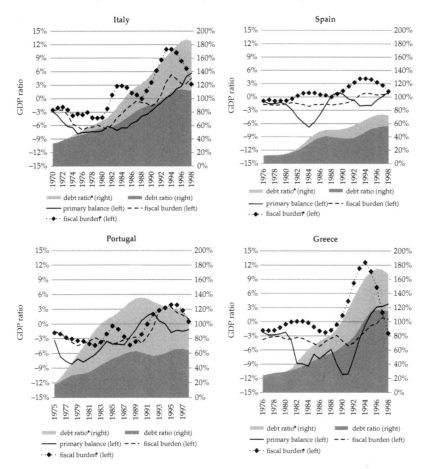

Figure 12.11. Realised vs. counterfactual fiscal burdens and debt paths.
Note: The fiscal burden is equal to the primary balance that would allow debt stabilisation at the existing level of the debt GDP ratio. Counterfactual series are denoted by an asterisk.
Source: Real borrowing costs: see Figure 12.8; Real GDP growth: The Conference Board Total Economy Database, available online at www.conference-board.org/data/economydatabase.

There was thus a compelling need to pursue fiscal adjustment – an especially difficult task for Italian and Portuguese governments, which had to run primary surpluses of 3 per cent of GDP or more compared to surpluses below 1 per cent in the case of Spain. By contrast, Greek governments, by further delaying financial reforms, managed to keep their fiscal burden slightly negative or at zero until the mid-1990s.

Table 12.6. *Deviation from debt-stabilising targets*

Country	Period (years)	Average deviation	Max. deviation	Cumulative deviation	Total (% of total years)
Italy	1971–80 (10)	1.4	2.6 (1972, 1973)	13.2	25 (82.6%)
	1982–96 (15)	2.7	4.5 (1987, 1994)	39.9	
Spain	1980–7 (8)	2.5	4.7 (1984)	19.8	14 (60.9%)
	1992–7 (6)	1.6	2.8 (1994)	9.6	
Portugal	1975–83 (9)	3.4	4.9 (1976)	30.8	18 (75.0%)
	1985–7 (3)	0.5	1.1 (1987)	1.5	
	1993–8 (6)	3.3	5.2 (1995)	20.0	
Greece	1981–93 (13)	4.1	7.2 (1990)	49.5	13 (56.5%)

Note: Downward deviations of realised primary balance from realised fiscal burden are expressed as percentage of annual GDP.
* Total years are 29 for Italy (1970–98) and 23 for Spain, Portugal and Greece (1976–98).

By comparing realised fiscal burdens and primary balances we can assess how long and by how much governments deviated from their debt-stabilising targets. The fact that primary balances systematically exceeded fiscal burdens for very long periods (even when debt was stabilised by running a primary deficit) provides evidence of a fiscal policy that ignored debt sustainability. As Table 12.6 summarises, Italy spent twenty-five years (86 per cent of the period since 1970) with an excess primary deficit, followed by Portugal, Spain and Greece (75, 60.9 and 56.5 per cent of the time since the completion of their democratic transitions). Between 1971 and 1996, Italian governments accumulated excess primary deficits that amounted to more than 53 per cent of their annual GDP. In spite of a gradual reduction in their primary deficits in the second half of the 1980s and a major adjustment plan launched in 1991, they managed to stabilise debt only in 1994/5 at around 120 per cent. In Greece departure from debt stabilisation occurred between 1981 and 1993, with cumulative excess primary deficits amounting to 50 per cent of annual GDP. Again, two major adjustment plans in 1992 and 1994 succeeded in stabilising the debt ratio at around 100 per cent in the mid-1990s. In the case of Spain and Portugal, after an initial period of fiscal laxity in 1982–6 and 1976–82, with cumulative excess primary deficits of 20 and 31 per cent of annual GDP respectively, governments pursued a policy of fiscal adjustment between 1988 and 1992, a period characterised in both countries by sustained growth. In response to the 1992–3 recession, both governments relaxed their fiscal stance, although to a much lesser degree in Spain than in Portugal. A new round of fiscal adjustment launched in 1996–7 managed to stabilise their debt ratio at around 60 per cent after joining the euro. Overall, the two Iberian governments deviated from their debt-stabilising targets significantly less than their Italian and Greek counterparts over the whole period.[62]

For all four governments the main gain from financial repression was to move their debt accumulation onto a less explosive path, enter the new macroeconomic regime based on low inflation and full financial liberalisation with a lower debt ratio, and pass on the burden of real fiscal adjustment and its distributional implications to future governments. Under the counterfactual scenario, Italy, which had an initial debt ratio of 33 per cent in 1970, would have switched to positive fiscal burdens by the early 1980s. By then the debt ratio would have been approaching 100 per cent and governments would have been forced to reverse their −7 per cent primary deficit to a 3 per cent primary surplus to prevent it from rising further. By delaying full financial liberalisation, Italian governments managed to postpone fiscal adjustment by a decade; yet the actual primary surpluses generated after 1992/3 would have stabilised the debt ratio at only around 180 per cent – a level comparable to Japan's in the early 2000s. In the mid-1980s Portuguese governments would have found themselves in a similar situation, with a debt ratio approaching 100 per cent (rising from a much lower initial level of 20 per cent in 1975), which could be stabilised only by turning their 4 per cent deficit into a balanced primary. The fiscal adjustment actually enforced in the early 1990s would have stabilised debt at around 130 per cent. The Greek debt ratio would have reached the 100 per cent threshold in 1990 rather than 1994, and stabilisation would have required a 1 per cent primary surplus – far removed from the primary deficit of 11 per cent running at that time. As in Italy, in Greece the protracted fiscal adjustment that started in the mid-1990s would have stabilised the debt ratio at a much higher level of around 170 per cent. The growth path of Spanish debt, which started from a very low level of less than 20 per cent, would have been much less explosive, and the two actual fiscal adjustments of the late 1980s and late 1990s would have managed to stabilise the debt ratio at around 50 and 75 per cent respectively.

---

[62] For details on the timing, composition and performance of large adjustment plans in Europe during the 1990s, see A. Alesina and R. Perotti, 'Fiscal Adjustments in OECD Countries: Composition and Macroeconomic Effects', *IMF Staff Papers* 44/2 (1997), 210–48; and A. Abbas F. Hasanov, P. Mauro and J. Park, 'The Performance of Large Fiscal Adjustment Plans in the EU: A Cross-Country Statistical Analysis', in P. Mauro (ed.), *Chipping Away at Public Debt: Sources of Failure and Keys to Success in Fiscal Adjustment* (Hoboken, NJ: Wiley, 2011), pp. 213–48.

Summary and Conclusions

During the golden age of economic growth of the 1950s and 1960s, southern European governments accumulated a significant gap in fiscal capacity compared to the advanced European economies. In the mid-1970s, the transition to democracy in Spain, Portugal and Greece accelerated social pressure for a far-reaching welfare state, which had been suppressed by the former dictatorships. In Italy, extreme political fragmentation and instability also led to a massive growth in the size of government. The political, socio-economic and institutional characteristics of the southern European countries – the role of fiscal policy in the consolidation of democracy, the use of the government budget as a patronage machine, lax budgetary rules that weakened controls on spending, widespread tax evasion and large black economies that undermined the tax effort – also contributed to fiscal instability. Buffeted by structural spending shocks of unprecedented magnitude, governments failed to adjust regular tax revenues, ran large and persistent primary deficits and embarked on rapid debt accumulation.

At the same time, two further shocks contributed to increasing their long-term fiscal fragility. On the one hand, their economies switched from the path of sustained growth of the preceding decades to the slow growth typical of the post-1970 era. On the other hand, the inflationary shock of the first half of the 1970s induced governments in the major advanced economies to adopt a new, market-oriented approach to monetary policy based on indirect instruments, such as central bank lending facilities and open market operations, and aimed at price stabilisation. This policy change implied the phasing out of direct instruments, such as regulated interest rates, credit ceilings and liquidity ratios, aimed at controlling the cost, volume and allocation of domestic credit, gave an unprecedented impetus to financial deregulation and liberalisation and brought to an end the era of low and stable nominal and real interest rates, which had prevailed since the Second World War.

High real interest rates and low growth would have dramatically increased the flow cost of government debt, leading to an explosive debt path in the absence of a sizeable fiscal adjustment. In order to improve their fiscal prospects, southern European governments maintained a macroeconomic policy regime of inflationary finance and delayed financial reforms as long as possible in an attempt to generate implicit revenues from seigniorage and financial repression large enough to put their debt on a more sustainable path. This option had only indirect distributive consequences and was therefore politically much easier to pursue than orthodox alternatives, such as scaling down government wage consumption and transfers, or bringing revenues into line with spending commitments by expanding direct and indirect taxation.

In turn, financial repression expanded the tax base on which seigniorage was levied and contributed to keeping governments' nominal effective borrowing costs below market rates. As a rule, policy-makers used revenues from financial repression as a complement to seigniorage, as theory suggests. However, they became a substitute during the process of disinflation in Italy in the 1980s and in Greece in the 1980s–90s. Aggregate revenues from implicit taxation peaked in the 1980s, when they contributed 3–7 per cent of GDP (10–25 per cent of regular tax revenues). Their size gives a measure of the fiscal costs that financial liberalisation would have required in terms of real fiscal adjustment.

Combined with relatively high – though gradually falling – inflation, financial repression kept real rates of government debt negative until the mid-1980s to the mid-1990s in the case of Greece. By partly offsetting the adverse shock to real output trend growth, negative borrowing costs enabled governments to maintain negative debt flow costs and fiscal burdens until the early 1990s. These reduced fiscal fragility and helped debt to move along a less explosive path. Gains in terms of flow cost savings were maximised in the 1970s and 1980s, and were significantly larger in Greece, which managed to keep them high until the mid-1990s, and Spain than for Italy and Portugal. Counterfactual flow costs, fiscal burdens and debt ratios show that full financial liberalisation would have implied an early switch to positive flow costs and fiscal burdens, leading Italy, Portugal and Greece into unsustainable levels of debt, in excess of 100 per cent over the course of the 1980s.

Financial repression, therefore, gave governments an opportunity to gain time and reduce the magnitude of the real fiscal adjustment required to stabilise their debt. The two Iberian governments exploited this opportunity during the expansionary growth cycle of the second half of the 1980s, corrected their fiscal stance and stabilised their debt ratios at moderate levels. This early adjustment gave them some leeway to slash spending in the aftermath of the 1991–2 recession and yet comfortably meet the Maastricht debt criterion in the run-up to joining the euro. Italian and Greek governments, on the other hand, wasted the financial repression bonus by running primary deficits in excess of their debt-stabilising targets almost uninterruptedly until the early 1990s. Debt ratios above 100 per cent left them with a heavy debt overhang and no room for fiscal manoeuvring for the rest of the decade and forced them to enter the EMU (with a delay in the case of Greece) with the onerous task of reducing their debt ratios.

Acknowledgement

This chapter is part of a wider research project on financial repression, liberalisation and integration in western Europe, supported by the Education, Audiovisual and Culture Executive Agency of the European Commission under the Jean Monnet Programme (Project 2010-2687). Additional funding from Fundación Rafael Del Pino is gratefully acknowledged.

Index

Note: Page numbers in **bold** refer to tables and those in *italic* refer to figures

Printed in Great Britain
by Amazon

73757587R00196